China in the World Market

China's increasing interaction with the world has had an enormous impact on its domestic economic reforms. In this book Thomas Moore examines the role of the outside world as a source of change in China in the decades since Deng Xiaoping instituted the country's Open Door policy. Moore assesses the impact of varying degrees of economic openness in the world trading system on the reform, restructuring, and rationalization of Chinese industries. Through the lens of two critical, internationally significant industries – shipbuilding and textiles – he investigates the opportunities and constraints presented by the world system.

Moore argues that scholars are wrong to focus narrowly on such factors as Chinese elite politics and industrial planning to explain the course of economic development and to extract predictions about China's future growth. International forces such as industry-specific trade regimes (the Multifiber Arrangement [MFA] in textiles, for example) have had a profound impact, disrupting the pattern of state intervention. The supervisory ministries that once played an intrusive role in the daily operations of industry now play a weakened role, allowing industries to adapt to world market conditions by undertaking the reforms necessary to thrive. As Moore amply demonstrates, the international environment most conducive to change in China's textile and shipbuilding industries during the 1980s and 1990s was one marked by moderate economic closure rather than openness. He also challenges the idea that China's recent economic success has been driven by a mainland version of the "East Asian" model, arguing that Beijing's ability to pursue strategic industrial policy is actually quite limited. Moore's finding that protectionist trade regimes such as the MFA have actually been a boon to industrial reform in China (when compared with other, relatively open international industrial sectors) has important implications for the study of "managed" versus "free" trade environments.

Based on extensive documentary and interview material, the book adds the Chinese case to a long tradition of country-based studies by political economists, historians, and area specialists that have chronicled the experience of developing countries as they enter specific industrial markets in the world economy. This is timely and provocative reading for anyone concerned with the nature of China's deepening participation in the world economy and its consequences for the country's development prospects, internal reforms, and foreign policy.

Thomas G. Moore is Associate Professor of Political Science at the University of Cincinnati. He is the author of numerous book chapters and scholarly articles on Chinese foreign policy and China's participation in the world economy, including publications in such journals as *Asian Affairs, Asian Perspective, Journal of Contemporary China*, and *Journal of East Asian Affairs*.

Cambridge Modern China Series

Edited by William Kirby, Harvard University

China in the World Market

Chinese Industry and
International Sources of
Reform in the Post-Mao Era

THOMAS G. MOORE

University of Cincinnati

CAMBRIDGE
UNIVERSITY PRESS

PUBLISHED BY THE PRESS SYNDICATE OF THE UNIVERSITY OF CAMBRIDGE
The Pitt Building, Trumpington Street, Cambridge, United Kingdom

CAMBRIDGE UNIVERSITY PRESS
The Edinburgh Building, Cambridge CB2 2RU, UK
40 West 20th Street, New York, NY 10011-4211, USA
477 Williamstown Road, Port Melbourne, VIC 3207, Australia
Ruiz de Alarcón 13, 28014 Madrid, Spain
Dock House, The Waterfront, Cape Town 8001, South Africa

http://www.cambridge.org

First published 2002

Printed in the United Kingdom at the University Press, Cambridge

Typeface Times New Roman 10/13 pt.   *System* QuarkXPress [BTS]

A catalog record for this book is available from the British Library.

Library of Congress Cataloging in Publication Data
Moore, Thomas Geoffrey, 1963– .
China in the world market: Chinese industry and international sources of reform in the
post-Mao era / Thomas G. Moore.
p. cm. – (Cambridge Modern China Series)
Includes bibliographical references and index.
ISBN 0-521-66283-4 – ISBN 0-521-66442-X (pb.)
1. Industries – China.   2. China – Foreign economic relations.   3. China – Economic
conditions – 1976–   4. Economic history – 1945–   I. Title: China in the world market:
Chinese industry and international sources of reform in the post-Mao era.   II. Title.
III. Series.
HC427.92 .M665   2001
337.51 – dc21   2001025634

ISBN   0 521 66283 4   hardback
ISBN   0 521 66442 X   paperback

Contents

Contents

Figures

ix

Figures

Abbreviations

Almanac	*Almanac of China's Foreign Economic Relations and Trade*
AFC	Asian Financial Crisis
APEC	Asia Pacific Economic Cooperation forum
ATC	Agreement on Textiles and Clothing
BMTs	bureaus of maritime transport
CBR	*China Business Review*
CCP	Chinese Communist Party
CCSI	China Corporation of Shipbuilding Industry
CHINASILK	China National Silk Import & Export Corporation
CHINATEX	China National Textiles Import & Export Corporation
CMRS	contract management responsibility system
CNTC	China National Textile Council
COSCO	China Ocean Shipping Company
CSIC	China Silk Industrial Corporation
CSSC	China State Shipbuilding Corporation
CSTC	China Shipbuilding Trading Corporation
CTR	*China Trade Report*
EC	European Community
FBIS	*Foreign Broadcast Information Service*
FBIS-CHI	*Foreign Broadcast Information Service, Daily Report-China*
FBIS-LAT	*Foreign Broadcast Information Service, Daily Report-Latin America*
FBIS-WEU	*Foreign Broadcast Information Service, Daily Report-Western Europe*

FDI	foreign direct investment
FEER	*Far Eastern Economic Review*
FIEs	foreign-invested enterprises
FTCs	foreign trade corporations
GATT	General Agreement on Tariffs and Trade
GDP	gross domestic product
GJMYWT	*Guoji Maoyi Wenti* [*Issues in International Trade*]
GSC	global surplus capacity
IMF	International Monetary Fund
JPRS	*Joint Publications Research Service*
KIEOs	keystone international economic organizations
KMT	Kuomintang
LLMA	*Lloyd's List Maritime Asia*
LMA	*Lloyd's Maritime Asia*
LNG	liquid nitrogen gas
LPG	liquid petroleum gas
LSE	*Lloyd's Shipping Economist*
LSM	*Lloyd's Ship Manager*
LTA	Long-Term Arrangement
MFA	Multifiber Arrangement
MMF	man-made fiber
MNCs	multinational corporations
MOFERT	Ministry of Foreign Economic Relations and Trade
MOFTEC	Ministry of Foreign Trade and Economic Cooperation
MTI	Ministry of Textile Industry
NICs	newly industrializing countries
OECD	Organisation for Economic Co-operation and Development
OMAs	orderly marketing arrangements
PLA	People's Liberation Army
PPP	purchasing power parity
PRC	People's Republic of China
SBR	*Seatrade Business Review*
SCMP	*South China Morning Post*
SETC	State Economic and Trade Commission
SEZs	special economic zones
SOEs	state-owned enterprises

SSIEC	Shanghai Silk Import and Export Corporation
STA	Short-Term Arrangement
STIB	State Textile Industry Bureau
SW&SB	*Shipping World & Shipbuilder*
TA	*Textile Asia [Yazhou Fangzhi Yuekan]*
TIBs	textile industry bureaus
TOI	*Textile Outlook International*
TVEs	township and village enterprises
VERs	voluntary export restraints
VLCCs	very large crude carriers
WTO	World Trade Organization
WTR&O	*World Trade Review and Outlook*
ZGFZGYNJ	*Zhongguo Fangzhi Gongye Nianjian [China Textile Industry Yearbook]*
ZGHY	*Zhongguo Haiyun [Maritime China]*
ZGJJNJ	*Zhongguo Jingji Nianjian [China Economic Yearbook]*
ZGJJXW	*Zhongguo Jingji Xinwen [China Economic News]*
ZGJXDZGYNJ	*Zhongguo Jixie Dianzi Gongye Nianjian [China Machinery and Electronics Industry Yearbook]*

Preface

In trying to interpret the momentous changes that have occurred in China since the death of Mao Zedong, one piece of the puzzle has been conspicuously missing – conceptually if not always empirically – from most scholarship on the so-called reform era: the impact of the outside world. Simply put, what influence have international forces had on the course of change in post-Mao China? Even in the literature on China's growing participation in the world economy, shifts in policy and behavior – both at home and abroad – have been attributed quite narrowly to domestic factors. While this tendency has begun to shift somewhat in recent years, the dominant approach remains Sinocentric in critical respects. Especially for the 1980s and early 1990s, the impact of the outside world continues to be seriously underestimated. Indeed, this book is intended less to highlight the *contemporary* pattern of external influence on China – one that is increasingly (if still sometimes inadequately) acknowledged in both the academic and popular literatures on China's political economy – than to document the significance of external influence during this earlier period.

More specifically, the overriding goal of this book is to begin work on a conceptual foundation for understanding how international forces have structured the choices China has faced as it has expanded its participation in the world economy while simultaneously undertaking reform of its state socialist economy. While scholars have typically acknowledged the "importance" of the Open Policy (*kaifang zhengce*) for China's economic development, few studies have examined with any specificity *how* international forces have actually influenced domestic change in China. At a theoretical level, I am especially concerned with how certain types of stimuli in the international political economy, such as varying degrees of economic openness in world industrial markets, feed back into the Chinese political economy by shaping reform efforts, industrial transformation, and general development strategy.

As it has reentered the world economy over the last two decades, China has had to operate in an international environment over which it exerts little influence. In the shipbuilding and textile industries, for example, its role was clearly that of a "regime-taker" rather than a "regime-maker." In shipbuilding, China was a latecomer to the international industry. As such, the fundamental dynamics of the world shipbuilding community were well-established prior to China's entry. In particular, the international political economy of shipbuilding has long been characterized by chronic surplus manufacturing capacity as the result of complex patterns of private sector initiative and public sector intervention. Even today, after more than a decade of sustained export success, China's share of the world shipbuilding market remains too small for it to have any significant influence over developments at an international level. Similarly, in textiles China found itself confronted with the Multifiber Arrangement, the eight-hundred-pound gorilla of industry-specific trade regimes. Despite China's recent emergence as a major player in world textile markets, the persistence of the Multifiber Arrangement – an institution that now dates back four decades – has defined the international marketplace throughout the post-Mao era.

The argument of this book is quite straightforward: global surplus capacity and the Multifiber Arrangement created incentives for a specific agenda of economic adjustment that profoundly shaped the course of reform, restructuring, and rationalization in the Chinese shipbuilding and textile industries, respectively, during the 1980s and early 1990s. I do not, however, claim that external forces provide a comprehensive explanation for developments in these industries. Quite to the contrary, my account emphasizes the interaction of international and domestic forces. In this vein, the case-study chapters show not only the catalytic effect that the Multifiber Arrangement and global surplus capacity had in triggering important changes in China's textile and shipbuilding industries, but also how domestic structure filters the impact of the outside world on China.

I owe thanks to many people for their help in making this book possible. My greatest intellectual debt is to my dissertation advisers at Princeton University: Lynn White, Robert Gilpin, and David Bachman (at the University of Washington since 1991). I am also grateful to Keisuke Iida for serving as fourth reader for the dissertation. Their comments and suggestions were useful at every stage of the project, and the study could never have been completed without their help and encouragement. Here, Lynn and David deserve special mention, not just for their advising, but also for the marvelous examples they set as scholar-teachers; no one could ask for better mentors. Another important influence since my days at Princeton is Sam Kim. While never a formal adviser, Sam has always provided me with scholarly inspiration and personal encouragement. I also cheerfully acknowledge the intellectual support and hearty friendship provided by my fellow graduate students, especially Solomon Karmel, Cheng Li, Jeff Sacknowitz, Dali Yang, and Kate Xiao Zhou. For sparking my interest in the subjects of Chinese politics and international relations as an undergraduate at Hamilton College, I am deeply indebted to Pete Suttmeier and Channing Richardson, respectively.

In the course of revising the dissertation into a book, I received valuable feedback from colleagues and friends too numerous to mention here. William Kirby (series editor), the late Michel Oksenberg, and David Zweig deserve special mention for their extremely careful readings of the entire manuscript. Their comments have improved the book tremendously. Dixia Yang provided able research assistance on several occasions. Remaining errors of fact, judgment, and interpretation are, of course, mine alone. At Cambridge University Press, I am very grateful to my editor, Mary Child, both for her initial interest in this project and for her patience in awaiting the final product. Similarly, I owe thanks to Mike Green, Holly Johnson, and Jonathan Munk for shepherding the manuscript through the various stages of the administration and production process.

Financial support in the form of a U.S. Fulbright grant was especially critical to the dissertation-stage research carried out for this project. (Here, I must also thank the Centre of Asian Studies at the University of Hong Kong for serving as my official host for the Fulbright-sponsored research.) For additional funding during my graduate career, all of which related in some way to the dissertation, I am grateful to the following institutions: U.S. Department of Education (FLAS program), Andrew W. Mellon Foundation, Council on Regional Studies (Princeton University), and Center for International Studies (Princeton University). I also gratefully acknowledge the C. P. Taft Memorial Fund at the University of Cincinnati for several faculty grants that enabled me to conduct additional research while revising the manuscript. Among the many other institutions that facilitated my research, I especially wish to thank the

Universities Service Centre at the Chinese University of Hong Kong for access to their outstanding library collection.

I would be most remiss not to thank the scores of individuals in Hong Kong, China, and the United States who generously took time out of their busy schedules to talk with me about my project. In forty-one cases, this contact resulted in formal interviews. Many of these informants also agreed to endure follow-up questions and other correspondence. In addition to these gracious individuals, countless others helped by identifying documentary sources, discussing research strategies, and even making personal introductions that led to extremely important interviews. Only I can fully appreciate their contribution to this book, and I extend my warmest thanks to everyone concerned.

Finally, I would like to acknowledge the tremendous support of my family. I could never thank them enough for indulging my stubbornness in sticking with this project. My parents always encouraged my studies, and I only wish that my father could have seen the finished product. My wife and three daughters have lived through the project with remarkably good humor, and for that I am deeply grateful. (In Karen's case, the standard injunction about spousal sacrifices is entirely inadequate. Indeed, there would be no book today without her unselfishness.) In many ways, this book is testimony to their patience. They have provided all the love and encouragement any husband and father could ever need.

1

China as a Latecomer in World Industrial Markets

REFORM CHINA: THE SLEEPING GIANT AWAKENS

With annual rates of growth in economic output and foreign trade that averaged nearly 10 and 16 percent, respectively, from 1978 to 2000, China's economic performance has in many ways become the envy of the developing world.[1] Although the creation of wealth has been most pronounced in coastal areas, the number of Chinese living in absolute poverty nationwide has been reduced by more than 200 million during the reform era.[2] While improvements in political life have been less signal, China has experienced a rise in material living standards that is, by most measures, unprecedented in the history of human civilization. According to the World Bank, China achieved the fastest doubling of economic output ever from 1978 to 1987, far outpacing both early industrializers (e.g., United Kingdom, United States, and Japan) and late industrializers (e.g., Brazil, South Korea, and Taiwan) alike. It then repeated the feat from 1987–1996.[3] While economic disparities have

[1] According to official Chinese statistics for economic growth, which are widely regarded as inflated, the rate averaged almost 10 percent per year over this period. Most independent experts suggest that growth was at least a couple of percentage points lower. By all accounts, however, China's economy has been among the world's fastest growing. Official growth rates for China's foreign trade are considered to be more reliable. For a brief discussion of Chinese statistics, see the Appendix. For a review of scholarly efforts to measure China's economic growth, see Lardy (1999).

[2] According to World Bank estimates, 60 percent of China's population lived on less than $1 per day (the international standard for poverty used by the World Bank and United Nations) at the beginning of the reform era. World Bank (1997a), pp. 1–3. For more detail, see World Bank (1996b) and World Bank (1992). Despite advances, an estimated 270 million Chinese remained in poverty by the late 1990s, with untold tens of millions living above this level, but only perilously so. See, for example, Daniel Wright, "The Other Side of China's Prosperity," *CBR* (September/October 1999), pp. 22–29.

[3] World Bank (1997a), p. 4. For a more detailed examination, see World Bank (1991), p. 12.

widened between both coastal and interior areas and urban and rural areas, it is also true that economic growth has been widely shared across China. In fact, the World Bank reported that if the thirty provinces of China (many of which would rank as average-size countries in both territory and population) were counted as individual economies, "the twenty fastest-growing economies in the world between 1978 and 1995 would have been Chinese."[4] Based on the purchasing power parity (PPP) methods used by the International Monetary Fund (IMF) since 1993, China has the world's second largest economy, trailing only the United States. China's ascent is fairly impressive even in per capita terms, with current estimates on a PPP basis figured at more than U.S. $3,000, up substantially from the Mao era. While this hardly qualifies China as a rich nation, it is testimony to the country's rapid progress in economic development.

China has not, of course, achieved this spectacular economic record in isolation.[5] Beginning in the early 1970s, and gaining momentum after Deng Xiaoping formally reassumed power at the Third Plenum of the Eleventh Central Committee in December 1978, China's economic rise has been inextricably linked to the outside world. Measured by foreign trade and investment flows, China's integration into the world economy has increased substantially as a result of the Open Policy (*kaifang zhengce*). Based on nominal figures for gross domestic product (GDP), Chinese trade has averaged about 35 percent of GDP each year since the mid-1990s, more than triple the 13 percent figure for 1980. By this yardstick, China's economy is today both significantly more open than in the past and relatively open by international standards. According to a World Bank study, by the early 1990s China already ranked in the top third of countries in terms of trade openness. By contrast, China was the least open of 120 countries studied for the period between 1975 and 1979.[6] While it should be noted that estimates using PPP as the basis for calculating GDP result in much lower absolute figures for trade openness (about 10 percent in recent years), all estimates (nominal and PPP-based) reveal an upward trend in China's integration with the world economy. Indeed, China's opening has been among the world's most rapid over the last two decades.[7]

[4] World Bank (1997a), p. 3.
[5] Parts of the following three paragraphs draw on Moore (2000).
[6] World Bank (1997b), p. 6.
[7] Ibid.

As a result of consistently high growth rates in foreign trade, China rose from thirtieth place among world traders in 1977 to a rank of seventh in 2000. If the countries of the European Union are combined for statistical purposes into a single economic entity, China jumps to fifth place, trailing only the United States, the European Union, Japan, and Canada. In a particularly telling statistic, China's exports in 2000 virtually matched those of India, Brazil, Indonesia, and Malaysia combined. Among other benefits, this success in exports has helped China maintain foreign exchange reserves that have ranked second only behind Japan's in recent years.

As spectacular as China's rise as a trading power has been, its success in attracting foreign capital has been equally or more impressive. As has been widely reported, since 1992 China has stood as the world's leading recipient of foreign direct investment (FDI) among developing countries. Indeed, from 1993 to 2000 China ranked no worse than third among all countries – advanced industrial and developing alike – in any given year. By the mid-1990s, FDI accounted for sizable (and growing) percentages of domestic investment, industrial output, exports, tax revenues, and jobs in China. Every year since 1996, for example, foreign-invested enterprises (FIEs) have accounted for more than 40 percent of China's total exports. All told, China received U.S. $372 billion in utilized FDI between 1979 and 2000, more than U.S. $300 billion of which was recorded since 1990. Long a leading recipient of loans from the World Bank and other sources of public finance, China has also emerged in recent years as a major borrower from private banks, taking in about 10 percent of the world's commercial debt flows. While its success in tapping into expanding cross-border flows of portfolio investment has been less notable, some progress has been made in this area as well.[8] Overall, China's participation in world capital markets is now quite substantial. That said, current levels of external indebtedness do not appear to pose a major problem, as evidenced by the fact that China's debt-to-service ratio remains well within international norms and compares quite favorably to those of most of its neighbors.

In sum, when consideration of China's economic openness is expanded to include measures such as inflows of FDI and dependence on FIEs for exports, as well as trade as a percentage of GDP, the magnitude of

---

[8] For further detail on the figures provided in this paragraph, as well as a comprehensive review of China's participation in world capital markets, see World Bank (1997b), pp. 19–27.

China's Open Policy over the last two decades becomes even more apparent. As early as 1994, in fact, Nicholas Lardy argued that China was "already somewhat more integrated into the world economy than Japan, Taiwan, or South Korea were at comparable stages of their economic development. By some measures, China is more open than these economies even on a contemporaneous basis."[9] For its part, the World Bank also published a study in 1994 in which it concluded that "China has become a relatively open economy."[10]

Whatever measure one prefers, therefore, evidence of China's deepening participation in the world economy is undeniable. Led by the economic takeoff of Guangdong, Shanghai, and other coastal areas, China has joined the latest generation of East Asian nations to emerge as newly industrializing countries (NICs). Chinese industries, once marginal actors in the world economy, have recently emerged as significant players in international markets, most notably in textiles, athletic shoes, household appliances, and toys, but also in areas such as power-generating machinery and office equipment. Indeed, one of the most striking aspects of China's rise as a trading power has been the changing commodity composition of its exports. In 1980, primary materials were the largest category of Chinese exports, with petroleum products leading the way. By contrast, manufactured goods constituted slightly less than 50 percent of total Chinese exports. Moreover, textiles alone accounted for almost half of China's manufactured exports. This basic pattern persisted until about 1985, when a significant shift in favor of manufactured exports began to occur. Over the next decade, China's export profile was steadily transformed as its links to the world economy expanded and deepened. By 2000, 90 percent of China's total exports were manufactured goods, with textiles comprising only about one-quarter of this category. Primary products had declined to a mere 10 percent of total exports.

China's success as an exporter is reflected in the merchandise trade surplus it has registered every year but one (1993) since 1990, surpluses that averaged nearly U.S. $30 billion per year between 1995 and 2000. Especially with its ballooning trade surplus with the United States, second only to Japan's since the early 1990s according to American data, the manufacturing juggernaut on the Chinese mainland has fueled concern in Washington that Beijing is (quite consciously) following in the mercantilist footsteps of its high-performing East Asian neighbors:

[9] Lardy (1994), p. 110.
[10] World Bank (1994), p. xv.

Japan, South Korea, and Taiwan.[11] While there has been great controversy surrounding the actual size and economic significance of China's
trade surplus with the United States – Beijing's figure is generally about
one-third of that claimed by Washington – all estimates reveal a dramatic
increase during the 1990s.[12] Using the statistics preferred by the United
States, for example, the trade imbalance increased more than eight-fold
between 1990 and 2000, when China's surplus reached an all-time high
of U.S. $84 billion and exceeded Japan's for the first time. As it turns out,
the Asian Financial Crisis (AFC) only exacerbated this trend; China's
surplus increased 14 percent from 1997 to 1998 on the strength of export
growth. (This occurred while Chinese exports worldwide were essentially flat, including a substantial decline in sales to Asia.)

Indeed, the surplus more than doubled between 1996 and 2000 according to American figures. In this sense, while the AFC took some of the
glimmer off the larger East Asian "economic miracle," this did not extend
in any significant way to China. In policy making and academic circles
alike, China continues to be seen as every bit the trade force it was prior
to the AFC. Indeed, the salience of China's economic rise remains one
of the most popular (and hotly debated) topics among observers of international relations, especially with Beijing's anticipated accession to the
World Trade Organization (WTO) in 2001. Simply put, the significance
of a richer, stronger China – and perhaps most importantly, a China
whose intentions outside its own borders are not yet clear – has not been
lost on either the scholarly community or government decision-makers
around the world.

THE PROBLEM FOR ANALYSIS

The inspiration for this book came from a series of observations I made
while considering possible dissertation topics at the beginning of the
1990s. First, I was struck by the mantra of Chinese officials that protectionism in world markets was having deleterious effects on China's
integration into the international economy. Chinese trade officials,
industrial bureaucrats, and diplomatic personnel routinely and at every

---

[11] In this sense, China's economic rise has long been viewed by some observers – especially prior to the Asian Financial Crisis – as yet another salvo in the mercantilist challenge from East Asia. For an early statement of this position, see Kleinberg (1990). For
a general examination of East Asian mercantilism, with special reference to the role of
Japan, see Fallows (1994).
[12] Two good reviews are Fung and Lau (2001) and Feenstra et al. (1998).

opportunity criticized the United States and other Western countries for trade policies that inhibited China's ability to sell products in their markets.[13] Among Beijing's numerous grievances, the Multifiber Arrangement (MFA) quickly became a lightning rod for its complaints about protectionism. Described in detail in Chapter 3, the MFA is *the* quintessential discriminatory regime against developing-country exports. In short, the MFA has provided the multilateral framework within which bilateral quotas on international trade in textiles will have been imposed for more than forty years by the time they are fully phased out in accordance with WTO agreements in 2005.[14]

As the international regime that had perhaps the greatest impact on China's participation in the world economy during the first two decades of the reform era, the MFA has long been held out for special opprobrium by Chinese observers. By restricting China's ability to export its most marketable products, so the argument goes, the MFA has stunted reform and restructuring within the textile industry and slowed China's integration into the world economy more generally.[15] Specifically, Beijing complained bitterly in the 1980s that the MFA unfairly restricted China's ability to earn much-needed foreign exchange. Chinese officials further predicted that the quota system would prevent the industry from advancing quickly into modern production. Indeed, Chinese officials routinely decried protectionism of all kinds, insisting that unfettered access to markets in advanced industrial countries was critical to prospects for economic growth, industrial restructuring, and market-oriented reform in their country.[16] The greater was China's ability to export without restriction, it was held, the more effectively (and expeditiously) China could undertake its domestic economic transformation and become more integrated into the world economy.

---

[13] It should be noted that these sentiments were overwhelmingly shared by Western economists, consumer rights advocates, and businesspeople.

[14] Technically, this forty-year period would include not just the time the MFA itself was in force, but also the time that the MFA's predecessor and successor – the Short-Term Arrangement/Long-Term Arrangement and the Agreement on Textiles and Clothing (ATC), respectively – were in force. The international regime is set to be dismantled permanently in 2005 when the ATC expires. For more detail, see Chapter 3.

[15] For two examples of official Chinese views on the MFA during the 1980s, see the interviews with Zhou Yunzhong and Wang Ruixiang, vice-presidents of the China National Textiles Import and Export Corporation, in *TA* 16:4 (April 1985), pp. 23–46, and *TA* 19:9 (September 1988), pp. 28–35, respectively.

[16] Similar arguments came from China's academic community as well. For the commentary of a noted Chinese scholar, see Zhang (1989).

While Chinese objections to the MFA were certainly understandable – the quota system was in fact designed to protect producers in advanced industrial countries from the impact of Chinese imports – these complaints also struck me as inconsistent with a growing body of academic research about the actual effects of quantitative restrictions on exporting countries. Specifically, one well-publicized lesson from the 1980s was that the voluntary export restraints (VERs) negotiated between Tokyo and Washington on Japanese automobile exports had, from the U.S. perspective, mostly backfired. Instead of strengthening American producers against Japanese companies, the VERs actually created more formidable competitors.[17] Limited in the *number* (but not the *value*) of cars they could export to the U.S. market, Japanese manufacturers quickly shifted their *Japan-based* production upmarket into luxury vehicles. Soon Japanese exports to the United States were generating substantially higher earnings per automobile. According to one study, 50 percent of the increased value of Japanese auto exports from 1980 to 1985 was attributable simply to product upgrading.[18] Indeed, most industry observers agree that Japan's long-term success in developing models like Toyota's Lexus and Nissan's Infiniti was accelerated by the VER with the United States in the early 1980s. By 1994, luxury models (defined as those with base prices above U.S. $30,000) comprised almost 40 percent of Japan's total automobile exports to the United States. Moreover, no Japanese luxury models were produced in the United States.[19]

In order to maintain their market share for inexpensive and midpriced cars, Japanese manufacturers built production facilities in the United States to circumvent the effects of the VER. In this sense, FDI was used as an instrument to avoid trade barriers. By 1985, Honda was already producing over 150,000 cars in its Marysville, Ohio plant alone.[20] Except perhaps from a very short-term perspective, the result of the VER was actually heightened, not reduced, competition for U.S.

---

[17] In May 1981, the first in what proved to be a series of VERs and other actions regulating U.S.-Japan trade in automobiles was announced, in which Tokyo agreed to limit the quantity of its vehicle exports to the United States. Japanese automobile manufacturers had tripled their share of the American market during the 1970s, although their sales remained almost exclusively in inexpensive compact cars – a market over which U.S. manufacturers expressed little concern until the 1979 oil crisis following the Iranian Revolution. When fuel-efficient cars became a larger segment of overall sales, Japanese competition became a more formidable threat to Detroit. The result, in short, was the VER negotiated by the Reagan administration. For a brief analysis of the period leading up to the VER on Japanese automobiles, see Yoffie (1983), pp. 221–230.

[18] Feenstra (1988). [19] Levinsohn (1995), p. 11. [20] Ibid, p. 7.

manufacturers. Through U.S.-based production, Japanese manufacturers were able to continue expanding their overall share of the American market despite the VER. And by concentrating its domestically based production on higher-end automobiles, Japan actually accelerated its entry into the most lucrative niche in the international industry. While the U.S. industry was eventually able to regain its competitiveness, the international automobile market was forever changed.

As it turns out, the case of Japanese automobiles was by no means an isolated one. Indeed, quantitative restrictions of various kinds – VERs, orderly marketing arrangements (OMAs), and formal quotas – had been emerging as an increasingly important institutional feature of the world economy since the 1960s. This so-called new protectionism – as distinct from the tariff-based "old protectionism" – was always associated most closely with the MFA in textiles, but the United States alone had nego- tiated VERs or OMAs on steel, footwear, and televisions with numer- ous countries prior to the Japanese automobile case in 1981. For their part, many Western European countries had also taken similar measures during the 1960s and 1970s. By the 1980s, the spread of the new protec- tionism had become a source of major friction in the international trading system. Striking the same note, governments in Europe and North America alike justified these measures as necessary to main- tain "orderly" (i.e., politically manageable) trade in a rapidly changing international economy. In this sense, quantitative restrictions were seen, paradoxically, as interim measures taken in defense of *free* trade, lest intense adjustment pressures in advanced industrial countries – which generally had the most open economies – lead to a return of the destruc- tively protectionist policies associated with the economic nationalism of the 1930s.

Taken as a whole, the pattern observed through the 1980s was one where many developing countries (and Japan) had been able to mitigate the effects of the new protectionism practiced by the United States and Western Europe.[21] Not all countries fared as well as the East Asian NICs, which set the standard for success in the face of export restraints, but most countries coped surprisingly well. In my view, these findings called into question Chinese complaints about the deleterious effects of VERs, OMAs, and other quantitative restrictions. Take the case of the MFA, for example. Numerous studies had shown that the quota system provided under the MFA could, at least under certain circumstances, have

---

[21] For the most comprehensive analysis, see Yoffie (1983).

salutary effects for exporting countries – this *despite* the admittedly discriminatory nature of the international regime. Beginning with Japan,
the original target of protectionism in textiles, many exporters were able
to adapt creatively within the confines of the MFA. In some cases, there
was strong evidence that NICs such as Hong Kong, Taiwan, and South
Korea had actually turned trade restraints to their own advantage,
exploiting weaknesses in the structure of the MFA to improve the long-
term competitiveness of their textile and clothing industries through
product upgrading, product diversification, market diversification, and
foreign investment in overseas factories. Nor were these results unique
to the MFA. South Korea and Taiwan, for example, duplicated this
success when faced with OMAs in footwear and television exports to the
United States in the late 1970s. Even earlier, European and Japanese
steel producers had skillfully mitigated the effects of VERs on steel
exports to the United States during the late 1960s and early 1970s.[22]

Based on the experiences of other countries, both with the MFA itself
and with similar trade restraints in other industries, it seemed reasonable
to question whether China, too, might ultimately find the effects of textile
quotas salutary in some respects. At the very least, Chinese complaints
about restricted market access under the MFA seemed at odds with the
growing body of evidence on how the new protectionism was affecting
performance in certain national economies, especially those of China's
high-performing neighbors. To be sure, not all exporting countries were
able to respond as effectively as Japan and the East Asian NICs had to
the challenge posed by the MFA, but there seemed to be a possibility
that China might not be as disadvantaged by the MFA as its officials
lamented. From Beijing's perspective, the MFA deprived China of valuable export markets for its goods, thereby limiting production and lowering growth. At first glance, however, it seemed to me that a strategy of
maximizing the volume of exports in an industry such as textiles, where
China had both enormous industrial capacity and an underlying comparative advantage in labor-intensive production, might reinforce the
status quo rather than contribute to substantive economic change. While
unfettered access to overseas markets might allow China to earn more
foreign exchange in the short term, the claim that it was also most conducive to economic reform and industrial modernization seemed questionable given the nature of China's economic system during the 1980s,
one that was only minimally transformed at that time.

[22] Feenstra and Boorstin (1991).

In my view, these issues raised more general questions about the kinds of industrial markets in the world economy that were most (and least) propitious for the reform and modernization of Chinese industries. Contrary to the comments of Chinese officials, my offhanded hypothesis at the time was that economic openness (unfettered exports) might actually be deleterious to industrial transformation. My hunch, in other words, was that "easy" exporting was not conducive to substantive economic change at an industry-specific level. Similarly, economic closure (forestalled or heavily restricted exports) also seemed likely to retard change since Chinese industries would be almost exclusively inward-looking. (Given bureaucratic inertia and other forces of stasis, industries lacking outside contact were unlikely to be pioneers of change.) By contrast, moderate economic closure (limited export restrictions, especially of the quantitative variety) might be more propitious for long-term industrial transformation and international competitiveness. In this sense, *moderately* hard times could be expected to elicit more economic reform and industrial restructuring than easy times. Based on the experiences of other countries that had faced similar restrictions in exporting to major markets like the United States and the European Union, there were reasons to expect that China might actually benefit in certain respects from "managed" rather than "free" trade with the advanced industrial countries. While the general literature on the new protectionism had never extended this argument beyond industrial restructuring to the possible benefits of managed trade for market-oriented economic reform, the causal mechanism seemed plausible in the Chinese context. At the very least, it seemed that the assumption that ideal-typic economic openness in the world economy was most conducive to change in China should not go unchallenged.

Consequently, this book addresses the following research question: what have been the effects of economic openness and economic closure in world trade on the reform, restructuring, and rationalization of Chinese industries? As I use the term, "economic closure" is anything that restricts or regulates access to world markets. As suggested above, examples would include not only trade embargoes (ideal-typic economic closure) but also instruments of managed trade (moderate economic closure), such as quotas, VERs, OMAs, and other forces that limit, but do not completely forestall, access to world markets. By contrast, ideal-typic economic openness is equivalent to free trade. Since the vast majority of academic studies and policy debates have focused on the effects of managed versus free trade environments, I examine only cases of economic openness and moderate economic closure rather than cases of extreme economic closure.[23]

In describing industrial change in China, the book does occasionally use generic terms such as transformation, adjustment, modernization, and competitiveness for descriptive purposes. More specific meaning, however, is attached to the most frequently used terms: reform, restructuring, and rationalization. By "reform" I mean the replacement of bureaucratic planning (broadly understood) with market-based economic activity. In this sense, reform includes not simply the decline of formal planning per se but also the reduction of direct administrative interference in economic decisions made by lower-level actors. As I use the term, "industrial restructuring" includes specific phenomena such as product upgrading (of existing goods), changes to the product mix (the introduction of new goods), diversification of export markets, and technological modernization.

In contrast, "rationalization" concerns the adjustment process whereby an industry raises its efficiency or competitiveness by improving its organizational structure, operational systems, and marketing capabilities. For example, rationalization is often associated with increased specialization within and among firms. In some cases, rationalization might also entail the consolidation of existing firms into larger operations with greater economies of scale. As a result, rationalization is often associated with both the closure of less efficient firms and government efforts to streamline an industry by channeling funding and other benefits to more competitive firms. (For this reason, the process is also often seen as being consistent with a more general shift toward a country's comparative advantage.) Furthermore, rationalization is not generally associated with increased industrial capacity. Instead, the goal is improved profitability among existing producers. (And if new capacity is added, we would certainly expect that less-profitable capacity be retired.) Finally, rationalization can also include the redistribution of industry geographically – domestically as well as internationally – in an effort to reduce escalating labor costs or move production closer to natural resources.

---

[23] In addition to my desire to make this project relevant to the existing literature, there were additional reasons for excluding ideal-typic economic closure from my research design. First, cases of extreme closure in world trading markets were difficult, if not impossible, to find for post-Mao China. Second, and more importantly, to my knowledge no one had argued that the international environment most conducive to the reform and modernization of Chinese industry was one of ideal-typic economic closure.

THE CASES

Based on the foregoing, this book uses a comparatively informed case-study approach to examine the impact of economic openness and economic closure in world trade on the reform, restructuring, and rationalization of Chinese industries. (For a comprehensive discussion of the methodological approach and sources of data used in this book, see the Appendix.) As far as the selection of cases is concerned, textiles is a fairly obvious choice given the existence of the MFA. (Unless otherwise specified, the terms "textiles" and "textile industry" refer broadly to the various product areas – textiles, clothing, apparel, and garments – that comprise this industrial sector.[24]) Not surprisingly, the impact of the MFA on developing countries has been widely studied, more so than any other example of managed trade. This, of course, allows us to put the experience of China's textile industry into broader comparative perspective. Moreover, textiles have been absolutely central to China's foreign trade throughout the post-Mao era. Although textiles finally relinquished its spot as China's leading export sector to the machinery and electronics sector in 1996, it continues to account for nearly 25 percent of China's total exports. Indeed, few industries are more important to the Chinese economy than textiles. Even with ongoing layoffs in state-owned enterprises (SOEs), the textile industry remains the country's leading employer and still accounts for about 10 percent of national economic output. As one might expect, the Chinese industry is universally regarded as the largest in the world.

For the purpose of this study, the textile industry possesses one other critical virtue: it serves as an example of both economic openness and moderate economic closure in the international trading system. Quotas against Chinese textile exports were gradually introduced on a product-specific basis over a period that lasted for more than a decade; from only a handful of goods in the early 1980s, China was by 1998 subject to quotas on more than one-hundred categories of goods worldwide.[25] In this sense, unrestricted sectors existed side-by-side with restricted sectors for many years, essentially representing free trade counterexamples to the managed trade conducted under the MFA. (One important area within

---

[24] For our purposes, the terms "clothing," "apparel," and "garments" are used interchangeably.
[25] *TA* 29:6 (June 1998), p. 114.

the industry, the silk sector, was entirely free of quotas until 1994.) The fact that product coverage under the MFA was expanded gradually provides an unusually rich opportunity to examine the effects of external forces on internal change, in this case the impact of expanding trade protectionism on China's textile industry.

As its second case study, the book examines China's shipbuilding industry. While there are no formal export restrictions in the world market for ships – unlike the VERs, OMAs, and quotas found in other industries – international shipbuilding in its own right is nonetheless characterized by a significant degree of economic closure. The world industry has been plagued by chronic surplus productive capacity for more than two decades, in large measure because the traditional maritime powers of Western and Northern Europe have vigorously resisted the decline of their shipyards. For commercial, political, and strategic reasons, governments in these countries slowed structural adjustment in the international industry by handing out generous subsidy packages and other measures designed to support shipyards that were experiencing increasing difficulty competing against upstarts in East Asia. In fact, the problem of global surplus capacity (GSC) was significantly exacerbated by the aggressive efforts of Japanese and South Korean producers to increase their share of the world market. To compound matters, the shipbuilding industry has also been buffeted by periodic recessions in international shipping, the worst of which led to a depression in world ship orders during the mid-1980s.

In sum, shipbuilding has proved to be one of the most intensely competitive arenas in international manufacturing in recent decades. For a new entrant such as China, in particular, the intensifying GSC found in the shipbuilding industry during the mid-1980s had an effect similar to other forms of moderate economic closure, such as the aforementioned VERs and OMAs. (In a definitional sense, GSC simply means that supply and demand are in substantial disequilibrium due to overcapacity. The result is a pronounced buyers' market.[26]) Specifically, the glut of shipbuilding capacity in the world market made it more difficult to secure export orders. Because there is no mechanism that *formally*

---

[26] Strange (1979, p. 304) defines GSC as "a situation in which demand is insufficient to absorb production at prices high enough both to maintain employment and to maintain profitability for all the enterprises engaged." Chronic GSC therefore exists when neither demand increases nor supply decreases.

limits the quantity of ships a country can export, a shipbuilder could in theory try to increase its market share by conducting an aggressive export campaign fueled by cut-rate prices. In practice, however, there has been a de facto limit on the number of vessels any single shipbuilding country could reasonably hope to export, especially in the short run, since rival governments have historically provided subsidies sufficient to protect much (or all) of the existing market share held by shipbuilding companies in their countries.

While the case study on the shipbuilding industry does not provide the same range of within-case variance (i.e., openness *and* closure) found in the textile industry, the degree of closure generated by GSC has, in fact, varied over time. GSC has been a problem for more than two decades, to be sure, but when the shipbuilding industry becomes truly depressed, as it did in the mid-1980s, the glut of manufacturing capacity takes on a different magnitude altogether. In this sense, *chronic* GSC turns into *severe* GSC. With government support flowing freely and ship prices dropping accordingly, a strategy of trying to *expand* the quantity of ship exports becomes not simply difficult, as it is during periods of chronic GSC, but virtually impossible.[27] All told, GSC represents a degree of moderate economic closure equivalent to the MFA. In this way, the shipbuilding case expands our examination beyond formal barriers (e.g., VERs, OMAs, and quotas under the MFA) to include other international forces associated with significant (but not extreme) economic closure.

Much like textiles, shipbuilding is an industry that has been the focus of considerable research in the fields of comparative development and international political economy, especially with regard to China's neighbors in East Asia.[28] As a result, the experience of the Chinese industry can be placed into international context quite readily. Collectively, the two case studies have several additional attributes. First, textiles and shipbuilding are both industries for which Chinese data sources are relatively comprehensive and plentiful. This is especially important for the "process tracing" research described in the Appendix. Second, these industries represent both heavy and light industry. While shipbuilding

---

[27] Indeed, governments have typically provided only the minimum level of subsidies necessary to *maintain* their country's relative market share, thereby making strategies to *increase* market share difficult for companies to pursue. Consequently, attempts to challenge the status quo during periods of *severe* GSC have been historically rare.

[28] See, for example, Amsden (1989), Chida and Davies (1990), Vogel (1985), and Strange (1979).

epitomizes heavy industry, the textile industry ranges from the capital-intensive production of advanced fabrics to the rudimentary, labor-intensive assembly of garments.[29] Finally, the two industries together cover the entire continuum of ownership types from large SOEs run by centrally controlled ministries to wholly foreign-owned enterprises managed from corporate offices in Hong Kong and Taipei.[30]

As part of introducing the case studies, a few words are in order about the time period chosen for this study. Aside from brief historical retrospectives for each industry, the case studies focus squarely on the post-Mao period. For shipbuilding, the greatest attention is paid to the period from the early 1980s to the early 1990s since the crisis in the international industry occurred in the mid-1980s. While the rest of the 1990s receives some coverage, primarily to update progress in the Chinese industry, this case study does focus mainly on the earlier period. In the textile industry, by contrast, there was no critical juncture, per se. Since the imposition of quotas under the MFA represented a "gradual crisis" for China, roughly equal attention is paid from the early 1980s to the late 1990s.

In both the textile and shipbuilding case studies, however, the period of investigation does end with 1997 – that is, prior to the full effects of the AFC. Simply put, the AFC introduced too many short-term distortions in industrial and trading activity to include this important, but generally unrepresentative, episode in the book. In textiles, China's exports declined for fourteen consecutive months from May 1998 to June 1999, while its export prices fell by an average of 16.5 percent in just the first five months of 1999 alone.[31] This conveys some sense of the dislocation caused by the AFC. While the impact on the textile industry was considerable, it paled in comparison to that on the shipbuilding industry, one of China's hardest-hit industries. While the South Korean won and Japanese yen depreciated substantially during the AFC, Beijing maintained its much-ballyhooed "no devaluation" policy for the Chinese *renminbi*. For China's shipyards, the result was virtually no new orders for several months and slow business for a full two years. Beijing did take

---

[29] For a good primer on the textile production process, from the fiber stage through the manufacture of end-use goods, see Dickerson (1999), Chapter 1.
[30] In fact, textiles alone encompasses the entire range of ownership types in China: large SOEs, urban collectives, township and village enterprises, private enterprises, joint ventures, and wholly foreign-owned enterprises.
[31] *TA* 30:11 (November 1999), p. 79, and *TA* 30:10 (October 1999), p. 94.

certain measures (e.g., raising substantially the export tax rebate for ships) to try to compensate for the effects of its currency policy, but these efforts provided little immediate help for an industry severely disadvantaged vis-à-vis its primary competitors. In addition to these short-term problems, the AFC is also likely to have significant long-term implications for China's textiles and shipbuilding industries. While much had returned to normal by 2000, the AFC introduced new dynamics into the industries' international and domestic environments, dynamics that could come to represent a major disjuncture from the past. For all of these reasons, the present study restricts its focus – except for the most basic of overview data – almost exclusively to pre-AFC developments.

Here, I should also note that the case-study chapters take a macrolevel approach in examining the Chinese shipbuilding and textile industries. The book's aim is not to examine firm-level processes or other subjects associated with a microlevel approach to industrial analysis. Rather, the case studies are designed to examine the experiences of the two industries in the aggregate, especially in terms of their integration into the world economy. For the shipbuilding industry, in particular, it certainly would have been possible to focus exclusively on the experience of a single shipyard. Indeed, other studies on China's economic reforms have demonstrated that much can be learned from an enterprise-specific approach. That said, the main theoretical argument of this book calls for a broader examination of how the shipbuilding industry has fared during the post-Mao era of reform and opening.

The limitations of a microlevel approach would be even greater in the case of the textile industry. While there are a relatively small number of major shipyards in China, the textile industry is so vast, so fragmented, and so diverse that any effort to focus on firm-level experiences (or local, regional, or product-specific experiences, for that matter) would be even less representative of the industry as a whole.[32] While a microlevel approach might be appropriate for other research agendas related to the textile industry, it is a poor fit for the theoretical interests of this book. Clearly, what is needed is a macrolevel perspective on the entire industry's integration into world markets under the MFA.

---

[32] The industry is so incomprehensibly large, in fact, that many experts have concluded that even aggregate data on the industry is incomplete. Only gross estimates are available. See, for instance, Chen and Jackson (1996).

INDUSTRY-SPECIFIC ANALYSIS AND THE STUDY OF CHINA'S
REFORM AND OPENING

In addition to the rationale described above, the industry-specific focus taken in this book also has the virtue of complementing existing strengths in the literature on China's growing participation in the world economy. Among the many different empirical approaches used to date, one prominent focus has been geographic. In addition to numerous studies of Shenzhen and the other special economic zones (SEZs), China scholars have also examined the experiences of various regions, provinces, and other localities under the Open Policy.[33] Similar works have also looked more broadly at China's integration into the East Asian regional economy.[34] Another popular approach has been to focus on a particular issue-area concerning China's growing participation in the world economy, such as foreign investment, foreign trade, or technology transfer.[35] A fourth perspective has been to examine China's relationship with international institutions, from its long-established ties with the World Bank, IMF, Asian Development Bank, and the Asia Pacific Economic Cooperation (APEC) forum to its still-evolving links with the WTO.[36] Yet another approach has been a focus on China's bilateral relations with its major economic partners.[37] All of this, of course, is in addition to the plethora of general studies on China's Open Policy.[38]

---

[33] The best work on China's SEZs remains Crane (1990). The classic account of Guangdong's early experience with reform is Vogel (1989).

[34] Two important works on the so-called Greater China phenomenon are Shambaugh (1995) and Naughton (1997).

[35] The literature on foreign investment in China has become huge. The leading scholarly work on the 1980s remains Pearson (1991). For a more recent analysis, see Rosen (1999); on foreign trade, see the book-length studies of Lardy (1992), World Bank (1988), and World Bank (1994); on technology transfer, see, for example, Feinstein and Howe (1997).

[36] For the classic account of the 1980s, see Jacobson and Oksenberg (1990). For a more recent survey, see Feeney (1998). On China's participation in APEC, see Moore and Yang (1999). On China's accession to the WTO, see Groombridge and Barfield (1999) and Pearson (2001).

[37] For a recent examination of Sino-American economic relations, see Saunders (2000). On economic ties with Hong Kong, one of the best analyses remains Sung (1991). For more recent overviews of China's major bilateral relationships, see the country-specific chapters in Kim (1998a).

[38] Important works include Shirk (1994), Howell (1993), and Lardy (1994). For a more recent treatment, see Economy and Oksenberg (1999), especially the chapters by Margaret Pearson and Nicholas Lardy.

By contrast, industry-specific analysis has received little attention thus far. While there have been many studies of China's industrial reforms, economic growth, and expanding foreign trade, these works have not typically concentrated on the experiences of individual industries.[39] Despite their significant strengths, analyses that focus on broad indices of industrial growth or changes in the commodity composition of foreign trade arguably do not capture fully the process of reform and opening in China's economic structure. Furthermore, the lack of industry-specific analysis of China is particularly surprising given the long tradition of both single-country studies and cross-national research in the field of comparative development that have chronicled the experiences of latecomers in particular industrial markets (e.g., textiles, steel, shipbuilding, pharmaceuticals). As many scholars have argued, one of the best ways to understand the nature of a particular country's economic development and integration into the world economy is by examining individual industries or industrial sectors.[40] Indeed, much of the most influential work in comparative development and international political economy in recent years has taken industry-specific change as its empirical focus.[41] Clearly, the time has come to study China in the same way. China's integration into the world economy is no longer a narrowly regional phenomenon, limited to a few pockets of development along its coast. The growing prominence of individual Chinese industries in the world market – from athletic shoes and toys to electronic appliances and machine tools – demonstrates that China's rise in the world economy is a broadly industrial phenomenon, increasingly like that of other contemporary latecomers in East and Southeast Asia.

Another advantage of an industry-specific approach is the way it effectively combines international and domestic levels of analysis. On the domestic side, trade and industrial policies are often formulated on an industry-by-industry basis. While there are certainly exceptions to this pattern, the incremental, uneven, and experiential process of economic reform in China certainly seems to correspond closely to this assumption. In this sense, industry-specific analysis is well-suited for the task of tracking how economic change actually takes place over time and space.

---

[39] Two excellent overviews of industrial reform are Tidrick and Chen (1987) and Naughton (1995). One book that does examine the reform experiences of individual industries is Byrd (1992a).

[40] For a recent statement of this position, see Shafer (1994). Two classic statements are Kurth (1979) and Cumings (1984).

[41] Some notable examples include Evans (1995), Wade (1990), and Amsden (1989).

On the other hand, it also has the important virtue of placing China's economy firmly into its international context. Given the rich diversity of industrial settings in the world market, a feature that makes useful generalizations about the effects of the international political economy on China frustratingly elusive, an industry-specific approach is arguably essential. As this book acknowledges, the contemporary world economy is characterized by a complex landscape for issue-areas such as foreign investment and international trade, one that varies considerably from industry to industry. As discussed earlier, this is especially true when one considers how the international trading system has come to reflect an increasing mix of both economic openness and economic closure over the last two decades as China's participation in world markets has grown. At the same time that much of the world's trade has become freer on both a regional and global scale, certain industries have become subject to various forms of managed trade. From quantitative restrictions, such as VERs and OMAs, to a proliferation of tariff-based instruments, such as antidumping duties, many industries have seen higher levels of regulation in international trade.

THE PLAN OF THE BOOK

The remainder of the book proceeds as follows: Chapter 2 examines in detail the role of the outside world as a source of change in post-Mao China. In addition to exploring key theoretical and conceptual issues, Chapter 2 also previews the book's main arguments about the interaction of international and domestic forces. Specifically, I argue that external factors significantly *restructured* the options facing officials in the shipbuilding and textile industries, in part by actually *widening* the range of politically feasible options to include a more market-oriented strategy of administrative deregulation previously unacceptable to bureaucrats who had resisted both the implementation of nationwide reform programs (i.e., reform from above) and reform experimentation at the firm or industry level (i.e., reform from below).

Consequently, Chapter 2 argues that the literature on China's growing participation in the world economy – as well as the general literature on international political economy – should place greater emphasis on the *structuring* of options more broadly, not just the *narrowing* of policy choices most often suggested by analysts. Indeed, international forces *enable* as well as *constrain* the options facing a country. For example, the case-study chapters show how the MFA in textiles and GSC in shipbuilding induced a change in the pattern of state intervention by simultaneously inhibiting a traditional "state socialist" approach and enabling a more "market-oriented" approach. (These ideal types are described later in this chapter.) In contrast to existing conceptualizations of China's reform process, the vast majority of which focus exclusively on domestic forces, Chapter 2 cites the case-study material as evidence of the need for an alternative "political economy of China's reform and opening," one that focuses explicitly on linkages between international and domestic forces. In this sense, the book is intended to represent a neglected perspective in the literature.

Chapters 3 through 6 focus on the textile industry, arguing that the industry achieved success in industrial restructuring (especially in "trading up" the international product cycle) *because* of, rather than *in spite* of, the protectionism of the MFA. Specifically, as the scope of textile quotas expanded, a pattern of export upgrading, product diversification, and market diversification emerged in restricted sectors of the Chinese industry. This was in stark contrast to the syndrome of "easy" exporting in which unrestricted sectors of the textile industry simply increased the volume of existing goods sold to established markets. While similar findings have been made in studies of other textile exporters, as discussed earlier, I take this finding a step further by arguing that the MFA actually provided an impetus for economic reform and other significant institutional change in the Chinese case. Most notably, the book argues that the expanding protectionism of the MFA induced a deregulated, market-oriented solution to the challenge of industrial adjustment in which the state withdrew substantially from its traditional role in the production and distribution of textile products. To be sure, the MFA was by no means the only cause of reform in the Chinese industry. Still, the moderate economic closure associated with the MFA was instrumental not only in sparking important instances of reform experimentation, but also in eliciting industry-level implementation of national reform programs. All told, apparent adversity was turned into an unexpected ally as the MFA came to represent a springboard for industrial modernization rather than quicksand.

Chapters 7 through 11 examine the shipbuilding industry, concluding that rather than lessening the effectiveness of China's entry into the world market, external pressure in the form of intensifying GSC actually facilitated China's long-term competitiveness by providing the impetus for a variety of far-reaching changes within the industry that would not otherwise have been undertaken. The irony, then, is that hard times in international shipbuilding – which had the same effect as restricting China's access to the world market – provided fortuitous, not disastrous, timing for its entry. Simply in order to compete, the Chinese industry was forced to change its basic development strategy, becoming more of a ship assembler reliant upon foreign designs, parts, and technology than a self-contained, autonomous shipbuilder. Unable to accept orders only for basic bulk carriers and tankers, as originally planned by industry leaders, China was impelled to trade up into more advanced ships. (As in textiles, the shipbuilding industry had also been characterized by the bureaucratic complacency associated with easy exporting.) In addition to experimenting with new ship types, Chinese shipyards also diversified into a wider range of marine and nonmarine products, increased their emphasis on shiprepair, and substantially reduced building periods to attract orders for new ships. As it turns out, international forces induced a change not only in development strategy (from import-substituting industrialization to greater export orientation), but also in the pattern of state intervention in the shipbuilding industry. Similar to the textiles case, central planning and other forms of direct administrative interference in the shipbuilding industry were increasingly replaced by more deregulated, market-oriented processes. While this change must be understood within the broader context of economy-wide reforms, GSC was instrumental – much like the MFA – both in spurring the implementation of existing reforms and in prompting new reform experiments.

While none of the sweeping changes witnessed in China's textile and shipbuilding industries would have been possible in the absence of the reform milieu that prevailed in the post-Mao era, the case-study chapters collectively argue that the basic policy of "reform and opening" represents only a partial explanation for industry-specific advances in enterprise autonomy, management practices, industrial restructuring, market-oriented economic activity, and technological modernization. From this perspective, a broadly proreform atmosphere – including the promulgation of particular reform programs – is best viewed as a necessary but not sufficient condition for the outcomes examined in this book. In this sense, the reform milieu associated with Deng's leadership in the 1980s and early 1990s served as an indispensable precondition for change.[42] As I argue in Chapters 6 and 11, respectively, it was the

---

[42] Indeed, the importance of this role should not be dismissed. For example, the general commitment to reform and opening is critical for understanding why China generally

underlying commitment to reform and opening, after all, that allowed the impact of external forces to play out as they did in textiles and shipbuilding.

Chapter 12 uses the concept of state capacity to construct a comprehensive explanation for the specific path of industrial change observed in China as it sought to cope with the challenges presented by the MFA in textiles and GSC in shipbuilding. While the case studies do show that external forces triggered important changes at an industry-specific level, the characteristics of world industrial markets cannot fully account for the outcomes observed. China's response was broadly consistent with incentives present in its international environment, to be sure, but domestic institutional constraints were also critical for explaining the timing, sequence, and specific content of policy choices. The book identifies three aspects of state capacity from the case studies – the organizational structure of the state, the nature of government-industry relations, and the transitional nature of China's economy during the 1980s and early 1990s – to show a policy "fit" between the particular challenges posed by international forces (i.e., GSC and the MFA) and the market-oriented solution for industrial adjustment that emerged in China's textile and shipbuilding industries. Conceptually, I argue that specific state capacities (and incapacities) profoundly shape the range of adjustment strategies available to a country in responding to international economic change.

Finally, Chapter 13 explores the implications of the book's findings and identifies areas for future research. First, I revisit the central thesis that moderate economic closure has been the most propitious international environment for industry-specific reform, restructuring, and rationalization during the post-Mao era by considering the generalizability and durability of this proposition. Second, I make a few observations concerning China's likely pathway to continued economic development in the twenty-first century. Specifically, I argue that China has only a very limited ability to pursue successfully the kind of "East Asian–style" industrial policy typically associated with Japan, South Korea, and Taiwan, thereby calling into question concerns – still prevalent even with Beijing's pending WTO accession – that China is following (or will be

---

undertook the adjustments necessary to improve its performance in the world economy, rather than simply retrench to the status quo ante, even in the face of external shocks such as the international crisis in shipbuilding and the imposition of textile quotas under the MFA.

able to follow) in the mercantilist footsteps of its high-performing neighbors. Lastly, I conclude by reiterating in final form my argument that the structuring impact of the international political economy represents one of the most conceptually important yet inadequately studied aspects of change in post-Mao China.

THE ARGUMENT IN BRIEF

Contrary to the received wisdom, my research on the Chinese textile and shipbuilding industries suggests that economic openness in world markets was not the most propitious international environment for industry-specific reform, restructuring, and rationalization during the first two decades of the post-Mao era. Indeed, economic openness was associated mainly with stasis while moderate economic closure was associated with significant change in the textile and shipbuilding industries. Specifically, moderate economic closure had two important effects. First, with the intensification of GSC in shipbuilding and the imposition of textile quotas under the MFA, both Chinese industries experienced an externally driven shift from a sellers' market (excess demand) to a buyers' market (excess supply).[43] Second, the MFA and GSC created incentives for a particular agenda of industrial adjustment that served as a substitute for world market signals that could not operate properly due to severe distortions in China's economic system. As mediated by domestic structure, these external stimuli led to substantial reform, restructuring, and rationalization at an industry-specific level.

Modern Economic Closure	→	Domestic Structure	→	Reform, Restructuring, Rationalization

This diagram is, however, only a simplified schematic representation of the book's main argument.[44] Embedded within the main argument are supplementary arguments that explain how and why the relationship between moderate economic closure and reform, restructuring, and rationalization held in these industries. Specifically, there are three supporting arguments.

---

[43] For an excellent primer on sellers' and buyers' markets, see Byrd (1987).

[44] These are not causal arrows, per se. Specifically, this diagram should not suggest that moderate economic closure *causes* domestic structure. Rather, the arrows are simply meant to indicate that the effect of moderate economic closure is mediated by domestic structure.

Moderate Economic Closure and the Emergence of a Buyers' Market in Textiles and Shipbuilding

Moderate economic closure contributed significantly to the emergence of a buyers' market in China's textile and shipbuilding industries. In textiles, to be sure, oversupply was an incipient problem even without the MFA.[45] That said, textiles was an industry where high levels of export growth could conceivably have offset, or at least softened, difficulties with excess manufacturing capacity. Due to the MFA, however, this was not a viable strategy. (Estimates vary widely, but some observers believe the MFA reduced the volume of China's textile exports by more than 50 percent over the last two decades.)[46] Consequently, while the textile industry might well have experienced problems with excess supply even in the absence of the MFA, quotas on Chinese exports certainly accelerated and intensified the emergence of a buyers' market. By contrast, there would have been no buyers' market whatsoever for Chinese ships without the severe GSC that developed in the wake of a major recession in international shipping. Previously, in fact, China's shipyards had faced a classic sellers' market, one that showed no signs of weakening prior to the externally induced crisis of the mid-1980s.

As previous studies have documented, the response of the Chinese government to industry-specific buyers' markets has typically been, in William Byrd's words, to force "producers to feel the impact of market forces directly."[47] Indeed, Byrd and his collaborators from a World Bank research team documented the importance of a buyers' market to the "marketization" of numerous Chinese industries in the 1980s. Specifically, they found that problems with excess supply often led to a higher share of self-marketing by enterprises.[48] Consistent with this pattern, the emergence of a buyers' market in textiles and shipbuilding led to a decreasing reliance on central planning in these industries as mid-level bureaucrats "discovered" an interest in market-oriented economic reform. Indeed, the myriad pressures associated with a buyers' market – in which (formerly guaranteed) sales become a difficult, unfamiliar task – are critical to understanding why the preferences of industry bureau-

---

[45] Indeed, Byrd (1987) identifies textiles as one of several Chinese industries in which a buyers' market emerged in the early 1980s.

[46] The restrictiveness of the MFA should not be underestimated. As one measure, China's quota utilization rates have generally been the highest of any major supplier to the United States and the European Union.

[47] Byrd (1987), p. 263.   [48] Ibid, p. 247.

crats changed. No longer facing the sellers' markets typically associated with state socialist economies, as captured so well in Janos Kornai's concept of a shortage economy, bureaucrats increasingly resisted the temptation to intervene in their accustomed fashion[49] Indeed their interest arguably shifted from the maintenance of administrative control to limited support for market-oriented deregulation as a way of deflecting unwanted bureaucratic responsibility. While the dynamics associated with a buyers' market were weakened somewhat by the relatively soft budget constraints that prevailed during the 1980s and early 1990s, the MFA and GSC did provide the basis for an increasingly hard market constraint.[50] Bearing greater responsibility for their own sales, producers became more attuned to customer demands and devoted more attention to the nonquantitative aspects of production (e.g., price, quality, and service) more generally. In this sense, the emergence of a buyers' market was critical in setting the process of reform, restructuring, and rationalization in motion for the Chinese textile and shipbuilding industries.

Why Moderate Economic Closure Was More Conducive to Industrial Restructuring and Rationalization than Economic Openness

In post-Mao China, foreign exchange has been king. Especially during the 1980s and early 1990s, financial profitability, efficiency of resource use, and other market-based considerations were minor concerns at best. For those involved in China's export business, "success" was defined mainly in terms of earning more foreign exchange. If world markets were characterized by economic openness, this objective was achieved most easily by selling more goods from the existing product mix rather than by trying to produce new, higher value-added goods.[51] (As alternative

---

[49] For the seminal work on shortage economies, see Kornai (1980).

[50] The concepts of "hard" and "soft" budget constraints were first introduced in Kornai (1980). A "hard" budget constraint is said to exist where the long-term viability of an enterprise depends on its profitability. Byrd (1987), p. 269, makes a similar point about weak financial discipline hindering the full impact of a buyers' market.

[51] This point is widely acknowledged. One Chinese analyst, writing in the trade ministry's official journal, expressed the point well: "In order to fulfill their foreign exchange earning quotas, foreign trade corporations did not consider ways to improve competitiveness in international markets; instead they focused on better [i.e., more] sales of primary [i.e., low value-added] products." This author also described foreign exchange earnings as the misplaced "strategic goal" driving Chinese trade in the 1980s, one that actually worsened "national economic returns"; Xu Kangning, "Formation of

export strategies, these options can be thought of as "volume-centered" and "value-centered" strategies, respectively.) In this sense, "success" was entirely possible within the parameters of the existing domestic economic system. Industrial restructuring and rationalization, however desirable in the abstract, were simply not necessary in order to generate more foreign exchange earnings. In the absence of an external impetus for change, several additional factors also reinforced the status quo: general bureaucratic inertia; the ingrained practice of "blind" production in state socialist systems; and the poor state of coordination between industry and trade that prevailed in the Chinese economy during the 1980s and early 1990s. Especially early in the post-Mao era, the country's economic and trade system was clearly best-suited for the kind of extensive-growth strategy permitted in unfettered export markets. (Indeed, this is one likely reason why Chinese officials objected so vociferously to international trade protectionism.)

All told, "success" in open world markets was possible without undertaking substantial industrial adjustment. Consequently, industries with unlimited access to the world market typically exhibited a pattern in which increasing quantities of existing goods were exported to generate higher foreign exchange earnings. If, by contrast, world markets were characterized by moderate economic closure, the ability to earn more foreign exchange was conditioned significantly upon a country's ability to trade up the international product cycle to higher value-added goods. Specifically, if the quantity of goods that can be exported is limited, then foreign exchange earnings depend on effective product upgrading and product diversification. In this sense, "success" requires that a specific agenda of industrial adjustment be achieved.

$$\text{Moderate Economic Closure} \rightarrow \text{Increased Incentive for Specific Agenda of Industrial Adjustment} \rightarrow \text{Change}$$

$$\text{Economic Openness} \rightarrow \text{No Increased Incentive for Specific Agenda of Industrial Adjustment} \rightarrow \text{Stasis}$$

As summarized in this schema, the book argues that economic openness in world industrial markets was, at best, a mixed blessing for China during the first two decades of the reform era. Specifically, the syndrome of easy exporting found initially in both textiles and shipbuilding could

International Economic Blocs and the Redirection of China's Foreign Trade Strategy," *GJMYWT* (October 1991), pp. 2–7, in JPRS-CAR-92-001.

be said to represent a Chinese version of "Dutch Disease," insofar as an ostensible windfall to China's economy proved ultimately to be a curse more than a blessing.[52] While China did earn impressive amounts of foreign exchange from these exports, there was little progress in trading up the product cycle toward higher value-added goods. The quality of existing goods remained poor, and the product mix was rarely expanded to include new or upgraded goods. Similarly, industrial rationalization was slow.

The key to this behavior was the partially reformed nature of China's economic system. As opposed to "comprehensive" reform, "partial" reform is characterized by incremental, *uneven* change across different dimensions of the economic system. Because partial reform is by definition nonuniform, various distortions are introduced. (Here, it should be noted explicitly that "partial" reform is not the same as "minimal" reform. Reform may be minimal in some dimensions of a partially reformed economic system, but partial reform indicates that the degree of reform differs considerably across dimensions.) Indeed, Chinese reform was characterized by profound asymmetries in the 1980s. For example, initiatives that established and broadened foreign exchange retention for China's foreign trade corporations (FTCs) were far more advanced than measures designed to make these FTCs responsible for their own financial performance. In the absence of a hard budget constraint, the primary incentive for FTCs was, therefore, quite narrowly to maximize their foreign exchange earnings. The result, not surprisingly, was an export-at-any-cost mentality in which FTCs focused on selling increasing quantities of ordinary goods – often below prevailing international prices – to established overseas markets. (This behavior explains, in part, why China became the world's most frequent target of antidumping cases in the late 1980s and early 1990s, trade actions in which Chinese exporters were accused of selling goods below their cost of production.)

Due to the distortions created by partial reform, some of which were even greater than those in the prereform system, the international market signals received by economic actors in China were severely

---

[52] In the Netherlands, a boom in gas exports during the 1970s (in the wake of the first oil shock) led to an appreciating currency and higher wages, both of which have clear benefits, but with these changes also eventually came higher inflation, mounting unemployment, and reduced competitiveness in other sectors of the economy. In the end, great success in gas exports – ostensibly a positive development – proved deleterious to the Netherlands, thus inspiring the term "Dutch Disease."

scrambled.[53] In fact, Chinese enterprises in the 1980s operated in what the World Bank once aptly called an "air lock" system.[54] As the case-study chapters describe in detail, the lack of more comprehensive reforms – or, in some cases, the incomplete *implementation* of existing reforms – created little incentive (and perhaps even a disincentive) for certain changes at the industrial level. While the sale of higher value-added goods made sense from the perspective of national economic returns – in part because this would result in larger foreign exchange earnings – this kind of industrial restructuring was unlikely to occur. Given the nature of the Chinese economic system, in which the prices paid to suppliers by FTCs were often fixed, there was actually a *disincentive* for many producers to upgrade their goods, whether that meant improving the quality of their existing goods or diversifying their product mix into more advanced goods. The additional expense of producing higher value-added goods simply could not be recouped in most cases. In this respect, reforms early in the post-Mao era did little to improve coordination between industrial and trading activities or otherwise alleviate the effects of the air lock system.

From this perspective, partial reform produced behavior that, while rational from the standpoint of individual economic actors, was clearly suboptimal from a societal or national perspective. According to the tenets of free trade theory, ideal-typic economic openness should be the most conducive international environment for the restructuring and rationalization of industries in a given country. As a matter of principle, their proponents would argue, unfettered markets provide the most efficient allocation of resources. Furthermore, economic openness would be expected to serve as an especially important impetus for industrial transformation in transitional economies since domestic markets are by definition not fully developed in these countries. In China's case, however, the nature of partial reform prevented world market signals from playing the transformational role expected under free trade theory. For industries characterized by economic openness in international trade, world market signals were not able to penetrate the air lock system.

In this sense, the book offers a potential qualification to neoclassical economic theories about modernization through allocative efficiency,

---

[53] Several economists have indeed argued that distortions introduced by partial reform were so severe in the 1980s that efficiency in resource allocation actually declined with the Open Policy. See, for example, Hsu (1989) and Lardy (1994).
[54] World Bank (1988).

especially with respect to the superiority of free trade. Specifically, the case studies suggest that the international environment most propitious for the reform, restructuring, and rationalization of Chinese industries during the first two decades of the post-Mao period was one marked by moderate economic closure rather than ideal-typic economic openness. Due to the nature of partial reform itself, which inhibited the responsiveness of Chinese economic actors to world market signals, a managed trade environment resulted, somewhat counterintuitively, in greater industrial competitiveness and export success by achieving a more efficient allocation of resources. Simply put, the specific agenda for industrial adjustment introduced by the MFA in textiles and GSC in shipbuilding served as a surrogate of sorts for the normal operation of world market signals, creating incentives for restructuring and rationalization.

From this analysis, the following argument can be made about the impact of free trade and managed trade environments on change at the industrial level: for partially reformed state socialist systems (and perhaps also for developing countries characterized by similar kinds of economic distortions), tight international markets may actually be beneficial to successful industrial development since they can induce countries – as we have seen in the Chinese case – to pursue more effective development strategies, strategies they would not otherwise be likely to adopt. As a result, the "free trade" environment advocated by neoclassical economic theory may not always be most conducive to industrial transformation. In the absence of explicit regimes (e.g., the MFA) or other forces (e.g., GSC) that have a similar effect in restricting or regulating access to world markets, other Chinese industries faced less pressure in the 1980s and early 1990s to undertake the kind of change achieved in the textile and shipbuilding industries.

Why China Responded to Moderate Economic Closure with Market-Oriented Reform

In a fundamental sense, policy responses for industrial adjustment can be classified according to one of three major approaches: (1) a "market-oriented" approach that emphasizes deregulation from direct government intervention in economic matters; (2) an "administrative guidance" approach in which political or bureaucratic decisions replace private, market-based decisions in a selective, discriminating manner; and (3) a "state socialist" approach in which industrial adjustment is attempted through the planning apparatus by means of central commands and other forms of direct administrative control. (Described more fully in Chapter 12, a real-world archetype of the administrative guidance approach would be the *developmental state* policies often associated with the postwar economic success of Japan, South Korea, and Taiwan.)

As detailed in the case-study chapters, China's responses to the MFA in textiles and GSC in shipbuilding are best characterized as relatively market-oriented approaches to the challenge of industrial adjustment. In shipbuilding, for example, China's strategy was considerably more market-oriented than the state-led policies adopted in Japan and South Korea. (As detailed in Chapters 8 and 12, regulation over the entire maritime sector – shipping as well as shipbuilding – increased in Japan and South Korea as government bureaucrats administered centrally coordinated plans to accelerate structural adjustment in domestic shipyards while protecting their market share abroad.) Here, I should note that my characterization of different national responses to the shipbuilding crisis (i.e., market-oriented versus state-led) emphasizes the direction of policy *within* individual countries rather than a relative assessment of total market-based economic activity *across* countries. Simply put, it could be argued that China's market-oriented response to GSC in shipbuilding belied the fact that state involvement in the Chinese industry was still greater, in an absolute sense, than in the Japanese or South Korean industries, where the trend was toward increased state intervention compared to the precrisis situation. So, while the organization of economic activity may still have been more market-based overall in the Japanese or South Korean industries, the trend in Chinese shipbuilding was clearly toward greater market orientation.

As one certainly would have expected, state socialist solutions were tried initially in responding to both GSC and the MFA. Over time, however, the direction of Chinese policy in coping with these external challenges shifted toward administrative deregulation. How much of this eventual market-oriented response in China can be attributed to moderate economic closure itself? Ceteris paribus, I argue that the specific incentives for industrial restructuring created by the MFA and GSC inhibited a state socialist approach while enabling either a market-oriented or an administrative guidance approach. According to this view, a traditional state socialist approach has limited utility for achieving the particular tasks of industrial adjustment – namely, upgrading existing goods and diversifying production to new (or less restricted) goods – introduced by moderate economic closure in world markets. By contrast, many would argue that a market-oriented approach is likely to be the most effective in accomplishing these tasks since markets ruthlessly pursue allocative efficiency. By the same token, however, there is considerable evidence that the administrative guidance approach associated with *developmental states* in East Asia can achieve industrial transformation just as effectively – and, by some accounts, more effectively – than a market-oriented strategy.[55]

In this sense, there are certainly limits to what can be attributed directly to moderate economic closure. While it explains quite satisfactorily the incentive for industrial adjustment facing China, even to the point of identifying the specific economic tasks classified here as "industrial restructuring," moderate economic closure is less compelling as a single-handed explanation for China's multidimensional response to the MFA in textiles or GSC in shipbuilding. As discussed further in Chapter 2, international-level variables – including moderate economic closure – are limited in their ability to explain specific outcomes in a given country. While a state socialist approach may be ill-suited for accomplishing the particular economic tasks necessary for coping successfully with, say, the imposition of textile quotas under the MFA, this kind of policy response is still certainly possible. As the case-study chapters document, elements of a state socialist approach were in fact tried in both the textile and shipbuilding industries. While moderate economic closure helped to induce a change in the pattern of state intervention, from direct administrative control toward greater reliance on market coordination of economic activity, it cannot alone satisfactorily account for this outcome. Even if the nature of the industrial challenge posed by moderate economic closure did constrain China's ability to pursue a traditional state socialist approach, why did a market-oriented approach ultimately prevail over an administrative guidance approach? From this perspective, there were still two viable options that could have been used to respond effectively to externally induced incentives for industrial restructuring.

In a fundamental way, therefore, China's response in textiles and shipbuilding requires reference to domestic factors. Specifically, I argue that the mediating impact of *domestic structure* is critical for understanding how and why moderate economic closure led to reform, restructuring,

---

[55] For a recent overview of the defining issues in this debate, see Woo-Cumings (1999). For the original literature on "market-oriented" versus "administrative guidance" approaches to late industrialization, with particular emphasis on East Asia, see my citations in Chapters 12 and 13.

and rationalization in these Chinese industries.[56] In general, the concept of domestic structure refers comprehensively to both state institutions and social structures. In the context of this book, however, domestic structure is conceived almost exclusively in terms of state institutions, broadly construed, since the nature of policy networks and other aspects of intrastate relations are the most important domestic causes of the changes studied here. In this sense, my use of the concept is consistent with the highly influential body of literature in comparative foreign economic policy that has used differences in domestic structure to explain variations in national responses to similar external challenges.[57]

As mentioned previously, I identify three aspects of domestic structure from the case studies – the organizational structure of the state, the nature of government-industry relations, and the transitional nature of China's economy during the 1980s and early 1990s – as critical for understanding why moderate economic closure led to reform, restructuring, and rationalization in the Chinese textile and shipbuilding industries. Specifically, I argue that these aspects of domestic structure effectively defined the capacities of the Chinese state in responding to intensifying GSC in shipbuilding and the imposition of textile quotas under the MFA. These capacities (and incapacities) in turn shaped the range of responses China could make. For example, I contend that domestic structure undermined the ability of the Chinese state to engage successfully in an East Asian–style industrial policy like that often ascribed to Japan, South Korea, and Taiwan. As a consequence, the viability of an administrative guidance approach to industrial adjustment was weakened. So, while Japan and South Korea responded to the crisis in international shipbuilding with a state-led policy, in which fine-tuned but wide-ranging administrative intervention in market-based economic activity increased, this approach was basically foreclosed for China. As explained in Chapter 12, the ability of government bureaucrats to act as strategic allocators of scarce resources was constrained by each aspect of domes-

---

[56] Of the three, restructuring can be attributed most directly to moderate economic closure, followed in order by rationalization and reform. While internal factors are important in each case, domestic structure is most important for understanding the specific nature of China's policy response, especially the market-oriented approach to industrial adjustment. In relative terms, therefore, reform is the outcome least easily attributed solely to international forces.

[57] Prominent book-length examples include Katzenstein (1978a, 1985), Gourevitch (1986), Ikenberry (1988), Evangelista (1988), and Ikenberry et al. (1988). For a useful review of issues concerning analysis of domestic structure, see Risse-Kappen (1995).

tic structure identified above. In much the same way, domestic structure also undermined China's capacity to employ a state socialist approach to industrial adjustment, regardless of whether such a strategy was even suitable – as discussed previously – for achieving the specific agenda of restructuring elicited by moderate economic closure.

All told, the book argues that domestic structure is an important concept for understanding the capacity of states to respond to external challenges. As the case-study chapters show, the range of adjustment strategies available to China was ultimately shaped by international and domestic forces alike.

Moderate Economic → Domestic Structure → Market-Oriented
Closure (Need for (Shapes capacity to Reform
Industrial pursue different
Adjustment) adjustment strategies)

As reflected in this schematic representation of the argument, domestic structure is a mediating variable through which the impact of the outside world is filtered. The relevance of internal factors notwithstanding, external factors should not be marginalized – as they often have been in the existing literature – as significant sources of change in post-Mao China. As both case studies document, the industry-specific changes examined in this book simply did not occur to the same extent (or even at all) in the absence of moderate economic closure. In this sense, the degree of economic openness in world industrial markets was clearly pivotal in charting the course taken by the Chinese textile and shipbuilding industries.

2

The Outside World as an Impetus for Change in China

The impact of the outside world must pass through an intellectual medium; and the only question is how strong is its refraction, to what extent it possesses independent vigor and can exert a counterweight. . . . We can – indeed, must – stress that in the life of peoples external events and conditions exercise a decisive influence upon the internal constitution. . . . There is a constant collaboration of the inner and outer world.

– Otto Hintze[1]

When you open the door, some flies inevitably come in.

– attributed to Deng Xiaoping

The international system, be it in an economic or politico-military form, is underdetermining. The environment may exert strong pulls but short of actual occupation, some leeway in the response to that environment remains. A country can face up to the competition or it can fail. Frequently more than one way to be successful exists. A purely international system argument relies on functional necessity to explain domestic outcomes; this is unsatisfactory, because functional requisites may not be fulfilled. Some variance in response to external environment is possible. The explanation of choice among the possibilities therefore requires some examination of domestic politics.

– Peter Gourevitch[2]

As Chapter 1 suggests, the case studies examined in this book provide substantial evidence that external factors were critical in inducing many of the far-reaching changes that took place in China's textile and

---

[1] Gilbert (1975), p. 162.   [2] Gourevitch (1978), p. 900.

34

shipbuilding industries. That said, an important question remains: what is it exactly that international forces *explain*? Indeed, the same case studies that reveal the powerful role played by the outside world also illustrate limits to what international-level variables can alone explain. In textiles, for example, national responses to the MFA have varied considerably across similarly situated countries.[3] In some cases, in fact, countries that shared important characteristics with China (i.e., developing countries, late entrants to world industrial markets, countries facing similar quota agreements under the MFA) either responded with different strategies or enjoyed varying levels of success in coping with the MFA. Furthermore, even countries that did adopt similar strategies sometimes employed different types of domestic policies for industrial adjustment (e.g., market-oriented versus state-led) in carrying out those strategies. Similarly, the crisis in international shipbuilding cannot by itself account for why a market-oriented solution for industrial adjustment was pursued in China's industry. As mentioned in Chapter 1, the same crisis elicited different strategies in other countries, including the more interventionist, state-led policies adopted in Japan and South Korea. In this sense, international-level variables offer an incomplete explanation for the specific nature of policy shifts witnessed in the Chinese, Japanese, and South Korean shipbuilding industries.

In trying to conceptualize the effects of international forces on change in post-Mao China, one possible source of guidance would be the burgeoning literature that has emerged on China's growing participation in the world economy. If there is a single dominant theme within this literature, however, it is that domestic politics have been the primary source of policy changes in China's reform and opening. Although their individual conceptualizations of the reform process have varied, most authors have used a political-institutional or political-social perspective to explain not only specific changes in the Open Policy (*kaifang zhengce*),

---

[3] By "similarly situated," I do not mean simply that a country is subject to textile quotas under the MFA. Even countries that face relatively uniform external stimuli (e.g., the moderate economic closure represented by the MFA) may not be similarly situated in other respects. For example, some may be small economies with a relatively high dependence on textile exports, while others may be large economies with a relatively low dependence on textile exports. In cases such as these, differential responses to the MFA can sometimes be explained by differences in their international circumstances. In other cases, however, the countries are similarly situated (albeit not identically situated) internationally. Here, of course, differential national responses to the MFA in textiles (or GSC in shipbuilding) cannot be explained satisfactorily without reference to domestic variables.

but also larger shifts in the nature of China's economic interaction with the outside world. With few exceptions, therefore, the general impression in the existing literature is that external forces were relatively insignificant in shaping China's reform and opening during the 1980s and early 1990s.[4] While a comprehensive review of this rich literature is beyond the scope of this book, it is worth examining how the issue of external-internal linkages has been handled thus far in scholarly work on post-Mao China.[5]

THE (UNDERESTIMATED) ROLE OF THE OUTSIDE WORLD IN EXPLANATIONS FOR CHANGE IN POST-MAO CHINA

Despite making a few obligatory references to the "importance" of international political and economic forces, the literature on China's growing participation in the world economy has not generally made a sufficient effort to identify the relevant external forces, describe the mechanisms by which their influence is felt, or specify exactly what it is that they can (and cannot) explain about change in China. The "outside world" is often featureless, existing only in some abstract sense. As a result, the "internationalization" of China's economy – a term that has gained increasing currency in recent years – usually means little more than the fact that certain firms or localities in China receive foreign investment, import equipment, or produce exports for world markets. For most authors, it is simply China's decision to "open up" – rather than any identifiable characteristics of, or processes within, the international political economy itself – that is seen as having transformed post-Mao China.

While recent and forthcoming work on China's participation in the world economy does place somewhat greater emphasis on how external factors have shaped China's reform and opening, this new focus applies mainly to developments in the last few years rather than retrospectively to the 1980s and early 1990s.[6] For this earlier period, the role of the outside world remains seriously underestimated. Even the most important books on China's integration into the world economy have downplayed international forces as causes of policy shifts and institutional

---

[4] The most prominent exception is Cumings (1989).
[5] For a more detailed review of this literature's strengths and weaknesses, see Moore (1997), Chapter 12.
[6] For examples of recent work that place greater emphasis on the role of the outside world, see Pearson (2001) and Zweig (2000).

change during this critical era. Especially at a conceptual level, a significant gap in our understanding of China's reform experience therefore remains.

One example of this weakness in the literature is the seminal work of Susan Shirk. In *How China Opened Its Door: The Political Success of the PRC's Foreign Trade and Investment Reforms*, Shirk offers a provocative application of the rational choice framework first introduced in her landmark book, *The Political Logic of Economic Reform in China*.[7] As the titles of her books suggest, Shirk's explanation for China's gradual opening in the Deng era is rooted squarely in domestic politics. Specifically, she argues that many salient features of the Open Policy – for example, gradualism, administrative decentralization, and particularistic contracting – are best understood as part of a political strategy designed to build support for reform by changing the preferences of various actors in the system. In this sense, reform policies were used selectively to extend new powers and resources to various groups during what proved to be an extended period of competition for leadership succession. Put another way, the gradualism and particularism of China's Open Policy during the 1980s and early 1990s reflected, in Shirk's view, political efforts to construct coalitions in anticipation of Deng's death, not experimentation with markets or an effort to test the waters of the world economy.[8]

To her credit, Shirk does offer one of the broadest empirical conceptualizations of the international system in the literature. Yet while she identifies a number of different external forces – multinational corporations, foreign governments, and international organizations among them – that have pressured China to undertake further reform, her account focuses narrowly on how the preferences of domestic actors were altered by the new opportunities and incentive structures created by Deng's strategy of "playing to the provinces."[9] What receives less attention, therefore, is how actual forces in the outside world – as distinct from the new domestic institutional arrangements and other internal reform measures that constitute the Open Policy itself – might themselves be reshaping the political and economic landscape by altering actor preferences. As Shirk herself has noted in a revised version of her argument, "Once the wall between China and the international economy was lowered, internationalization exerted a powerful influence on the reform process

---

[7] Shirk (1993, 1994).   [8] Shirk (1994), p. 18.   [9] Ibid, p. 24.

during the 1980s and '90s."[10] Yet, in her analysis "internationalization" is still conceived narrowly as a process of domestic coalitional change in which new strategic possibilities emerge for political entrepreneurs. The impact of external factors on the course of the Open Policy is dismissed: "international factors did not determine the specific content and style of reform policies; the domestic institutional setting did."[11] While this is perhaps true in a narrow sense, the story of China's reform and opening is much more than just one of its leaders, political institutions, or economic system.

For all its strengths, Shirk's analysis is representative of how the literature generally underestimates the impact of the international political economy on China's reform and opening. With very few exceptions, the "political economy of China's reform and opening" is almost exclusively a *domestic* political economy.[12] There is, in fact, a strong sense that China was launched onto a reasonably clear, albeit broadly defined, internal trajectory of change under Deng, a trajectory from which external forces have not significantly deflected China. The international environment, where relevant, has only marginally reinforced the existing trajectory of change. Even if the initial decision to open up was internally driven – a point that can be debated – there is no reason to assume that the resulting course of events was driven only (or even primarily) by internal factors. For example, while studies of Soviet reform under Mikhail Gorbachev have also focused largely on domestic forces, there has also been much greater emphasis on the impact of international-level variables than that found in the comparable literature on China.[13] Indeed, it would seem to make little sense conceptually to study China's deepening integration into the world economy without examining thoroughly the external environment to which China has opened. There is, after all, presumably something "out there" in the world. What is it, and how does it matter for China?

Although there are books in the literature that have devoted insufficient *empirical*, as well as *theoretical*, attention to the impact of the outside world, in most cases the lack of emphasis on external forces has been a result instead of conceptual shortcomings concerning the nature of external-internal linkages.[14] Specifically, most authors have adopted

---

[10] Shirk (1996), p. 187.   [11] Ibid, p. 206.
[12] Again, the clearest exception is Cumings (1989).
[13] See, for example, Snyder (1989), Deudney and Ikenberry (1991), and Evangelista (1995).
[14] See, for example, Crane (1990) and Kleinberg (1990). In an otherwise excellent political and economic history of the SEZs, Crane devotes only two paragraphs in his entire study

what I would call an "all-or-nothing" conceptualization of the impact of the outside world on China: either international-level variables *determine* domestic outcomes or they are largely dismissed analytically. In *China's Participation in the IMF, the World Bank, and GATT. Toward a Global Economic Order*, their landmark study of Beijing's early participation in the keystone international economic organizations (KIEOs), Harold Jacobson and Michel Oksenberg warn against placing too much explanatory weight on international forces, reminding us strongly that China's "policies were chosen by the leaders of China and were not forced upon them by the KIEOs."[15] As they put it, "Chinese participation in the KIEOs . . . was not an automatic outcome dictated by the structure of the international system."[16] From this perspective, one entirely consistent with the larger literature on China's reform and opening, external forces carry independent explanatory weight if (and only if) they alone *determine* the outcome. Due to their use of this all-or-nothing conceptualization, Jacobson and Oksenberg are unable to advance significantly our understanding of how the outside world affects China: "analysis of the interaction between two sets of political-economic systems, those of China and those of the KIEOs . . . shows how the interaction becomes an 'added ingredient' in the process of change on both sides."[17]

While they do document instances in which the KIEOs "contributed" not only to changes in official policy, but also to the policy process itself (and even to the emergence of specific institutions) in China, Jacobson and Oksenberg resist assigning any meaningful role to international forces in the reform process (i.e., anything more than as an "added ingredient"). How exactly did the KIEOs "contribute" to change in China? Simply put, Jacobson and Oksenberg see external factors as having reinforced – not created, impelled, or induced – internal developments. Put another way, the international system only contributed to changes that in their view would have happened anyway.[18] Yet, they never give any

---

to the role of international factors, this despite the fact that the express purpose of the book was to explain changes in China's SEZ policy in the 1980s. As the author himself notes: "It [his approach] tends to downplay international forces, a posture which may be questionable for an issue, such as the SEZs, so obviously influenced by world-systemic pressures" (p. 14). For his part, Kleinberg also relies almost exclusively on domestic forces in explaining the course of China's Open Policy, except for a rather cryptic observation (p. 4) in which he suggests that incentives in the international political economy were encouraging China to pursue a neomercantilist development strategy.

[15] Jacobson and Oksenberg (1990), p. 168. [16] Ibid, p. ix.
[17] Ibid, p. viii. [18] Ibid, pp. 129, 145.

real indication of how significant (or trivial) this reinforcing effect was for outcomes, except to state that "it is possible . . . to *list* changes the KIEOs helped to produce in China."[19]

Margaret Pearson takes a similar approach in *Joint Ventures in the People's Republic of China: The Control of Foreign Direct Investment Under Socialism*, a book that remains the definitive study of China's experiments with foreign direct investment in the 1980s.[20] While Pearson consistently recognizes the importance of external pressure in bringing about changes in China's policy on foreign investment, she, too, ultimately downplays its explanatory power by concluding that Chinese reformers, not foreign investors, made the actual decisions to liberalize. In describing many of the changes as mere "by-products" of ongoing reforms, she concludes that "the liberalizations in controls over foreign investment that filtered through from broader domestic reforms were results of decisions made by the Chinese government itself; they were not responses to foreign pressures to improve the investment environment."[21] As if to underscore her point that the external environment did not dictate change to China, she warns that "to focus *solely* on one factor – and particularly to focus solely on direct pressure for liberalization by foreign investors – is misleading."[22] Not surprisingly, then, Pearson ultimately constructs her explanation around domestic factors, this despite repeated observations like the following: "There was little indication that without pressure from foreign investors reformers would have liberalized unilaterally."[23] While she does strike a fairly even *descriptive* balance between international and domestic factors, Pearson's *analysis* ultimately focuses on the growing influence of economic reformers at the top of the system.

The focus in Jude Howell's *China Opens its Doors: The Politics of Economic Transition* is also on how domestic political dynamics have shaped the Open Policy and China's integration into the world economy.[24] In her formulation, China's reform and opening has been a cyclical process in which "each cycle draws the bamboo curtain open further."[25] Simply put, recentralization becomes increasingly difficult as the number of beneficiaries under the Open Policy grows over time. The cycles of centralization and decentralization continue but with weakened downswings since previous levels of centralization are never fully reestablished. In this sense, the opening essentially fuels itself. For Howell, therefore,

[19] Ibid, p. 130, emphasis added.   [20] Pearson (1991).   [21] Ibid, p. 207.
[22] Ibid, p. 213, emphasis in original.   [23] Ibid.   [24] Howell (1993).   [25] Ibid, p. 41.

the key is how reform and opening gains political momentum. As she puts it:

> Each cycle moves the policy either a few steps forwards or a few steps backwards. However, each cycle leaves a residue of policies, structures and interests in its wake, which prevent a return to point zero and lay the conditions for the advance of the next cycle. In this way the Open Policy keeps moving forward. As opening up becomes more firmly established, any attempts to reverse the policy become systemically and politically more complicated.[26]

To her credit, Howell does acknowledge the impact of the Open Policy on various aspects of China, including the "character and institutional fabric of the state."[27] In a chapter entitled "Towards a Market-facilitating State," she describes how new state institutions were created by the Open Policy and how existing institutions have adapted to China's reform and opening. In the external sector of the economy, for example, Howell sees the roots of a market-facilitating state becoming deeper and stronger with each successive cycle in the Open Policy. As a result, she argues that a "spiral course of institutional change thus shadows the spiral path of the Open Policy."[28] Specifically, Howell notes that "[t]he course of the Open Policy has been shaped . . . by the willingness of foreign capital to trade and invest in China."[29] In fact, she finds that "disappointment amongst reformist leaders [with the level of foreign investment] . . . provided a significant impetus to further changes in the policy favourable to the foreign investors. . . . [T]he influence of foreign capital on the content of policy has risen."[30] In the end, however, she, too, deemphasizes the independent impact of the outside world: "Although foreign capital is crucial to the realisation of the Open Policy, it is not directly involved in the policy-making process."[31]

BETWEEN CHOICE AND CONSTRAINT: CHINA CHARTS ITS COURSE IN THE WORLD ECONOMY

As these important works reveal, the literature places too much emphasis on whether Chinese leaders *could* have made other choices. To be sure, they did "choose" these policies; the decisions were certainly not forced upon them in any literal sense. As it is, however, the all-or-nothing

[26] Ibid, p. 6.   [27] Ibid, p. 181.   [28] Ibid, p. 7.
[29] Ibid, p. 23.   [30] Ibid, p. 24.   [31] Ibid, p. 26.

conceptualization deflects attention away from what could have been a much more important finding analytically: the circumstances – domestic and international alike – under which particular choices were made and why. As Pearson herself acknowledges with regard to foreign investment regulation, "under the conditions, the reformers had little choice but to liberalize."[32] Indeed, this is precisely the direction in which the literature needs to move. Instead of relegating international-level variables to second-class status analytically because they cannot single-handedly explain China's domestic and foreign economic policies, the scholars reviewed above could have specified more systematically the domestic conditions under which external pressures had their greatest (and least) impact on China. Moreover, they could have explored in greater depth the nature of linkages between external and internal forces.

Too often, the literature sets the standard for external influence in terms of control or coercion. In effect, the question asked is: are state actors, intergovernmental organizations, or nonstate actors – for example, the United States, the World Bank, and foreign investors, respectively – able to use coercive power to impose their preferences for economic policy or institutional reform on China? As the literature correctly points out, many important policy decisions concerning China's reform and opening have *not* been made under concerted foreign pressure on specific issues, let alone as the result of foreign control. (In this sense, China's bilateral agreements with the United States and the European Union on WTO accession may be an exception rather than the norm.) As Pearson has argued in a recent overview of China's integration into international economic regimes, most policy changes during the 1980s and 1990s "were made readily and at the initiative of Chinese policymakers, who seemed convinced of their benefits."[33] The fact that, convinced of their economic benefits, China's reformers voluntarily made policy changes does not, however, negate an explanation in which international forces play a central role. Indeed, the fact that changes were made voluntarily rather than by coercion obscures the more relevant issue: would they have occurred in the absence of international factors? Would the policy changes have been made, for instance, if they were not necessary in order to reap more fully the benefits of participating in the world economy? Simply put, policy changes do not have to be the result of foreign pressure – either in the form of direct coercion

---

[32] Pearson (1991), p. 213.   [33] Pearson (1999), p. 175.

or explicit conditionality – in order for external factors to figure prominently in their emergence.

To be sure, Chinese leaders *could* have eschewed virtually every change made during the post-Mao era. Contrary to the literature, however, the fact that China's leaders have had a choice, and in fact have often willingly undertaken specific reforms, does not mean that international forces have been marginal to the process. International forces may not be ineluctable, but if decisions repeatedly fit a pattern in which China "chooses" a policy that facilitates deeper integration into a liberal, market-based international economic system, how significant is the narrow issue of "choice" relative to other conceptualizations of how the outside world affects China's development? If Chinese policy is, as most experts now acknowledge, increasingly (albeit still imperfectly) convergent with international economic regimes, surely this weakens the significance of "choice" as such for understanding the course of China's reform and opening. An analytic framework that marginalizes the role of international forces, as the all-or-nothing conceptualization does by setting such a high standard for external influence, proceeds as if China's reform and opening has taken place in a vacuum. Yet China's deepening integration into the world economy over the last two decades has in many ways been defined by the fact that its international environment is neither one of its own making nor one over which it has enjoyed much influence. Indeed, as Pearson has recently pointed out, Beijing has had no viable alternative but to interact with the liberal trade and investment regime that in effect governs the world economy.[34] In this sense, the international environment has not simply been *conducive* to China's reform and opening – it has also *impelled* policy changes in certain critical respects. As I have argued elsewhere, the structuring impact of the international political economy has been seriously underestimated in the literature on post-Mao China.[35]

INTERNATIONAL-CENTERED PERSPECTIVES ON CHINA'S
REFORM AND OPENING: TOWARD A "SECOND IMAGE
REVERSED" CONCEPTUALIZATION

As this chapter has discussed, the most neglected perspective in the literature on China's growing participation in the world economy is

[34] Ibid, p. 165.   [35] Moore (1996).

an approach that focuses squarely on external-internal linkages, to say nothing of an *international*-centered perspective as such. An example of the latter is what I have elsewhere called the "global logic" of China's reform and opening.[36] This approach, which follows in the tradition of what Peter Gourevitch has termed "second image reversed" analysis, starts from a simple premise: there is much about the changing nature of economic activity in China that can be understood as a function of its position in the international political economy.[37] As a latecomer, it should be no surprise that China's participation in world capital and goods markets has followed the basic course it has. While it is certainly difficult to identify specific imperatives that all latecomers must heed, China's behavior fits the basic pattern of its contemporaries that have become more integrated with the world economy, especially those countries with sizable internal markets, inefficient economic systems, and backward technology. While this argument can easily be overstated, the idea of a global logic does provide a welcome contrast to the domestic-centered analyses of China's reform and opening that have attributed virtually all change to internal causes and processes.

While this book is less extreme in its embrace of an international-centered perspective, it too, falls broadly in the tradition of second image reversed analysis. As Gourevitch notes, "The international system is not only a consequence of domestic politics and structures but a cause of them. Economic relations and military pressures constrain an entire range of domestic behaviors, from policy decisions to political forms. International relations and domestic politics are therefore so interrelated that they should be analyzed simultaneously, as wholes."[38] With this insight as its inspiration, the book argues that the experiences of the Chinese textile and shipbuilding industries cannot be understood without reference to the international environments in which they have operated.

---

[36] The notion of a "global logic" was first examined in Moore (1996). For a more recent treatment, see Moore and Yang (2001).

[37] By "turning around" the second of Kenneth Waltz's three images, Gourevitch identified a long tradition of diverse scholars, from Otto Hintze and Alexander Gerschenkron to Theotonio Dos Santos and Immanuel Wallerstein, whose work shared a thematic recognition that international forces can have a profound impact on domestic politics, policies, and institutions. For Waltz's three images, see Waltz (1954). For Gourevitch's propositions, see Gourevitch (1978).

[38] Gourevitch (1978), p. 911.

Even at the beginning of the post-Mao era, reform was never a program of specific policies to be implemented from above by central leaders. Rather, it was (and still is) what Cyril Zhiren Lin once called an "open-ended" process, one influenced internally by, among other actors, mid-level bureaucrats, local governments, and nonstate firms – as well as by central leaders.[39] While external forces are obviously not the only salient factors involved in China's reform and opening, the empirical record suggests that they have played a more critical role than that indicated in the literature. Especially for the coastal areas and trade-oriented industries, the "field of play" in China's political economy has broadened progressively to include more and more of the outside world. The strategic terrain over which politics in China is conducted now extends beyond domestic structures to regional, international, transnational, and even global structures. As the case studies in this book show, the characteristics of specific world markets have proved to be critical in charting the course of reform, restructuring, and rationalization in Chinese industries. More broadly, international factors have clearly given shape to the "political economy of reform and opening" in post-Mao China. With the expansion and intensification of various external-internal linkages over the last two decades, the source of policy shifts and other kinds of ostensibly "domestic" change in China is no longer (if indeed it ever was) either narrowly external-systemic or internal-societal.[40] Indeed, many of the changes that have accompanied China's growing participation in the world economy are consistent with the notion of reform and opening as a "discovery process" in which learning, experimentation, and various types of external-internal feedback mechanisms have been critical.

Clearly, a new approach is needed in order to conceptualize the interaction of international and domestic processes more fully. The concept of a feedback mechanism does indeed provide one useful way to think about how international forces, such as those operating at the industrial level, can shape domestic change.[41] How do external stimuli, such as the

---

[39] See Lin (1989).

[40] Samuel S. Kim has consistently trumpeted this theme in his work on Chinese foreign policy over the years. Although he argues that neither set of factors can alone explain changes in China's foreign relations, he does provide an excellent overview of both external-systemic and domestic-societal factors as sources of change in Chinese foreign policy. For his most recent statement along these lines, see Kim (1998b).

[41] Also drawing on Gourevitch's "second-image reversed" analysis, Samuel S. Kim has pointed to the utility of thinking in terms of a "a circular feedback process in which external influences become part of the conceptual, definitional, policymaking, and institution-building processes of Chinese foreign policy"; ibid, p. 23.

moderate economic closure associated with the MFA in textiles and GSC in shipbuilding, feed back into the Chinese political economy? As the case-study chapters will show, the introduction of these international forces induced a change in the pattern of state intervention toward greater reliance on deregulated, market-oriented solutions for industrial adjustment. As this example suggests, it is necessary to incorporate both the international environment and the domestic environment in defining the context of China's reform and opening.

CONCEPTUALIZING THE "OUTSIDE WORLD"

In discussing the impact of the outside world, China scholars have used several terms relatively interchangeably in the literature: the international system, the international environment, and the international dimension. Among these, the term "international environment" is used as the primary reference in this book. Unlike the term "international system," which holds specific theoretical meaning for some scholars of international relations, the term "international environment" refers broadly to the external context in which China operates. Unlike general references to "international forces," "international factors," or "international pressures," the term "international environment" effectively indicates the larger milieu in which China finds itself, rather than a narrow focus on any particular set of actors or processes. In this sense, the term is used synonymously with the notion of an international-external dimension, as opposed to a domestic-internal dimension.

In many respects, the term "external" is preferable to the term "international" since the latter arguably overemphasizes the primacy of inter-governmental relations and transactions in contemporary world affairs. Indeed, terms such as "external," "world," "transnational," and "global" suggest a much wider range of actors and activities than the state-centered paradigms often associated with the study of "international" relations. While each of these terms has its strengths and weaknesses, "external" has the virtue of being the most neutral, both normatively and theoretically.[42] Consequently, this book refers frequently to China's

---

[42] The term "global," for instance, suffers from the opposite problem of the term "international" – namely, it overstates the degree to which state actors have lost control over outcomes in world affairs. While distinct from both "globalization" and "globalism," "global" arguably brings its own viewpoint, too. Similarly, the term "world," while

"external environment." At the same time, it also makes wide use of the term "international environment." In part, this is done simply to inject variety into the book's phraseology. Moreover, since the "external" factors examined in the book – namely, the MFA in textiles and GSC in shipbuilding – are in fact largely "international" (i.e., inter-state) phenomena, this usage is also analytically meaningful. In sum, "international" and "external" have no specific difference in meaning unless otherwise indicated.

How are we to operationalize the concept "external environment"? As used in this book, it is actually an umbrella concept comprised of the myriad forces that operate in the outside world. While the term is useful as a shorthand reference, we should distinguish between several basic realms in world affairs: political, military, economic, and social-cultural. Within any given realm, we might then examine factors such as the distribution of power, the policies of leading states and intergovernmental organizations, and the actions of nonstate entities (i.e., transnational or nongovernmental actors).[43] Even if we restrict our focus to the world economy, therefore, it is very difficult to generalize about the effects of China's external environment given the diversity of forces present even within narrowly defined issue-areas such as international trade, investment, and technology transfer. For this reason, it is desirable to be as precise as possible in identifying the international forces that one studies. As described in Chapter 1, this book examines the international environment primarily in terms of the degree of economic openness found in specific industrial markets.

Like many studies of China's foreign relations, especially those concerned with traditional political-security affairs, this book conceives of the international environment at least partly in structural terms. Specifically, the moderate economic closure represented by the MFA in textiles and GSC in shipbuilding is treated not simply as a function of, say,

---

perhaps less ideological than "global," is still associated to some degree with the politicized literatures on world order and world society. While the cases studied in this book certainly do contain an element of "transnational" relations, understood as exchange which takes place outside the traditional state-centric realm, the recent experiences of the Chinese textile and shipbuilding industries are still best understood from the perspective of "international" rather than "transnational" political economy.

[43] This discussion draws on Deudney and Ikenberry (1991), especially pp. 77–78, and Breslauer (1997), especially p. 5.

U.S. or Japanese government policy, but also as a structural feature of the industrial markets China encounters in the world political economy. Take the MFA for example. As important as the bilateral textile agreements negotiated with the United States have been in shaping China's participation in international textile markets, the external environment Beijing faces in this industrial sector cannot be reduced simply to foreign pressure from Washington. Indeed, the moderate economic closure that characterizes world trade in textiles today is the product of decades of complex interaction among exporting and importing countries. As detailed in Chapter 3, the regulation of textile trade has been governed by a series of formal international regimes, most notably the MFA. In shipbuilding, GSC also represents a structural feature of the industrial market, albeit one not formalized by an explicit international regime. Even more than in the textile industry, moderate economic closure in shipbuilding is the result not of policies adopted by any particular national government (let alone an international institution), but rather of the long-term interaction of governments and firms both within and among shipbuilding countries. In this sense, GSC reflects the ongoing interaction of myriad state and nonstate actors in the world shipbuilding industry.

Many studies on China have examined the international environment in structural terms.[44] For example, Chinese foreign policy is often analyzed from a balance-of-power perspective associated with neorealism. According to this view, the international system – defined in terms of the distribution of material power capabilities – significantly constrains China's interaction with other states.[45] In a different but related way, the international forces examined in this book – the MFA in textiles and GSC in shipbuilding – can also be conceived in structural terms. For this study, then, the "external environment" consists of distinct international structures in the textile and shipbuilding industries. In terms of what Kenneth Waltz would call "system" effects, therefore, the book examines a specific industrial market as a structure in the international political economy that, "once formed . . . becomes a force in itself, and a force that the constitutive units [that is, individual countries] acting singly or in small numbers cannot control."[46]

---

[44] For an excellent overview, including an application of structural analysis to norms, see Johnston (1998).

[45] For two examples from different periods, see Goldstein (1998) and Ng-Quinn (1984).

[46] Waltz (1979), p. 90.

THE EFFECTS OF EXTERNAL FORCES: TOWARD A
CONCEPTUAL FRAMEWORK

In order to improve upon the all or nothing conceptualization currently found in the literature, we must begin by making a clear distinction between two analytically different phenomena: first, the "effects" of forces in the international environment; and, second, the "responses" of individual countries to these external forces. As China scholars have been quick to point out, external forces do not *determine* the political and economic choices made at the domestic level, except perhaps in extreme cases such as foreign invasion, international occupation, or formal colonization. Under most circumstances, international forces only *shape* or *condition* the range of action available.

As even a devout systems theorist like Waltz has noted, the international environment has little power to explain specific outcomes in a particular country.[47] Consequently, the "effects" of the international environment cannot be defined, even just for operational purposes, simply as the "response" taken by a country to certain external forces. How, then, can we conceptualize the "effects" of international forces on China? Since international forces can only be said to explain fully the external situation countries face rather than the specific policies they adopt in response to these constraints, the "effects" of international forces are perhaps best conceived in terms of the "structuring" impact they have on the options available to states.[48]

The case studies examined in this book do, in fact, suggest that the emphasis conceptually should be placed on the *structuring* of options more generally, not just the *narrowing* of policy choices often suggested by analysts. As the chapters on the textile and shipbuilding industries show, international forces can *enable* as well as *constrain* the options facing a country such as China. For example, by creating a buyers' market in ships and putting a premium on the production of advanced ships, GSC in shipbuilding fundamentally altered the incentives facing state officials, thereby making some options – namely, a market-oriented

---

[47] Waltz (1986), pp. 343–344.
[48] This does not suggest that international-level variables are unimportant for explaining the "responses" of states. Rather, it simply means that external forces cannot single-handedly explain unit-level responses. Put another way, international-level variables may well be important for explaining state responses, but they cannot provide a complete explanation for such action. In this sense, many (but not all) scholars agree, all structural explanations are necessarily incomplete.

approach to industrial adjustment – more viable politically. Previously resistant to change, industry bureaucrats "discovered" an interest in administrative deregulation as a result of hard times at home and abroad. At the same time, by introducing economic tasks associated with intensive (rather than extensive) growth, GSC also inhibited China's ability to pursue the traditional state socialist approach familiar to centrally planned systems. In this sense, the impact of external forces was to *restructure* the range of policy options available to China. This finding is especially important since moderate economic closure has been assumed, as discussed in Chapter 1, only to narrow, not expand, the range of options available, principally by working against the prospects for market-oriented reform.

In fact, inasmuch as external challenges for industrial adjustment created (or, at the very least, significantly exacerbated) internal crises that forced domestic actors in China to consider increasingly radical solutions to the problems associated with partial reform in state socialist systems more generally, international forces not only *restructured* the options available, but also *accentuated* the choices among the remaining possibilities. Specifically, it could be argued that the forces of moderate economic closure examined in this book served to sharpen the dichotomy between the following choices: increased market-oriented reform, with as much reliance as desired on an externally oriented development strategy; and (2) retrenchment toward greater direct administrative control over economic activity with correspondingly less emphasis on an externally oriented development strategy (or, at the very least, a less *successful* externally oriented development strategy). While the status quo remained an option, the international environment had effectively raised the opportunity cost of inaction for the Chinese textile and shipbuilding industries.

LIMITS TO INTERNATIONAL-CENTERED PERSPECTIVES ON
CHINA'S REFORM AND OPENING

International-centered perspectives offer a welcome contrast to Sinocentric analyses that attribute virtually all change to internal causes and processes. Yet even if one thinks the world political economy exerts a powerful influence, we still need to account for why China did in fact make adjustments necessary for more successful participation in the world economy, adjustments not always made by other countries. As Peter Gourevitch observes, "meeting the demands of the [international] system . . . requires explanation."[49] For that matter, there is also the issue of explaining the specific adjustments made by China, adjustments that differed from those made even by other successful countries. As Chapter 1 explores in detail, some countries have concentrated more on certain strategies (e.g., product upgrading) than others (e.g., market diversification) in responding to incentives present under the MFA. Similarly, as mentioned in this chapter's opening paragraph, even countries that have focused on the same strategy have often employed different policy orientations (market-oriented versus state-led) in pursuing their objective.

Consequently, while this book does encourage greater use of international-centered perspectives as we seek to understand China's recent experience as a latecomer in the world economy and a reformer from state socialism, it does not suggest that international-level variables can single-handedly explain either the evolution of the Open Policy or China's foreign economic policy in general, to say nothing of the myriad changes within China itself. Even if the path ultimately taken was profoundly shaped by outside forces, and often not in the ways originally expected by China's leaders, internal causes and processes were certainly important as well. As discussed above, the outside world explains only the (restructured) options Chinese decision makers face, as well as the changing costs and benefits attached to those policy choices, *not* the country's responses per se. In Peter Katzenstein's words, "International factors . . . are funneled through domestic structures that are shaped by different histories and embody different political possibilities."[50] In this sense, there is a chain of causality in which the impact of international forces is mediated by domestic forces.

In Chapter 12, I follow the lead of Katzenstein and others writing in this vein by focusing primarily on domestic structure – especially the organizational structure of the state, the nature of government-industry relations, and the transitional nature of China's economic system during the 1980s and early 1990s – in my examination of internal forces. These are not, of course, the only domestic factors that could be used to explain a country's response to the external environment. Ideational variables, for instance, are largely absent from my argument. Similarly, informal politics, party politics, and factional power models – three mainstays among China scholars – receive little attention in this book. Nor do broader societal or regional interests weigh heavily in my analysis.

---

[49] Gourevitch (1986), p. 235.   [50] Katzenstein (1985), p. 37.

For my case studies, I found that a focus on the specific institutional capacities of the state proved to be most important for understanding how domestic politics shaped China's response to its external environment.

Even though the central argument of this book is that greater attention should be paid to the international context within which China operates, domestic agency certainly matters. Indeed, one of the main limitations of a purely international-centered perspective is how the "politics" of reform and opening tend to disappear. To the extent that Chinese decision-makers retain significant leeway in their actions, however, this maneuvering room is arguably best understood in terms of the political autonomy they possess and the specific institutional capacities they enjoy. In this sense, the book eschews the "strong state" versus "weak state" debate in favor of the political science literature that emphasizes the specific capacities (and incapacities) that characterize a given state. It is these domestic constraints, I contend, that gave shape to China's responses to the MFA in textiles and GSC in shipbuilding. From this perspective, internal factors are always critical in explaining the timing and specific content of individual country responses, even when external factors arguably serve as the main impetus for change.[51] In sum, the international environment does not single-handedly *determine* state policies. Rather, these choices must be explained in terms of both external and internal factors.

FUTURE RESEARCH: BROADENING AND DEEPENING
THE STUDY OF CHINA'S REFORM AND OPENING

For all the reasons suggested above, the research agenda should now turn more explicitly to the study of *how* and *when*, rather than merely *if*, external factors have influenced China's reform and opening. For a simple conceptualization, consider the imagery of a funnel in which remote and

---

[51] In a fundamental sense, therefore, "international" and "domestic" explanations are best conceived as complementary explanations for specific outcomes in a particular country. For an interesting analysis that assesses international and domestic explanations as "rival" and "complementary" explanations for labor politics and regime change in Latin America during the 1940s, see Collier (1993). While my case-study chapters reveal clear instances where international forces (e.g., GSC-related incentives to export advanced ships) were at *cross-purposes* with certain domestic forces (e.g., the original plans of industry officials), there were other domestic forces (e.g., the reform milieu of the post-Mao era) that *reinforced* the direction of external influence.

proximate causes play complementary roles in shaping outcomes. As this notion of causality suggests, we need conceptual models that integrate several levels of analysis: subnational, national, and international. (These levels, of course, can in turn be further disaggregated.) Indeed, the case-study chapters argue that the reform, restructuring, and rationalization of China's textile and shipbuilding industries was the result of both external and internal factors. At the very least, China scholars need to be more self-conscious in trying to trace policy shifts, institutional change, and other related outcomes back to "remote" factors in the funnel of causality when they construct explanations for China's reform and opening. For example, given the rapid growth in China's participation in the world economy over the last two decades, it is surprising that Sinologists have not yet developed their own version of the longstanding *gaiatsu* (outside or foreign pressure) literature found in Japanese studies.[52] Indeed, this raises a broader question: Under what circumstances – internal and external alike – do specific international forces have the greatest (and least) impact on Chinese domestic and foreign policy? While some research has addressed this question with regard to China's participation in the world economy, much work remains.[53]

For the study of China's reform and opening to advance, moreover, we need to move away from the "external versus internal" controversy itself.[54] While the case-study chapters do argue that change in the textile and shipbuilding industries was the result of discretely external and internal factors, they also suggest – far more importantly – that developments in these industries were the product of *interaction* between external and internal factors. For example, both case studies contend that moderate economic closure altered the policy preferences of bureaucratic actors within the industrial apparatus. In this sense, the simple image suggested by a funnel of causality (or, to use an alternative visualization, a chain of causality) does not fully capture the interactive linkages between international and domestic factors. As helpful as the funnel image may be for visualizing causal processes – with its wide top (broadest environmental influences), tapered middle (institutional context),

---

[52] For a recent example, see Schoppa (1997).

[53] Two preliminary efforts are Moore and Yang (2001) and Pearson (2001).

[54] As noted by Gerald Segal, this division has long characterized the China field: "There remains a basic tension between the student of international relations who sees the international system as the primary determinant of change in foreign and even domestic policy, and the area specialists who tend to see the domestic environment as the source of reform and each country as unique." Segal (1990), p. 3.

and narrow bottom (final decision-making agents) – it conveys only a simple understanding of how the various "inputs" are related.

Whereas the existing literature overstates the distinction between international and domestic factors, rarely even classifying external factors as "remote" inputs in the funnel of causality, future work must regard China's external environment as more than just a set of confining conditions. In the spirit of James Rosenau's call three decades ago for greater emphasis on "linkage politics," research on China's deepening involvement in the world economy must seek to identify patterns in which factors at one level repeatedly impinge upon behavior at the other level.[55] As China's currency policy during the Asian Financial Crisis showed, "international" and "domestic" processes have become increasingly interrelated.[56] Indeed, it can be argued that many "domestic" processes in China cannot be fully understood today as analytically separate from their "international" or "regional" contexts, especially with regard to the formulation of policies for further economic reform.

At the same time, new conceptual frameworks must not inadvertently "crowd out" the role of domestic actors and institutions in an effort to better incorporate the relevance of international forces. What is needed, therefore, are theories that by their very design integrate data from both levels of analysis. As stated by Robert Putnam, whose seminal work on "two-level games" was a major contribution to this effort, "we need to move beyond the mere observation that domestic factors influence international affairs and vice versa, and beyond simple catalogs of instances of such influence, to seek theories that integrate both spheres, accounting for areas of entanglement between them."[57] As Gabriel Almond observed in a review article on linkage politics, "the picture which emerges [from such analysis] . . . is one of a complex dynamic process which offers no simple answers or solutions."[58] As Almond's comment suggests, the danger is that greater richness is achieved at the expense of analytical rigor. To guard against this outcome, China scholars would do well to continue drawing upon frameworks already developed in the general literatures in comparative politics and international relations, a strategy employed to good effect in recent work by Margaret Pearson and David Zweig.[59] From this perspective, it is encouraging to note that

---

[55] See Rosenau (1969).   [56] See Moore and Yang (2001).
[57] Putnam (1988), p. 433.   [58] Almond (1989), p. 257.
[59] Pearson has applied the literature on transnationalism to China's behavior in international economic regimes. See, for example, Pearson (2001). For his part, Zweig has on

studies formulated at a single level of analysis – international *or* domestic – continue to give way in the fields of international and comparative political economy to projects aimed at bridging the external-internal gap.[60]

One endeavor that deserves particular attention in future research is greater efforts at specifying the various mechanisms by which the international environment affects China. As already noted in the literature, China is influenced by a widening array of external factors. By almost any measure, their number has grown tremendously across issue-areas as China's participation in world affairs has expanded over the last two decades.[61] Less studied, however, are the different mechanisms by which external influence is exerted. Put another way, we currently have a better understanding of *what* forces affect China than of *how* these forces affect China. As critiqued above, the existing literature on China's participation in the world economy focuses far too narrowly on control as the primary means by which the outside world can influence China. Indeed, any analysis of external influences should also explicitly include mechanisms such as contagion and conditionality.[62] While not especially relevant to the case studies examined in this book, contagion has been an important mechanism by which the outside world has influenced change in post-Mao China. From the general demonstration effects of export-oriented industrialization among China's neighbors in East Asia to the transfer of specific concepts such as *chaebol*-style conglomerates and the notion of a *developmental state*, one should not underestimate the extent to which the diffusion of ideas and norms has shaped China's reform and opening.

More germane to this book is a conceptualization focusing on conditionality, whether that conditionality is formal or informal in nature. There is, for example, a *private* conditionality driven by market forces that operates similarly to the *official* conditionality imposed on developing countries (and the so-called transitional economies) by foreign

several occasions applied a general analytical framework on the "internationalization of domestic politics" to China's Open Policy. See, for example, Zweig (1995, 2000).

[60] Important landmarks in the development of this literature include works as diverse as Cumings (1984), Katzenstein (1985), Gourevitch (1986), Haggard (1990), Putnam (1988), and Rogowski (1989).

[61] For an excellent overview, see Economy and Oksenberg (1999).

[62] This discussion draws on analysis found in Whitehead (1996b) and Schmitter (1996), both in Whitehead (1996a). It should be noted, however, that my use of the terms "control," "contagion," and "conditionality" modifies both Whitehead's and Schmitter's usage.

governments and multilateral economic institutions.[63] Just as China's accession to the WTO is conditioned upon meeting certain regime requirements, so too is China's participation in capital and goods markets conditioned in a similar way upon domestic reforms and changes in foreign economic policy. Consider, for example, China's laws governing foreign investment. Beijing has not been forced (in the literal sense) to improve China's investment environment for foreign capital, but failure to do so carries with it significant risks – namely, that capital flows might be diverted over time to more investor-friendly developing countries. In this sense, China can certainly avoid x if it so chooses, but then y may not happen. In this way, private conditionality exerts pressure on China along a wide variety of economic fronts, from macroeconomic stability and trade policy to industrial restructuring and the protection of intellectual property rights.[64]

As an alternative to the all-or-nothing conceptualization that has thus far dominated the literature, a focus on conditionality recognizes the potential importance of international factors while still acknowledging the voluntary nature of Chinese action. In contrast to control, which emphasizes the use of coercive power and even implies a diminution of sovereignty, conditionality focuses on external-internal linkages that can be conceived, at least in part, in terms of feedback loops in the policy-making process. As detailed in the case-study chapters, the MFA in textiles and GSC in shipbuilding restructured the policy options available to Chinese decision-makers at the industrial level, both by changing the costs and benefits of specific policy choices and, perhaps even more fundamentally, by changing the preferences of certain bureaucratic actors.

Yet in neither case was "control" the operative mechanism of international influence. Even in the textile industry, where there is a formal international regime under which trade is regulated by bilaterally negotiated agreements (e.g., Sino-American textile pacts), direct control plays almost no role. The MFA itself has virtually no reach within China, nor have Washington, Brussels, or other major trade partners dictated specific policy changes to Beijing through any authority granted under the MFA. Yet the external environment has had a significant impact on China's textile industry. However conditional in nature, external incentives for change have been powerful indeed. The opportunity costs of

---

[63] This use of the term "private conditionality" draws on Stallings (1995), p. 362.
[64] For additional discussion, see Moore and Yang (2001).

inaction, while undoubtedly survivable, would have been painful at an industry-specific level.

The fact that conditionality is associated with voluntary rather than coercive change does not, therefore, render external forces marginal. One method for assessing their explanatory power is counterfactual analysis. As Miles Kahler has observed in discussing the impact of IMF and World Bank programs, "The best measure of influence is the degree to which external actors change the trajectory of national policy from what it would have been in the absence of their intervention."[65] Put in the context of this study, the relevant question is whether the changes observed in the Chinese textile and shipbuilding industries would have occurred in the *absence* of moderate economic closure. As described in Chapter 1, the gradual nature of product coverage under the MFA is well-suited for examining the impact of varying degrees of economic openness on China's textile industry. Where quotas were in place, the industry experienced significant reform, restructuring, and rationalization. For unrestricted sectors of the industry, change was largely absent. While this pattern was evident throughout the industry, it was most easily seen in the silk sector. A similar argument applies to shipbuilding, where intensifying GSC in the international industry during the mid-1980s triggered changes that were not only unprecedented in the Chinese shipbuilding industry but also unlike anything witnessed in other heavy industries such as automobile manufacturing. In both textiles and shipbuilding, therefore, external forces clearly "changed the trajectory" of policy at the industry-specific level. For this reason, the book argues that the most powerful causal chain in each case runs from the international environment to the reform, restructuring, and rationalization of these Chinese industries.

CONCLUSION

With few exceptions, the salience of international factors has been an under-studied (or at least under-conceptualized) subject in the literature on China's integration into world markets during the 1980s and early 1990s. To a more limited extent, that same critique also applies to studies of China's more recent participation in the world economy. Ironically, there is a major disjuncture between the scholarly community's emphasis on domestic forces as the primary (and, in some cases, almost

[65] Kahler (1992), p. 96.

exclusive) determinant of change in post-Mao China and the underlying premise of Western policy for the last two decades – by national governments and intergovernmental organizations alike – that policies of "engagement" in China's external environment can be an important source of internal change. A handful of recent contributions notwithstanding, most of the vast literature on China's reform and opening has essentially bracketed the international system. (In this respect, the books reviewed in this chapter actually hold up fairly well. While they downplay the role of international forces at a theoretical level, these otherwise excellent books do devote considerable empirical attention to China's external environment.)

All told, the outside world is not a constant that can be ignored in comparative or country-specific analysis. Indeed, the external environment is a dynamic set of forces with which internal forces interact and not simply a static set of opportunities to which internal actors respond. If one measure of influence is the extent to which policy would have been different in the absence of a specific international factor (e.g., the MFA in textiles or GSC in shipbuilding), then the salience of the outside world should be clear. While too much significance should not be assigned to the relative importance of international versus domestic variables, lest China scholars repeat the mistakes often found in other country-specific studies, the case studies examined in this book do suggest that international forces can be decisive in certain respects.

3

Tailor to the World: China's Emergence as a Global Power in Textiles

CHINESE TEXTILES: AN INDUSTRY WITH A DISTINGUISHED PAST AND A BRIGHT FUTURE

There is perhaps no industry in the history of Chinese civilization as storied as the textile industry.[1] For this study, however, our concern lies mainly with the industry's development in the post-Mao era and its experience with the MFA.[2] Over the last two decades, textiles has served as a leading sector as China has undergone domestic commercialization and deepened its integration into the world economy, a role similar to that played in Japan and elsewhere in East Asia.[3] Indeed, historians, economists, and political scientists have long recognized the critical role of textile manufacturing in the process of economic development.[4]

During the Mao era, the textile industry not only met the basic clothing needs of China's large, predominantly poor population, but it also served as an important source of capital for projects in other industrial sectors. Indeed, the textile industry has borne an enormous tax burden in the half century since the People's Republic of China (PRC) was

---

[1] For general background on the history of China's textile industry, see *Dangdai Zhongguo de Fangzhi Gongye* (1984) and Harris (1993), Chapter 14. For a primer on the textile industry during Late Imperial China, see Feuerwerker (1995b).

[2] The contemporary period is not, of course, the first in which China's textile industry has been significantly influenced by the outside world. For a detailed examination of the late 19th and early 20th centuries, see Reynolds (1975) and Hou (1965).

[3] See, for example, Smitka (1998).

[4] For the classic argument that the development of textile manufacturing allowed Great Britain to dominate the world economy, and in so doing spurred Britain's industrial revolution more generally, see Hobsbawn (1968). For an economist's view, see Anderson (1992), pp. 2–14. As far as political science is concerned, Kurth (1979) represents a highly influential political economy perspective on the textile industry.

established.[5] During the reform era, moreover, the industry has also been the country's leading source of net foreign exchange earnings, with the trade surplus in textiles (exports minus imports) exceeding U.S. \$250 billion over the last two decades.[6]

As far as the size of the textile industry is concerned, estimates range widely. Especially as the share of textiles produced by enterprises under the administration of the Ministry of Textile Industry (MTI) has fallen, official figures have been increasingly regarded as grossly understated. As one foreign study of statistical coverage in the industry concluded, problems of data capture – especially at lower levels of administration (e.g., township and village enterprises [TVEs]) – make comprehensive coverage impossible.[7] Employment estimates vary tremendously but a conservative figure for the late 1990s would be about 20 million workers.[8] (This does not include natural fiber production, which is considered agricultural work.) Put another way, the industry's workforce is roughly the size of Australia's entire population. Unfortunately, estimates of the number of textile factories in China range just as widely as employment estimates. By some accounts, there are more than 100,000 factories engaged in some aspect of textile production, with much of the growth in recent years attributable to garment sewing.[9] All told, China's textile industry is universally regarded as the world's largest. In fact, the claim is still sometimes made, even if just for effect, that "there are more sewing machines in China than people in the United States." As the government has proudly proclaimed, China produces some 20 billion garments a year, or roughly three garments for every person on earth.[10]

Most important to this study, China has emerged as one of the leading international traders of textile products. According to official statistics compiled by the WTO, China was the world's largest exporter of both textiles *and* clothing in 1999, accounting for 9 percent and 16 percent of the international market, respectively. (Overall, China leads the world

---

[5] For a revealing look at this issue, see the interview with Ji Guobiao, China's Vice-Minister of Textile Industry, in *TA* 19:5 (May 1988), pp. 18–23.

[6] *TA* 31:12 (December 2000), p. 43.

[7] See Chen and Jackson (1996).

[8] *TA* 31:3 (March 2000), p. 59. This figure might be too low, however. For example, some estimates in the mid-1990s placed some 5 million garment workers in Guangdong province alone; *TA* 27:9 (September 1996), p. 99.

[9] See, for instance, *TA* 28:2 (February 1997), p. 69. One recent estimate placed the number of textile and garment factories at 130,000. *TA* 31:3 (March 2000), p. 59.

[10] *Xinhua*, 3 April 2000, in FBIS-CHI-2000-0403.

industry with a total market share of 13 percent.) While China is not a big importer of clothing, it is the world's second largest importer of textiles (many of which are reexported after processing), taking in 7 percent of total international sales in 1999.[11] By any measure, therefore, China has become a major player in the world industry. Indeed, textile trade is critical not just to the Chinese industry itself (e.g., exports account for slightly more than one-half of China's production of textiles and clothing by value), but to the entire Chinese economy, as well.[12] While the share of textile and clothing products in China's total exports had declined to 22 percent by 1999 from a high of 30 percent in 1994, it was still close to the 23 percent share recorded in 1980. (Indeed, textile and clothing exports still account for nearly one-half of China's total light industrial exports.) This record is especially remarkable given the quantity-based restrictions placed on China under the MFA. Indeed, it suggests how successful the industry has been in moving upmarket. While the relative share of textile and clothing products in China's total exports has declined modestly over time, the absolute value of these sales has continued to rise steadily, reaching U.S. $43 billion in 1999. In fact, only in 1996 did the textile sector finally relinquish its leading position in China's export profile to the machinery and electronics sector. Rather amazingly, therefore, nearly U.S. $1 out of every U.S. $4 of Chinese exports is still earned from the sale of textiles and clothing, this despite the rapid growth of Chinese exports across an increasing number of industrial sectors.

Any history of the textile industry in the PRC must begin with the establishment of MTI in 1949. One of the original four industrial ministries set up under the supervision of the State Council, MTI was charged with consolidating an industry whose resources were not only fragmented but also inefficiently deployed. While the regional concentration in coastal areas like Shanghai, Qingdao, and Tianjin made sense when Chinese producers relied upon foreign supplies for their raw materials, it required significant change after 1949 when the new government decided to rely on cotton grown in China's inland provinces. MTI's mandate to exert central control over the industry notwithstanding, much of the industry's history from the mid-1950s onward was one of partial decentralization. In the Great Leap Forward, for instance, direct

---

[11] For a summary of the 1999 textile data contained in the WTO's annual publication *International Trade*, see *TA* 31:11 (November 2000), pp. 50–66.

[12] *TA* 29:4 (April 1998), p. 58 and *Zhongguo Xinwen She*, 18 November 1999, in FBIS-CHI-1999-1999.

supervision over most textile enterprises was transferred from MTI to authorities at the provincial and city level.[13]

While some control reverted back to MTI in the 1960s, especially over the largest enterprises, much of the day-to-day decision making remained below the national ministerial level. In this sense, MTI's role was restricted to one of general oversight for much of the Mao era. One area in which central influence was felt, however, was the afore-mentioned effort to shift textile production to fiber-producing areas in China's interior. While this policy met with mixed results and coastal provinces continued to enjoy the majority of textile-related economic activity, it did represent a significant episode of government intervention in the industry's development. A related aspect of central influence was the heavy tax burden imposed on traditional textile-producing areas such as Shanghai during the 1950s, 1960s, and 1970s.

It is difficult to make generalizations about China's textile industry given its enormous size and scope. Even in the prereform era, during which greater uniformity in the economic system might have been expected, tremendous diversity existed. In fact, this was probably more true for the textile industry than for most industries. That said, some general statements can be made in describing the prereform textile industry. First, the industry was basically divided into a state-run sector and a collective-run sector. In the state-run sector, textile factories were operated by the central government under the direction of MTI. In the collective sector, textile factories were operated by provincial or local governments, with the latter defined as municipal, county, or township governments. (Until the reform era, there was no significant private or foreign-invested sector.) Even within the state-run sector, moreover, key decisions such as production assignments were actually made by the local or provincial textile industry bureaus (TIBs) rather than in Beijing.

The relative decentralization of the industry notwithstanding, planning was significant all the same. Implementation of the plan for textiles was divided among the different ministries, local and provincial bureaus, and commercial and foreign trade departments responsible for various aspects of production, procurement, distribution, and pricing. In the area of natural fibers, for instance, production was carried out under the supervision of the relevant agricultural department. The output of natural fibers was then procured by state purchasing and supply bureaus; these inputs were in turn distributed to textile enterprises under the

---

[13] For an excellent discussion of one textile mill's experience, see Sabin (1992).

supervision of MTI (or, alternatively, the provincial or local textile bureaus). The allocation of imported materials was organized by foreign trade departments and then distributed to factories according to a system similar to the one used for the allocation of domestically produced inputs. Finished fabric was generally distributed to garment factories (or similar next-stage users) by MTI itself. The distribution of finished goods, however, was handled by the relevant branches of the Ministry of Commerce system.

State dominance, of course, applied not only to domestic sales but also to traded goods. In fact, foreign trade in textiles was controlled exclusively by the central government; neither MTI itself nor the TIBs enjoyed import or export rights. Authority over this activity was vested in the Ministry of Foreign Trade. Under this ministry's supervision, the China National Textiles Import and Export Corporation (CHINATEX) was established in 1961 as one of the handful of state-controlled FTCs, each of which enjoyed a monopoly in the import and export business for its product area.[14] Over time, CHINATEX opened offices in nearly twenty countries and established eight specialized subsidiaries to handle different areas of China's textile trade. All told, MTI and CHINATEX wielded considerable influence even though central planning was less comprehensive in textiles than in many other industries, especially heavy industries such as machine-building. Even where the direct supervisory role of MTI was fairly limited, for example, it continued to cast a considerable shadow over the industry through its bureaucratic influence on issues ranging from the allocation of capital and equipment to decisions involving pricing and distribution.

SINO-AMERICAN RELATIONS, THE MULTIFIBER ARRANGEMENT, AND CHINA'S TEXTILE INDUSTRY

Few observers would disagree that the two most important influences on China's growing participation in international textile markets over the last two decades have been its experience as a signatory to the MFA and its tumultuous bilateral relations with the United States over textile issues. As introduced in Chapter 1, the MFA is the quintessential protectionist regime against developing country exports. In fact, the emergence and institutionalization of a restrictive trade regime in textiles

---

[14] For background on the origins and early history of CHINATEX, see the interview with its vice-president, Zhou Yunzhong, in *TA* 16:4 (April 1985), pp. 23–46.

during the 1960s and 1970s was a direct, albeit contradictory, response to the broad liberalization of tariff rates for manufactured goods that occurred during these decades, an outcome achieved through successive negotiating rounds conducted multilaterally under the auspices of the General Agreement on Tariffs and Trade (GATT).[15] Although the United States and other countries did place restrictions on textile imports from certain suppliers (e.g., Japan) both before and after World War II, the adoption of the Short-Term Arrangement (STA) in 1961 marked an important first step in establishing an international regime designed to limit the "market disruption" caused by competitive goods from the developing world. The success of the STA – a one-year pact – led to the adoption of the Long-Term Arrangement (LTA) in 1962, an agreement that provided similar protection to domestic producers of cotton products for five years. The LTA was itself renewed twice, first in 1967 and again in 1970.

While the STA and the LTA allowed only modest growth in cotton goods, neither made any provision for products made from other fibers. Not surprisingly, developing countries diversified their production, especially with respect to man-made fibers. As these countries became increasingly competitive in artificial fibers and wool products, pressure began to mount in the advanced industrialized countries to expand product coverage beyond that provided for under the LTA. The result was the MFA. First negotiated in 1973, it provided a regulatory framework within which textile importers and exporters were to conduct periodic bilateral negotiations concerning the "orderly development" of their trade.[16] The MFA was designed to address problems of market disruption in the major importing countries while still allowing modest growth in developing country exports. By authorizing quantitative restrictions to regulate trade flows, the MFA represented an important exception to the tariff-based principles of trade liberalization pursued under the GATT.

After the original agreement (1974–1977) expired, the MFA was renegotiated three times: MFA II (1977–1981), MFA III (1982–1986), and

---

[15] Cline (1990) provides a useful discussion of how trade protection in the textile industry has evolved over recent decades.

[16] It should be noted, however, that the MFA provides for unilateral action by importing countries if an acceptable agreement with a given exporting country cannot be reached. Among several excellent overviews of the LTA and the MFA, see Aggarwal (1985) and Friman (1990).

MFA IV (1986–1991). Only a month after MFA IV was signed in August 1986, the Uruguay Round negotiations of the GATT were launched with great fanfare. One of the main objectives of these multilateral talks – the eighth in a series dating back to the Geneva Round in 1947 – was the return of textile trade to the GATT framework. Along with liberalization in agriculture, services, and intellectual property, a phase-out of the MFA was identified as a top priority by the nearly 120 countries participating at the ministerial meeting in Punta del Este. The Uruguay Round was originally scheduled for completion by December 1990, thus allowing plenty of time for a quota-dismantling plan to be in place when MFA IV expired on July 31, 1991. Due to a number of roadblocks, most notably the disagreement between the United States and the European Union over agriculture, the Uruguay Round was not concluded until December 1993, preventing the MFA phase-out from beginning until January 1, 1995. As a result, the MFA had to be extended twice on an interim basis to provide a continued framework for international textile trade for the period from August 1, 1991 to December 31, 1994. While many observers still refer generically to the MFA, the Agreement on Textiles and Clothing (ATC) technically replaced the GATT-affiliated MFA as the governing regime for international textile trade with the founding of the WTO on January 1, 1995. This new regime, which is itself set to expire on December 31, 2004, was created to preside over the phase-out of the international quota system. For the sake of convenience, references to the MFA in this book include both its precursors (the STA and LTA) and its successor (the ATC) unless otherwise noted.

Since the normalization of diplomatic relations between the United States and PRC in 1979, Washington and Beijing have concluded a series of five bilateral textile agreements. The first agreement, which covered the period from January 1, 1980 through December 31, 1982, placed limits on Chinese exports to the United States in eight categories of goods. With so few products covered, China easily shifted its exports to unrestricted goods – a development that led the United States to seek more restrictive terms the second time around. Unable to reach a new agreement, Washington unilaterally imposed a much wider range of quotas when the first pact expired at the end of 1982. For its part, Beijing retaliated by reducing imports of wheat and artificial fibers from the United States. By August 1983, the two sides signed a second bilateral agreement, one that covered more than half of Chinese textile exports, double that under the first agreement. The second agreement was in force (retroactively) from January 1, 1983 to December 31, 1987. It was during this second agreement, in December 1983, that China became a signatory to the MFA.

Even with a second Sino-American textile agreement in place and China participating as an active member of the MFA, the next few years proved to be increasingly contentious on the textile front. First, groups representing the U.S. textile industry petitioned both Congress and the Reagan administration for various forms of import relief from Chinese goods. For example, antidumping and countervailing duty cases were filed with the Commerce Department and U.S. International Trade Commission by domestic interest groups that alleged that Chinese textile producers were selling goods unfairly in the American market, injuring U.S. producers. Lobbying efforts also focused on Capitol Hill, where several proposals sought to control the level of textile imports by legislation. (While these bills were not motivated exclusively by imports from China, China's emergence as a major supplier was a leading factor.) In one particularly high-profile case, only a veto by President Reagan prevented the so-called Jenkins Bill from becoming law in 1985.

The years covered by the second Sino-American textile agreement also saw the emergence of a new issue concerning "country-of-origin" regulations and Chinese textile exports. As the result of a 1984 decision that changed the standards by which customs declarations were made in the United States, many items that had formerly been classified as Hong Kong exports were subsequently counted against Chinese quotas.[17] Even more importantly, this period witnessed a massive increase in "consultation calls" by the United States, the device by which an importing country is entitled under MFA rules to request negotiation with an exporting country to establish import limits for previously unrestricted products in which a surge in trade can be documented. "Calls" made during the second Sino-American agreement resulted in a doubling of the number of categories covered and raised the percentage of Chinese exports subject to quotas to nearly 75 percent.

The final notable development that occurred during the second Sino-American textile agreement was China's decision to sign MFA IV in 1986 (MFA III had already been in force when China joined the MFA in 1983), a move Beijing made with considerable reluctance. First, China was dissatisfied with the lack of progress toward any meaningful liber-

---

[17] Specifically, the U.S. government shifted from a cutting-based standard to an assembly-based standard for determining country of origin. This had the effect of increasing the number of Chinese exports.

alization of textile trade, one of the stated long-term goals of the MFA. Second, Beijing vehemently objected to the inclusion of ramie and other previously unrestricted fibers into the new MFA extension, an effort it believed was designed (with considerable input from Washington) primarily to limit China's ability to expand its textile exports.

It was, therefore, in the context of this rather stormy relationship that the United States and China needed to forge a third bilateral textile agreement to take effect when their second agreement expired on December 31, 1987. The third agreement, originally scheduled to run for four years, but later extended for an additional two years (thus running through December 31, 1993), resulted in the most comprehensive product coverage yet for Chinese exports, as virtually all major categories other than silk were subject to quotas.[18] In terms of growth rates, however, China received somewhat lenient treatment compared to other exporters. In fact, the average annual growth rate of 3 percent permitted under the third bilateral textile agreement was quite healthy compared to pacts reached by the United States with Hong Kong, Taiwan, and South Korea that limited growth to 1 percent annually. On the other hand, China's growth rates continued to be substantially below the 6 percent ceiling suggested by the MFA.

Even with the new agreement, however, textile issues remained a point of friction in Sino-American trade. It was during this third agreement that issues such as transshipment and the use of prison labor became serious irritants between Washington and Beijing. The transshipment issue, in particular, raised negotiation over a new pact to a high-stakes game. With Clinton administration officials accusing China of transshipping U.S. $2 billion of textiles annually to the United States through third countries, all in an effort to circumvent quota restrictions, Washington took an unusually aggressive position in trying to set the terms for a fourth Sino-American textile agreement that would be in force from January 1, 1994 to December 31, 1996. The United States issued a number of threats, including one that it would slash China's textile quotas unilaterally by as much as one-third if an agreement could not be reached bilaterally. In the end, an agreement was reached, one that included both lower overall growth rates (zero in 1994, 1 percent thereafter) and an expedited procedure for dealing with transshipment problems that allowed Washington to, among other things, take unilateral action where it had "clear evidence" of infractions. (Previously, the

---

[18] *TA* 19:2 (February 1988), p. 14.

United States was required to wait for the Textile Surveillance Board of the MFA to review transshipment cases, a process in which dispute resolution often took more than a year.) While agreements reached with other developing countries in the mid-1990s also contained provisions for surprise inspections, triple deductions, and other measures designed to control quota circumvention, China was alone in having its growth rate cut back so severely by the United States. In an unprecedented step, silk products were included in a separate memorandum of under-standing that permitted the imposition of quotas by Washington. (Even though the United States has almost no silk industry, American officials justified their position on the grounds that imports of Chinese silk gar-ments had been expanding very rapidly and were beginning to compete directly with a variety of U.S. garments in other fiber categories.) While the Chinese won some concessions during negotiations for the fourth agreement, these consisted mainly of earning a reprieve from the even harsher terms originally sought by the United States.

As it turned out, the tough conditions of the fourth agreement were no fluke. The fifth Sino-American textile agreement – signed in Febru-ary 1997 after several months of difficult negotiations failed to produce a new accord prior to the expiration of the fourth agreement on Decem-ber 31, 1996 – reflected a series of unprecedented demands by the American side. First, the agreement, which covered the period from January 1, 1997 to December 31, 2000, contained new market access pro-visions in which China agreed to gradually reduce and bind tariffs on textile imports. In the past, Sino-American textile agreements had focused solely on the issue of Chinese exports to the United States. With the fifth agreement, however, China's continued access to American markets was made explicitly conditional upon Beijing's willingness to lower its own trade barriers. Hailed by the Clinton administration as a major achievement, the extension of Sino-American negotiations to include reciprocal market access represented a watershed in the history of U.S. trade policy in textiles.

By contrast, China did not succeed in having country-of-origin issues included in the new agreement. Effective July 1, 1996, the United States adopted new rules that, while applicable to all countries, were widely regarded in the international textile community as an effort to limit Chinese exports. In short, these rules changed the standard by which the nationality of finished garments is determined for customs purposes. While the technical aspects of this policy shift are irrelevant to this study, the result was a legal standard that increased substantially the quantity of "Chinese" goods imported into the United States. In this way, the existing quota system became even more restrictive since more transnationally produced goods counted against China's quotas. Much to Beijing's chagrin, the fifth agreement ultimately contained no upward adjustment in quota levels to compensate for the adverse effect that the new "country of origin" rules would have on Chinese exports.

In fact, the fifth agreement actually provided for quota *reductions* (ranging from 1 percent to nearly 50 percent) on at least 14 categories of Chinese exports, including several top-selling products like cotton trousers, knit shirts, and underwear. Washington justified this as compensation for continued (and, by some accounts, worsening) transshipment problems during the fourth agreement. (Indeed, the quota reductions targeted categories where there had been repeated violations.) At the same time, the United States also retained its rights in the fifth agreement to assess triple damages and take other punitive actions in response to fraudulent activities. While Beijing did obtain small quota increases for other product categories, the net result was an agreement that reduced China's access to the U.S. market by 2.6 percent in 1997 compared to what would have resulted if the (modest) growth rates in the fourth agreement had simply been carried over for an additional year.[19] Overall, the new pact provided for an annual average growth rate of 1 percent over the life of the agreement, an expansion rendered especially negligible given the new, lower starting point for the categories in which China's quota base had been reduced. In addition, Washington and Beijing agreed that restrictions on silk products would continue to be covered by a separate document, with the quotas imposed in 1994 to be eliminated on January 1, 1999, two years after the date originally agreed for removal. In sum, the fifth agreement represented – by any available measure – the most restrictive textile accord reached between Washington and Beijing in two decades of bilateral negotiations.

Even more significantly, the fifth agreement also permitted the United States to restrict China's textile exports for eight additional years *after* the pact itself was set to expire on December 31, 2000. Pursuant to the ATC, the use of quotas in international textile markets is to be eliminated gradually during a period from January 1, 1995 (the date the WTO superseded the GATT) to December 31, 2004. On January 1, 2005, world

---

[19] Much of the analysis in this paragraph, including the calculation of a 2.6 percent reduction in China's access to the U.S. market, draws upon Brenda A. Jacobs, "Talking Textiles," *CBR* (March/April 1997), pp. 30–37.

textile trade is supposed to be free of quantitative restrictions for the first time in four decades. That said, the fifth Sino-American textile agreement essentially provided for twelve years of total coverage: the four years (1997–2000) formally covered by the accord; four more years (2001–2004) under the terms of the ATC (assuming that China became a WTO member by December 31, 2000); and an additional four-year period (2005–2008) *beyond* the scheduled end of the ATC. Specifically, the fifth agreement allowed Washington to invoke a special safeguard mechanism to protect against surges in Chinese exports to the United States through December 31, 2008. Although the safeguard mechanism called for consultations between Washington and Beijing, the United States did retain the right to impose quotas unilaterally on an emergency basis if agreement could not be reached bilaterally on how to manage the alleged market disruption.

Not surprisingly, textile trade became a major sticking point in negotiations leading to the Sino-American bilateral agreement on China's accession to the WTO reached in November 1999. The fifth agreement notwithstanding, China demanded a complete end to all U.S. textile restrictions in 2005 as provided by the ATC – that is, with no subsequent safeguard mechanism. For its part, Washington pushed Beijing to accept the maintenance of formal textile quotas – reportedly up to 90 percent of current quota levels – until 2010 as a condition for American support of China's membership in the WTO. As was widely reported, the textile issue was part of the final stumbling block: Washington refused to yield on a U.S. provision allowing 51 percent foreign ownership in Chinese telecommunications companies, while Beijing insisted upon an end to textile restrictions. The compromise, so the story goes, was a 50-percent ceiling on foreign ownership in exchange for a four-year safeguard mechanism for textiles after the ATC expires in 2005.[20] As far as textiles are concerned, therefore, the WTO negotiations basically reconfirmed the terms of the fifth agreement. If invoked, this safeguard mechanism could leave the Chinese industry subject to textile restrictions long after its developing country competitors enjoy quota-free exporting.

[20] See, for example, "Watershed Pact," *New York Times*, 16 November 1999, p. A1. To be precise, the Sino-American agreement provides for two separate safeguard mechanisms. The first is specific to textiles and will remain in effect until December 31, 2008. The second applies to all types of products and will be in force for twelve years after China accedes to the WTO. Under the agreement, the United States also reserves the right to treat China as a nonmarket economy in monitoring Chinese dumping of textiles.

SPRINGBOARD TO SUCCESS: A REVISIONIST ACCOUNT OF
THE MFA'S IMPACT ON CHINESE DEVELOPMENT

Not surprisingly, most observers assume that the MFA has been bad for China. As the classic example of "managed" trade against developing country exports, the MFA has been held out for special opprobrium by Chinese officials, Western economists, consumer rights advocates, and international traders alike. Consequently, each group has also heralded the ATC as a major step forward for global economic welfare. In short, China will be able to export more goods and foreign consumers will enjoy cheaper prices for their clothing. By restricting China's ability to export its most marketable product, so the argument goes, the MFA has stunted reform and restructuring within the textile industry and slowed China's integration into the world economy more generally.[21]

As economists have shown, the MFA has created severe distortions in the allocation of global resources. Since the markets of advanced industrial countries are partially closed, trade *between* developed and developing countries (e.g., the United States and China) is suboptimal from the standpoint of market efficiency. Yet another distortion exists in the location of world economic activity *among* developing country exporters. Here, efficiency is impeded by the nature of quota entitlement under the MFA, a system based primarily upon past performance. As a result, economic activity in the international textile industry is driven as much by the availability of quota as by cost advantages. Hong Kong and South Korea, for instance, continue to be major centers of clothing production long after their other light industries have migrated to the next generation of NICs in East Asia. Simply put, these time-honored suppliers remain "competitive" in large part due to the significant allocations of quotas they continue to receive from the United States and the European Union.

Consequently, one of the primary criticisms leveled at the MFA is that it provides entitlements not only to producers in traditional importing countries, but also to producers in traditional exporting countries such as Hong Kong, Taiwan, and South Korea. The presumed losers in this system, in addition to consumers who end up paying higher prices, are rising exporters with a comparative advantage – developing countries

---

[21] For two examples of official Chinese views, see the interviews with Zhou Yunzhong and Wang Ruixiang, vice-presidents of CHINATEX, in *TA* 16:4 (April 1985), pp. 23–46, and *TA* 19:9 (September 1988), pp. 28–35, respectively.

such as China – whose exports are subject to restrictions. Rather than identifying China as a victim, however, this book argues that the Chinese textile industry has achieved its export success *because* of, rather than *in spite* of, the MFA. While the protectionist nature of the MFA is beyond debate, I argue that its effects on China have been largely beneficial and, most importantly, bode well for the industry's performance in the post-MFA world market. While similar findings have been made in studies of quantitative restrictions imposed on exports of textiles, automobiles, and steel products from other developing countries, this book adds an additional wrinkle by arguing that the MFA has, in the Chinese case, provided an impetus not just for industrial restructuring and industrial rationalization, but also for economic reform.[22] Using these three issues as an organizing theme, what follows is a preview of the arguments developed more fully in Chapters 4 and 5.

Industrial Restructuring

The MFA did prove to be a restraint on China, but one that actually accelerated the restructuring and modernization of its textile industry. Unable to export at will, China had a powerful incentive to upgrade its exports to higher value-added goods, diversify its production toward unrestricted goods, and explore new export markets in which there were no quotas. By restricting the volume of China's exports to the world market, the MFA effectively shifted the basis of China's competition with other textile-producing countries from price to quality. The result was a race not to sell the most lower-end goods at the cheapest prices, but rather to secure the most orders for upmarket goods. In this sense, competition was posed in qualitative rather than quantitative terms. With quotas in place, the parameters of China's export expansion were well-defined. Expansion was possible mainly by increasing the unit value of exports. Under the MFA, the premium for export success was on more sophisticated goods, higher productivity, better and more reliable quality, and prompt delivery. Just as Japanese manufacturers responded to VERs on automobile exports by shifting production from subcompact vehicles to luxury vehicles, many Chinese textile factories have significantly upgraded their production to higher value-added goods. According to interviews and press accounts alike, this aspect of industrial restructur-

---

[22] A particularly important contribution to this literature is Yoffie (1983).

ing has proceeded further in the textile industry than in other comparable Chinese industries.

Economic Reform

For the most part, the upgrading described above was accomplished through market-oriented deregulation. Simply put, China's economic system during the early to mid-1980s did not serve the country's textile exports well at all. For example, coordination between industry and trade was so poor that it all but precluded a successful response to the incentives for export upgrading and product diversification present under the MFA. In order to penetrate the air lock system that existed between Chinese factories and the world market, fundamental changes were necessary in areas such as the management of foreign trade. As documented in Chapter 5, reform *experiments* were often undertaken with the explicit purpose of improving China's performance under the MFA. In other cases, the presence of the MFA facilitated the *implementation* of existing reforms that had never been fully carried out. Given the powerful incentives present under the MFA, it is no coincidence that the textile industry served at times as a laboratory for economic reform in China. While specific reform efforts in the textile industry must obviously be understood within the larger context of an economy-wide reform program, so, too, did the experience of the textile industry shape the evolution of reform in areas such as the export agency system and the extension of direct export rights to factories. As these examples illustrate, several important initiatives were either developed in the textile industry or received early implementation there.

Briefly put, the logic of the MFA – albeit not the one intended by its protectionist creators – is to induce changes that facilitate intensive rather than extensive growth strategies in the targeted countries. In this way, the imposition of quotas on Chinese exports simply exacerbated the basic diseconomies of the prereform system in the textile industry. As mentioned above, increases in the unit value of exports are at a premium under the MFA. Furthermore, changes in the international business environment have placed increased emphasis on the flexibility needed to produce small orders on a "quick response" basis. All told, there is considerable pressure to decentralize economic decision making to lower levels of administration in order to become (or remain) competitive. For China, especially, this has made deregulation the order of the day, especially with regard to market-oriented reform.

In the end, the imposition of quotas under the MFA accelerated, and in some respects even induced, movement in China's textile industry from a system dependent largely upon planning and other administrative measures to a system of greater market-based economic activity. The decentralization of economic authority, however imperfect, extended from the purchase of materials and equipment to decisions concerning production and distribution. Along the way, mandatory targets eroded into guidance targets, and over time the role of planning became truly negligible. In 1996, for example, the annual plan for the textile industry drawn up by the China National Textile Council (MTI's successor), provincial governments, and the State Planning Commission officially declared that the market should decide both annual output levels and the product mix.[23] In fact, production had been increasingly unplanned for years, especially above the local level. While hierarchical ties between government departments and enterprises have not been completely severed, they, too, have been substantially weakened over time.

Industrial Rationalization

By restricting China's ability to sell overseas, the MFA exacerbated the more general problems of labor oversupply and idle production facilities that have plagued so many Chinese industries. Specifically, the MFA eliminated the option of coping with chronic overproduction in textiles simply by increasing exports. Unlike the silk sector, where problems associated with the blind expansion of production or preexisting excess capacity could be managed in part by increasing the quantity of exports (until quotas were finally imposed in 1994), product areas covered by the MFA faced strict limits on a volume-centered export strategy. In this way, the MFA intensified the consequences of a vicious cycle characteristic of many Chinese industries in which stockpiling led in turn to debt chains and mounting financial losses. As discussed at greater length in Chapter 5, it is no coincidence that the textile industry was identified as the centerpiece of China's three-year plan for SOE reform launched in 1998.

Here, it is worth noting that the MFA was by no means the only factor that contributed to growing problems with excess capacity in the textile industry. Another important, long-term impetus for industrial readjustment in textiles was the loss of guaranteed procurement by the Ministry

---

[23] *TA* 27:5 (May 1996), pp. 80–81.

of Commerce in the early 1980s. Shortly before China joined the MFA, and at a point when the original bilateral textile agreement with the United States was not yet seriously restrictive, the Ministry began contracting only for specified quantities of output. Faced with an increasing oversupply of goods, the government ended its practice of purchasing all output.[24] Not surprisingly, this shift in policy pushed the textile industry toward a greater reliance on exports as a way to cope with the growing problem of overproduction. While the significance of the government's procurement policy should not be overlooked, its impact was arguably modest until the MFA began to place limits on the ability of the Chinese textile industry to export its way out of difficulty.

In this sense, the MFA and the end of guaranteed procurement represented mutually reinforcing pressures for readjustment in the textile industry. Especially as quota coverage expanded and tightened over time, increased exports simply could not substitute for the rationalization of the industry. While reductions in production capacity proved quite difficult to achieve, especially at first, significant progress was made in areas such as technical renovation. Given its size alone, to say nothing of its importance as a mainstay of the Chinese socialist economy, China's textile industry is anything but an easy target for change. From this perspective, its record of reform, restructuring, and rationalization – however uneven and incomplete – is actually quite impressive. In accounting for these changes, I argue that the impetus to modernize equipment, improve management practices, and reorganize the industry in general can be traced back in large measure to the discipline introduced by the MFA.

THE MULTIFIBER ARRANGEMENT, FOREIGN DIRECT INVESTMENT, AND THE DEVELOPMENT OF CHINA'S TEXTILE INDUSTRY

The MFA is long-noted for its distorting effects on the pattern of FDI in the international textile industry. On the one hand, the MFA has in some cases accelerated the product cycle internationally, serving as an impetus for the transfer of production from traditional suppliers to new manufacturing centers. For example, the first wave of FDI within the East Asian textile industry, which occurred during the late 1970s and early

---

[24] For an account of these developments, see Naughton (1995), pp. 125–126.

1980s, was spurred almost exclusively by the pressure of binding quotas on regional leaders such as Hong Kong, Taiwan, and South Korea. Restricted in their ability to export by the MFA, manufacturers in the East Asian NICs added production facilities in unrestricted (or substantially less-restricted) countries as a strategy for increasing their overall business. In this sense, the MFA is widely regarded as being responsible for transforming many small- to medium-sized textile companies in Hong Kong, Taiwan, and South Korea into diversified multinational companies.[25] Similar migrations of economic activity did not occur in other light industries until considerably later when push-factors (e.g., appreciating currencies, higher wages, and rising costs for land and raw materials) led to a second wave of FDI across a wide range of industries such as toys, footwear, sporting goods, and consumer electronics.

On the other hand, the MFA discourages FDI in countries currently covered by export restrictions, especially if product coverage is relatively comprehensive and if quota utilization is already high. Obviously, there is little incentive to move export-oriented production to a new location from which export to the desired markets (e.g., the United States and the European Union) may not be possible. In this sense, the MFA casts a very wide shadow, indeed. One irony of the MFA, therefore, is that it was both a driving force behind the initial flow of FDI into China in the early 1980s and a major obstacle to continued FDI in the textile industry in the late 1980s and 1990s. Interviews consistently revealed that the textile industry was a primary target of Hong Kong industrialists early in the reform era as they sought to avoid restrictions imposed on their Hong Kong–based production under the MFA. While the textile industry was once a leading target of FDI in China, it has lagged badly in recent years in comparison with other industries. By the end of 1997, contracted FDI in the textile industry stood at U.S. $33 billion on a cumulative basis, only about 6 percent of total contracted FDI.[26] As early as 1994, moreover, only 24 percent of China's textile exports came from FIEs. By contrast, 37 percent of China's exports in other industries were supplied by FIEs.[27] Especially compared to other light industries, FDI plays a relatively small role in the textile industry. In garments, for example, some observers estimate that the share of exports produced by

---

[25] For an interesting discussion of this phenomenon, see *TA* 26:12 (December 1995), pp. 78–80.

[26] *Xinhua*, 18 November 1998, in FBIS-CHI-98–321.

[27] *TA* 26:5 (May 1995), p. 77.

FIEs might be nearly double its current level (less than one-third) if not for the presence of the MFA.

Interviews left no doubt that the MFA has weakened the "Greater China" phenomenon in the textile industry. While many Hong Kong and Taiwan textile manufacturers have relocated to Guangdong and Fujian provinces, respectively, interviewees repeatedly stressed that uncertainty about the availability of quota was the major factor inhibiting FDI on the scale seen in other light industries. Given the positive role FDI is seen as having played in China's reform and opening, the impact of the MFA is often judged to be negative for this reason as well. There is, however, some evidence of a silver lining in the cloud the MFA has created over FDI in China's textile industry: Due to the problem with quota availability, there has been less foreign investment in production and a relatively greater emphasis on the importation of foreign machinery and technology. As a result, China's textile industry is by all accounts less reliant upon processing arrangements and more autonomous in the provision of logistical services than light industries for which there is no system of export restraints.

Non-PRC informants, including several business consultants who follow the industry full-time, stressed that China has made considerable strides in developing integrated production of finished products for sale overseas. While Hong Kong and Taiwan manufacturers remain important middlemen for a significant portion of China's exports to important markets like the United States and the European Union, the textile industry is still less reliant upon outside partners for its export business than are China's other leading industries. According to interviews and press reports alike, some textile factories have actually shifted out of processing work into their own design, production, and direct export, a phenomenon whose occurrence is much less frequent in other industries.[28] To be sure, Chinese manufacturers have enjoyed only modest success in establishing name-brand garment products overseas, but it appears that they are somewhat less dependent on the transnational manufacturing networks that have come to dominate so many industries in East Asia.

Even where FDI is involved in China's textile industry, the MFA may still have offered China some advantages. While the MFA prevents China from attracting the level of FDI it otherwise would, there is evidence that the terms of FDI in the textile industry may be superior in

[28] See, for example, *TA* 27:5 (May 1996), p. 72.

some cases to FDI in other Chinese industries. On the one hand, many foreign investors have apparently refused to commit their capital to Chinese factories without explicit promises that they would be entitled to use a share of China's quota in specific product categories. On the other hand, many informants argued that the quota system under the MFA actually *increased* China's bargaining leverage with foreign investors, enabling it to extract concessions in exchange for a commitment to make quota available to new joint ventures or wholly foreign-owned enterprises. Several informants spoke authoritatively about cases in which certain production locations in China were so desirable that potential foreign investors found themselves in effect bidding for the right to produce in China using a specific allotment of quota. To ensure long-term access to quota, prospective investors have sometimes had to offer a quid pro quo in the form of equipment, training, or technology.

All told, China appears well-positioned to thrive in the reconfigured world market that will emerge with the phase-out of the MFA. Whatever benefits China's textile industry has enjoyed under the MFA, it is likely to perform even more effectively in an international environment characterized by greater economic openness, this as a result of the sweeping changes the industry has undergone over the last two decades. While reform, restructuring, and rationalization are by no means complete, the industry is arguably not far from the point where the positive impact of export restrictions will diminish considerably or even cease to exist altogether. By the time all quotas on Chinese textile exports are finally removed, an event that remains several years away, the industry is likely to be in excellent position to benefit from more open competition internationally. Indeed, the textile industry is widely regarded as a beneficiary of China's accession to the WTO. According to official Chinese government estimates, textile exports are expected to double by the time quotas are completely eliminated in 2005, with more than 5 million new jobs created as a result.[29] This, it is hoped, will compensate in part for predicted losses in sectors such as agriculture and automobile manufacturing. While some dislocation will occur in the textile industry as a result of WTO membership – mainly among domestic fiber producers who will face a stiffer challenge from foreign materials as China lowers its import

[29] These estimates, which are consistent with estimates by the World Bank and independent researchers, come from the State Council's Development Research Center; *TA* 30:12 (December 1999), p. 59.

78

duties – even this may increase the competitiveness of Chinese finished goods since access to cheaper inputs should translate into lower production costs.

With the phase out of the MFA, therefore, China will have greater opportunities to export what Beijing continues to regard as its "most competitive commodity" for the foreseeable future.[30] I would argue, of course, that Chinese factories are likely to be highly successful in a "free trade" environment precisely *because* of, not *in spite* of, their experience coping with the "managed trade" environment in which the industry found itself during a critical transitional period in China's economic development. As far as the stability of world textile markets is concerned, international management of China's rise has been largely successful. For all the undeniable global economic costs that result from regulating trade politically, the MFA has at least allowed China to emerge as the world's dominant supplier with minimal – indeed, perhaps *unnecessarily* minimal – disruption to the domestic markets of advanced industrial countries. In the case of the textile industry, therefore, the dislocation caused by the awakening dragon has been allowed to unfold in an "orderly" fashion, one that has also fortuitously served China's long-term interests.

---

[30] As this quote suggests, most official analyses regard textiles as an industry in which China will flourish with greater economic globalization. *Zhongguo Xinwen She*, 18 November 1999, in FBIS-CHI-1999-1119.

4

Beating the System with Industrial Restructuring: China's Response to the Multifiber Arrangement (MFA)

DEVELOPING COUNTRY STRATEGIES FOR COPING WITH THE MFA

The experiences of other developing countries suggest several ways that exporters can adapt to restrictions under the MFA: product upgrading to achieve higher unit values for goods subject to quotas; product diversification toward unrestricted goods; increased exports to countries that do not impose quotas under the MFA; improved utilization of existing quotas; moving production abroad legally via foreign investment to avoid quotas; and illegal transshipments of domestic production through third countries to avoid quotas.[1]

First, with regard to product upgrading, there is a strong incentive under the MFA for exporters to trade up into higher-end goods since the quantity of their sales is strictly limited. If a specific product (e.g., men's cotton dress shirts) becomes subject to quotas, one strategy is to move upmarket from cheaper shirts sold at discount department stores to more expensive shirts sold at upscale department stores. Second, the imposition of quotas in one product line (e.g., women's cotton sweaters) frequently results in greater exports of unrestricted products (e.g., women's ramie sweaters). Third, the presence of quotas in one export market (e.g., the United States) often leads to increased exports to unrestricted markets (e.g., Japan). Fourth, another common response to the MFA is to ensure that quota allocations are fully utilized, a strategy that often requires both improved administrative coordination and adjustments to

[1] Major works that examine the experience of developing countries under the MFA include Yoffie (1983), Hamilton (1990), and Cline (1990). For a particularly insightful account of developing country experiences, see Cable (1990).

the product mix. Finally, the impact of restrictions can also be mitigated by avoiding quotas altogether, either by moving production overseas or through customs fraud.

Given the incentive structure presented by the MFA, one could reasonably expect China's response to reflect some combination of the strategies used by other developing countries.[2] Especially as quotas expanded over time to cover an increasing share of China's exports to critical MFA signatories such as the United States and the European Union, a pattern of, say, product upgrading and market diversification could well be expected to emerge. All things being equal, this pattern – or whatever combination of strategies emerged instead – would be expected to apply with less force to product lines (or even entire sectors) unaffected by the MFA. Finally, while there might be changes made in anticipation of quotas, not to mention spillover effects from product areas where upgrading and diversification had already started, one would generally expect the pattern to be most pronounced *after* MFA coverage has been formally extended to a particular product or sector.

Made to Order: China Goes Upmarket in Response to the MFA

As it turns out, product upgrading has been one of China's primary responses to the imposition of quotas under the MFA. Product upgrading can take many different forms, from improved quality in existing goods to the manufacture of new higher-end goods. While most countries exhibit at least some movement up the product cycle as the effect of quotas becomes more restrictive over time, upgrading is by no means the dominant response for all developing countries. As indicated by the comparative data shown below, and documented in greater detail in the various existing studies on the MFA, product upgrading has *not* occurred evenly across all countries.[3] Indeed, some have focused more on diversifying production to unrestricted goods and diverting exports to

---

[2] By all accounts, Chinese officials identified very quickly the basic strategies available in responding to the MFA. While much of the early assessment was restricted to internal (*neibu*) reports, prominent foreign affairs journals such as *Guoji Maoyi Wenti* (*GJMYWT*) [Issues in International Trade], the official publication of the Trade Ministry, eventually provided detailed analyses of China's options in coping with the quota system. See, for instance, Shi Yunjia, "Making the Most of Limited Quotas under the Multifiber Agreement," *GJMYWT* (June 1989), pp. 46–50, in JPRS-CAR-89-102, and Peng Yuanxun, "The Multifiber Arrangement and China's Textile Trade," *GJMYWT* (April 1992), pp. 2–6, in JPRS-CAR-92-056.

[3] See Yoffie (1983), Hamilton (1990), Cline (1990), and Anderson (1992).

countries that do not impose quotas. Still others have responded primarily by improving the utilization of their existing quotas or by trying to capture as much of the potential quota rent as possible. The main point is simply that product upgrading is not automatic. As a result, the finding that China has achieved significant upgrading under the MFA requires detailed examination.

While serious problems remain with the quality of its textile exports, China has made substantial progress in several key areas: purity of fiber content; better dyeing techniques; improved packaging; quicker production schedules; more reliable delivery; and greater uniformity in color, shrinkage, and measurement. Informants – including several foreign buyers who were otherwise quite critical of the Chinese industry – repeatedly emphasized that high quality production was possible in China by the late 1980s and early 1990s, in no small measure due to incentives provided under the MFA. Specifically, many interviewees stressed that *country* reputations, as prevalent as they are, are less important to businesspeople interested in stable, long-term relationships than *factory* or *company* reputations. For an enterprise in China to trade up in the world market, it needs to become the source of choice for foreign buyers looking to place orders for higher-end goods. In this sense, reputations are earned and lost by performance.[4]

From this perspective, product upgrading takes place not just one factory at a time, but one order at a time. In the long run the result is an enhanced reputation for the country more generally. Consider how China fared in the results of a major international survey conducted in 1990, in which buyers for department or specialty stores such as Saks Fifth Avenue, The Limited, and Macy's were asked about their sourcing decisions for mid- to higher-price garments. While perennial powerhouses such as Italy and Hong Kong remained at the head of the class, "China, South Korea, and Taiwan were earmarked by buyers of apparel goods in the top half price segment, which is indicative of the perceived improvement in [the] quality of exports from these low cost countries."[5] Indeed, all of the buyers surveyed – American, Canadian, and European alike – ranked China close to its high-performing East Asian neighbors

[4] Press reports also confirm the importance of factory-specific reputation to upgrading. See, for instance, *TA* 23:11 (November 1992), p. 65, which documents how certain enterprises in Guangdong were actually in a position to choose their work, no longer having to scramble to secure attractive orders from foreign buyers.

[5] "Apparel Sourcing: A Survey of Retail Buyers' Attitudes in Canada, the USA, and Western Europe," *TOI* (November 1991), p. 87.

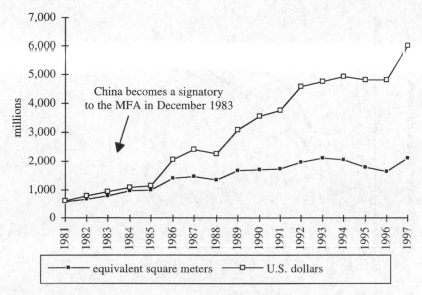

Figure 4.1. U.S. textile and apparel imports from China. *Source: U.S. Imports of Textiles and Apparel Under the Multifiber Arrangement*, various years.

and consistently ahead of countries like Belgium, Spain, and Ireland for private label and designer label products.[6]

At a very basic level, China's product upgrading can be seen in the trend toward increased exports of finished goods relative to primary goods. Clothing, for instance, has come to represent a far more important segment of China's export business than raw materials or semi-finished goods such as basic fabrics. While there are several ways to gauge a country's progress in trading up the international product cycle, the most commonly used measurement is change in the unit value of exports. As shown below, China's success in product upgrading within the textile industry has been well above average overall and even outstanding in certain areas.

At the broadest level, consider China's overall export profile to the United States. In 1981, shortly after the normalization of Sino-American relations and the subsequent conferral upon China of most-favored-nation trade status, growth in the quantity and value of China's textile exports to the United States was remarkably even. As Figure 4.1 shows,

[6] Ibid, pp. 91–92, presents summary tables of survey results.

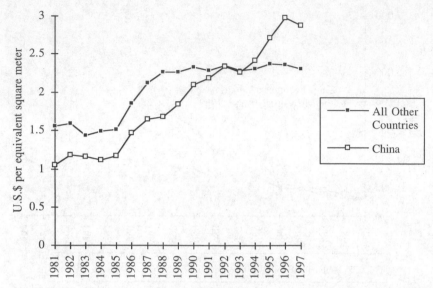

Figure 4.2. Unit value of U.S. textile and apparel imports. *Source:* Calculated from data in *U.S. Imports of Textiles and Apparel Under the Multifiber Arrangement*, various years.

growth in the U.S. dollar value of Chinese exports soon began to out-strip increases in physical volume, a gap that has continued to widen over time. Even in aggregate terms, therefore, the power of China's move upmarket is apparent.

Given the incentive for developing countries to increase the unit value of their exports under the MFA, it is important to place China's experience in comparative perspective. As impressive as the record shown in Figure 4.1 would seem, how has China fared relative to its competitors? As Figure 4.2 documents, by 1994 China had fully erased the 50 percent gap in unit value that had existed in 1981. In fact, the unit value of Chinese exports now consistently exceeds the world average – a world average that, it should be noted, includes advanced industrial as well as developing countries.

Comparison of China's performance to that of specific peer groups is also revealing. First, consider China's high-performing neighbors in East Asia. While Hong Kong's ability to move upmarket is absolutely unrivaled, Figure 4.3 shows that by 1996 China had overtaken both Taiwan and South Korea. Indeed, informants claimed that nowhere else in light

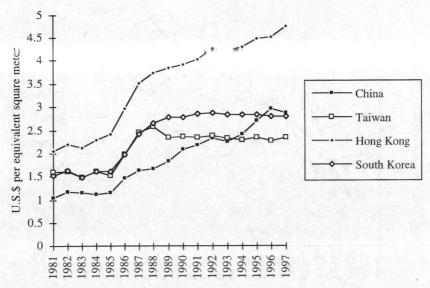

Figure 4.3. Unit value of U.S. textile and apparel imports from China and the East Asian newly industrializing countries. *Source:* Calculated from data in *U.S. Imports of Textiles and Apparel Under the Multifiber Arrangement,* various years.

industrial manufacturing has China performed as effectively vis-à-vis its neighbors as it has in textiles.[7] In fact, Hong Kong's continued climb in unit value suggests that China's upgrading is *not* due mainly to relocated production of high-priced goods from its neighbors. (As discussed in Chapter 3, the MFA has slowed the relocation of production from Hong Kong and Taiwan compared to the migration witnessed in other light industries. Given the large quota allocations that Hong Kong, Taiwan, and South Korea enjoy as long-established participants in the MFA, and the dearth of available quota in China, foreign industrialists from these countries have a powerful incentive to retain some production at home, particularly at the high end of the market.)

---

[7] Since trade in products such as toys, footwear, sporting goods, and consumer electronics is not always recorded consistently, especially with regard to data on the quantity of exports, it is difficult to confirm that gains in unit value have been greater in textiles. That said, several interviewees were foreign traders with experience in different product areas, so considerable weight has been given to their views. In their opinion, upgrading has been greatest in textiles, in large part due to the presence of quotas under the MFA.

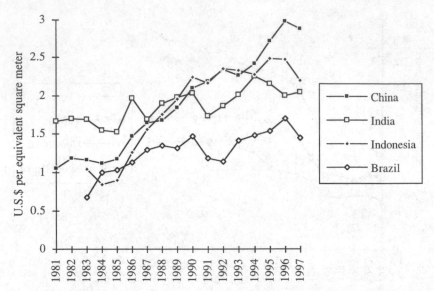

Figure 4.4. Unit value of U.S. textile and apparel imports from large developing countries. Country data unavailable in this series for Indonesia and Brazil prior to 1983. *Source:* Calculated from data in *U.S. Imports of Textiles and Apparel Under the Multifiber Arrangement*, various years.

Compared to other large developing countries, China certainly holds its own. As Figure 4.4 documents, China has, since the mid-1990s, consistently enjoyed higher unit values for its textile exports than India, Indonesia, or Brazil. While Indonesia kept pace with China until 1993, India long ago surrendered the sizable margin it once held. Meanwhile, Brazil has continued to lose ground in relative terms.

Finally, China also stacks up well against the most prominent small country suppliers to the U.S. market. As Figure 4.5 shows, it achieved more growth in unit value than Malaysia, Thailand, or Pakistan over the fifteen-year period studied here. In absolute terms, moreover, by 1996 China had drawn nearly even with Malaysia, a strong, upscale supplier that once enjoyed a significant advantage over China.

Dressed for Success: Chinese Factories Work Their Way into Saks Fifth Avenue and Macy's

While Chinese-made goods remain staples on the racks at J.C. Penney and The Gap, to say nothing of Wal-Mart and K-Mart, clothes from

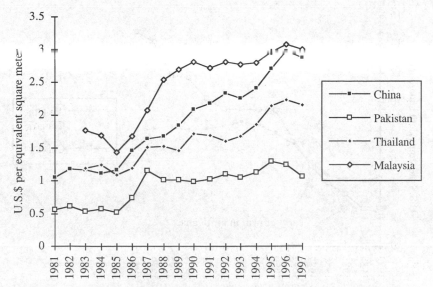

Figure 4.5. Unit value of U.S. textile and apparel imports from China and leading small countries. Country data unavailable in this series for Malaysia and Thailand prior to 1983. *Source:* Calculated from data in *U.S. Imports of Textiles and Apparel Under the Multifiber Arrangement*, various years.

Chinese factories can now regularly be found in upmarket department stores, specialty shops, and even independent boutiques. Furthermore, product upgrading has not been limited to garment exports: the unit value of textile fabrics has improved steadily, too.[8] The most remarkable development, however, remains China's track record in trading up into higher-end fashion apparel, a process in which the MFA has proved to be a springboard, not quicksand. Although this phenomenon has been documented in general terms above, the nature of China's success can be seen most vividly by examining its experience in individual product categories, many of which represent the modern-day battleground on which reputations for light manufacturing in the international economy are won and lost.

Consistent with the hypothesis suggested at the beginning of the chapter – namely, that upgrading should be most pronounced for those product areas where the impact of quotas is greatest – China's move

---

[8] According to published reports, the unit value of a metric ton of Chinese textile fabrics rose from $4,000 in 1990 to $10,000 in 1995; *TA* 26:12 (December 1995), p. 81.

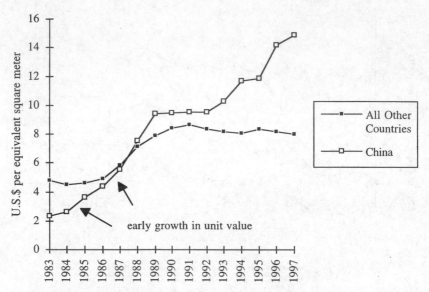

Figure 4.6. Unit value of U.S. imports of women's and girl's cotton knit shirts.
Data either incomplete or not comparable for this series prior to 1983.
Source: Calculated from data in *U.S. Imports of Textiles and
Apparel Under the Multifiber Arrangement*, various years.

upmarket began in products made of cotton, the fiber category in which
the MFA first became truly restrictive.[9] As Figures 4.6–4.10 show, the
pattern of increasing unit values for key Chinese exports of cotton goods
typically began during the second Sino-American bilateral textile agree-

[9] Foreign traders interviewed on the subject concurred that some of China's most impressive gains came in the most restrictive categories; that is, where quota was most scarce.
With quota utilization rates for virtually all of China's exports at nearly 100 percent, it
is difficult to assess the relative restrictiveness of the quota system across products. Some
analysts suggest that "hot" categories (i.e., those for which quota is exhausted quickly)
are the most restrictive. There is some merit in this view, but idiosyncrasies in the markets
for certain products render time-based analysis highly imperfect. As it turns out, utilization rates are not an entirely satisfactory measure of restrictiveness anyway. Since limits
exist on aggregate categories as well as on specific product lines, quotas sometimes
become binding for a given product, such as girl's cotton knit shirts, well before the formal
limit for that particular MFA category is reached. This would not, of course, be apparent just by examining quota utilization rates. While definitive statements about restrictiveness across product areas is difficult, it is safe to say that the MFA is unusually
restrictive vis-à-vis China's exports since quota utilization rates in the United States and
the European Union are substantially higher for China than for any other country. See,
for example, *TA* 24:11 (November 1993), p. 15, and *TA* 27:1 (January 1996), p. 87.

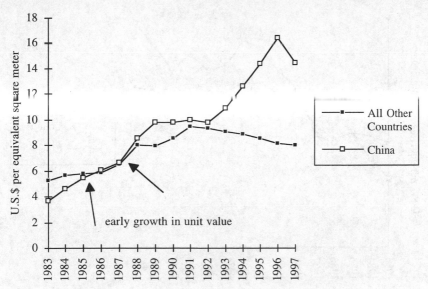

Figure 4.7. Unit value of U.S. imports of men's and boy's cotton knit shirts. Data either incomplete or not comparable for this series prior to 1983. *Source:* Calculated from data in *U.S. Imports of Textiles and Apparel Under the Multifiber Arrangement*, various years.

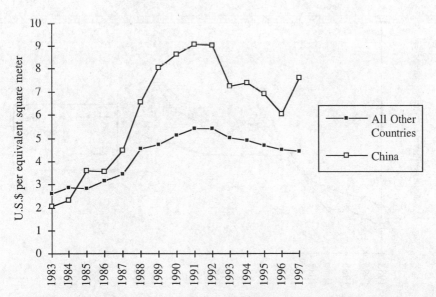

Figure 4.8. Unit value of U.S. imports of cotton sweaters. Data either incomplete or not comparable for this series prior to 1983. *Source:* Calculated from data in *U.S. Imports of Textiles and Apparel Under the Multifiber Arrangement*, various years.

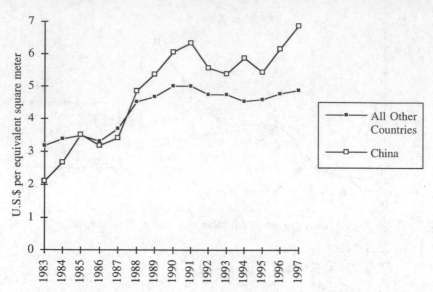

Figure 4.9. Unit value of U.S. imports of women's and girl's cotton trousers. Data either incomplete or not comparable for this series prior to 1983. *Source:* Calculated from data in *U.S. Imports of Textiles and Apparel Under the Multifiber Arrangement*, various years.

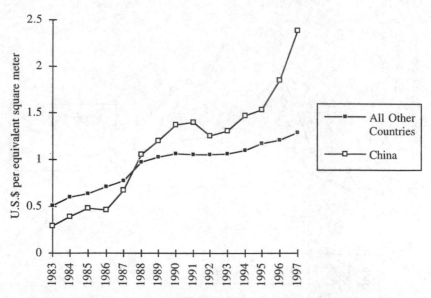

Figure 4.10. Unit value of U.S. imports of cotton underwear. Data either incomplete or not comparable for this series prior to 1983. *Source:* Calculated from data in *U.S. Imports of Textiles and Apparel Under the Multifiber Arrangement*, various years.

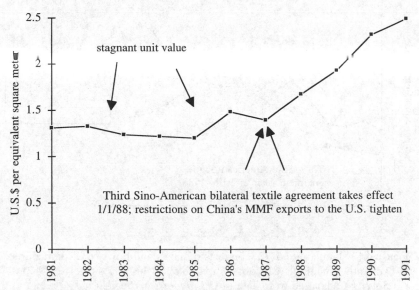

Figure 4.11. Unit value of U.S. imports of man-made fiber (MMF) products from China. Data for this series (total MMF imports by country) ended in 1991; the continued increase in the unit value of U.S. MMF imports from China can be seen in Figures 4.12–4.14 below which present data for individual product categories. *Source:* Calculated from data in *U.S. Imports of Textiles and Apparel Under the Multifiber Arrangement,* various years.

ment (1983–1987), an agreement that did in fact emphasize restrictions on cotton products. Each of the popular apparel items documented in these figures represents a critical area of competition among foreign textile suppliers to the United States. Contrast this record with that of man-made fiber (MMF) products, shown in Figures 4.11–4.14, where unit values were relatively stagnant until coverage of MMF products became more restrictive with the third Sino-American textile agreement (originally negotiated for 1988–1991, later extended through 1993).

Living within the Rules: China Diversifies to Cope with the MFA

Product diversification has proved to be another effective strategy in maximizing China's ability to export under the MFA. Consistent with a pattern identified in many (but not all) developing countries, the export

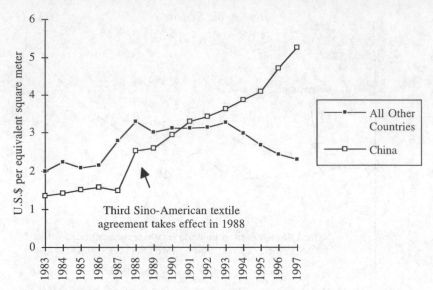

Figure 4.12. Unit value of U.S. imports of men's and boy's MMF knit shirts. Data either incomplete or not comparable for this series prior to 1983. *Source:* Calculated from data in *U.S. Imports of Textiles and Apparel Under the Multifiber Arrangement*, various years.

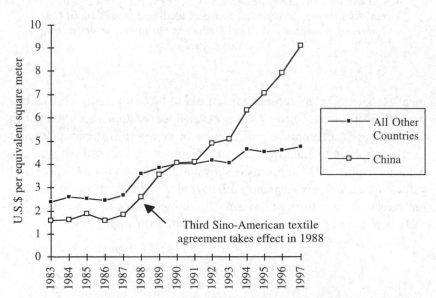

Figure 4.13. Unit value of U.S. imports of men's and boy's MMF coats. Data either incomplete or not comparable for this series prior to 1983. *Source:* Calculated from data in *U.S. Imports of Textiles and Apparel Under the Multifiber Arrangement*, various years.

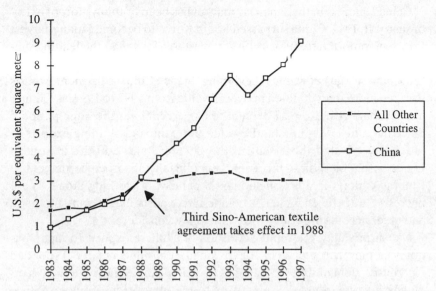

Figure 4.14. Unit value of U.S. imports of women's MMF dresses. Data either incomplete or not comparable for this series prior to 1983. *Source:* Calculated from data in *U.S. Imports of Textiles and Apparel Under the Multifiber Arrangement*, various years.

profile of China's textile industry reveals an unmistakable shift over the years toward nonquota countries and nonquota goods.

Nonquota Countries. With so much of the world's trade already regulated under the MFA, market diversification is a limited strategy in coping with the regime. Simply put, most non-MFA countries are either too poor (e.g., the developing world) or too small (e.g., Switzerland) to absorb any significant level of exports from China. While trade with Eastern Europe and the countries of the former Soviet Union did grow in the 1990s, this hardly represented a major market-expanding opportunity. In fact, only one substantial option remained: Japan. Although Japan is a signatory to the MFA, most of its experience with the regime has been as an exporter rather than as an importer. (As discussed in Chapter 3, the STA and LTA were instituted in the 1960s largely with Japanese exports in mind.) Even as the competitiveness of Japanese textile producers began to wane over the decades, Tokyo never imposed import quotas as authorized under the MFA, in part because other import barriers seemed to provide adequate insulation.

China's success in the Japanese market has been nothing short of extra-ordinary. In 1991, China surpassed South Korea to become Japan's largest source of imported textiles; in 1992 it overtook Taiwan as the leading supplier of foreign clothing to Japan.[10] As it turns out, China's dominance of the Japanese market was just beginning. In fact, Chinese garment exports to Japan more than doubled in overall value from 1992 to 1997, as China's market share rose from 47 percent to 64 percent over the same period.[11] Since the mid-1990s, in fact, the value of textile and clothing exports to Japan have rivaled those sent to the United States and the European Union.[12] Together, these three markets officially absorbed 65 percent of Chinese exports in 1997, including 78 percent in clothing alone. These figures would be even higher, of course, if reexports, illegal transshipment, and other accounting issues were taken into consideration.

Not surprisingly, the rapid expansion of Chinese exports to Japan has not been met with silence in Tokyo. Japanese producers have responded vigorously, demanding on several occasions that Tokyo launch fact-finding investigations as a precursor to the imposition of quotas. Since 1994, in fact, China and Japan have been engaged in an ongoing dialogue over how to manage the surge in Chinese exports. On at least two separate occasions, Beijing has "volunteered" to restrict its exports of certain products to avoid the use of actual quotas by the Japanese government. In the first case, however, Beijing refused to announce specific ceilings on the eight individual product categories that were to be restricted effective January 1, 1995. From Japan's perspective, this arrangement left unclear the question of how much – or even whether – the Chinese government was keeping exports below the level that would otherwise have resulted. Similar to the U.S. case, there were also allegations that Chinese goods were simply being transshipped through Hong Kong and other third parties to avoid further conflict with Japan. These tensions grew until November 1996 when China, again after lengthy and often tense negotiations, committed itself once again to adopting more effective

---

[10] *TA* 23:8 (August 1992), p. 52.

[11] *TA* 28:1 (January 1998), p. 86, and *TA* 28:4 (April 1998), p. 17.

[12] According to official WTO statistics, Japan is in fact the leading market for Chinese exports. For a summary of 1999 data, see *TA* 31:11 (November 2000), pp. 50–66. The issue of reexports through Hong Kong, to say nothing of the transshipment problem discussed in the next section, makes definitive statements about the actual level of exports to the United States, the European Union, and Japan difficult, but there is every indication that years of higher overall growth in exports to Japan have rendered the three markets roughly equal in importance.

"export management standards." China has thus far avoided the imposition of actual quotas, and the voluntary restraints to which it has agreed apply only to a small number of product categories. In other cases, however, China has not proved so lucky. Brazil, for example, established quotas in 1996 designed to reduce the volume of Chinese imports by half over a three-year period. This came after Chinese clothing exports increased 237 percent between 1995 and 1996.[13]

Nonquota Goods. As far as product diversification is concerned, consider the case of MMF products. While each of the five Sino-American bilateral textile agreements covered a wide range of goods, including MMF products, the first two agreements concentrated primarily on Chinese exports of cotton goods. Although U.S. restrictions were quite liberal in some respects – as evidenced by the significant growth in China's exports of cotton goods over the last two decades – access to the U.S. market for these products has been limited compared to other fiber categories. As Figure 4.15 shows, while exports of Chinese cotton products doubled by volume from 1981 to 1991, exports of Chinese MMF products increased five-fold over the same period. Most significantly, almost all of this growth occurred during the first and second bilateral agreements, when MMF products were relatively unrestricted.[14] Similarly, note the explosive growth in Chinese exports from the "other fibers" category as both cotton and MMF products became subject to increasingly restrictive coverage over time. So great was the surge in Chinese exports from unrestricted categories – growth rates from the mid- to late 1980s were typically about four times that for restricted categories – that goods made from "other fibers" (ramie, linen, and silk blends) were included in the third Sino-American textile agreement (1988–1991) for the first time.

In sum, the gradual expansion of product coverage under the MFA (or, more specifically, under the Sino-American bilateral agreements negotiated within the MFA framework) led China to diversify its product mix away from restricted categories. Figure 4.16 documents this shift, first toward MMF products at the expense of cotton goods, and then

---

[13] *Brasilia Correio Braziliense*, 13 June 1997, in FBIS-LAT-97-116.

[14] Realizing that MMF products represented a growth area for Chinese exports, even if quotas were imposed in later agreements, 80 percent of investment in the textile industry during the Seventh Five-Year Plan (1986–1990) went into the MMF sector, doubling production capacity; *TA* 22:4 (April 1991), p. 59.

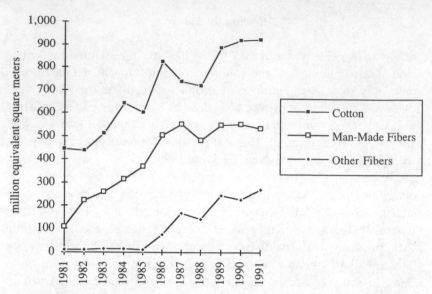

Figure 4.15. Volume of U.S. imports from China by fiber category. Data by fiber category discontinued in this series after 1991. *Source:* Calculated from data in *U.S. Imports of Textiles and Apparel Under the Multifiber Arrangement*, various years.

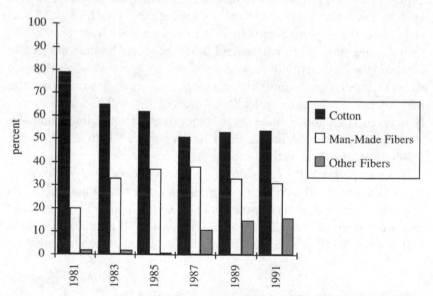

Figure 4.16. Share of U.S. imports from China by fiber category. Data by fiber category discontinued in this series after 1991. *Source:* Calculated from data in *U.S. Imports of Textiles and Apparel Under the Multifiber Arrangement*, various years.

toward products made from "other fibers" at the expense of both cotton goods *and* MMF products.

Flouting the Rules: China Transships to Circumvent the MFA

China quickly exhausted improved quota utilization as a strategy for coping with the MFA. Whatever slack might have existed in certain categories was rapidly eliminated. Except for a few temporary administrative glitches, China has not suffered from any chronic failure to utilize its quota allocations fully. Quite to the contrary, in fact, Beijing has long had to guard against *overshipment* to major export markets. Indeed, the scarcity of available quota has led directly to one of the most controversial aspects of China's response to the MFA: the illegal transshipment of production to the United States and the European Union through third parties. (While there was some Chinese investment in overseas production facilities in the 1990s, a strategy that represents a legal way to circumvent quotas on Chinese exports, these efforts were very small in scale.) Especially as quotas became more restrictive during the late 1980s and early 1990s, allegations emerged that an increasing share of exports from Hong Kong were actually manufactured in China, this in clear violation of the quota system.

In this sense, China has engaged in what might be called "fraudulent" diversification. The third parties involved in this activity typically enjoy either an abundant supply of quota (e.g., Hong Kong and other traditional suppliers who are mired in a losing struggle to remain competitive) or no restrictions whatsoever (e.g., developing countries in Latin America or Africa). This behavior should not be confused with *legal* reexports that are properly charged against Chinese quotas – goods sent through an entrepôt like Hong Kong en route to their final destination, often to take advantage of superior quality control, packaging services, or transportation linkages. Estimates for illegal transshipment during the early 1990s, when the problem first reached international prominence, ranged as high as nearly U.S. $11 billion a year, a figure equivalent to 45 percent of China's total exports of these products at the time.[15] Put another way, for every U.S. $100 of men's dress shirts legally exported to the United States, there may have been another U.S. $45 of shirts made in China that entered the United States for customs purposes as imports from another country, bearing a fraudulent certificate of origin from that third country.

[15] U.S. Customs Service (1994), p. 4.

While illegal transshipments are widely acknowledged to be less prevalent in textile fabrics than finished garments, clothing now represents nearly 70 percent of China's total exports from the industry.[16] Circumvention is not a peripheral issue, therefore, in China's textile trade. In the view of industry consultants and trade experts, there has been incontrovertible proof for many years that Chinese exports are significantly underreported. For evidence, many observers note the fact that half of the fast-growing foreign apparel suppliers to the United States in the early 1990s had little or no production capability for export. According to United Nations data, most of these countries also reported large increases in clothing imports from China.[17] In a few cases, U.S. customs officials traveled to small countries newly active as exporters, only to find no garment factories whatsoever. Informants familiar with these operations told stories about tropical countries in Central America or equatorial Africa that would import from China four or five winter sweaters for every man, woman, and child annually.

Simply put, the numbers do not add up when it comes to China's trade in textiles. Substantial exports have long been diverted to third countries for eventual passage into the United States and the European Union. One informant claimed that the number of people employed in the production of illegal garment exports could conservatively have been estimated at one million in South China alone during the early 1990s. While there was considerable disagreement among interviewees about the percentage of Hong Kong's garment exports to the United States that were actually produced in China and illegally relabeled "Made in Hong Kong" (estimates ranged from 25–75 percent), most concurred that Hong Kong industrialists and traders were the masterminds behind the bulk of China's transshipment, including the production diverted to obscure third countries far removed from East and Southeast Asia.

SILK EXPORTS: A CONVENIENT "FREE TRADE" COUNTEREXAMPLE TO "MANAGED TRADE" UNDER THE MFA

How much of the industrial change described in this chapter should be attributed to the MFA? While it would be an exaggeration to suggest

---

[16] One interviewee familiar with U.S. government investigations estimated that two-thirds of Chinese transshipments in the early 1990s involved garments.

[17] U.S. Customs Service (1994), pp. 3, 9–11.

that China's participation in this international regime was the sole impetus behind the restructuring of its textile industry, the impact of the MFA should not be underestimated. As mentioned previously, one advantage of studying the textile industry is the opportunity it provides to examine the effects of trade protectionism on export performance and industrial restructuring in developing countries. The fact that product coverage under the MFA was phased in gradually enhances the ability of a researcher to isolate the effects of quotas on China's exports. Here, the silk sector provides the single best case since China's exports of silk products to the United States and the European Union became subject to restraints only in 1994.[18] Until that time, the silk sector represented a convenient "free trade" counterexample to the "managed trade" conducted under the MFA. In contrast to the rest of the industry, where the imposition of quotas was followed by export upgrading, product diversification, and exploration of new overseas markets, the quota-free silk sector was marked by declining unit values for exports and sluggish economic adjustment. Similarly, while other sectors of the textile industry saw a significant shift toward market coordination and at least preliminary efforts to rationalize the industry's resources, topics examined at length in the next chapter, the silk sector was characterized by continued reliance on bureaucratic coordination and only fainthearted gestures toward industrial rationalization until the mid-1990s. While factors other than the absence of quotas surely contributed to the different experience of the silk sector, developments following the imposition of quotas on silk products in 1994 seem to confirm just how important the "MFA effect" has been for change in China's textile industry. Specifically, it appears that the silk sector has now entered a phase of externally induced restructuring similar to that experienced previously in other sectors of the textile industry.[19]

The silk industry has a long, illustrious past in China, one especially important to the history of its foreign economic relations. By most accounts, Chinese production of silk goods dates back approximately 5,000 years. Today, the export of silk products (raw silk, silk fabric, and silk garments) has grown into a multibillion dollar business with,

---

[18] Silk was never formally included in the MFA. In 1994, quotas on Chinese exports of silk products to the United States and the European Union were introduced (in March and April, respectively) by means of separate bilateral agreements that were technically independent of the MFA.

[19] *TA* 27:5 (May 1996), p. 76.

according to conservative estimates, roughly 1,000 factories and 800,000 employees in the state-run sector alone. If rural and collective enterprises were included, the totals would exceed 3,000 factories and 1.6 million workers.[20] The China National Silk Import and Export Corporation – the first incarnation of the entity now commonly referred to as CHINASILK – was established in 1949 immediately after the Communist Party's victory, although control over China's lucrative silk trade was never completely centralized over the first three decades of the PRC.[21] For most of that period, CHINASILK was simply the silk-related division of CHINATEX. In 1982, it became a distinct entity, administratively separate from CHINATEX but still subordinate to the Ministry of Foreign Economic Relations and Trade (MOFERT, the successor to the Ministry of Foreign Trade).[22] While ministerial reorganization was not unusual at the time, interviews indicated that this particular move was made partly in anticipation that China would soon become a signatory to the MFA, as it did in December 1983. As a fiber category not covered under the MFA, silk was to be hived off into a separate entity.

Five years later, in 1987, CHINASILK was again overhauled as part of a general trend toward industrial reorganization that accompanied a package of foreign trade reforms designed both to make state trading entities more responsible for their own financial performance and to increase competition in handling China's foreign trade. As described in greater detail below, the effect of these changes was mixed. On the one hand, there was some sporadic liberalization in China's silk trade, especially for garments. On the other hand, industrial and trading activities became increasingly unrelated within China, contributing to the outbreak of the so-called cocoon wars of the late 1980s and 1990s. In short, efforts to find an effective balance between decentralization and recentralization in the silk sector were unsuccessful. Overall, CHINASILK retained considerable authority long after its analog, CHINATEX, found itself greatly weakened in other sectors of the textile industry. In addi-

---

[20] *TA* 26:10 (November 1996), p. 87. Another 20 million are reported to be engaged in silk cocoon farming. Similarly, by some accounts there are up to 6,000 factories just for the manufacture of silk *garments*; *TA* 29:4 (April 1999), p. 88.

[21] The Ministry of Textiles and Ministry of Commerce also apparently engaged in some trade in silk products.

[22] For more on the prereform history of CHINATEX and CHINASILK, see the interview with Zhou Yunzhong, then–vice-president of CHINATEX, in *TA* 16:4 (April 1985), pp. 23–46.

tion to CHINASILK, the other main bureaucratic player during the 1990s was the China Silk Industrial Corporation (CSIC), an agency that reports directly to the China National Textile Council (CNTC), the successor to MTI. As elsewhere in China, then, the major bureaucratic fault lines in the silk industry lie between the (partially reformed) foreign trade apparatus and the (institutionally revamped) ministerial chain of command that oversees production and technical modernization in the industry.

Problems in China's Silk Industry

Many problems found in the silk sector over the last two decades have been typical of China's light industry more generally: poor quality, weak design capabilities, unreliable delivery, backward technology, inadequate funds for investment, overproduction, inefficient management, chaotic supply channels for raw materials, and cutthroat competition among export channels. While each of these problems is important, several merit special discussion. By all accounts, low-quality output has been a chronic problem in the silk industry over the years, far greater than in many other export-oriented Chinese industries, including the rest of the textile industry. Almost every informant queried on the subject asserted that little progress had been made in producing higher-quality goods during the late 1980s and early 1990s, observing that strides had been more rapid elsewhere in the textile industry. Indeed, it is telling that China had failed to establish brand-name silk products for itself by the early 1990s, unlike the situation in cotton, wool, and man-made goods where there had already been some movement, however modest, away from manufacturing exclusively under foreign labels. Interviewees, including several major foreign buyers, remarked on the poor workmanship, shoddy materials, and mediocre design of Chinese silk products, noting once again the difference vis-à-vis other sectors of China's textile industry. Most unacceptable, in their view, were shipments that clearly failed to meet quality standards stipulated in contracts.

Lack of reliable delivery has also traditionally plagued the silk sector, a problem that especially frustrates foreign buyers who must cope with short selling seasons in fashion-conscious markets. Needless to say, the silk sector enjoyed virtually no success in producing small batches of specialized goods on short notice to foreign customers. Rather, mass production of standard goods continued to reign supreme. Compared to other sectors of the textile industry, the silk sector failed to demonstrate any ability to alter production plans quickly to meet changes in world demand.

Another related problem is overproduction. To those interviewed, it was apparent that quality suffered partly as a result of "blind" expansion. Indeed, the overdevelopment of China's silk industry has been a common focus among industry observers, a problem less pronounced in other sectors of the textile industry, where quantitative restrictions have been imposed on Chinese exports under the MFA.[23] In short, the de facto (and, until the late 1980s, de jure) strategy in silk was to increase revenue simply by exporting *more* products, not *better* products. By all accounts, CHINASILK imposed far too little discipline over the various export channels under its jurisdiction. Especially in the late 1980s and early 1990s, press reports were replete with anecdotes about different silk-trading entities – many of which were subsidiaries of CHINASILK – engaged in cutthroat price competition.[24] In the absence of meaningful financial accountability, and spurred on by powerful export incentives such as foreign exchange retention, the rush to sell more goods all but consumed the silk sector.

Silken Sorrows: Unrestrained Exports and China's Failure to Trade Up in the World Market

Relying mainly upon exports, China's silk industry has enjoyed robust growth in output throughout the post-Mao period. For example, production increased almost 16 percent per year between 1988 and 1994, a period that Yu Xiasong, a vice-minister of the State Economic and Trade Commission (SETC), has referred to as the "blind and chaotic expan-

---

[23] This issue receives particular attention from foreign analysts of China's industry. See, for instance, *TA* 26:1 (January 1995), p. 67.

[24] CHINASILK and its subsidiaries have branches in 30 provinces, autonomous regions, and municipalities, as well as representative offices worldwide. To put it mildly, "coordination" among these actors was poor. The incentives to export were so strong, in fact, that the competition spread to unauthorized trade channels. Especially with the partial relaxation of centralized foreign trade authority in 1987, part of a larger package of foreign trade reforms implemented that year, new exporters entered the scene to challenge CHINASILK. Intended to improve efficiency, this effort at partial reform spurred the so-called cocoon wars in which intense bidding lowered prices, reduced quality, and disrupted delivery schedules. As described later in the text, the State Council eventually intervened (in 1988) to reimpose central control over silk exports. While this episode was secondary in importance to the syndrome of "easy" exporting as a cause of China's stagnant unit prices and general failure to "trade up" in silk products over time, it certainly only made matters worse.

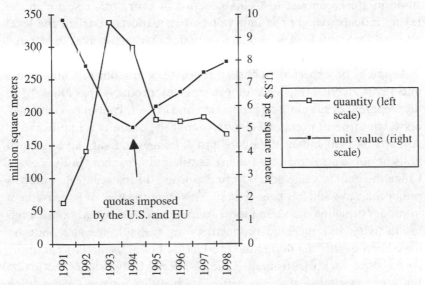

Figure 4.17. Chinese exports of silk garments to the United States. *Source:* Calculated from data in computer printouts provided by the Office of Textiles and Apparel, U.S. Department of Commerce.

sion" of the sector.[25] From 1990 to 1993 alone, Chinese exports of silk garments increased from 70 million pieces to 310 million pieces.[26] During this same period, the unit value of these exports fell by roughly 40 percent.[27] As depicted in Figure 4.17, the unit value of U.S. imports from China declined 48 percent from 1991 to 1994, while at the same time rising meteorically in volume. While world prices were descending from a pronounced spike at this time, the unit value of U.S. imports from all other countries declined by only 18 percent during the same period. By the mid-1990s, silk garments from China commanded only one-half of the price received by South Korean manufacturers.[28] This performance

[25] *TA* 26:10 (November 1996), p. 72.

[26] *China Daily*, 27 March 1994, reprinted in FBIS-CHI-94-059. Later reports had 1993 exports of silk garments as high as 350 million pieces; *TA* 29:4 (April 1999), p. 88.

[27] Calculated from data provided in *TA* 27:3 (March 1997), p. 85. In fact, this trend was well-established prior to the 1990s. According to data presented at a meeting of the International Silk Association in 1991, the average export price of Chinese silk blouses declined by 14 percent from 1985 to 1990; *TA* 23:11 (November 1992), p. 107.

[28] *TA* 26:1 (January 1995), p. 67. For additional data that suggests an even greater decline for this period, see *TA* 27:5 (May 1996), p. 76.

stood in stark contrast to China's record in every other sector in the textile industry, where the unit value of its exports matched the level attained by South Korean products in major markets such as the United States (as shown in Figure 4.3).

As might be expected, published reports coming out of China in the mid-1990s decried the lack of progress in product upgrading: "The development of silk clothing production and exports cannot be called successful in terms of profit and quality, even if the quantity is impressive."[29] As early as 1990, in fact, the Economist Intelligence Unit had concluded in its periodic assessment of China's textile industry that "in the case of China the gain in value added from exporting downstream silk products rather than raw silk has been limited."[30] Noting the lack of improvement in product quality, the same report found "indications that both labour productivity and machine productivity in the silk weaving industry have been decreasing during the production boom of the last decade."[31] As a group of scholars from the China National University of the Textile Industry concluded more recently, "unhealthy internal competition among silk exporting enterprises [had] caused the steady fall of selling prices on foreign markets."[32] By all accounts, a vicious circle emerged in which burgeoning production over time led to excess manufacturing capacity, which in turn resulted in declining prices and mounting financial losses in the industry.[33] In fact, a senior silk official has publicly acknowledged that much of the industry's problems through the mid-1990s can be traced back to the rush to set up facilities for silk production in the 1980s in response to the seemingly limitless opportunity to export to the world market.[34]

Informants consistently commented upon the lack of discipline in China's silk industry in the early 1990s. Even foreign buyers, who at China's expense benefited from the price wars, acknowledged how much better the industry could have performed over time. Needless to say, those associated with the industry itself lamented the self-destructive chaos. All agreed that the silk sector had failed to diversify its product mix satisfactorily and needed to upgrade its existing products. In an

[29] Ibid.
[30] Economist Intelligence Unit, "The Textile Industry in China," *TOI* (July 1990), p. 44.
[31] Ibid.
[32] *TA* 27:3 (March 1997), p. 85. The figure on declining unit values of silk exports is calculated from data provided in the same article.
[33] For one such account, see *TA* 27:9 (September 1997), p. 112.
[34] *TA* 28:8 (August 1998), p. 71.

interesting note, several of the foreign businesspeople and consultants interviewed on the subject observed that one of the things the silk sector lacked was the discipline imposed on the rest of the textile industry by the MFA. In their view, this externally imposed restraint was important for explaining the different records of achievement in the silk and nonsilk sectors of China's textile industry.[35]

Smooth as Silk: The Dangers of "Easy" Exports to the World Market

In many ways, the silk sector epitomizes the dangers that accompany an ability to sell products rather easily on the world market. As the Open Policy unfolded in the early 1980s, officials in the silk industry quickly recognized the favorable export opportunity that awaited them: China's traditional niche in the silk trade could be expanded dramatically. With no coverage for silk products under the MFA, the amount of foreign exchange earned could be increased simply by exporting more goods. For officials in the silk industry, this meant that there were basically no incentives – internally or externally – to abandon bureaucratic coordination as the primary mechanism for organizing economic activity in the industry. As long as silk exports continued to grow, industry officials could be expected to ignore (or at least minimize the implementation of) most reform measures. And even where reform did proceed, its partial nature insulated silk officials from serious considerations about profitability and other concerns that might have weakened their natural affinity for bureaucratic coordination.

While the silk sector was not without its problems, life was comfortable there in comparison with other sectors of the textile industry that had to cope with quantitative limits on their exports to major markets such as the United States and the European Union. It is telling, for example, that the *value* of silk exports was targeted by Chinese officials to increase by only 5 percent during the Seventh Five-Year Plan (1986–1990), whereas the *volume* of silk exports was planned to increase by 10 percent.[36] Facing a relatively easy environment, one that could

---

[35] This does not mean that these individuals were supporters of the MFA. In fact, they generally condemned the MFA in every other respect, arguing that protectionism created economic inefficiency in the advanced industrialized countries and limited their own business opportunities as textile traders.

[36] *ZGJJXW*, 24 February 1986, p. 2.

even be characterized as a sellers' market, the export of silk products remained heavily regulated by government bureaucrats at several levels of administration. Exports grew with little consideration for improving quality, raising efficiency, or shifting the commodity composition of China's silk exports toward a greater proportion of finished goods. Overall, the industry lacked the discipline necessary to curtail over-production and upgrade its goods for export. This was in stark contrast to developments in others sectors of the textile industry where, as Chapter 5 will document, market-oriented solutions to the challenge of economic adjustment emerged with increasing frequency. Since the silk sector was able to achieve significant export growth without undertaking fundamental changes in its operation, there was little impetus for reform and rationalization.

When problems such as poor product quality and indiscriminate exports were addressed, bureaucrats relied mainly on traditional administrative means rather than experimentation with new reform initiatives or greater implementation of existing reform programs. The problem of product quality, for example, was addressed by education programs and efforts to intensify inspection procedures, not by reforms that would have increased the responsibility of decentralized economic actors. Interviews and press reports alike indicate that bureaucrats relied heavily on newly established "quality networks" and various campaigns to enhance quality awareness at the local level.[37] To improve the variety of silk goods manufactured for export, efforts were often made to readjust the product mix through central commands.[38] Furthermore, CSIC was created in 1990 to coordinate the production of higher quality goods and carry out technical modernization.[39] As one interviewee put it, "their response [in the silk industry] is always to 'strengthen administrative management.'" Other interviewees indicated that even foreign joint ventures – some of which theoretically enjoyed direct export rights – were expected to "coordinate" their activities with industry bureaucrats in ways not commonly found in other sectors of the textile industry.[40]

---

[37] *TA* 23:7 (July 1992), p. 96.
[38] See, for instance, *ZGJJXW*, 1 July 1991, pp. 15–16.
[39] *TA* 23:5 (May 1992), p. 106.
[40] By the early 1990s, in fact, there was an official movement to discourage foreign investment in the silk sector. Interviews and press reports alike suggest that administrative measures were taken to control new projects as a way of handling the problem of excessive exports at low prices. See, for instance, *TA* 23:8 (August 1992), p. 10.

The central government also tried to deal with the problem of excess productive capacity in silk goods through administrative measures. In 1989, for instance, Beijing issued a well-publicized edict forbidding the "blind expansion" of silk production. Not only was this command ignored, but state-run silk producers were among the worst offenders in contributing to even greater overproduction. Even the president of CHINASILK observed that

> the industry is in a state of latent crisis, due not so much to foreign competition as to its own structural problems. Lack of coordination between its agricultural, manufacturing and trade sectors has caused serious over-capacity. . . . Some newly established small enterprises look only for quick success and instant profit, neglecting technical updating, new product development, and the improvement of quality. . . . As a result, the basis of China's industry has been weakened, and it is now lagging further behind the developed countries, or even some of the developing countries such as Brazil.[41]

Overall, it was bureaucratic coordination rather than market coordination that served as the primary mechanism for adjustment in efforts to change the commodity composition of China's silk exports from raw silk to finished goods. While fairly successful in achieving the desired shift in the sector's product mix, little progress was made in upgrading production *within* specific categories of goods.[42] For example, China began to export relatively more silk blouses than raw silk or silk fabric, but those additional garments were usually of the same mediocre or poor grade. While this shift represented an advance of sorts, from unfinished to finished goods, the ultimate prize – higher unit value for individual product lines – remained elusive.

Time and again, therefore, the government tried to increase centralization over the management of silk exports. From 1987 to 1995, the State Council issued eight separate directives designed to strengthen central control over the purchase and supply of silk products.[43] Several of these directives either reiterated CHINASILK's existing authority or even

---

[41] *TA* 27:5 (May 1996), p. 70.

[42] Exact estimates differ depending on the source of the data, but in approximate terms China's exports of raw silk, silk fabric, and finished silk garments achieved an even balance by the early 1990s, each representing one-third of exports. As late as the mid-1980s, raw silk had accounted for between 40 and 50 percent of silk exports.

[43] *TA* 27:5 (May 1996), p. 76.

expanded its control over silk exports.[44] In this sense, difficulties in the silk sector were met not with reform, but rather with counterreform. Efforts to implement recentralization in China's silk trade included licensing systems and tax rebates.[45] In the end, these efforts failed to stem the flood of silk exports, at least to the degree desired by officials who recognized the opportunity cost that China incurred by settling for exporting more goods at stagnant or even declining unit prices. Put simply, administrative measures were often ignored from below. At best, they were incompletely implemented. China's silk exports continued to grow in uncontrolled fashion, often through unauthorized channels. In the absence of restrictions like those imposed under the MFA, there was no effective mechanism to discipline actors operating in a partially reformed economic system.

Quotas to the Rescue?: Advances in China's Silk Industry in the Wake of Restricted Exports

By all accounts, reform and rationalization of the silk industry did not become a serious issue until the United States and the European Union imposed quotas on Chinese silk exports in the spring of 1994. In early 1996, after nearly two years of increasingly hard times, industry officials formally applied to the State Council for rescue assistance. As an article in the official media explained the sector's predicament at the time, "The silk industry was advantageous to China [in the past] . . . [because] silk output and exports ranked first in the world. However, since the second half of 1994 the industry has faced unprecedented difficulties."[46] While many of the silk industry's underlying difficulties were chronic, the imposition of quotas intensified these problems significantly, mainly by eliminating the previous strategy of constantly increasing exports as a way for the industry to stay afloat amid its troubles.

By 1996, the hard times experienced by the silk industry began to receive concerted attention from high-ranking leaders. Vice-Premier Li Lanqing, for example, issued a call for reform of the silk industry at a

---

[44] For additional background, see *ZGJJXW*, 17 October 1988, p. 15.

[45] For more information on these schemes, see "Silk Spins out of Control," *CTR* (July 1989), pp. 8–9.

[46] "PRC Silk Industry Seeks Government Assistance," *Zhongguo Xinwen She*, 22 January 1996, in FBIS-CHI-96-015.

national conference in May 1996.[47] As described by Chen Youzhe, CHINASILK's president, the quotas imposed on silk products by the United States and the European Union have increased the "urgency of reforming the current system."[48] Indeed, the State Council convened a series of special meetings in 1996 in response to declining exports of silk garments. Although several measures were taken, the most important was the establishment of the State Cocoon and Silk Coordination Group to oversee affairs in the entire sector. As its name suggests, this new entity was designed to better coordinate silk production and exports given the newly restrictive nature of world markets created by quotas from Washington and Brussels. By all accounts, the quota-induced crisis experienced by the silk industry served as the impetus for reform and rationalization at several levels of administration.[49]

While many initiatives originated in Beijing, such as a revamped inspection and licensing system designed to close below-grade production facilities, others came from the local level. To cite just one example, officials in Shanghai attempted to reintegrate the city's silk production and silk export by merging the Shanghai Silk Import and Export Corporation (SSIEC) and the Shanghai Jinda Silk Company into the Shanghai Silk Company Limited in October 1997. In the words of Xu Weimin, the new company's general manager: "In the past, the city's silk production and export were operated by two companies and overseen by two government departments. Neither side cared much about the other."[50] SSIEC had set up its own production factories or simply joined forces with TVEs. For their part, Shanghai Jinda and other existing manufacturers of silk garments had sought direct export rights as the primary means for developing overseas markets on their own. From a national perspective, the outcome of this dynamic was quite unsatisfactory and, given the quotas imposed on Chinese exports beginning in 1994, increasingly unsustainable. Shanghai Silk, the new company designed to coordinate the city's production and trading business in silk goods, was self-consciously patterned after Japan's *Sogoshosha*.[51] From all indications, this local effort in Shanghai was a fairly typical development as

---

[47] For more detail, see "Vice Premier Li Lanqing Urges Silk Industry Reforms," *Xinhua*, 17 May 1996, in FBIS-CHI-96-099.
[48] *TA* 27:5 (May 1996), p. 71.
[49] For more detail, see *TA* 27:10 (October 1996), p. 73.
[50] *TA* 29:7 (July 1998), p. 49.   [51] Ibid.

China's silk industry attempted to cope with the imposition of quotas by the United States and the European Union.[52]

While the magnitude of reform and rationalization should not be over-stated – indeed it remains too early to evaluate the long-term trajectory of the silk sector – there are encouraging signs of industrial adjustment in the wake of these quotas. As shown in Figure 4.17, the unit value of China's silk garment exports to the United States rose steadily from 1994 to 1998. Moreover, the 57 percent increase registered during this period compares favorably with the 40 percent gain enjoyed by all other countries. Indeed, this result reverses the trend between 1991 and 1994, when the unit value of Chinese exports declined far more than that of its competitors (48 percent as opposed to 18 percent). Furthermore, the lower volume of export sales – a direct result of quotas – has led to a partial rationalization of the industry, one that appears to have slightly preceded the nationwide program begun in 1998. A "National Plan" was drawn up in 1997 under which 65 major SOEs in the silk industry were restructured through bankruptcy, mergers, and other forms of administrative reorganization. According to press accounts, this rationalization included substantial workforce reductions.[53] While the majority of enterprises in the silk sector were still suffering losses in 1997, there was some evidence that the percentage of loss-making firms had actually declined compared to the period from 1994 to 1996.[54]

CONCLUSION

All told, recent events in the silk sector provide additional evidence that change in China's textile industry cannot be understood without reference to the MFA. Specifically, this chapter has emphasized the close connection between the imposition of product-specific textile quotas and a distinct pattern of industrial restructuring. The next chapter examines the impact of the MFA on reform and rationalization in China's textile industry. Here, as well, the experience of the silk sector serves as an important benchmark for assessing the effects of various degrees of economic openness on change at the industrial level in China.

---

[52] In Jiangsu, for instance, producers and traders formed the Jiangsu Province Silk Group as a vehicle to improve their performance on the world market. *Xinhua*, 20 May 1997, in FBIS-CHI-97-354.

[53] *TA* 28:12 (December 1997), p. 84.

[54] *TA* 28:9 (September 1997), p. 113, and *TA* 28:11 (November 1997), p. 92.

5

China Looms Large: Reform and Rationalization in the Textile Industry

THE previous chapter documented China's successful response to the MFA, a response marked by export upgrading, adjustments to the product mix, and market diversification among export destinations. This chapter will explore how that record of industrial restructuring was built, with special emphasis on the policy environment. It begins by reviewing the problems that China's textile industry faced as it sought to cope with quotas. It then discusses the various administrative measures and economic reforms that were taken in an effort to improve the industry's performance. Here, the main argument is that bureaucratic coordination gave way over time to market coordination as the primary means for pursuing economic adjustment in the textile industry, albeit only after administrative measures failed to produce the desired changes. Next, the chapter provides an overview of rationalization efforts within the industry. Lastly, it examines the system of quota allocation as a detailed case study of China's adjustment to life under the MFA.

HANGING BY A THREAD: CHINA COPES WITH THE MFA

Although legendary for their immensity, the problems affecting the textile industry are little different from the basic challenges that all Chinese industries have faced during the post-Mao era. Indeed, the textile industry has at one time or another suffered from just about every affliction one could mention: stockpiled output; idle equipment/surplus capacity; unplanned development; outmoded technology; deteriorating physical plant; a crushing tax burden; redundant workers; poor management; an unreasonable price structure; the heavy burden of providing wages and other support for huge numbers of retired employees; wasted investment funds; lack of financial profitability; and persistent shortages

111

of raw materials, power, capital, and foreign exchange. All of this is in addition to industry-specific problems such as impure fiber content, poor quality fabrics, and a lack of uniformity in color, shrinkage, and measurements. To make matters worse, China has also lagged in areas particularly important for international marketing, such as reliable delivery and proper packaging.

It is almost a truism among scholars of comparative and international political economy that a successful national response to an external challenge – for example, the imposition of quotas under the MFA – requires a flexible economic and political system that allows a country to adjust quickly and skillfully to changing conditions in the world market.[1] It should surprise no one, therefore, that China's (largely unreformed) economic and foreign trade system did not serve the country's interests well in directing quota-restricted textile exports in the early 1980s. Indeed, China's response was at first simply more of the same: continued reliance on bulk orders of low-grade goods. Rather than moving upmarket toward higher value-added goods, China's exports actually became the subject of dumping allegations, an indication that the industry's de facto strategy retained an emphasis on underselling foreign competitors. Furthermore, this competition also began to pit Chinese goods against other Chinese goods, often in the most cutthroat manner. While the antidumping cases brought against China may have been motivated in part by politics, especially domestic politics in the United States, the mere fact that China could credibly be charged with dumping is extremely revealing given the incentive it faced under the MFA to achieve higher unit values for its restricted exports.

China's adjustment to life under the MFA was also hampered by a number of problems common to new signatories, including an understandable (but painfully evident) lack of experience in managing its export quotas. China's quota utilization was relatively poor at first, as evidenced by problems with overshipment in some categories and unused quotas in others. Furthermore, textile officials had difficulty learning how to use the MFA's carryforward, carryover, and swing provisions to maximize China's export position.[2] To make matters worse,

---

[1] On the issue of trade protectionism, see, for instance, Yoffie (1983). For a sampling of more general treatments, see Gourevitch (1986), Katzenstein (1984, 1985), and Loriaux (1991).

[2] Carryforward allows the exporting country to borrow quota from the next year for application to the present year. Carryover involves the reverse, as the exporting country applies a portion of unused quota from the present year to the following year. Finally,

poor management of export growth resulted in massive surges for specific product categories that triggered so-called consultation calls by major importers such as the United States and the European Union. As a result, more products became subject to export restraints than were required by the letter of bilateral agreements negotiated under the MFA. Overall, the result was heightened tension in China's textile relations with its major trading partners. While there is no doubt that Washington and Brussels would have requested consultations occasionally to estab-lish a "managed" import level on new products for which China was enjoying increasing market share, Beijing's mismanagement of quota utilization and its failure to control sharp increases in particular imports from year to year inflamed bilateral relations and, as a result, made the MFA more restrictive in practice than was required in theory.

The constraints of the MFA proved significant indeed. Problems with fabric quality, manufacturing design, and the long lead time required for production and overseas delivery remained, but now China could no longer compensate simply by trying to sell more goods. As early as 1982, a year before China became a signatory to the MFA and a mere two years into the first Sino-American textile agreement, there was recogni-tion among Chinese officials that the industry would have to move upmarket in order to achieve sustainable export growth.[3] More broadly, it was understood among industry analysts that China would need to accomplish several things if the textile industry was to continue as the country's leading foreign exchange earner: shift production to unre-stricted goods, diversify its export markets, redress the supply problems that hindered high-quality production for export, and otherwise trade up the international product cycle.[4]

The issue, therefore, was not so much *whether* China understood the nature of the challenge presented by the MFA as much as *how* it would attempt the necessary economic adjustment. As might be expected, China at first relied mainly on bureaucratic coordination, shifting to market coordination only when the former failed to satisfactorily improve the industry's performance. This initial emphasis on bureau-cratic coordination is not surprising given that market-oriented reforms were extremely modest in the country's industrial sector at the time of

swing allows the exporting country to transfer unused quota for one category to another category for which quota is either exhausted or nearly exhausted, thereby enabling con-tinued exports of those goods.

[3] *TA* 18:9 (September 1987), p. 170.

[4] For more detail, see note 2 in Chapter 4.

China's accession to the MFA. Even after 1984, when the second phase of China's economic reforms began, it took several years for substantial marketization to occur outside of agriculture.[5] In this sense, the situation in the textile industry did not differ much from other industries at the time, and it would have been shocking if China's early response to the MFA had not included significant reliance on central commands issued through the planning apparatus, political campaigns designed to change bureaucratic behavior, and other *dirigiste* policies. In the end, however, it was only with the successful implementation of economic reforms – thereby shifting the balance significantly (albeit not completely) from bureaucratic to market coordination – that the desired results in industrial adjustment were achieved to any substantial degree in China's textile industry.

THE ROAD TO REFORM

Business as Usual: Administrative Measures in Response to the MFA

Rather than attempt to catalog all of the myriad administrative efforts undertaken in response to the MFA, this section will simply provide examples that illustrate the wide-ranging forms of bureaucratic coordination that were used in trying to effect adjustment in the Chinese textile industry. One method was institutional change. In classic state socialist fashion, Beijing created several new bureaucratic agencies over the years to administer changes in the industry, changes designed at least in part to respond more effectively to incentives present under the MFA. For example, the China National Garments Research and Design Centre was established in late 1983 – simultaneously with China's signing of the MFA – to help the industry identify and develop higher value-added products for export.

Other efforts at bureaucratic coordination included attempts to move China's production upmarket through central planning. Although the planning apparatus was already somewhat diminished in its scope and effectiveness by the mid-1980s, it remained an important means by which bureaucrats could attempt economic adjustment in certain segments of the textile industry. Informants recounted numerous instances in which industry officials tried to readjust the product mix and improve quality

[5] For a comprehensive study of China's economic reforms, see Naughton (1995).

114

through central directives, especially in the early to mid-1980s. In many cases, these commands were either incompletely implemented or simply ignored. In other cases, production did in fact shift to unrestricted or less restricted product categories, but usually without the requisite improvement in quality. The result, therefore, was some success in minimizing the impact of quotas by diversifying production, but typically with goods that were as poor (or worse) than those produced in the past.

This failure of central planning revealed, among other things, a lack of coordination between industry and trade in China. Because export contracts were secured by representatives of CHINATEX and other authorized trading entities, in most cases there was little prospect of substantive contact between foreign customers and textile factories. This arrangement all but eliminated the valuable flow of marketing and design information, managerial expertise, and other spillover effects that typically accompany business relationships between foreign buyers and textile producers in developing countries. To put it mildly, it proved difficult for textile factories to produce high-fashion goods, comprehend the seriousness of quality specifications, or understand the importance of timely delivery when their contact with the outside world was so limited. To be sure, China's traders had decent access to information about world textile markets, but few of these bureaucrats had either the professional background or the narrow self-interest (i.e., personal incentive) to apply that knowledge to China's fullest benefit. In short, the lack of coordination between industry and trade represented a fundamental problem for China's position in the world market.

Political campaigns were another vehicle used by the Chinese government in trying to effect industrial adjustment. As reported widely in the press and reiterated in interviews, the textile industry was the focus of numerous campaigns designed to remedy problems such as output stockpiling, low worker productivity, the poor use of investment funds and foreign exchange allocations, and bad management in general.[6] Time and again, the government exhorted the industry to change its ways, although often to little avail. These efforts culminated with the designation of 1990 as "The Year of Quality and Fashion" in the textile industry. While hardly the last effort of its kind, the use of slogans and media coverage as an instrument of economic change declined in importance after the widely-acknowledged failure of this high-profile campaign.[7]

---

[6] See, for example, *TA* 22:10 (October 1991), p. 60.
[7] *TA* 21:10 (October 1990), p. 117.

115

Even as the importance of market coordination grew throughout the late 1980s and early 1990s, government policy continued to play a significant role in the textile industry. (As in all economies, of course, China reflects elements of both bureaucratic and market coordination.) Under the Seventh Five-Year Plan (1986–1990), for example, certain textile firms were eligible for preferential access to raw materials, transportation, and energy sources. There were also press reports of a special foreign exchange fund to help textile-exporting enterprises finance technology imports.[8] While these efforts may have contributed marginally to China's success in textile exports, most interviewees – especially non-PRC informants – were highly skeptical of China's ability to pursue (with any success) the type of strategic industrial policy often ascribed to Japan, South Korea, and Taiwan. As evidence, many cited the superior performance of nonstate firms (FIEs, TVEs, and private firms), the sector that has benefited the least during the post-Mao era from government efforts at export targeting. According to these observers, a state-led approach to industrial adjustment was virtually doomed to failure in China. (PRC interviewees were more divided on this point.) Based on their experience with China's textile industry, and their impressions of dynamics within the state more generally, non-PRC informants saw little basis for optimism that government resources could be harnessed for developmental (as opposed to particularistic) ends without fundamental, long-term changes to the economic and political system.

Even as the trend toward market coordination became clear, reform was occasionally offset by counterreform in the textile industry. Regarding the export of cotton yarn and cloth, for example, directives were passed in 1987 and again in 1990 that recentralized foreign trade authority in an effort to increase the proportion of finished textile goods in China's overseas sales.[9] Other bureaucratic efforts ranged from policies that sought to limit output by controlling spindleage to threats of sanctions against companies that failed to achieve foreign exchange targets.[10] As an indication of the textile industry's importance as the country's

[8] *CTR* (March 1988), p. 3.
[9] See, for instance, *TA* 18:9 (September 1987), p. 170, and *ZGJJXW*, 19 November 1990, pp. 8–9.
[10] For representative press reports, see *TA* 21:7 (July 1990); *TA* 19:10 (October 1988), p. 93; *TA* 20:10 (October 1989), pp. 70, 94; and *TA* 21:3 (March 1990), p. 76. Even in the early 1990s, TIBs were trying to deal with overproduction simply by instructing enterprises to cut production, albeit with the threat of penalties; *TA* 23:2 (February 1992), p. 106.

leading foreign exchange earner, these actions often came directly from the State Council itself. Indeed, the Eighth Five-Year Plan (1991–1995) included provisions that tightened control over production of certain textile goods.[11]

Between a Rock and a Hard Place:
The Perils of Partial Reform

Even though the shift from bureaucratic coordination to market coordination in the textile industry eventually became so pronounced that several interviewees described it as a "reform pioneer," textiles was not always on the fast track for administrative deregulation. While the general reform measures adopted nationally in the late 1970s and early 1980s appear rather minor in retrospect, even these simple steps were often ignored or incompletely implemented. Here, one of the main impediments to change was the TIBs and other administrative departments that jealously guarded their supervisory roles.

Even if these bureaucrats had been willing agents of change, however, early reform measures were simply too limited to have made a significant difference in China's export performance. Enterprise autonomy was circumscribed by production targets, an inability to import machinery and raw materials directly, and little effective control over retained profits. With inadequate supplies, ineffective financial incentives, and a planning system that remained surprisingly comprehensive, it would have been very difficult for firms to shift their production to meet market demand – even if that had been their primary objective. In an economic system that was only partially (and, at that point, also minimally) reformed, textile enterprises were confronted with a set of inherently conflicting goals concerning output targets, quality standards, and profit criteria. Meeting even one of these goals sometimes excluded progress on the others.

If there was a single problem that inhibited China's ability to cope with the MFA for much of the 1980s, it was the glaring lack of coordination that existed between industry and trade described in the previous section. In the partially reformed Chinese economic system, one in which international market signals were severely scrambled, the modus operandi for CHINATEX and other FTCs was simply to export as much as possible, thereby maximizing their foreign exchange revenue. Given

---

[11] *CTR* (December 1990), pp. 8–9.

their limited financial responsibility at the time, concerns about profitability were relatively minor. The result was an "export-at-any-cost" mentality in which FTCs engaged in cutthroat price competition overseas, often eliciting allegations of dumping from the United States and other countries. The FTCs financed this self-destructive competition mainly by squeezing China's textile producers, sometimes managing to secure purchase prices that were even below the already low, state-set prices authorized by the State Council.[12] Unable to export their goods directly, and in many cases with foreign exchange targets or other obligations to uphold themselves, enterprises were in effect forced to sell their goods to FTCs at prices that did not cover any meaningful approximation of cost.

For nearly forty years, the Chinese government had strictly controlled prices for most textile goods in an effort to provide stable living standards. Minor adjustments notwithstanding, prices remained unchanged for decades. In the early and mid-1980s, the government raised the prices of certain raw materials (e.g., cotton) to support agriculture. The prices of most finished goods, however, were not raised to reflect the increased cost of material inputs. As a result, textile producers were hit with a double whammy: skyrocketing prices for raw materials and low-ball purchase prices by FTCs.[13] Given this predicament, it should not be surprising that textile enterprises failed to pay more attention to quality control and timely delivery. Nor should it be surprising that they were generally unwilling to absorb the extra cost necessary to secure the highest-grade raw materials. Better goods cost more to produce, but this added expense could not be recouped given the partial nature of reform in China at the time. Indeed, in the absence of significant price reform, there was arguably a *disincentive* for producers to upgrade the quality of their goods. Customer service lagged, therefore, not just because of a dearth of buyer-producer contact, but also because of the discrepancy between production costs and the prices paid to textile factories by CHINATEX and other authorized trading entities.

Even where small advances in moving upmarket were achieved, this came at a hefty cost: financial losses mounted as the FTCs competed vi-

---

[12] *TA* 22:11 (November 1991), p. 63.

[13] Furthermore, textile producers faced a sellers' market in purchasing raw materials since the supply of decent quality inputs always lagged behind domestic demand. By contrast, textile producers faced a buyers' market in distributing their finished goods, since surplus productive capacity at home and export restrictions abroad combined to ensure that supply always outstripped demand.

gorously for the restricted volume of export sales China was allowed to make under the MFA. In many cases, Chinese goods competed against Chinese goods in the world market with little or no regard for the cost of producing each U.S. dollar of exports. As long as decentralization in decision making outpaced any meaningful concept of financial accountability, the result may have been rational for individual economic actors, but it was clearly suboptimal from the perspective of national welfare.

True to form, the initial response was to address problems of economic adjustment through bureaucratic coordination. One administrative measure taken in this case was a reduction in the number of FTCs authorized to sell certain products; this step was taken in the hope that fewer competitors would mean less destructive pricing behavior. At the same time, the government also tried to re-regulate purchase prices, raising them to a level more consistent with the cost of production incurred by textile enterprises. While this administrative adjustment was undoubtedly better than no adjustment, the system still lacked the flexibility necessary to cope with the ongoing structural changes in the Chinese economy. Simply put, the situation in the textile industry was extremely fluid, and sporadic price corrections by bureaucrats proved unable to manage the transition effectively. (Extreme fluctuations, especially in the supply of certain raw materials, made the task of effective bureaucratic coordination all the more difficult.) What is more, the system of state-fixed prices – even if adjustable – still did not allow prices to rise with quality for a given product. Even when prices were adjusted, they were adjusted across the board, with no provision made for prices to reflect quality. Given the premium on unit value in a world market dominated by the MFA, this limitation constituted a major handicap.

When administrative changes accomplished little, the emphasis began to shift more decisively toward market coordination. It was not enough simply to reduce the number of actors and occasionally adjust prices. For China to participate effectively in world textile markets, more comprehensive reform was necessary. As discussed in Chapter 1, partial reform often introduces new distortions that create serious dilemmas for economic policy, dilemmas that accentuate the basic choice between backsliding toward the prereform system and moving forward with greater market-oriented reform.[14] For example, it was publicly acknowledged by

---

[14] From this perspective, dilemmas of partial reform represent a policy disequilibrium in which the proverbial halfway house between plan and market, while theoretically

government officials that the only way to ensure that textile factories were rewarded for producing high-quality goods was to increase the role of market coordination in determining prices.[15] In this way, the partially reformed nature of the economic system proved to be a major impediment as China tried to upgrade its existing production and diversify to new goods and markets.

Efforts to Link Industry and Trade: The Case of the Export Agency System

As described above, the single biggest problem China encountered in adjusting to life under the MFA was the lack of coordination between industrial and trading activities in textiles. Simply put, the air lock system introduced in Chapter 1 made an effective response to the MFA difficult indeed. Textile factories lacked the proper incentives to upgrade production and pay greater attention to quality and timeliness of delivery. For their part, the FTCs were driven almost exclusively by the prospect of foreign exchange earnings, relatively oblivious to concerns of either their own profitability or the export cost of earning each U.S. dollar. As this section documents, one of the major reform initiatives undertaken to address this set of problems was the export agency system.

Interviews indicated that the textile industry had been used to experiment with the export agency system prior to the plan's formal approval by the State Council as part of the larger package of foreign trade reforms promulgated in 1984. According to these accounts, the textile industry was selected not only because of its role as the leading foreign exchange earner, but also because officials understood the need to reduce, if not eliminate altogether, the isolation of Chinese enterprises that resulted under the air lock system. If the industry was to thrive in a world market dominated by export restrictions under the MFA, change would be especially necessary in this sector.

The agency system was designed to introduce several substantive changes from previous arrangements for China's exports. First, the responsibility for profits and losses was to fall on the producers them-

---

possible, is difficult to sustain in practice. At the very least, it is very costly to sustain this halfway house. In this sense, the opportunity cost of inaction – either back to a greater emphasis on bureaucratic coordination or decisively forward toward market coordination – is made high by dilemmas of partial reform.

[15] *TA* 23:1 (January 1992), p. 90.

selves, with the FTCs simply acting as sales agents on a commission basis. Second, and perhaps most importantly, the prices received by textile producers were to be based on world market prices. With the advent of the agency system, therefore, the air lock system was to be (at least partially) penetrated. As long as textile enterprises had to sell through FTCs, however, their autonomy was still limited in a fundamental way. Interviews yielded stories of FTCs withholding market information and otherwise manipulating business relations with their "clients" (i.e., the textile factories). Even pricing remained less than fully market-determined as the result of asymmetries in information and other elements of imperfect competition that continued under the agency system.[16] After all, while the number of authorized FTCs increased dramatically as the result of foreign trade reform, producers were still required to export through FTCs.

To make matters worse, the agency system was never fully implemented due to considerable resistance from the FTCs. Understandably, the FTCs preferred the traditional system in which they actually took title of the goods and thus were entitled to a portion of the foreign exchange earnings. Under the agency system, they had no such claim and therefore refused to cooperate whenever and however they could. While the textile industry certainly was not immune to this problem, the percentage of textile exports handled on an agency basis was apparently almost double the national average.[17] By this measure, at least, the textile industry was at the forefront of reform.

Even though the agency system was never fully applied, it did weaken the air lock system to some degree. Prices were more consistent with international levels, producers had access to more information about specific foreign buyers and general trends in the world market, and factories had a somewhat greater financial incentive to pursue upmarket goods and improve the quality of their production. Even where the agency system was employed, however, it by no means eliminated all distortions. At best, it represented a halfway house along the road to reform.

The next step, as it turns out, was to grant direct export rights to textile enterprises, a move that allowed them to negotiate autonomously with

---

[16] In a major study of China's foreign trade system under reform, the World Bank found many instances in which enterprises received prices for exports well below the prevailing international price for the relevant products. See World Bank (1994), p. 114.

[17] For general data, see ibid, p. 113. For data specific to the textile industry, see *TA* 21:6 (June 1990), p. 69.

foreign buyers, thereby circumventing FTCs altogether.[18] As with the agency system, the extension of direct export rights had been under experimentation in the textile industry for years.[19] Interviews revealed that different schemes had been tried over a lengthy period that allowed textile enterprises to cultivate buyer-seller links and export their goods directly. Indeed, published reports indicate that eight textile firms in Shanghai enjoyed some form of autonomous export rights on a trial basis between 1981 and 1988.[20] The results were apparently so favorable that the system was devised and adopted not just throughout the textile industry but across the economy. This is another example of how the textile industry has served as a reform pioneer in China. Textile exports are so critical to China's trade – and the MFA represented such a significant external challenge – that experiments in the industry have repeatedly had a wider influence on the larger process of reform.

By all accounts, the granting of direct export rights produced superior results. Published reports, generally confirmed by interviews, indicate that enterprises working under the autonomous export system upgraded their product mix more quickly, improved quality substantially, achieved greater worker productivity, enjoyed better financial performance, and recorded greater export earnings.[21] In fact, one factory in Shanghai claimed an increase of U.S. $1 per equivalent square meter for its goods compared to what it received when its exports were handled indirectly through FTCs.[22] Other data for Shanghai show a whopping 40 percent annual increase in export growth for enterprises with direct export rights during the early 1990s.[23] Reports from other provinces indicate similar results.[24] While the number of textile factories enjoying autonomous export rights initially was limited, it did grow to more than 600 leading enterprises by early 1995.[25]

---

[18] Under the original formulation of direct exporting, the only special obligation enterprises had was to fulfill an export target and remit a certain percentage of their foreign exchange earnings. In exchange for enjoying direct export rights, they gave up not only assigned orders from foreign trade bureaucrats but also – at least in theory – their access to subsidized raw materials and cheap credit.

[19] It was publicly acknowledged that the textile industry had been chosen to test the autonomous export system before possible adoption in other sectors. During one critical period leading up to the wider adoption of the policy, the system received the support of Shanghai's then-Mayor Zhu Rongji; *TA* 20:7 (July 1989), p. 146.

[20] *TA* 23:7 (July 1992), pp. 130–131.   [21] Ibid.   [22] Ibid.

[23] *TA* 26:3 (March 1995), p. 44.

[24] For information on Jiangsu, see *TA* 24:6 (June 1993), p. 53.

[25] *TA* 26:4 (April 1995), p. 71.

The Decentralization of Foreign Trade Authority

As the result of a series of reforms in the foreign trade system, beginning with the landmark measures adopted in 1984, the number of FTCs in China grew from the original dozen centrally controlled entities that enjoyed monopolies in the prereform era to nearly 4,000 companies by the mid-1990s, down from a peak of more than 5,000 companies in the early 1990s. As part of another set of reforms carried out in 1988, a contract system was instituted in which direct control over foreign trade transactions was significantly decentralized to the burgeoning FTCs and provincial-level units of MOFERT. More reform followed in 1991, when the contract system was further adjusted in an effort to make trading entities more responsible for their own profits and losses. The key feature of this initiative was the announced elimination of export subsidies that previously had been paid from central coffers to reimburse trading entities for domestic currency losses incurred in buying goods for export.[26]

While the erosion of CHINATEX's monopoly was obviously a critical development for the industry, a subject to which the book returns in Chapter 6, an equally significant turning point was the decentralization of decision-making authority *within* CHINATEX as the result of the 1988 foreign trade reform. As Zhou Yunzhong, CHINATEX's president at the time, observed:

> Till the end of 1987 our Corporation controlled all sales. Of course we had branches all over the country, but the basic control was in our hands. However, our foreign trade system is undergoing a reform this year. . . . Both depthwise and widthwise this reform is the most significant since 1949; it covers not only the textile trade but our entire trade structure. We had some modifications eight or nine years back, but nothing compared to this present reform.[27]

While there is no evidence that the decentralization of foreign trade authority was tried on an experimental basis in the textile industry prior to its application elsewhere, there is some evidence that these reforms were designed to address problems in the textile industry. According to some informants, dissatisfaction with China's performance in world

---

[26] For an excellent discussion of these reforms, see World Bank (1994), Chapter 2.

[27] For a text of the interview with Zhou Yunzhong, see *TA* 19:9 (September 1988), pp. 35–39. The statement quoted here appears on pp. 35–36.

textile markets was a motivating factor behind the 1988 reform of the foreign trade system, a sentiment consistent with the statements of CHI-NATEX officials at the time.[28] With the exception of a handful of goods (raw cotton, cotton yarn, polyester-cotton blended yarn, greycloth, and polyester/cotton blended cloth), decision making for trade in textiles was decentralized to the provincial and local subsidiaries of CHINATEX, not to mention other trading entities unaffiliated with CHINATEX.

Even though trading entities were supposed to become financially self-sustaining as part of the 1988 reform, in reality the central government continued to subsidize CHINATEX and its branches for the losses they incurred in selling to the world market. Indeed, it was only with the elimination (or at least the substantial reduction) of these subsidies in 1991 that trading entities finally became more responsible for their own performance. Although the Chinese government never released data on its direct export subsidies, in part to avoid giving its trading partners ammunition during negotiations over China's accession to GATT/WTO, interviews and press reports suggested that textile products had traditionally received high levels of subsidies. Not surprisingly, then, the loss of these subsidies hit CHINATEX and other textile traders quite hard, although some of the extra cost they faced was defrayed by the higher rates of foreign exchange retention granted to textile traders by the government.[29] All in all, the industry coped remarkably well with the new arrangements, mainly by improving management, both at the factory level and among the trading entities.[30] As one Hong Kong trader with extensive contacts in the Chinese industry put it, "Now the calculation of costs is taken much more seriously by all parties before a contract is accepted."

Yet another important measure in the decentralization of China's textile trade was the standardization of trade incentives in 1991, a move that went a long way toward eliminating the advantages formerly enjoyed by the SEZs and other officially designated "open" areas. No longer would trade entities in these locations enjoy preferential arrangements for foreign exchange retention that enabled them, in effect, to offer lower bids for the products they purchased domestically for export. Finally, competition in China's textile trade was further enhanced when regional CHINATEX branches were permitted to buy goods from

---

[28] Ibid. See also the interview with the then–vice-president of CHINATEX, Wang Ruixiang, in *TA* 19:9 (September 1988), pp. 28–35.
[29] *CTR* (June 1991), pp. 10–11.   [30] *TOI* (May 1992), p. 55.

factories outside their home province.[31] The increased competition did, as one would expect, prove felicitous for product upgrading, quality improvements, and efficiency gains.

Import Liberalization and Reform in Raw Materials Allocation

One of the biggest problems facing Chinese industries in recent years has been chronic shortages of raw materials, particularly high-grade inputs. The presence of the MFA – with the incentives it provides for developing countries to increase the unit value of their exports – has made the need for high-quality yarns and fabrics especially urgent in the textile industry. In the early and mid-1980s, Chinese enterprises had great difficulty acquiring raw materials of the quality required to secure contracts from foreign buyers interested in the manufacture of upmarket products. Furthermore, even the supply of low-grade materials often proved to be sporadic; as a result, Chinese firms were not always able to fulfill their contracts, even for ordinary, cheap goods. Since quota allocation is both product-specific and time-bound, chronic shortages of raw materials meant that China occasionally squandered some of its precious quota.

This intolerable outcome, as well as the desire to access higher-quality inputs to facilitate the industry's move upmarket, led directly to both greater import liberalization and reform in the allocation of raw materials. In order to pursue the intensive growth strategy encouraged by the MFA, the government enacted a series of measures that allowed duty exemptions for imports of certain raw materials used in export processing. Import relief was also provided for the purchase of foreign equipment that would enhance China's own capacity to produce high-quality inputs. This relaxation of controls also extended to foreign exchange, as retention ratios were increased to provide enterprises with greater access to funding for their purchases of imported materials and equipment.

This trend toward import liberalization and foreign exchange reform was not, of course, unique to the textile industry, but there is evidence that the impetus for broader changes in the external sector of the economy once again came in part from developments in China's textile trade and the effects of its participation in the MFA. According to a number of informants, including several with connections in Beijing, the

---

[31] *CTR* (December 1991), p. 10.

textile industry figured prominently in decisions concerning economic reform and changes in the Open Policy. Given the industry's importance, as well as the particular challenge it faced in the form of the MFA, this role should not be surprising. While it would be a huge overstatement to suggest that the performance of the textile sector drove the reform process in foreign trade, neither should its impact be underestimated.

In addition to these changes, the need to improve the industry's access to higher-quality raw materials – a need made particularly urgent by the incentive structure of the MFA – also resulted in reforms to the domestic sector of the economy. The import of superior inputs provided a short-term solution, but the preference of top leaders and central bureaucrats was clearly for China to supply its own inputs in the long run. While a variety of administrative measures were taken in an effort to make the supply of domestically produced raw materials more stable, over time the policy emphasis shifted increasingly toward greater market coordination.[32] While some reports indicate that central control over the allocation of raw materials was greatly reduced by the late 1980s for much of the textile industry, the role of the market still varied significantly from region to region and from fiber to fiber well into the 1990s.[33] By most accounts, in fact, reform in the distribution of raw materials lagged behind reform efforts in other areas of economic activity related to the textile industry. Still, there was undoubtedly more reform in this area than there would have been in the absence of the MFA.

TRIMMING THE COLOSSUS: RATIONALIZATION EFFORTS IN CHINA'S TEXTILE INDUSTRY

Struggling with Overcapacity

By the early 1990s, it was painfully clear that the quota system under the MFA precluded a strategy in which the full utilization of China's textile industry could be achieved through increased exports. Specifically, the textile industry could not follow the path of the silk industry, which had relied upon a huge expansion of exports to cope with chronic (and,

---

[32] Space does not permit a lengthy discussion of the various administrative efforts taken to improve the bureaucratic allocation of raw materials in the textile sector. Indeed, a thorough examination of the chaos surrounding the supply and distribution of various fiber groups in the post-Mao era could fill an entire book. For an analysis of the wool sector, see Findlay (1992).

[33] *TA* 19:12 (December 1988), p. 100.

indeed, worsening) overcapacity. While some growth in the volume of exports was possible, even to major MFA markets like the United States and the European Union, the situation in textiles was quite different from that in most other industries. To be sure, overcapacity became so great that no export push probably could have resolved it satisfactorily, but the existence of the MFA did make the need for rationalization especially pressing.

While there had been sporadic efforts to reorganize the industry during the 1980s, the early 1990s saw a confluence of forces both inside China (e.g., mounting losses among SOEs) and outside China (e.g., increasing constraints as a result of more stringent accords with the United States) that led to intensified efforts to implement a rationalization program for the textile industry. In 1991, for instance, the State Council launched a long-term program for reducing capacity and limiting production that is still ongoing today, albeit substantially revised from its original conception. Indeed, the strategy for the textile industry was regarded as a pilot scheme for rationalization programs in Chinese industry more generally.[34] (While ill-defined in the view of many industry observers, this plan did lay the groundwork for the current effort, one that will likely extend at least a decade into the twenty-first century.) As part of the state's initiative, MTI proposed in the early 1990s that large, export-oriented syndicates and multinational companies be created within the industry, both to reorganize China's productive capacity into more profitable firms and to increase China's ability to compete in world markets with other giant commercial entities. Some progress, however modest, was made toward that goal. For instance, textile firms such as Shanghai's Shenda Textile and Garment Group were leading participants in pilot schemes for the contract and joint stock systems later implemented more widely across the industrial landscape.[35] Indeed, Shanghai's TIB was one of three units chosen as part of the city's first experiment in forming state holding corporations.[36] Continuing problems in the industry notwithstanding, these examples provide further evidence that the textile industry has served as a reform pioneer in certain critical respects.

---

[34] For details of the plan in textiles, see "Interview with Minister of Textile Industry Wu Wenying," *Liaowang*, 30 September 1991, in FBIS-CHI-91-232.

[35] See, for example, Minister Wu Wenying's comments in *Renmin Ribao*, 20 November 1992, in JPRS-CAR-93-006, and Li Qian, "Seize the Opportunity to Leap Forward – Commenting on Strategic Readjustment of Shanghai's Textile Industry," *Renmin Ribao*, 14 September 1994, in JPRS-CAR-92-078.

[36] McNally and Lee (1998), p. 37.

Since the overall pace of readjustment in the industry was slow, however, renewed efforts were made to intensify the rationalization program. This process culminated in an August 1994 National Conference on Textile Work in Beijing at which Vice Premier Li Lanqing announced that textiles would be considered a "priority industry in the country's experiment with the bankruptcy process."[37] The State Council subsequently issued a circular calling for a comprehensive rationalization of productive capacity, a major restructuring of industry output to meet market demand, and technical renovation targeted at leading enterprises. This directive outlined a plan for reducing production (e.g., by retiring spindles), producing more top-quality goods (e.g., high-end garments for export), and transferring production from coastal areas to interior provinces where raw materials such as cotton were produced.[38] For its part, CNTC – which had replaced MTI in 1993 – reiterated its vision to reorganize the textile industry into fifty large textile enterprise groups that would achieve greater long-term competitiveness in cut-throat world markets. Here, in fact, there appeared to be some tangible progress. Wu Wenying, chairwoman of CNTC at the time, reported that 129 shareholding companies had been established in the textile industry by the end of 1994, with 26 entities having stock market listings.[39] As modest as these changes were, they at least provided the prospect for longer-term change.

That said, rationalization in China's textile industry was still quite limited through the mid-1990s. While there was some reduction in productive capacity, the actual retirement of spindles was far less than that required for the substantial reorganization of the industry intended by Beijing. In many cases, spindles were simply sold by SOEs to TVEs (or otherwise "reallocated") rather than genuinely idled. Losses continued to mount industry-wide, with the greatest concentration of financial difficulty found, not surprisingly, among SOEs. One of the main problems was the lack of central control exercised in the textile industry. Even as early as 1991, when Beijing began its most recent push to downsize the industry, less than one-quarter of China's textile enterprises were accountable in any meaningful way to MTI. As Wu Wenying admitted

[37] *Xinhua*, 25 August 1994, in FBIS-CHI-94-166.
[38] For more on the State Council circular, see *Xinhua*, 22 October 1994, in FBIS-CHI-94-207.
[39] *China Daily*, 26 January 1995, in FBIS-CHI-95-017.

at the time, rationalization depended critically upon compliance from government departments at lower levels of administration.[40] Although each iteration of Beijing's rationalization program during the early and mid-1990s included some reward for enterprises successful in reducing textile production, the employment implications (and related social considerations) of enterprise downsizing slowed – and, in some cases, prevented altogether – key steps such as spindle retirement. Implementation of central edicts was avoided not only through the relocation of "retired" productive capacity to TVEs but also through the outright falsification of data.

While less than optimal overall, the rationalization program was not without its successes. For example, one-third of all enterprises under Shanghai's TIB had reportedly shifted to service businesses by 1996. Moreover, the city achieved a 20-percent reduction in textile production capacity from 1994 to 1996. As a consequence of this downsizing during the 1990s, 240,000 employees in Shanghai's textile industry, or roughly half its workforce as of 1992, were reportedly laid off by 1996.[41] Despite this downsizing, Shanghai's industry suffered growing losses throughout this period. Nationally, the financial story was the same, especially among SOEs. While the nonstate sector reportedly ran a profit in 1996, SOEs fell deeper into the red with each passing year. By 1996, CNTC reported losses for the industry at 10.6 billion yuan, with 42 percent of SOEs in the textile industry classified as loss-makers. Indeed, 17 percent of all money-losing SOEs nationwide were reportedly from the textile sector. Moreover, deficits among textile SOEs were estimated to represent 10 percent of all SOE deficits.[42] In keeping with policies formulated at the 1994 National Conference on Textile Work, bankruptcies were pursued as a means to promote rationalization in the industry. Bankruptcies were often carried out simply to dispose of bad debt, however, so in many cases factories remained open with their workforces intact and production levels relatively unchanged.[43]

[40] "Interview with Minister of Textile Industry Wu Wenying," *Liaowang*, 30 September 1991, in FBIS-CHI-91-232.

[41] *TA* 26:9 (September 1996), p. 18, and *TA* 27:10 (October 1997), p. 68.

[42] *TA* 28:5 (May 1998), pp. 73–74. According to some reports, more than 50 percent of textile SOEs were losing money by 1997. See, for example, "Fighting a Battle to Alleviate Difficulties of the Textile Industry," *Xinhua*, 3 January 1998, in FBIS-CHI-98-012.

[43] *TA* 28:1 (January 1998), p. 76.

The Textile Industry and Zhu Rongji's Three-Year Plan
for SOE Reform

While some progress was made toward the rationalization of China's textile industry during the early 1990s, many problems – especially financial problems – persisted and even worsened over time. As mentioned above, losses among SOEs were at record levels. The workforce remained highly redundant. The industry continued to be plagued by production oversupply. For all of these reasons, not to mention the industry's continued importance to China's export base, Zhu Rongji made the textile industry the flagship of his three-year plan to reform SOEs. In November 1997, then–Vice Premier Zhu identified textiles as an industry that could provide "a breakthrough for the reform of the state sector" despite its myriad problems.[44] Calling for mergers to address the problem of chronic overcapacity in the industry, Zhu declared during one of a series of public comments that "[i]f we can successfully achieve our goal of revitalizing the textile industry, we can say we found the key to helping state enterprises in all other industries out of difficulty."[45] When Zhu assumed the premiership in March 1998, the textile industry officially became the centerpiece of his three-year plan for SOE reform. Highly publicized targets were set for the elimination of 10 million spindles (a 25 percent decrease) and a reduction of 1.2 million workers (a 30 percent decrease) over three years, including 4.8 million spindles and 600,000 layoffs in 1998 alone. The rationalization of enterprises, which was to be accelerated substantially, would be achieved through the merger, acquisition, and liquidation of firms.

In order to retain greater control from the top, the SETC – not MTI/CNTC, as in the past – was designated to direct the implementation of this latest effort at SOE reform in the textile industry. Vice-Premier Wu Bangguo was reportedly given special responsibility by Zhu for overseeing this initiative. For day-to-day matters, the SETC official in charge was Shi Wanpeng, former chair of CNTC before that entity was replaced by the State Textile Industry Bureau (STIB) as part of the ministerial shakeup that occurred at the Ninth National People's Congress in March 1998 as part of the broader governmental restructuring introduced by Zhu. To elicit greater compliance than that achieved by previ-

---

[44] *TA* 27:12 (December 1997), p. 78.
[45] "Zhu Rongji Urges Reforming State-Run Textile Firms," *Xinhua*, 3 November 1997, in FBIS-CHI-97-307.

ous rationalization programs, this plan provides more financial resources to write off bad loans and rewards for enterprises that meet targets for employment and production cutbacks.[46] In addition, funds have been made available for technological renovation in textile factories as compensation for production cuts.[47] It is hoped that this incentive will elicit greater compliance at lower levels of administration. While it would be premature to make definitive conclusions, initial results from this most recent rationalization program look more promising than efforts from earlier in the 1990s. On the whole, most of the targets set for 1998 and 1999 were reportedly achieved.[48] Spindle elimination and workforce layoffs were both on pace or slightly ahead. Deficit reduction fell short by 10 to 15 percent in 1998, but this was not surprising given the economic slowdown caused in part by the Asian Financial Crisis. In 1999, the government claimed that the industry made a small profit, its first since 1993.

TO GET RICH IS GLORIOUS: THE ALLOCATION OF TEXTILE QUOTA IN CHINA

Textile Quota as a Political Commodity

As a final example of evolving market coordination in China's textile industry, this section examines changes in the quota allocation system since the early 1980s. By all accounts, textile quota has been among the most valuable assets in China over the last two decades. It was widely acknowledged, for example, that the People's Liberation Army (PLA) has received textile quotas as compensation for its support of particular political leaders. In fact, several informants claimed that certain elements within the military were rewarded with huge quota allocations for their support of the regime during the Tiananmen crisis in 1989. As one foreign diplomat observed, "In an economy short on foreign exchange, quota rights are the next best thing." This anecdote illustrates an important point: by creating the need for a quota system, the MFA made the

---

[46] To facilitate bankruptcies and mergers, of which there were literally hundreds – more than 350 in 1998 by one account – the government provided 12.6 billion yuan to write off bad loans; *TA* 29:3 (March 1999), p. 73.

[47] The reported figures were 20 billion yuan in direct government support plus 14 billion yuan in bank loans; *TA* 31:3 (March 2000), p. 61.

[48] *TA* 29:3 (March 1999), p. 73, and "How the 'Point of Breakthrough' for State Enterprise Reform Came out of Difficulty," *Xinhua*, 25 January 2000, in FBIS-CHI-2000-0129.

issue of who has access to world markets – always a critical question in China – all the more pronounced. Quota holding in effect confers a property right to export China's most successful product: textiles. Due to the vast riches involved, control over quota allocation is an enormously powerful political resource.

In keeping with the organization of the prereform foreign trade system, which was still essentially unchanged when China entered into the first Sino-American textile agreement in 1980, the vast majority of quota was simply handed over to CHINATEX, the FTC that enjoyed a monopoly over the country's foreign trade in textiles. Except for a small percentage retained at the national level by MOFERT, CHINATEX controlled all of the quota. Officially, CHINATEX allocated the quota to its provincial branches based on their previous performance, with the provincial branches in turn distributing the quota directly to deserving textile factories.[49] According to interviewees familiar with the system, however, the process was dominated by rent seeking. Not surprisingly, CHINATEX officials allocated as little quota by merit as possible, reserving the balance for allocation based on political favoritism. As one informant chuckled, "Quota allocation wasn't serving the best interests of the nation in those early years, but many individuals were getting rich."

In the late 1980s, control over quota allocation was transferred from CHINATEX directly to MOFERT. Informants were divided on whether this change was simply a power play designed to enrich one entity at the expense of another, or whether it reflected a genuine desire on the part of the central leadership to improve the industry's export performance. Either way, little changed. MOFERT allocated quota directly to its provincial foreign trade bureaus, bypassing the national office of CHINATEX entirely. The provincial branches of CHINATEX still received sizable allocations, but these now came from the provincial foreign trade bureaus. According to some interviewees, the new arrangement simply perpetuated the pattern of rent-seeking behavior. According to other interviewees, several of whom had extensive experience trying to obtain quota in China, the allocation of textile quota was somewhat more merit-based under MOFERT than CHINATEX. One Hong Kong indus-

---

[49] For two good descriptions of the quota allocation system consistent with the information gleaned from interviews, see Jerome Turtola, "Textile Trade Tensions," *CBR* (September/October 1986), p. 32, and *TA* 19:7 (July 1988), pp. 91–92.

trialist claimed that quota was allocated "mostly according to the past record," although he acknowledged that this sometimes meant the size of previous allocations more than the strength of recent export performance. As he put it, "Local officials and factory managers were not in much of a position to resist; they can try to make their case and even negotiate some, but ultimately they have to take what they are given." Another veteran of the China market estimated that 60 percent of quota was allocated on merit under MOFERT. That, of course, left the other 40 percent of China's multibillion dollar textile business to be guided on the basis of personal or political ties.

Front companies were often set up in Hong Kong to arrange export orders using politically allocated quota. In other cases, quota was simply sold illegally. Either way, the profiteering that occurred during the 1980s and early 1990s is legendary among industry observers. According to interviews, families of high-ranking officials became fabulously wealthy through such activities. As one industry insider observed in the early 1990s, "the corruption goes very, very high in the Party."

The Evolving System of Quota Allocation in China: From Political-Bureaucratic Administration to Corrupted Market

Not surprisingly, early efforts to improve China's export performance in textiles focused on strengthening the administrative management of quotas. Specifically, several steps were taken to make the existing system of bureaucratic allocation more rational. First, as indicated above, control over quota allocation was transferred from CHINATEX to MOFERT. Political abuse continued, to be sure, but MOFERT was arguably more successful in linking quota allocation to performance. In 1987 MOFERT established an inspection system that required exporters to file monthly reports. This data, which was used as the basis for computerized monitoring of China's textile exports, enabled trade officials to improve their management of quota utilization. In 1988 MOFERT began a system of reserve quota allocation, setting aside some 30 percent of quota in most categories at the beginning of each administrative cycle to reward high-performing exporters as the year unfolded. MOFERT also claimed it would reduce (or even eliminate) quota given to underperforming exporters, a threat several informants claimed was actually carried out occasionally. Indeed, press reports and interviews indicate that MOFERT was committed to allocating a larger share of quota based on value-added considerations related to product upgrading.[50]

Even if MOFERT's intentions were good, the system of quota allocation remained fraught with problems. According to one published report, for example, MOFERT relied largely on "its branches to 'double check' the export performance of manufacturers in their respective province or municipality."[51] It is easy to understand how corruption continued to flourish in the textile industry given this method of bureaucratic oversight. In an apparent attempt to further rationalize the quota allocation process, the State Council established the Chinese Textile Chamber of Commerce in 1989; one of its primary missions was "to supervise the utilization of textile quotas and export licenses by its members, besides making recommendations for quota allocation."[52] While this organization may have been designed to increase the transparency of the quota allocation process, or at least to provide greater oversight of MOFERT's behavior, it turns out that the Chamber was in fact dominated by MOFERT itself. Never important as an independent entity – many interviewees were not even familiar with it – the Chamber may actually have increased the reach of central bureaucrats in certain ways.

The air lock that existed between textile factories and the world market made it difficult for China to improve its export performance under the MFA. Even if the bureaucratic allocation of China's quota had not been tainted by corruption, the results would still surely have been suboptimal. As discussed earlier, the problem of the air lock system was ultimately addressed – with mixed results – by reform experiments such as the export agency system and the granting of autonomous export rights. Pioneered to a substantial degree in the textile industry, these initiatives were designed to improve China's export performance by giving factories more incentive to respond effectively to the world market. In the case of the MFA, of course, this meant increasing the unit value of exports and otherwise moving upmarket.

These reforms in the foreign trade system had several important implications for quota allocation in China. Most notably, there was the problem of how enterprises that wanted to sell their products on an export agency basis – to say nothing of autonomously – would secure

---

[50] Walter C. Lenahan, a former Deputy Assistant Secretary of Commerce for the U.S. government, addressed this issue before the American Chamber of Commerce in Hong Kong. For a transcript of his comments, see *TA* 19:7 (July 1988), pp. 88–91.

[51] *TA* 19:7 (July 1988), p. 92.   [52] *TA* 20:8 (August 1989), p. 116.

quota. For obvious reasons of self-interest, CHINATEX and its branches vigorously resisted these reforms, as did MOFERT to a somewhat lesser extent. Not surprisingly, quota went primarily to goods exported by the traditional method. According to published reports, CHINATEX's branches – still the major recipients of quota from MOFERT – were allowed to decide the ratio between quotas for their own use and quotas for trading under the export agency system.[53] The result, not surprisingly, was that enterprises interested in exporting under the export agency system had great difficulty securing quota. The same held true for enterprises that wanted to export directly. According to informants, entities affiliated with CHINATEX used their quota holdings as leverage to secure goods through the conventional arrangement. All told, it was hard to reconcile the bureaucratic allocation of one of China's scarcest resources – textile quota – with growing decentralization in foreign trade authority.

One illicit means of obtaining quota was to buy it on the vibrant black market that began to emerge shortly after the imposition of restrictions in the early 1980s. For example, while export success in some coastal areas outstripped the supply of quota, there was a surplus of quota in many interior provinces. The result was two-fold: the emergence of a black market in legal quota and a proliferation of counterfeit visas.[54] Interviews suggest that the volume of transactions in the black market was small at first but grew quickly as the result of two trends: first, continuing decentralization in China's domestic political economy; and second, the steady increase over time in the number of products covered under China's bilateral textile agreements with the United States and the European Union.

By all accounts, quota trading was widespread by the late 1980s. Because it was illegal, there is no hard data on what percentage of quota was traded or what the rate of turnover was for certain popular items. As forthcoming as most informants were on other issues, they were extremely reluctant to discuss the subject of quota trading. That said,

---

[53] *TA* 20:7 (July 1989), p. 146.

[54] A brief primer on the customs process for textile goods under quota is necessary here. When quota is allocated, an export visa is issued by one of MOFERT's 37 regional offices (MOFERT was renamed MOFTEC in 1993). When the product is actually exported, one copy of the export visa is surrendered by the exporting company to China's Customs Bureau. A second copy is sent to the importing company, which must present the export visa in order for the product to be released in the country of destination. For more detail, see *TA* 25:5 (May 1994), p. 53.

several observations can be made about this era. First, the quota markets for specific goods were often quite volatile depending on quota utilization rates in China and demand conditions in the world market. Especially in the 1980s, when the black market in quota was still developing and information about quota availability and global demand were relatively poor, it was not unusual for quota costs to fluctuate by 40 to 50 percent per year. Second, the premium for quota was by all accounts quite high. U.S. officials estimated that the cost of quota in China represented, on average, 20 to 50 percent of the selling price of a good.[55] In fact, many traders and business consultants reported that the cost of quota was often as high (or even higher) in China than it was in Hong Kong by the early 1990s. Even where the absolute cost of obtaining quota was lower in China, the premium paid to secure quota frequently represented a higher percentage of the total selling price than in Hong Kong. Third, trade in textile quotas was especially lucrative since these transactions were invisible to tax authorities. Interviews and press reports indicate that sales of export quota were often contingent upon foreign currency payments deposited into Hong Kong bank accounts.[56] Importers often became directly involved in financing the purchase of quota necessary to fill their orders. Several informants acknowledged that foreign retailers routinely provided foreign exchange for Chinese textile factories to buy quota.

As this last example suggests, foreign businesspeople tried a variety of methods to cope with the uncertain availability of quota in China. Some large companies, especially those from Hong Kong with strong connections in China, sought to make stable access to quota part of their agreements to move production to China. In some cases, informants said, the "quota fee" was built into "offers" negotiated by the two sides. Concerned about having to buy quota at high prices on the black market, or even finding themselves saddled with goods they could not export at all, foreign businesspeople became involved in a complex series of formal and informal relationships with exporters, importers, and various government agencies in China. For their part, however, perennial quota-holders in China were not always eager to commit themselves to a long-term quota arrangement with foreign businesses. Consequently, executives from large international companies expressed considerable

---

[55] *TA* 22:10 (October 1991), p. 10. Interviews confirmed cases where the quota premium ranged as high as 50 percent.
[56] *TA* 24:8 (August 1993), p. 66.

frustration with the quota system. As one American executive put it during an interview:

> The fact that we are a multibillion dollar company seems to mean precious little in China sometimes. Everywhere we went [when we first entered China] we were offered ridiculously low quota, just like any other player trying to get in. And often the quota we got was for categories we didn't even want! Even today, it's very hard to do business on a year-to-year basis. We've tried everything. One year we went into a province and tried to buy the entire quota for a particular category from the officials who controlled it, offering them considerably more than they had received the year before. We were rejected, however. The whole process remains a mystery a lot of the time.

Continuing Change in Quota Allocation: Toward a Formal Auction System

As described above, the heart of the problem was the disjuncture between access to quota and the ability to produce upmarket goods for export in an efficient, profitable manner. Throughout the 1980s and early 1990s, the fruits of economic reform and industrial adjustment enabled many textile factories to upgrade their production and modernize their business operations. While some were granted export autonomy rights in an effort to alleviate the air lock problem and rectify other dilemmas of partial reform associated with China's transitional economy, this status had little meaning without the ability to secure quota. Clearly, the existing quota allocation system was no longer appropriate for a textile industry undergoing substantial decentralization and reform in other areas of economic activity. While the burgeoning black market represented an improvement over a purely bureaucratic system of allocation, especially one in which quota was often doled out as political patronage, by the early 1990s it was clear that problems related to quota allocation continued to hamper the industry's progress. To be sure, China had achieved significant gains in the unit value of its textile exports overall. Indeed, the black market often allowed quota to find its way to export orders that could command relatively high prices on the world market, since these orders could absorb the highest quota premium. That said, the black market was an expensive, and in many ways inefficient, allocation mechanism. The route by which quota migrated to high value-added export orders was often quite circuitous. Moreover, the black market did not always work; valuable quota was still too often used to export relatively unsophisticated goods. As interviews and press reports confirmed, producers of goods with high unit prices could not always secure quota, either in the black market or through administrative channels on the basis of merit.[57] In this sense, the unrealized potential of textile exports continued to represent a substantial opportunity cost for China under the MFA.

According to interviews, Chinese officials had considered instituting a quota auction for a number of years. While central leaders reportedly had reservations about reducing such an important aspect of China's participation in the world economy to an open – albeit officially sanctioned – bidding contest, the success of quota auctions in other countries finally swayed their opinion in favor of implementing such a system on an experimental basis. Not only would a quota auction lead to higher unit prices for China's exports, and thus higher foreign exchange earnings, but the rents generated by auctioning quota would benefit the national treasury.[58] While high-ranking families had prospered under the old system, the benefits were apparently becoming less concentrated at the top. Particularly for categories in which quota was repeatedly resold, a growing portion of the premium actually accrued to lower-level actors. Quota auctions had their detractors, to be sure, but in the end the decision was made to proceed on a limited basis.

Not surprisingly, MOFERT – which along with CNTC was given responsibility for implementing the experimental system – engaged in considerable footdragging as it set up the auction system. The central directive was issued in December 1992, and other changes outlined in the "Regulations on the Management of Textile Export Quotas" went into effect on January 1, 1993, but it was not until March 1994 that

---

[57] One published account related the story of a garment factory that had to turn down large orders for luxurious dresses to be sold in the United States that would have been worth *four times* the amount eventually earned by the dress factory that held the relevant quota, a factory that obviously exported much more ordinary dresses; *TA* 27:5 (May 1996), p. 72.

[58] I use the terms "quota auction" and "quota bidding system" interchangeably, as does the Chinese government and industry observers. Technically speaking, an auction system awards quota rights based on the value of contracts without levying an actual charge for the quota itself. A bidding system often connotes that a fee is paid for the acquisition of quota. In other words, prospective exporters submit price bids to buy quota rights for a year. In the Chinese case, a fee is actually paid to the government for securing quota.

auctions actually commenced, and then only for thirteen categories that were not among China's leading exports. According to the new regulations, the rationale for experimenting with the bidding system was "to encourage the development and export of high-grade garment products, increase the economic returns from using the quotas, and provide enterprises capable of engaging in export trade with an opportunity for competition."[59] As explained later by a MOFERT official, the initiative was designed to "encourage fair competition among domestic exporters and also promote the export of upmarket products."[60]

By all accounts, one of the main rationales behind setting up a bona fide auction system was a desire to limit the speculation and profiteering that plagued the black market. For instance, only entities actually engaged in the production or export of textiles were to be allowed to bid under the auction system. Whatever the difficulty of enforcing this provision in practice, it was designed to eliminate actors whose participation was premised on making use of political connections for commercial advantage. This group included not only rent-seeking bureaucrats, but also a considerable number of SOEs that had essentially abandoned production to concentrate on quota trading. Favored under the old system of allocation, these firms often generated much of their revenue simply from trading their quota holdings. As one informant involved in FIE production put it, these companies found it "more profitable and less trouble to deal in quota entitlement than to actually make anything."

Under the new regulations, quota-holding firms were permitted to transfer up to 20 percent of their quotas in any given product category to another firm without penalty, but the original quota-holding firm was obligated to inform the Ministry of Foreign Trade and Economic Cooperation (MOFTEC, MOFERT's new name as of 1993) and secure prior approval of local authorities as necessary. Another important condition was a limit of one transfer for each set of quotas. Retransfer of quota was strictly prohibited according to the new regulations. Additional provisions included performance-based awards and penalties. Quotas were to be awarded for high-priced exports, increases in nonquota exports, and exports using a high percentage of Chinese-made materials. By contrast, penalties were to be assessed for low-priced exports, speculation or other unauthorized use of quotas, illegal transshipments to avoid quota

[59] "Regulations on the Management of Textile Export Quotas," *Guoji Shangbao*, 31 December 1992, in FBIS-CHI-93-020.
[60] *China Daily*, 14 June 1993, in FBIS-CHI-93-112.

requirements, and violations of country-of-origin rules issued by China's leading trade partners.

Even though most of China's textile quotas initially remained outside the bidding system, the new regulations also included provisions to improve quota management under the old system.[61] For example, firms were now required to utilize at least 90 percent of their quota allocation for a given year or face lower quota allocation in following years. There were also incentives for firms to return unused quota, rather than simply allow them to expire, so that it could be reallocated before year's end to firms ready to make shipments overseas. In these and myriad other ways, the criteria for merit-based bureaucratic allocation were tightened, in theory if not always in practice. For quota not subject to the bidding system, MOFTEC continued to allocate directly to firms under state management while provincial-level foreign trade bureaus received quota for allocation to local firms.

The bidding system was extended from 13 to 27 categories between 1994 and 1996. In June 1996, the bidding system was also modified to make it easier for new firms to qualify as bidders. For example, new exporters were allowed to join the bidding only two years after obtaining basic MOFTEC authorization to engage in textile trade, with no requirement of past export experience in particular product categories.[62] Later in 1996, the long-anticipated Committee on Textile Quota Auctions was finally established under MOFTEC. While this committee's purpose was to provide more independent administration of the bidding process, its association with MOFTEC made many industry observers skeptical.[63] Indeed, until 1998 quota allocation remained divided into two separate processes: an "open bidding" system and a "bidding by agreement" system. Under the second scheme, which was largely a euphemism for the established practice, quota was reserved mainly for state-owned entities guaranteed quota in the past. The main criteria for allocation under this system were high-priced sales (as determined by past performance)

---

[61] For details, see the text issued by MOFERT entitled "Regulations on the Management of Textile Export Quotas," *Guoji Shangbao*, 31 December 1992, in FBIS-CHI-93-020.

[62] For more detail on these changes, see *TA* 26:7 (July 1996), p. 92.

[63] Although MOFTEC was originally given primary responsibility for implementing the experimental bidding system, CNTC was also supposed to play an advisory or coordinating role. More importantly, reports had persisted for more than two years that a new government department would be established to oversee the auctioning of quota due to the conflict of interest MOFTEC would experience in moving from bureaucratic allocation to a more market-oriented auction system. See, for instance, *TA* 25:3 (March 1994), p. 69.

and a good record of quota utilization. According to published reports, the development of brand-name clothing lines was reportedly well-rewarded by generous quota allocations.[64] To be fair, therefore, it should be noted that "bidding by agreement" in the mid-1990s was probably more merit-based than bureaucratic allocation in the past. Officially, the justification for continuing this practice was that these "inheritance" exporters represented the country's most important links to overseas buyers. From this perspective, prudence dictated a gradual transition to a truly competitive bidding system for all of China's textile quotas.

By 1998, "open bidding" had been expanded to include 37 product categories, and nontraditional exporters were increasingly well-represented.[65] By all accounts, this system achieved considerable success in channeling more quotas to actual quota-users rather than to mere quota-traders. Entities qualified to participate were either authorized FTCs or manufacturing enterprises with autonomous export rights. Most notably, the percentage of quotas allotted through the bidding system to firms with autonomous export rights increased from 16 percent in 1998 to 30 percent in 2000.[66] By 2000, in fact, 393 textile enterprises with autonomous export rights enjoyed quota allotments, less than one-third of which were SOEs.[67] While still in development, the new bidding system offers a process in which TVEs, FIEs, and other entities formerly at a disadvantage can secure quota on a relatively even playing field. In this respect, it represents a significant improvement over the black market. Now more than ever, there is a premium on high value-added goods since the bidding process imposes an unprecedented degree of commercial discipline.

While China's participation in the MFA did generate rent seeking, it also impelled the creation of a black market in quota trading. Despite its illegality, this vibrant institution was tolerated since quota-holders, many of whom had powerful political connections, received a handsome premium for surrendering their property right. While this kind of politically corrupted market is far from a ideal mechanism for resource allocation, it did over time significantly reduce the day-to-day role played by state trading companies and various ministerial entities. Imperfections aside, the black market for textile quota worked to ensure that China's exports moved upscale. Moreover, the adoption and ongoing

---

[64] See, for instance, *TA* 29:10 (October 1998), p. 63.
[65] *TA* 29:4 (April 1998), p. 57.   [66] *TA* 31:0 (January 2000), p. 48.
[67] *TA* 31:0 (January 2000), p. 48, and *TA* 31:3 (March 2000), p. 58.

institutionalization of the quota auction system augers well for continued progress in this area.

CONCLUSION

All told, the impact of the MFA on reform and rationalization in China's textile industry was less signal than the impact of industrial restructuring documented in Chapter 4. While reform has advanced to the point where the industry can be characterized as something of a pioneer, the trend toward market coordination – however impressive – is less directly attributable to the MFA than is the pattern of product upgrading, readjustment to the product mix, and diversification of export markets. Compared to industrial restructuring, economic reform in the textile industry arguably reflects the broader policy environment more closely. That said, this chapter has shown how China's participation in the MFA not only *reinforced* existing reform initiatives, but also helped to *induce* new experiments with reform in the textile industry. By demonstration effect, in fact, these reforms modestly influenced the Chinese economy as a whole.

A similar observation can be made about rationalization efforts in China's textile industry. Even if recent developments suggest that decent progress is being made, the fact remains that rationalization in the industry was fairly modest for most of the 1980s and 1990s. While the MFA does exert pressure for industrial rationalization by contributing to overcapacity in newly affected developing countries, this pressure was weaker than pressure for industrial restructuring. Even if the restrictive effects of the MFA, which eliminate an export push as a solution for overcapacity, are credited with inducing whatever rationalization did occur during the period studied in this book, the impact would still be fairly limited given the lack of extensive results.

That said, we should also consider the possibility that rationalization would have been even slower in the absence of the MFA. Given the textile industry's central role in China's economy, in which it has borne a sizable burden in supporting retirees and absorbing surplus personnel, it is reasonable to ask what degree of rationalization would have been accomplished if China's exports to the world market had been unfettered by MFA restrictions. The experience of the silk industry suggests a bleak picture. While the silk sector has special circumstances of its own that render comparison with the rest of the textile industry imperfect, its experience as an unfettered exporter until the mid-1990s provides an interesting glimpse into the disastrous capacity woes other sectors might have encountered. From this perspective, the MFA provided sufficient pressure to elicit modest rationalization in China's textile industry, this by accentuating the underlying problem of overcapacity.

Rather than dismiss the impact of the MFA, therefore, it is perhaps better to identify its limitations. Insofar as the reform and rationalization of the Chinese textile industry was (and still is) so deeply intertwined with the very essence of China's political economy, the reach of the MFA has understandably been fairly shallow. For example, while the need to cope with the imposition of quotas has contributed significantly to specific reforms in the production and trade of textile goods, the effects of the MFA have not yet extended to, say, an overhaul of the distribution system for cotton. Nor, of course, should this have been expected. In many ways, the reform and rationalization of China's textile industry represents one of the country's greatest developmental challenges in making the transition to a modern economy with extensive linkages to world markets. This is a fact Zhu himself acknowledged in making textiles the flagship for SOE reform: "If we successfully solve the problem of the labor-intensive textile industry . . . we will surely be able to solve the problems of other industries also."[68]

[68] "Zhu Rongji on Textile Industry Reform," *Xinhua*, 3 November 1997, in FBIS-CHI-97-317.

6

Industrial Change in the Shadow of the MFA: The Role of Top-Level Strategy, Mid-Level Intervention, and Low-Level Demand in China's Textile Industry

EVEN if we accept that the international environment was a powerful influence in impelling certain changes in the textile industry, we must still account for the response within China. Did the reforms and other policy changes in the industry mainly reflect strategy made by the top leadership to cope with life under the MFA? Or were they fundamentally the result of bureaucratic intervention by MTI/CNTC, CHINATEX, or MOFERT/MOFTEC at either the national or provincial level? Or, finally, did the main impulse for change come from below as enterprises (and other local actors) reacted to changing market conditions at home and abroad? In other words, are the changes that occurred in the textile industry best conceptualized as the outcome of top-level strategy, mid-level intervention, or low-level demand? This question will serve as the primary focus of this chapter. Before addressing this important topic, however, we must first examine more closely the evolving role of various bureaucratic players involved in China's textile industry. Only by surveying this "alphabet soup" of institutions, a subject not comprehensively explored in previous chapters, is a full assessment of their role in the system possible, especially vis-à-vis higher- and lower-level actors.

RESHAPING THE ORGANIZATIONAL LANDSCAPE OF THE CHINESE TEXTILE INDUSTRY

As with all eras of change, there were both winners and losers in China's textile industry during the 1980s and early 1990s. Of the three leading bureaucratic players, MOFERT gained the most strength. (For the sake of convenience, the remainder of this book will refer simply to MOFERT given the relative triviality of the trade ministry's numerous name changes since the founding of the PRC. For most of the period studied here, MOFERT was the contemporary name.)[1] By contrast, CHINATEX and MTI were both substantially weakened as the result of institutional developments that significantly transformed the government's role in the industry. (Similarly, this chapter will refer to MTI and its successors – CNTC and STIB – simply as MTI.) While these changes in bureaucratic power cannot be attributed exclusively to the impact of the MFA, China's participation in this international regime certainly contributed to organizational restructuring within the industry.

By all accounts, MTI was the biggest loser during the reform era. While it experienced the same challenges encountered by other ministries – e.g., increasing independence on the part of regional textile bureaus and textile factories – MTI also faced a rather unique threat: the MFA. Almost from the first day of China's participation in the MFA, export quota became one of the most coveted commodities in China. "In the textile industry, quota is king," observed one informant. When the privilege of administering China's quotas was given to MOFERT, the balance of power within the textile industry shifted substantially. Never among China's most powerful industrial ministries, MTI's standing was further weakened by its lack of control over the country's export quotas.

MTI's marginalization was gradual but unmistakable. By all accounts, MTI repeatedly petitioned China's leadership for a greater role in quota management. These pleas were not answered, and MOFERT in turn excluded MTI as much as possible from matters concerning China's textile trade. As one interviewee, a Hong Kong businessman with life-long ties to the Chinese industry, put it: "The introduction of the quota issue completely distorted relations within the industry – the rivalry became most unhealthy." Given the value of quota, MOFERT became the organization with whom everyone wanted good relations. Some of this decline would, of course, have taken place even in the absence of

---

[1] After the founding of the PRC in 1949, the Ministry of Trade was established to oversee both domestic and foreign trade. This entity was split in 1952, with the regulation of foreign trade transferred to a new Ministry of Foreign Trade. In 1982, the Ministry of Foreign Trade was merged with the Ministry of Foreign Economic Cooperation to become the Ministry of Foreign Economic Relations and Trade (MOFERT). Finally, as mentioned in Chapter 5, MOFERT was renamed in 1993 to the Ministry of Foreign Trade and Economic Cooperation (MOFTEC) as part of a more general bureaucratic restructuring of the State Council.

the MFA. To some greater or lesser degree, the reform era eroded the power of central ministries in almost every industry. Moreover, MTI's power was inherently limited by the size and diversity of China's textile industry. Even in the Mao era, it had always been too big for a single ministerial body to control effectively. That said, the MFA clearly *accelerated* MTI's decline by empowering its rivals in the trade bureaucracy.

By the early 1990s, MTI played little more than what one informant termed "an advisory role" in the industry. Factories paid a nominal, lump-sum fee annually to MTI to maintain their association, but MTI exercised no effective control over most local entities. Except for technical assistance and some limited investment funds, MTI had little to offer most factories. As a result, most entities became rather disinterested in their relationship with MTI; again, it was MOFERT that mattered bureaucratically given its control over export quotas. In 1993, the diminution in MTI's role was formalized by its elimination in favor of CNTC. That said, MTI's institutional demise was mostly in name. Except for a reduction in staff from 500 to 280 and some minor management reforms, CNTC operated almost identically to MTI – even Minister Wu Wenying and other top personnel were retained.[2] Policy changes were fairly minor. In this sense, the transfer from MTI to CNTC did not signify a new course institutionally as much as an acknowledgment of MTI's diminished stature. As described in Chapter 5, CNTC's successor, STIB, was created in April 1998 alongside the likes of the Bureau of Machine Building Industry (formerly a ministry) and the Bureau of Light Industry (formerly a council, as for textiles). Compared to CNTC, STIB is charged with reducing even further Beijing's advisory role in matters such as production planning and the allocation of raw materials. Over time, administrative authority is to be decentralized completely to provincial and local authorities. STIB's duties include oversight of industry regulations, provision of research and marketing services, and, most importantly, oversight of SOE reform. With its staff reduced from 280 to 80, STIB is slated to be absorbed completely into SETC once SOE reform is complete.[3]

CHINATEX, the other mainstay in China's textile industry for decades, underwent its own transformation during the 1980s and early 1990s. Its role in the industry changed markedly and its power declined

---

[2] See, for example, *TA* 24:8 (August 1993), pp. 56–58, and *TA* 25:11 (November 1994), p. 11.

[3] *TA* 29:8 (August 1998), p. 67.

palpably, although not as precipitously as MTI's. Needless to say, CHI-NATEX was weakened by its loss of control over China's export quotas. While it continued to receive a fairly generous allocation of quota from MOFERT – the ministry to which it reported until 1993 – CHINATEX has been an entity with a declining function ever since the mid-1980s. Again as described in Chapter 5, MOFERT's Foreign Trade Administration circumvented CHINATEX's central bureaucracy entirely by allocating quota directly to its own provincial-level foreign trade bureaus. The local branches of CHINATEX ultimately received a portion of the quota from these foreign trade bureaus, but this mechanism eliminated CHINATEX's head office from the proverbial administrative loop.

Further reducing the head office's role, ten CHINATEX departments that had been directly administered from Beijing were transformed into independent subsidiaries for specialization in discrete areas of China's textile trade, such as yarn and fabrics, garments, and raw materials. While CHINATEX still exists, it is substantially decentralized in an operational sense. In addition, CHINASILK was removed entirely from the jurisdiction of CHINATEX. Similarly, CHINATEX's provincial and municipal-level branches also became significantly more autonomous as a result of various reforms carried out in the textile industry during the 1980s. The result is that CHINATEX's head office was reduced over time to a predominantly advisory body that coordinated a shrinking number of foreign trade transactions each year. As early as 1988, Wang Ruixiang, vice-president of CHINATEX, captured the essence of this change well:

> [I]n line with the change of its functions, the headquarters is putting more stress on trade promotion overseas. Formerly we were mainly an administrative organization, now we've become more commercial and operational. We are trying to become more international, multifunctional, comprehensive, and group-orientated.[4]

The trend only intensified in the 1990s. By mid-decade, in fact, CHI-NATEX was handling only about 8 percent of China's total textile export value. That said, it remained China's single largest FTC involved in textile trade and ranked second overall among Chinese exporters.[5] As described by Wang, the steadily declining share of China's textile trade has "forced [CHINATEX] to shift its strategy from acting as a dedicated

---

[4] *TA* 19:9 (September 1988), p. 29.   [5] *TA* 17:12 (December 1996), p. 92.

trade company to a business with multiple focuses, including trade and heavy investment in manufacturing."[6] In keeping with this shift, CHINATEX began building its own factories – both at home and abroad – in a bid to develop its own name brands.[7] As part of this endeavor, CHINATEX has become quite active in raising capital in international markets. In fact, CHINATEX became only the fifth Chinese company to issue commercial paper in the United States when it successfully raised U.S. $100 million in 1997.

This discussion of MTI and CHINATEX makes clear the firm grip on power that MOFERT has enjoyed over China's textile trade since the late 1980s. Indeed, interviews indicated that MOFERT used its power over quota not only in the Byzantine world of bureaucratic politics, but also for financial gain. Formally and informally, agencies within MOFERT and its local foreign trade bureaus developed commercial stakes in textile factories. As confirmed by interviews, positions within MOFERT's Foreign Trade Administration were among the most powerful and lucrative bureaucratic positions in China during the late 1980s and early 1990s. Informants of widely varying backgrounds told of a succession of deputy directors and other high officials within MOFERT who were sacked due to corruption in the early 1990s. (Several shared the story of one official who lost his position but was allowed to move to Hong Kong. Once there, he simply continued to conduct business with his former colleagues at MOFERT.) The feeling among most observers was that Beijing was serious about stemming the worst abuses but unwilling to crack down completely. Indeed, some informants intimated that too many top leaders and their families were advantaged by these dealings for the political allocation of quota ever to be eliminated completely.

WHO DID WHAT TO WHOM?: AGENTS OF CHANGE IN CHINA'S TEXTILE INDUSTRY

Weakening the Ties That Bind: Bureaucrats and Market Coordination in China's Textile Industry

The remainder of the chapter explores, in turn, the role of top-level strategy, mid-level intervention, and low-level demand in bringing about

---

[6] Ibid.

[7] See, for instance, "Chinatex to Branch Out Round the World," *China Daily*, 26 January 1995, in FBIS-CHI-95-17.

far-reaching change in China's textile industry. While each was important in its own right, thereby negating the idea that any single level could be accurately identified as the decisive agent of change, the chapter does argue that a critical turning point in the reform of the industry involved overcoming resistance among mid-level bureaucrats. For this reason, the analysis pays special attention to the crucial question of why mid-level bureaucrats – in violation of their basic affinity for *bureaucratic* coordination – increasingly adopted *market* coordination as a means for pursuing economic adjustment in the textile industry. Here, in fact, the moderate economic closure associated with the MFA came into play. By exacerbating the adjustment challenges facing the industry, textile quotas in the world market created incentives for mid-level bureaucrats both to support reform impulses from below and to comply with reform from above, to say nothing of experimenting with reform initiatives of their own. In this way, the MFA – in conjunction with other factors – can be said to have actually *widened* the range of politically feasible options to include a more market-oriented strategy of deregulation than was formerly possible.

Reform from Above: The Role of China's Central Leadership

As a potential explanation for the sweeping changes that occurred in China's textile industry, the impact of the central leadership could have been felt in three principal ways: first, the creation of a generally proreform atmosphere in China, highlighted by Deng Xiaoping's personal support for the policy of reform and opening; and second, the promulgation of (and subsequent support for) various nationwide programs for enterprise reform, industrial reorganization, and foreign trade reform; and lastly, specific actions designed to spur the reform, restructuring, and rationalization of the textile industry.

Proreform Atmosphere. The basic commitment to a policy of reform and opening was an essential precondition for the changes that occurred in China's textile industry. This may be an obvious point, but its salience is so great that it bears repeating. Support for economic reform ebbed and flowed over time, but the political climate was generally favorable to the course of events that unfolded in the industry. To be sure, this proreform atmosphere did not translate into uniform change across industries, but its importance as a necessary (although not sufficient) condition for economic adjustment should not be overlooked.

Nationwide Reform Programs. How well can change in the textile industry be explained by the general reform programs introduced by the central leadership? Put another way, was reform in the textile industry primarily a function of nationwide reform programs? Reform measures promulgated at the national level clearly *facilitated* change in the textile industry, in part by providing new courses of action that had already been legitimized from above, but the mere *existence* of these programs does not fully explain either why (or when) they were initially adopted or their successful implementation over time. Furthermore, as discussed in Chapter 5, the textile industry often served as a laboratory for reform in China. In this sense, the proposition that reform in the textile industry reflected programs adopted at the national level reverses the direction of influence in certain cases.

Industry-Specific Actions. By all accounts, China's top leaders were fairly engaged in matters concerning the textile industry. Given the size of the industry, and its importance to China's foreign trade, their interest in policy making on textile-related issues is not surprising. According to interviews and press reports, the Chinese leadership was aware of the challenge posed by the MFA, although perhaps most pointedly in terms of bilateral frictions with Washington and Brussels over textile trade. That said, a wide range of informants asserted that high-ranking government officials – and perhaps even certain members of the top leadership – understood that improved export performance under the MFA was contingent upon trading up the international product cycle to goods with higher unit values. As a result, so the argument would go, China's leaders were relatively tolerant of broad change in the textile industry since it was one of the country's leading employers and foreign exchange earners. On this issue, informant views ranged considerably, from characterizations of the Chinese leadership as a fairly important agent of change to an image of the leadership as a skeptical – or even reluctant – follower in the industry's reform process.

As this suggests, evidence concerning top-level support for reform and rationalization in the textile industry is mixed. Not only was there no singular policy consistently espoused by the central leadership, but interviews and press reports indicated that even individual leaders were identified with different policy positions at different times. (This includes key leaders in the reform coalition such as Zhao Ziyang in the 1980s and Zhu Rongji in the 1990s.) What can be said unequivocally is that China's top leaders did participate frequently in national conferences on the textile industry. As suggested earlier, the situation in textiles was frequently examined as a microcosm of change in Chinese industry more generally.

In the absence of more decisive evidence, a reasonable conclusion would be that China's top leaders played a significant *supporting* role in the reform, restructuring, and rationalization of the textile industry. While the course of change may not always have been consistent with their initial preferences, they generally supported pragmatic measures designed to improve the performance of the industry, both in domestic markets and internationally. Indeed, the central leadership's most important role as an agent of change was arguably to validate (and, in some cases, apply more widely) reform experiments initiated from below in the textile industry. Consider, for example, the July 1992 State Council "Directive on Regulations for Transforming the Operational Mechanism of State-owned Enterprises." This document, which identified the responsibilities expected of SOEs, as well as the fourteen "autonomies" granted to them, affirmed a policy first developed at the local level in the textile industry.[8] While this directive ultimately met with mixed success itself, its promulgation illustrates well the kind of corroborative role Beijing often played vis-à-vis industry-specific reform.

By contrast, the central leadership played a fairly minor role in initiating change within the textile industry. Even when attempted, top-down reforms typically encountered uneven implementation (or worse) at lower levels of administration. Consider, for example, the State Council's March 1987 decision to transfer control over garment production from the Ministry of Light Industry to MTI. By all accounts, this move was designed to improve coordination between the textile and garment sectors of the industry. The State Council had studied the performance of other developing countries during the early 1980s, finding that their achievements in product upgrading and other aspects of industrial restructuring were often superior to China's. In an effort to rectify this situation, particularly in light of the increasingly restrictive quotas imposed on China under the MFA, the central leadership imposed this bureaucratic reorganization as an administrative solution to industry-specific problems. The nominal transfer of garment production to MTI did not, however, substantially improve coordination between the textile and garment sectors. Problems with the supply of fabric, for example, persisted and arguably even worsened. Organizational flowcharts

---

[8] *TA* 24:1 (January 1993), pp. 62–63.

notwithstanding, bureaucratic resistance within the textile and garment sectors meant that MTI never exercised the kind of institutional coordination envisioned in top-level strategy. Export performance improved, to be sure, but this resulted mainly from continued decentralization and other measures associated with broader economic reforms.

As this example suggests, the mere promulgation of national policy does not necessarily translate into change on the ground. As described by one industry observer, central policy is often like "loud thunder without raindrops."[9] Indeed, the importance of local initiative and local compliance underscores the degree to which the support of the central leadership is more often a lubricant for reform than an irresistible force for change. On the other hand, neither did China's top leaders – whatever their reservations about the scope or pace of change – stand in the way of market-oriented economic and trade reforms (and, to a lesser degree, rationalization) as successful tools for improving the performance of the textile industry. In this sense, the central leadership should perhaps be characterized as a somewhat grudging, but increasingly supportive, agent of change. The story of China's textile industry is not, however, one primarily of "reform from above," especially in terms of industry-specific adjustments.

Reform from the Middle: Overcoming Bureaucratic Resistance in China's Textile Industry

MTI, CHINATEX, and MOFERT. As described earlier, the national offices of MTI, CHINATEX, and MOFERT were generally resistant to most change in the textile industry, especially at first. CHINATEX, in particular, clung rather desperately to every vestige of its former monopoly in China's textile trade. While CHINATEX identified the basic strategy China should employ under the MFA quite early, it wanted to implement that strategy entirely on its own.[10] In fact, the only respect in which CHINATEX proved to be an agent of change was in pushing for its own autonomy from MOFERT, a self-interested agenda that hardly constituted a comprehensive reform program.[11] MOFERT's record as an

---

[9] *TA* 24:5 (May 1993), p. 88.

[10] Press reports indicate that CHINATEX outlined the elements of a successful strategy in response to the MFA as early as 1983. See, for example, *TA* 14:4 (April 1983), p. 68.

[11] For insight into CHINATEX's position in the mid-1980s, see the interview with Zhou Yunzhong, president of CHINATEX, in *TA* 17:5 (May 1986), pp. 45–49.

agent of change was better than CHINATEX's but still mixed. As noted in Chapter 5, MOFERT was a strong opponent of reform to the quota allocation system. While MOFERT's resistance on this issue did hamper the industry's progress, it was not an unqualified opponent of reform. It did, after all, preside over considerable reform within the foreign trade system, even if many of these changes were either introduced from above or the result of experimentation from levels below the national office.

As might be expected from its interest in maintaining the bureaucratic status quo, MTI was hardly a reform pioneer either. That said, several informants – none of whom had direct ties to the ministry – expressed regret that MTI had, by the late 1980s, become so marginalized within the industry. In their view, MTI could have contributed positively to the development of the industry, even if only by following its own self-interest on certain issues. As one interviewee put it, "MTI had a much better idea about the national interest of the industry than MOFERT." Indeed, it was in the context of bureaucratic politics that MTI played its most important role as an agent for change, serving as a partial counterweight to the MOFERT-CHINATEX alliance. In the late 1980s, for example, CHINATEX strongly resisted the extension of autonomous export rights to textile factories, a move it feared would reduce its business rather drastically. MTI, for its part, fought on behalf of the factories, arguing that autonomous export rights were an important means for better coordinating industry and trade.[12] What would this change mean for MTI? First, it would likely improve China's performance in world textile markets. Second, MTI also had a more narrow self-interest: the ability for textile factories to export directly would allow prices to reflect their costs more accurately. Squeezed between rising prices for raw materials and the low purchase prices they received from CHINATEX (and other authorized trading entities), textile factories sought autonomous export rights as a way to better protect their interests.

Provincial- and Municipal-Level Initiatives. True to their reputation, provincial- and municipal-level officials proved at times to be formidable roadblocks along the path to reform. For example, some government departments reportedly opposed the export agency system since it threatened to reduce the role of regional FTCs to mere processing agents

---

[12] See, for instance, the interview with Ji Guobiao, vice-minister of MTI, in *TA* 19:5 (May 1988), pp. 18–23.

in China's foreign trade.[13] Especially in the 1980s, mid-level bureaucrats frequently resisted reform initiatives both from above and from below. Over time, however, this resistance weakened in certain respects. In fact, provincial- and municipal-level bureaucrats at times became rather important agents of change, even with regard to market-oriented reform. This turn of events, while it should not be overstated, is critical for understanding why China's textile industry was able to achieve significant industrial adjustment.

Why did provincial and municipal-level bureaucrats – as well as others at the national level – increasingly accept market coordination as a means for economic adjustment in the textile industry? This weakening of the classic affinity between bureaucrats and bureaucratic forms of coordination is perhaps best understood through a series of examples. First, the spread of quotas on Chinese textile exports led to growing disenchantment with the existing procurement system, one that saddled bureaucrats in local foreign trade bureaus (and, later, other authorized FTCs) with more goods than they could export. Whereas other light industries could continue with a volume-centered export strategy, this was not an option for the textile industry. Given the nature of the MFA, what bureaucrats wanted were slowly increasing volumes of high-quality goods, not torrents of mediocre (or even shoddy) goods. As a result, bureaucrats who would otherwise have been expected to favor bureaucratic coordination came over time to support greater reliance on market coordination, a position that would enable them to operate on a more selective basis in procuring goods for export. In this way, the MFA helped to change the policy preferences of mid-level actors, thereby making market-oriented reform a more viable alternative, politically speaking.

A relevant case here would be the adoption of a selective purchase system (as opposed to guaranteed procurement) as part of the larger package of foreign trade reforms in 1991. With greater responsibility for their own profits and losses, foreign trade departments under MOFERT placed smaller orders for textile goods. This change was critical to the deepening of a buyers' market in textiles, a development that increased competition within the industry and set off a chain effect of restructuring and reform among enterprises interested in positioning themselves favorably in a more rigorous commercial environment. With a less reliable supply of orders, as well as increasing expectations of financial

---

[13] For examples, see *TA* 19:6 (June 1988), p. 120.

responsibility and growing uncertainty about supplies of subsidized raw materials, enterprises began to push harder for greater operational autonomy.

In some cases, the changes carried out by mid-level bureaucrats entailed little more than the belated implementation of reform programs promulgated at the national level. In other cases, they merely represented the broader application of reform initiatives first tried on an experimental basis at lower levels of administration. In some instances, however, provincial- and municipal-level bureaucrats undertook new initiatives on their own. Shanghai officials, for example, were reportedly instrumental in spearheading important reforms such as the export agency system.[14] Shanghai was also one of the first places to experiment in granting greater autonomy to textile-exporting enterprises in a bid to improve their performance in world markets (and, not incidentally, to relieve some of the financial responsibility borne by the Shanghai municipal government, as well).[15] Nor was this behavior somehow unique to Shanghai. According to published accounts, provincial and municipal governments were important agents of reform in Tianjin, Guangzhou, Jiangsu, and other textile centers throughout China.[16] As much as they valued their traditional institutional prerogatives, mid-level bureaucrats apparently acted out of necessity – or even desperation – as they improvised their way through the wrenching process of economic transition in local textile sectors.

Another factor that made bureaucrats at the provincial or municipal level more willing to support reform initiatives over time was the increasingly dire fiscal situation in the bloated, inefficient textile industry. According to interviews, there was a clear relationship between growing financial accountability and the willingness of officials to increase the role of market coordination. The general trend, therefore, was one in which greater (although still limited) responsibility for profits and losses – coupled with restricted opportunities for export growth due to the MFA – led to a declining interest among bureaucrats in the textile industry in protecting their traditional role. For instance, Shanghai authorities

[14] For more detail on the role played by Shanghai authorities in the export agency system, see *TA* 20:7 (July 1989), pp. 145–146.

[15] By some accounts, these experiments began as early as 1981, many years before such a system was even considered at the national level. See *TA* 23:7 (July 1992), pp. 130–131, and *ZGJJXW*, 11 April 1988, p. 19.

[16] For an interesting discussion of measures taken in Tianjin, see *TA* 25:8 (August 1994), p. 63.

became significantly more active in implementing economic reform and carrying out industrial adjustment in the textile sector once they were vested with significant financial responsibility for managing state-owned assets at the municipal level. In an effort to revive the industry and stem the flow of financial losses, bureaucrats in Shanghai oversaw numerous mergers and began plans to allow some firms to go bankrupt. As early as 1996, long before Zhu's national program for SOE reform was in place, a total of nearly 200,000 textile workers had reportedly been dismissed in Shanghai.[17]

Financial performance in the textile industry was poor everywhere, of course, not just in Shanghai. SOE losses grew steadily throughout the early and mid-1990s, this in stark contrast to the relative success and profitability of many TVEs and FIEs.[18] As it turns out, the declining financial performance of SOEs owes much to the vitality of non-state enterprises. As discussed in the final section of this chapter, the heightened competition provided by TVEs and FIEs has only exacerbated the fundamental dilemmas facing SOEs. Furthermore, it also appears that the poor financial performance of the state-run sector, which has been worse in textiles than in many other industries, is due in part to the MFA, since export restrictions have indirectly contributed to the unusually high levels of surplus manufacturing capacity found in textiles.[19] As discussed earlier, idle capacity and stockpiled output are two of the major problems China's textile industry has faced in the post-Mao era.

Over time, these difficulties have certainly reduced opposition to various kinds of reform, including formerly radical solutions such as quasi-privatization. Indeed, press reports in the mid-1990s routinely documented cases in which textile factories were restructured under private management after being allowed to fail.[20] Where officials were once reluctant to lay off workers or shut down unprofitable plants, the new environment of greater financial responsibility at the local level produced uncharacteristically blunt statements, such as the following

---

[17] *TA* 27:5 (May 1996), pp. 72–73.

[18] Estimates of SOE losses in the textile industry vary widely. Most estimates suggest that the proportion of loss-making SOEs roughly doubled in the early 1990s from approximately one-third to two-thirds. Other estimates are more extreme, claiming that fully 75 percent of all SOEs in the textile sector registered a loss in 1995; *TA* 27:5 (May 1996), pp. 72–73. For the record, the remaining enterprises are typically characterized as "barely profitable."

[19] *TA* 22:8 (August 1991), p. 132.   [20] For example, see *TA* 27:5 (May 1996), p. 75.

observation from the chairman of the Shanghai Textile Holding Company, the entity that manages SOEs in the municipality: "Some moribund enterprises are like rotting apples. We must cut off the good part before the whole apple goes bad."[21]

By one interpretation, the increasing use of market coordination represents not so much the liberation of textile enterprises as much as their abandonment by mid-level bureaucrats. Given the general failure of administrative measures to address many of the problems facing the textile industry, including the need for economic adjustment in response to quotas imposed under the MFA, deregulation by bureaucrats is arguably best characterized as an abdication of responsibility in which the burden of reform, restructuring, and rationalization is shifted increasingly toward lower-level actors.[22] In this sense, the willingness of bureaucrats to grant greater decision-making autonomy to entities under their supervision reflects a desire to avoid unwanted responsibility. Indeed, the delegation of operational autonomy also protects bureaucrats from complaints that their supervision is the culprit impeding enterprise performance. If firms still encounter difficulty, so the argument goes, it is more difficult for them to fix the blame on their superiors.

Several interviewees also pointed to a learning process in which mid-level bureaucrats began to see how reform and restructuring in the non-state sector, as well as some fairly successful experiments among SOEs, led to improved performance. There was, in other words, a fairly strong emulation effect. Along the same lines, one cannot underestimate the phenomenon in which local officials decided to "plunge into the sea" (*xia hai* [i.e., go into business]), particularly after the substantial boost the reform program received from Deng's "Southern Tour" in the summer of 1992. Having seen others become rich by opening new textile factories (or taking over the management of existing plants), and sensing the progressive withdrawal of higher levels of administration from direct supervision over economic activity, many officials all but relinquished their former supervisory responsibilities to become entrepreneurs. With this, an important source of bureaucratic resistance to reform was weakened, even if not eliminated entirely.[23]

---

[21] *TA* 27:5 (May 1996), p. 73.

[22] Byrd (1987) makes a parallel argument.

[23] In the view of many observers, local officials retain too much influence for economic activity in China to be considered fully consistent with market-based conceptualizations as understood in the West.

Reform from Below: Enterprise Initiative in the Textile Industry

Familiar only with the prereform system, most factory managers were understandably wary of change at first. By all accounts, enterprises generally became reform advocates only as they became more accountable for their own performance. At that time, frustration with the *partial* nature of reform led many factory managers to petition their supervisory agencies for more *comprehensive*, integrated reform. In some cases, in fact, upstart enterprises directed by talented, ambitious managers called for a wide range of decision-making rights and other freedoms that were significantly ahead of their time.[24] It is difficult to assess the impact that these requests had on policy trends, but the cumulative effect of complaints received from below may have contributed over time to the weakening of bureaucratic resistance discussed in the last section.

Especially as the air lock system became increasingly penetrated, and the requirements for success in the world market consequently came into clearer focus, textile enterprises became quite vocal in demanding certain changes in how the industry was administered. To be sure, the distortions created by partial reform were, in some cases, actually beneficial to enterprise interests. (Here, we are reminded that factory managers can resist as well as embrace reform depending on its effect.) In other cases, however, partial reform left factory managers in the untenable position of having to meet an export target, turn over a set amount of foreign exchange to the government, and make a profit – all while doing business at low, state-set prices without the benefit of direct access to foreign buyers. According to one informant with first-hand experience in the Chinese industry, the standard refrain from factory managers to their superiors was, "If you expect us to be responsible for our own profits and losses, we have to be able to export directly, not just take orders from CHINATEX." Along the same lines, textile enterprises were at the forefront of efforts to change the system for quota allocation.[25] Frustrated by their inability to secure quota, sometimes even if they were willing to buy it illegally on the black market, factory managers long urged those higher in the system to adopt either a more strictly performance-based system of bureaucratic allocation or, better

---

[24] See, for instance, *TA* 19:6 (June 1988), p. 125, and *TA* 19:5 (May 1988), p. 108.
[25] For recent examples in published accounts, see *TA* 27:4 (April 1996), p. 96, and *TA* 27:5 (May 1996), p. 72.

still, an auction system in which all enterprises would bid on an equal basis.

However articulately enterprises petitioned for change, reform in China's textile industry was certainly more than a case of the proverbial mouse that roared. Indeed, "self-reform" was probably the most important contribution they made as agents of change. Often without authorization, enterprises simply undertook the changes their managers believed were necessary for success, bending the rules farther and farther either until someone stopped them or until further reform no longer suited their interests. In the words of one informant, "The rules for the new Chinese economy are being made at the ground [factory] level as we go along." While that comment may have been an overstatement, and there certainly were limits to this strategy for effecting change, it did capture the dynamism that characterized many enterprises in China's textile industry.

While the degree of self-reform varied tremendously from enterprise to enterprise, some textile factories virtually remade themselves by undertaking sweeping changes in business practices, production processes, and other areas of enterprise operation. In many instances, self-reform was achieved in close association with foreign clients. In fact, even when there was no formal joint venture arrangement or other financial stake held by foreign partners, the outside world still often proved instrumental in eliciting change among Chinese textile factories. As mentioned in Chapter 4, the real measure of global standing in the textile industry is defined at the factory level. While the reputation of the national industry certainly matters, what really matters – especially in a huge, enormously diverse industry such as China's textile industry – is factory-specific reputation. Since textiles is a buyer-driven industry in the world market, foreign companies seeking to source their goods from Chinese factories can play an enormous role in inducing wide-ranging changes at the factory level.

While this is true for other buyer-driven light industries – for example, toys, consumer electronics, and athletic footwear – it is even more true for textiles due to the presence of the MFA. If, for example, a foreign company is a high-volume, upmarket merchandiser whose business is greatly coveted by officials at the national or local level, it can influence which factories receive certain allocations of quota. As several interviewees stressed, this dynamic provided tremendous leverage to foreign buyers in securing compliance from Chinese factories. As one Hong Kong tycoon with textile operations in nine Chinese provinces boasted,

"If their performance is not suitable, we can threaten [to use our connections] to have their quota taken away from them. Without quota, of course, they will be unable to export." Some interviewees even suggested that foreign-induced reform at the enterprise level is greatest when the relationship does *not* involve an equity stake. Where FDI is involved, so the argument goes, the leverage of the foreign partner is sometimes actually reduced since any threat to sever the relationship is less credible than if there is only an arms-length, buyer-producer relationship. If this is true, then the dampening effect of the MFA on FDI may actually have been a fortuitous condition for change in China's textile industry.

REFORM BY ATTRITION: THE ROLE OF THE NONSTATE SECTOR IN RESHAPING CHINA'S TEXTILE INDUSTRY

By all accounts, nonstate enterprises have been an important agent of change in China's textile industry, especially during the 1990s. Their emergence as dynamic producers and highly successful exporters created pressure throughout the industry – especially on SOEs – for further reform, restructuring, and rationalization. The role of nonstate enterprises in China's textile industry has increased dramatically in the post-Mao era. In the 1970s, SOEs produced almost 90 percent of China's textile production. By 1985, that figure had fallen to 67 percent, followed by further declines to 54 percent in 1991 and 29 percent in 1995.[26] In this respect, much of the tide had already shifted by the early 1990s. In Jiangsu province, for example, TVEs alone (i.e., not including FIEs and private enterprises) accounted for as much as half of total textile production by 1993.[27] Similarly, CNTC reported that TVEs produced 60 percent of garments nationally during the Eighth Five-Year Plan, 1991–1995.[28] In yet another telling statistic, nonstate firms contributed more than half of the profits tax paid by the industry in 1993.[29] Employment in TVEs alone trebled in the first 15 years of the post-Mao era to more than 6 million individuals working in some 53,000 textile enterprises.[30]

By the mid-1990s, nonstate enterprises had in certain respects established themselves as the leaders of China's textile industry. Economic reform and industrial restructuring were without question deepest

---

[26] *TA* 29:1 (January 1998), pp. 75–76.   [27] *TA* 25:5 (May 1994), p. 59.
[28] *TA* 27:4 (April 1996), p. 101.   [29] *TA* 24:6 (June 1993), p. 53.
[30] *TA* 23:12 (December 1992), p. 73.

among TVEs and FIEs. Interviewees repeatedly stressed that economic activity in the nonstate sector was almost completely market-oriented, arguing that TVEs and FIEs should therefore be considered bona fide commercial entities. Furthermore, small- to medium-sized TVEs and FIEs proved to be the most effective group in coping with life under the MFA. By all accounts, the most success in product upgrading was accomplished by these entities, especially with their entrance into lucrative areas such as high-fashion garments. These same firms also made the greatest strides in shifting from generic processing work to designing, producing, and directly exporting their own merchandise.[31] Interviews were rife with paeans to nonstate enterprises. To be sure, there were occasional remarks about fly-by-night firms that failed to honor their contracts or otherwise damaged the international reputation of China's industry, but even informants with close ties to the state-run sector acknowledged the important role played by TVEs and FIEs in moving the whole industry upmarket.

The TVEs proved so successful, in fact, that they eventually began to penetrate the state-run sector through business alliances that frequently expanded over time from loose production agreements to virtual corporate takeovers. In order to expand production capability, acquire technological expertise, or simply gain access to export quotas, TVEs entered into a wide variety of business pacts with large SOEs in urban areas. For their part, the SOEs reached out to the TVEs as part of a desperate strategy to avoid economic collapse. As one report from Liaoning province put it:

> Almost all rural textile enterprises are making profits, leaving the government officials with a sense of shame. Hence the state-run enterprises [by] necessity team up with rural plants. The new alliance is expected to show profitable results within one year.[32]

In this way, TVEs changed the behavior of SOEs not only by providing heightened competition and otherwise underscoring their deficiencies, but also by carrying out the "market socialist" equivalent of corporate takeovers.[33] Indeed, TVEs often became the more powerful

---

[31] See, for example, *TA* 23:8 (August 1992), pp. 54–55, and *TA* 27:5 (May 1996), p. 72. As the first of these articles indicates, TVEs have also been leaders in diversifying China's export markets to countries that are not signatories to the MFA. This owes in part to the greater difficulty TVEs often encounter in securing export quota.

[32] *TA* 24:11 (November 1993), p. 61.

[33] See, for instance, *TA* 25:5 (May 1994), p. 58, and *TA* 24:11 (November 1993), pp. 60–61.

partner in these relationships, usually on the strength of their management skills, reputation for quality production, competitive pricing, and, in some cases, more extensive market contacts outside China.

Another effort to improve the performance of SOEs was the so-called state-owned but civilian-run arrangement in which officials would contract out the operation of a factory, rather than either endure further loss making, or simply close the plant. In essence, the civilian managers leased the state-owned factory, paying rent and undertaking the responsibility to pay the relevant profits tax. In many cases, the results of this arrangement were quite impressive despite minimal changes in personnel, equipment, or production.[34]

The state sector was, of course, too big for this process of cooptation to provide a comprehensive solution to the industry's need for reform and rationalization. In fact, several interviewees noted a trend in the early 1990s toward the bifurcation of the industry into two increasingly distinct segments: an advanced, outward-looking sector comprised of competent factories capable of producing high-quality goods; and a backward, largely unreformed sector comprised mainly of inefficient SOEs whose only hope was to produce for the lower end of the domestic market. For the first segment, the sky remains the limit; international observers expect to find some Chinese factories at or near the top of the global industry in the near future. The fate of the second segment, by contrast, is grim indeed. While the demise of unreformed (or slowly reforming) enterprises has been relatively slow, at least until recently, the reality of two worlds within China's textile industry could already be seen in the substantial flow of experienced managers, engineers, and other technical personnel from SOEs to TVEs and FIEs during the 1990s.[35] "Reform by attrition" is a slow process, to be sure, but it is powerful all the same.

---

[34] For more details on this variant of "privatization" in China's state-owned textile industry, see *TA* 24:12 (December 1993), pp. 62–63, and *TA* 25:3 (March 1994), pp. 69–70.
[35] *TA* 24:7 (July 1993), pp. 84–85.

7

Chinese Shipbuilding: The Modest Origins of an Emerging Industrial Giant

BEHEMOTHS IN THE MAKING?: CHINA'S SHIPYARDS ON THE RISE

In the space of a single decade, from the early 1980s to the early 1990s, the Chinese shipbuilding industry was transformed from a technologically backward, poor-quality manufacturer of basic ships to a bona fide force in the world industry. Although Japan and South Korea still far outclassed the rest of the field, China had risen by the early 1990s to a position atop the middle-ranking shipbuilding powers, a group that included such notable European builders as Germany, Poland, Denmark, Spain, the Netherlands, and Finland. In fact, the Chinese industry had by that time already eclipsed such traditional maritime powers as Britain and Italy, as well as promising developing countries such as Brazil and Taiwan. Ranked only sixteenth among world ship exporters in 1982, the year in which the China State Shipbuilding Corporation (CSSC) was formed to oversee the country's major shipyards, China moved into third place only a decade later, a position in which it quickly became ensconced. For several years prior to the Asian Financial Crisis, an episode that threw the regional (and indeed global) shipbuilding industry into turmoil, China had averaged about 15 percent of the world market. While far behind Japan and South Korea, which jockey perennially for the top spot and together account for 60 to 70 percent of the world market, China typically enjoyed a comfortable lead over fourth-place Taiwan.[1] As Figure 7.1 shows, China's ship exports grew by 1997 to more than 30 major vessels a year, totaling more than 1.3 million deadweight tons. Indeed, exports have accounted for more than 50 percent

[1] See, for instance, "South Korean Shipyards Retain Top Rank," *Journal of Commerce*, 1 February 2000, p. 14 (Maritime section).

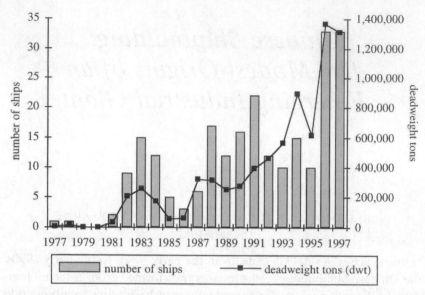

Figure 7.1. Ship exports by the China State Shipbuilding Corporation (CSSC).
Source: Calculated from data in computer printouts supplied by CSSC.

of total Chinese ship production on average since the mid-1980s.[2] In 1996, in fact, the China Shipbuilding Trading Corporation (CSTC) – CSSC's trading arm – reached a rank of fifteenth among Chinese import and export companies.[3] As this rank would indicate, ships have become an increasingly important export item in China's overall trade profile. By the mid-1990s, in fact, ships were among the largest foreign exchange

[2] This is an average figure by deadweight tonnage; the actual percentages vary fairly widely from year to year due to idiosyncrasies in the shipbuilding industry. (For example, a single order for a series of ships by a foreign shipowner can skew a given year's production heavily to exports.) Export data were calculated from computer printouts supplied by CSSC. Data for total domestic production were taken from *ZGJJNJ*, various years. If anything, the 50-percent figure understates the role of exports since the export data only includes oceangoing ships greater than 2,000 deadweight tons, whereas the data for total domestic production includes all ships (i.e., coastal and river vessels as well as oceangoing ships.) In some years, exports have comprised as much as 85 percent of production.

[3] Since 78 percent of CSTC's total trade in 1996 was accounted for by exports, its rank as an exporter is undoubtedly much higher. CSTC is not a major importer; its imports consist mainly of advanced equipment and raw materials needed for specialized vessels. Data on CSTC's trade can be found at http://www.chinaships.com.

earners in the entire machinery and electronics sector, averaging about U.S. $1.5 billion annually.[4]

While China's shipyards still face many problems, especially in improving economic efficiency, most observers agree that China's standing in the international industry will only grow. CSSC cannot yet match the technological expertise and product quality of Western Europe or South Korea, to say nothing of Japan, but it can produce a serviceable vessel both on schedule and at a good price. Perhaps most significantly, China has diversified its production of ships from traditional bulk carriers and oil tankers to virtually every major type of advanced vessel, including several state-of-the-art freighters, liquid petroleum gas (LPG) carriers, and very large crude carriers (VLCCs). By the early 1990s, Chinese shipyards had already built shuttle tankers, product-chemical tankers, refrigerated containerships, roll-on–roll-off vessels used to transport goods such as automobiles, and a host of other specialized ships. While a few of these advanced ships were built for use by Chinese shipping companies, most notably the state-owned China Ocean Shipping Company (COSCO), most were built for foreign shipowners.

As discussed in Chapter 1, the present examination of the Chinese shipbuilding industry pays greatest attention to the period from the early 1980s to the early 1990s since the crisis in the international industry occurred in the mid-1980s. Given this book's analytic focus on varying degrees of economic openness in world industrial markets and their effects on the reform, restructuring, and rationalization of Chinese industries, our primary interest lies with the moderate economic closure – represented here by severe GSC – created during the international shipbuilding crisis. While the remainder of the 1990s does receive some coverage, this is mainly to update progress in the Chinese industry. Another reason to focus mainly on the decade from the early 1980s to the early 1990s is the AFC, which began in 1997. In addition to introducing short-term distortions, the AFC also created new long-term dynamics for China's participation in the world shipbuilding industry. Depending on events in Japan and South Korea, as well as developments in China itself, the contours of these new dynamics will not be clear for several more years. Consequently, post-AFC events are treated as a significant disjuncture from developments earlier in the post-Mao era.

---

4 *Xinhua*, 10 September 1997, in FBIS-CHI-97-253, and *Xinhua*, 26 February 1998, in FBIS-CHI-98-057.

As shall be examined in Chapter 8, severe GSC in the mid-1980s had a direct and substantial impact on China's shipping and shipbuilding industries. As foreign yards began to offer fire sale prices and highly concessionary financing to prospective buyers, all in a desperate bid to attract work, COSCO placed increasing numbers of its ship orders overseas, sometimes even canceling plans for domestic projects. With this, of course, it became increasingly difficult for CSSC to pursue its original strategy of building ships primarily for the domestic market, a plan outlined later in this chapter. Moreover, due to the idiosyncrasies of the international shipbuilding market during the mid-1980s, remaining world demand for new vessels, however modest, was concentrated in relatively advanced ship types rather than the basic bulk carriers and oil tankers Chinese yards were already able to produce. As a result of the international shipbuilding crisis, therefore, CSSC had to turn not only to greater reliance on export orders but also to the construction of advanced ship types. As shall be documented in Chapters 8 and 9, these changes – and especially the shift toward more sophisticated vessels – led to a level of foreign involvement in China's shipbuilding industry far greater than originally envisioned. Indeed, by the early 1990s CSSC was well on its way to becoming substantially integrated into the international division of labor.

In addition to trading up the international product cycle toward more advanced ship exports, China's shipbuilding industry could list several other notable achievements by the early 1990s: the level of technology was significantly upgraded through licensing with foreign companies; the industry's product mix was diversified to include not only different types of ships, but also more emphasis on shiprepair and a greater variety of marine products (e.g., ship engines, deck machinery); product quality and customer service were improved; the number of clients, especially in new export markets, was greatly expanded; delivery times became more reliable; and higher rates of productivity were achieved (although these remained modest overall). Moreover, as Figure 7.2 shows, CSSC diversified its economic activities significantly into nonmarine production.

CSSC's success in these areas is especially noteworthy since shipbuilding is a state-owned heavy industry located primarily in major urban centers such as Shanghai, Dalian, Guangzhou, Tianjin, and Wuhan. At the beginning of the post-Mao era, shipbuilding was firmly entrenched in the traditional system of central planning. It also suffered from so-called multiheaded leadership, as bureaucratic power was divided principally among the Sixth Ministry of Machine Building, the

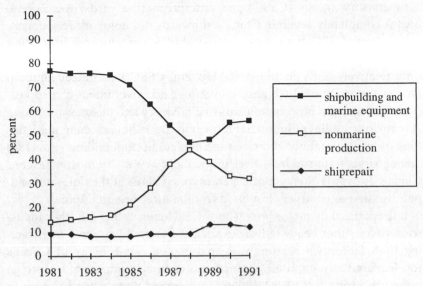

Figure 7.2. Sector shares of CSSC's industrial output. *Source: Zhongguo Jingji Nianjian*, various years.

Ministry of Communications, the PLA Navy, and various municipalities and provinces. As a result of this fragmentation of authority, as well as Mao's idiosyncratic development strategy, the industry operated on very low economies of scale since individual yards strove for self-reliance. Technology was backward by international standards and the quality of Chinese-built ships was poor.

While the industry still suffered from many problems a decade after CSSC's creation, the production and distribution of ships and other marine equipment was almost entirely market-based by the early 1990s. Reorganization within the industry, highlighted by the greater special-ization of individual shipyards, eliminated some of the main disec-onomies that had plagued Chinese shipbuilding in the past. By the early 1990s, in fact, the industry had made substantial advances by importing critical equipment, using modern computer-aided design technology, and introducing more sophisticated production processes and management practices at the yard level.

Equally impressive was the degree to which government intrusion in enterprise activities was reduced by the late 1980s and early 1990s. Although the classic state socialist pattern of hierarchical ties between a supervisory agency (CSSC) and enterprises (the yards) were by no means completely severed, China's shipyards did enjoy more independence from CSSC than most comparable SOEs enjoyed from their supervisory agencies at the time.[5] By allowing its yards greater autonomy relatively early in the post-Mao era, CSSC was indeed unusual among the traditional Chinese ministries and government-owned corporations that combined administrative, advisory, and business functions. As previous studies of industrial reform in China have documented, this kind of transformation – however incomplete in shipbuilding – was rare among large, state-run industries in the early 1990s.[6] By most measures, China's shipyards did not fit the stereotype of SOEs at the time – uncompetitive dinosaurs largely insulated from market-oriented forces.

Indeed, the only major area where CSSC lagged behind other industries – even other heavy industries such as automobiles – was in attracting FDI. Here, two reasons were paramount. First, many of China's top leaders flatly opposed opening the country's shipyards to foreign investors during the 1980s. While compromises were made in order to allow FDI in other industries considered to be "mainstays" of China's socialist economy, including automobiles, these accommodations came much later for shipbuilding. According to interviews, even the production of commercial vessels was deemed to be inappropriate territory for foreign investors. Second, the supply of potential foreign investment was meager. Given the dire situation in the international shipbuilding industry, one defined by chronic overcapacity, few foreign investors were interested in building new capacity (or even modernizing existing capacity) during the 1980s. That said, these sorts of discussions were not encouraged by Beijing even when partnerships between CSSC and foreign investors did in fact seem possible. In any event, there were no significant joint ventures until the establishment of the Shanghai Edward Shipbuilding Company in the Pudong Development Zone in 1991, a relatively small, experimental entity formed between two Shanghai yards (Zhonghua and Jiangnan) and a German shipbuilder, Schierack Beteiliguns.[7] While foreign investment has picked up considerably

---

[5] For points of comparison, see the detailed case studies examined in Byrd (1992a).

[6] See, for instance, Tidrick and Chen (1987) and Byrd (1992a) for the research findings of the World Bank based on a decade of intensive study of change in Chinese industry.

[7] A joint venture had been formed in 1980 between the China Corporation of Shipbuilding Industry (CSTC's predecessor) and a group headed by Sir Yue Kong Pao, a Hong Kong tycoon and owner of World-Wide Shipping, one of the world's largest shipping companies. While an important gesture at the time, this venture – the International United

since the mid-1990s, as shall be discussed in Chapter 9, it still represents the weakest area of China's participation in the world shipbuilding industry.

A BRIEF HISTORY OF CHINA'S MARITIME DEVELOPMENT

Although China's modern shipbuilding industry was not established until the mid-1800s, its maritime history goes back virtually to the beginning of recorded Chinese civilization. While most historians agree that wooden sailing boats were almost certainly in use during the Han Dynasty (ca. 200 B.C. to A.D. 200), there is also evidence that simple plank boats may have existed in the Shang Dynasty (ca. 1766 B.C. to 1122 B.C.). During the Ming Dynasty (1368–1644), Zheng He, the famous Chinese navigator, made several historic voyages, the farthest of which apparently reached the eastern coast of Africa.[8]

China's maritime achievements all but ended with the Ming Dynasty, however, and the Qing Dynasty (1644–1911) and the Chinese Republic (1911–1949) saw few noteworthy advances in shipbuilding and waterborne transportation. Although the Qing government did set the modern Chinese shipbuilding industry in motion by establishing the Jiangnan Manufacturing Bureau in Shanghai in 1865 to produce ships and ammunition, foreign shipping companies dominated maritime affairs in China in the century prior to the founding of the PRC in 1949. Indeed, historians identify the shipbuilding and shiprepair sector as the leading recipient of foreign investment in manufacturing during the second half of the eighteenth century.[9] While the British dominated the industry, Americans and other foreign nationals were also involved in expanding China's shipyard capacity. By 1929, there were 13 shipyards in Shanghai alone, most of them foreign-owned.[10] Despite this growth, however, China is

---

Shipping and Investment Company – was a broad-based concern involved in the buying, selling, chartering, and managing of ships. While it did order some ships from Chinese yards, the venture was only marginally engaged in ship manufacturing. In fact, eleven years later, even the semi-official *Zhongguo Haiyun* [*Maritime China*] referred to the Shanghai Edward venture in Pudong as China's "first joint venture in shipbuilding"; *ZGHY* 10:1 (Spring 1992), p. 70.

[8] For more detail on China's maritime history, see *Dangdai Zhongguo de Shuiyun Shiye* (1989), Spence (1990), and Deng (1999). Additional overviews of China's modern maritime history can be found in Heine (1989), Muller (1983), and Swanson (1982).

[9] See, for example, Feuerwerker (1995a), p. 44, and Hou (1965), p. 80.

[10] Hou (1965, pp. 879–883) provides a good primer on the role of foreign investment in China's shipyard development.

still estimated to have built only 500,000 deadweight tons of steel ships from 1865 to 1949, less than the typical output for a *single* year in the 1980s.[11] (Much of the activity in Chinese yards was obviously repair work.)

When the PRC was established in 1949, the Chinese fleet had only a few oceangoing vessels. While China's merchant marine had never exactly flourished under the Nationalist government, the meager fleet that did exist was further depleted by a combination of Japanese and Kuomintang (KMT) plundering. First, Japan either confiscated or destroyed much of China's fleet during its notorious occupation of the coastal regions during the 1937–1945 war period. The small fleet that did survive was, in turn, further decimated by retreating KMT forces during the final stages of the civil war. As the KMT fled the mainland, most of China's remaining merchant and naval ships sailed with them. All that remained were the few vessels too unseaworthy to make the voyage to Taiwan; even these derelict ships were often sunk or sabotaged by the KMT as they fled. For China's shipyards, the story was painfully similar. As the KMT fled the mainland, they plundered China's main yards (in Shanghai, most notably), seriously damaging the facilities and destroying whatever machine-building equipment they were unable to take with them. With the founding of the PRC in 1949, China only had about twenty shipyards capable of building steel ships, fewer than one thousand machine tools for shipbuilding, and at most ten thousand trained workers.[12]

In order to rebuild an industry that lay in complete ruin, the new Communist government established the Shipbuilding Industry Bureau in 1950 under the control of the Ministry of Heavy Industry.[13] (In 1952, the Bureau was put under the authority of the newly created First Ministry of Machine Building.) Due to both national security concerns and China's transportation needs during the period of national reconstruction, the shipbuilding industry received a fairly high priority immediately after the Revolution. Throughout the 1950s, and during the First Five-Year Plan (1953–57) in particular, the basic policy was to rebuild and expand China's shipyards by taking advantage of aid from the Soviet

[11] *China's Shipbuilding Industry in Progress* (1991), p. 4. Cheng (1971, p. 297) also uses the 500,000-deadweight-ton figure, citing a Soviet study on Chinese shipbuilding.
[12] Ibid.
[13] This administrative unit was renamed several times during the 1950s, but it was, in effect, always a bureau under the Ministry of Heavy Industry, an entity also sometimes referred to as the Ministry of Machine Building.

Union.[14] In 1953, a naval agreement was signed with Moscow that provided not only for technical and financial assistance, but also for the transfer of finished vessels and the parts and equipment needed to upgrade Chinese yards. Not surprisingly, ship construction during this time concentrated on projects for the PLA Navy, which had established its own Shipbuilding Division shortly after 1949. Indeed, the navy also established its own enterprises for the research and production of various kinds of naval equipment.[15] It is also no coincidence that the PRC's early maritime efforts focused on the shipyard at Dalian (Port Arthur) near the Lushun naval base, occupied by Soviet forces until 1955.[16]

Since domestic construction of merchant ships was slow at first, China began adding to its fleet in the mid-1950s by buying a few used ships each year from abroad. For the most part, however, China's need for ocean-going vessels was minimal in the 1950s. Until the Sino-Soviet split at the end of the decade, the Soviet Union was China's dominant trading partner, and, as a result, goods were exchanged almost exclusively by rail rather than by sea. Furthermore, the U.S.-led trade embargo on China, a result of the Korean War, prohibited China from using Chinese-flag ships for most of its non-Soviet foreign trade. Instead, China had little choice but to charter foreign-flag ships to carry its foreign trade.[17] For all these reasons, China's demand for merchant ships was not strong in the 1950s.

With Soviet help, China began to produce decent-sized merchant ships on a regular basis by the late 1950s. According to the U.S. Defense

---

[14] For a good overview of Soviet assistance, see *Dangdai Zhongguo de Chuanbo Gongye* (1992), p. 39–45. Indeed, the main objective for shipbuilding under the First Five-Year Plan was to transform the existing major yards in Shanghai, Guangzhou, Dalian, Wuhan, and Tianjin from facilities that were predominantly engaged in shiprepair into viable shipbuilding bases. Toward this end, the Plan also saw the establishment of ship research and design organizations. For more detail, see Hong (1982).

[15] Excellent background sources on China's naval programs include Lewis and Xue (1994), *Dangdai Zhongguo de Guofang Keji Shiye* (1992), and *Dangdai Zhongguo de Haijun* (1987).

[16] While the Dalian shipyard on Bohai Bay in Liaoning province was founded by the Qing government in 1898, it was controlled alternately by Japan and Russia for most of the pre-1949 period. A Sino-Soviet shipbuilding company was set up in 1952 at Dalian, in which Soviet ships were repaired in exchange for technical help and Soviet equipment to rebuild the yard. The agreement was dissolved when Soviet forces withdrew in 1955.

[17] To this end, the China National Chartering Corporation (Zhongzu or Sinochart) and the China National Foreign Transportation Corporation (Zhongwaiyun or Sinotrans) were formed in 1951, as was the Chinese-Polish Joint Stock Shipping Company (Chipolbrok).

Intelligence Agency, China was launching approximately ten merchant ships per year by 1960.[18] Indeed, accounts from China also confirm that it was capable by this time of building significant oceangoing vessels, such as the *Yuejin* ([Great] Leap Forward) and the *Hongqi* (Red Flag), each well in excess of 10,000 deadweight tons.[19] The most celebrated arrival, however, was the legendary *Dongfeng* (East Wind), a 16,000-deadweight-ton vessel launched in 1960, complete with a claim that it was manufactured exclusively with Chinese designs, equipment, and materials.[20]

With the Sino-Soviet split in 1960, however, China's shipbuilding industry suffered tremendously. As was the case with so many Chinese industries, the withdrawal of Soviet aid forced a thorough rethinking of the policies for (and organizational structure of) the shipping and shipbuilding industries. In 1960, the Shipbuilding Industry Bureau was moved to a newly created Third Ministry; Beijing also began sending shipyard managers to Western Europe for study in lieu of the expertise formerly provided by Moscow. Despite these efforts, however, merchant ship production fell from about ten ships per year in 1959 and 1960 to two ships in 1961, one ship in 1962, and none at all in 1963.[21] (It was during this period, in fact, that COSCO was established under the Ministry of Communications as the national shipping company responsible for carrying China's foreign trade.)[22] In 1963, the Shipbuilding Industry Bureau was hived off from the Third Ministry to become a separate, self-standing ministry – the Sixth Ministry of Machine Building – in an effort to coordinate naval and merchant ship construction, each of which was experiencing a crisis in its development.[23]

---

[18] U.S. Defense Intelligence Agency, *Defense Intelligence Digest*, June 1967, p. 13, cited in Muller (1983), pp. 117–118.

[19] *Dangdai Zhongguo de Haiyang Shiye* (1985), p. 285.

[20] *FBIS Daily Report-China*, 24 September 1976, p. G1, and *FBIS Daily Report-China* 27 September 1976, p. G7.

[21] U.S. Defense Intelligence Agency, *Defense Intelligence Digest*, June 1967, p. 13, cited in Muller (1983), pp. 117–118.

[22] Formed in 1961 to increase China's independence in foreign trade and to reduce the substantial costs of foreign chartering, COSCO augmented its fleet mainly through purchases on the second-hand market. Since Chinese-flag ships were only permitted in about a dozen foreign ports (scattered mostly among developing countries in Africa and Asia) in the early 1960s, however, China found it still had to rely extensively on chartering foreign ships. As a second-best solution, the Ministry of Communications set up the Ocean Tramping Company and Yick Fung Shipping Company as front companies in Hong Kong to carry China's goods under so-called flags of convenience. In this way, China was able to gain greater control over the transportation of its foreign trade.

[23] For a full accounting of this change in organizational structure, as well as many others that followed, see Lewis and Xue (1994), especially pp. 81–83.

By all accounts, the new Sixth Ministry put relatively little emphasis on merchant ship production in the early 1960s. The policy implemented by its first minister, Fang Qiang, a vice-admiral in the navy and a close political associate of President Liu Shaoqi, was clearly designed to meet military needs first and foremost, at least in part because civilian needs could be met by buying and chartering ships abroad. Chinese and Western accounts agree that Liu was the central figure behind the Ministry's shipbuilding policy throughout the early 1960s; thus, his lack of support for an active merchant shipbuilding program was critical. Indeed, it was Liu who is said to have observed: "Building a ship is not as good as buying one and buying one is not as good as chartering one."[24]

The shipbuilding industry suffered considerable, although intermittent, disruption during the Cultural Revolution (1966–1976). In fact, Chinese shipyards at times served as key battlegrounds in the struggle for power between the "radical" and "moderate" factions within the Communist Party. Because Liu's imprimatur was so clear on China's shipbuilding policy, Fang Qiang and the Sixth Ministry itself were quickly targeted by leftist radicals critical of Liu. By 1967, Fang had been purged along with Liu, and many of China's shipyards were paralyzed by political extremism. At several points, the infamous Gang of Four was apparently able to bring most of the main Shanghai yards under their control, reportedly even using the Zhonghua yard as a makeshift political prison.[25] Ultimately, the navy was forced to intervene to restore order at several yards since work there had ceased altogether, leaving both the construction of new ships and critical repair projects unfinished. According to John Lewis and Xue Litai, the navy in fact took control of the Sixth Ministry in 1967, as well as all research institutes and other related marine production facilities.[26] In 1969, two new links in the administrative chain were created above the Sixth Ministry: a Shipbuilding Industry Leading Group formed under Li Zuopeng, first political commissar of the navy, and a National Defense Industry Leading Group – which reported directly to the Central Military Commission (rather than the State Council) – to oversee ordnance, aviation, and telecommunications as well as shipbuilding.[27]

---

[24] Accurate or not, this statement is still widely quoted and has been consistently attributed to Liu. See, for instance, *FBIS Daily Report-China*, 5 March 1975, pp. G7–8. Regardless of whether Liu actually said this, no Chinese or Western analyst has suggested that his policy was substantially different from the spirit of this statement.

[25] *FBIS Daily Report-China*, 15 November 1977, pp. G7–8.

[26] Lewis and Xue (1994), p. 83.   [27] Ibid, pp. 81–88.

By 1970, the political situation in the industry had improved some-what, although the yards remained occasional targets for the radicals, again particularly in Shanghai, but also in Dalian and elsewhere. Zhou Enlai had made an important speech in 1970 in which he renewed his earlier call for the development of China's merchant fleet and an end to foreign chartering. In order that domestic yards could meet more of China's need for ships, he instructed that the number of 10,000-deadweight-ton berths be expanded considerably.[28] Consequently, China began to import foreign ship technology, piecemeal at first and then eventually in entire units. Not surprisingly, domestic production was still inadequate to meet China's immediate shipping needs – particularly given the long-term expansion of foreign trade that began in the early 1970s. Acknowledging the necessity of importing vessels, the State Council in 1974 reaffirmed the earlier policy of buying ships abroad whenever "favorable market conditions" existed.

After a brief respite in the early 1970s, the shipbuilding industry again became a focal point of intense political struggle during the final years of the Cultural Revolution. By the summer of 1974, the Gang of Four had resumed the offensive, elevating the maiden voyage of the Chinese-built *Fengqing* to a test of political correctness and national loyalty. The cargo ship's triumphant voyage to Europe was seized by radicals as evidence that the policy of buying ships abroad was not only unnecessary, but indeed tantamount to "worshipping things foreign" and a "national betrayal." According to Chinese press accounts, Jiang Qing (Mao's wife and a key member of the Gang of Four) was herself instrumental in using the *Fengqing* case to attack Premier Zhou.[29]

After Zhou's death in January 1976, Zhang Chunqiao led the Gang of Four in using its stronghold in the shipbuilding industry to engineer a political controversy over the purchase of the *Gengxin*, a 14,000-deadweight-ton passenger-cargo vessel bought for training purposes at a price barely above the scrap-metal rate. Referring to this ship as a "discarded yacht" bought to ferry privileged cadres around on pleasure cruises, the Gang of Four put the dilapidated vessel on display in Shang-hai and used it as a pretext for attacking the policies of Deng Xiaoping, Zhou's protégé and their primary political rival.[30]

---

[28] *China Machinery Industries Yearbook* (1991), p. 71.
[29] *FBIS Daily Report-China*, 15 November 1977, pp. G7–8.
[30] *FBIS Daily Report-China*, 27 January 1977, p. G5.

Although Mao's death in September 1976 – followed soon thereafter by the purge of the Gang of Four itself – greatly reduced elite support for radicalism, sporadic political incidents continued at some yards in Shanghai, at least until a navy officer, Su Zhenhua, was appointed that city's mayor later in the year.[31] Following the fall of the Gang of Four, the China Corporation of Shipbuilding Industry (CCSI) was formed in 1977 under the auspices of the Sixth Ministry of Machine Building in an attempt to introduce more organizational coherence into the industry, especially with respect to its incipient foreign economic relations. All told, however, responsibility for China's major yards in the period after the Cultural Revolution became, by all accounts, increasingly contested and fragmented among the Sixth Ministry, the navy, the Ministry of Communications, and various provinces and municipalities. The administrative future of the industry was very much in doubt.

REORGANIZING PRODUCTION FOR THE FUTURE:
THE CREATION OF THE CHINA STATE
SHIPBUILDING CORPORATION

As far as formal institutional change is concerned, the creation of CSSC in May 1982 is, without question, the most important single effort by the central leadership to reorganize China's shipbuilding industry in the post-Mao period. With this move, the Sixth Ministry of Machine Building was abolished and CSSC assumed total control of its shipyards, marine institutes, and related equipment factories. In addition, authority over additional shipbuilding facilities was transferred to CSSC from both the Ministry of Communications and various municipal and provincial governments. As a result, CSSC presided over virtually all significant civilian shipbuilding capacity in China: 26 shipyards, 66 factories and equipment plants, 33 research and development units, and 3 institutions of higher education. The total workforce in 1982 was conservatively estimated at 300,000.

One important question raised by the creation of CSSC was how the relationship between civilian and military production would be handled. Over the first three decades of the PRC's existence, civil-military relations in the shipbuilding industry had taken several different forms. On the one hand, the Chinese shipbuilding industry has always been

---

[31] *FBIS Daily Report-China*, 13 April 1977, p. E3.

characterized by a split between civil and military production. Although the Shipbuilding Industry Bureau worked closely with the navy for much of the 1950s, even then there was a division of labor. The navy, for example, had a parallel set of administrative offices, including its own shiprepair and shipbuilding department and various research and technical institutes. Except for periods when authority over civilian and military construction was formally consolidated into a single organization, such as when the Sixth Ministry of Machine Building was originally created in 1963, the structure of the shipbuilding industry has always been at least partially bifurcated into merchant and naval production.

While the line has often been blurred, the structure of China's defense establishment is divided into two sides: the ministries and corporations ("defense industries") under the direction of the State Council; and PLA factories and other organizations ("military industries") under the direction of the Central Military Commission.[32] Shipbuilding, represented since 1982 by CSSC, is one of six defense industries under the direction of the State Council. (The others are the nuclear, ordnance, aviation, space, and electronics industries.) Entities such as CSSC – and CSSC in particular – have evolved from traditional machine-building ministries heavily influenced by the military to a wide array of predominantly civilian-run, profit-seeking corporations. (Indeed, as was widely reported, many PLA-owned industries were themselves focused significantly on commercial production until the military was ordered to divest itself of its commercial operations in July 1998.)[33] While CSSC's shipyards have always engaged in some naval construction, and are responsible in fact for most of the major ship projects undertaken in China, they should not be mistaken for the PLA's yards – of which several remained in the 1990s – that operate under the authority of the Central Military Commission.[34]

---

[32] For an excellent overview of China's defense establishment, see Frankenstein (1997).

[33] The navy, for instance, has its own conglomerate related to maritime activities, the China Songhai Industrial and Commercial Corporation. At this writing, it remains unclear how successful efforts have been to achieve the withdrawal of the PLA from its commercial activities.

[34] Several informants referred generically to the "PLA yards" during interviews, but no details were offered. Since the subject of these interviews was civilian shipbuilding, often with the understanding that military construction was too controversial for discussion, I did not press for further information. Two published reports in the 1990s also mentioned naval shipyards. According to one press account in Hong Kong, a company named "Reliable Shipbuilders" was set up in 1992 in Hong Kong to represent the 13 shipyards belonging to the navy, which had reportedly been given permission in 1989 to dedicate 50 percent of their facilities for commercial activities. The Hong Kong company claimed

Officially, CSSC is *classified* as a ministerial-level corporation under the authority of the State Council. More importantly, however, CSSC does, from all indications, actually *operate* as a state-run corporation independent of direct military control. In short, CSSC's yards are not military yards per se. Indeed, responsibility for the standardization and certification of military and civilian ships has long been administratively separate.[35] Moreover, while virtually all of CSSC's major yards have undertaken naval construction from time to time – including Dalian, Jiangnan, Hudong, and Guangzhou – the vast majority of work for every yard is civilian construction.

While CSSC obviously works closely with the PLA in the production of warships, to the point where the navy maintains representative offices in several of CSSC's major yards, the financial relationship was designed in 1982 to be arms-length.[36] While it is hard to evaluate such claims, the most comprehensive report published in China on the shipbuilding industry reports that civilian and military projects have indeed been subject to separate accounting since CSSC was created.[37] Interviews were not particularly revealing on this issue, but it appears that work done for the military since the mid-1980s has been handled on a separate basis from CSSC's commercial work on merchant ships for foreign and domestic clients. In fact, there is little evidence that CSSC has enjoyed preferential access to energy, raw materials, funding, or any other kind of advantage due to its role in naval construction. Quite to the contrary, CSSC's predicament in the 1980s and 1990s – one defined largely by having to fend for itself in an era of intense competition outside China and defense conversion within China – makes the apparent lack of governmental largesse particularly striking.

that the naval yards had between 30 and 100 years of experience, thereby further indicating that a division of existing facilities between civilian and military construction had persisted with the creation of CSSC. For more detail, see *SCMP* (Freight & Shipping Post), 13 July 1992, p. 10. The other published reference, also to "13 naval yards," appeared in Nagatsuka (1995), p. 35.

[35] Naval ships are overseen by the National Defense Science Commission while civilian ships are handled by CSSC itself; *Dangdai Zhongguo de Chuanbo Gongye* (1992), pp. 633–637.

[36] In fact, the contractual relationship also extends to design and engineering work conducted by CSSC research institutes. While the navy has its own departments as well, CSSC entities continue to complete work for the navy on a contract basis. In the mid-1980s, the national defense research budget was formally divided between military and civilian agencies, with only 30 percent of the budget given to CSSC for basic research and development. The remaining 70 percent was allocated to the navy; ibid, pp. 628–631.

[37] Ibid, pp. 605–608.

Indeed, CSSC's independence from military control is perhaps best understood within the context of defense conversion in post-Mao China. Positioned last among Deng's Four Modernizations, defense was not a priority in the late 1970s and early 1980s. Moreover, shipbuilding was always something of a laggard among defense industries. According to some accounts, in fact, declining orders for naval ships contributed significantly to the decision in 1982 to reorganize shipbuilding assets (shipyards, repair facilities, equipment factories, and research institutes) into a commercial entity – CSSC – that could address civilian construction more efficiently.[38] As early as 1981, civilian output already accounted for more than 60 percent of total output in the shipbuilding industry. Given their overall military priorities, Chinese decision-makers may have been able to foresee that civilian output would reach 80–90 percent by the late 1980s.[39] In this sense, shipbuilding was fairly unique among defense-related industries. After all, the reorganization of China's shipyards into a ministry-like corporation preceded the transformation of other defense industries into similar corporations by a full decade. Unlike the other numbered ministries in the defense sector, for which oversight was consolidated into the newly formed Commission of Science, Technology, and Industry for National Defense in 1982, the Sixth Ministry was simultaneously transformed into CSSC *and* placed under the authority of the State Council. Furthermore, shipbuilding was the only sector *not* to undergo subsequent change during later rounds of defense industry reorganization.[40]

CSSC: A MODEL FOR INSTITUTIONAL REFORM IN CHINESE INDUSTRY?

Given China's considerable success in entering the international market for new ships during the 1980s, the creation of CSSC is often cited as the beginning of China's ascent toward the upper echelon in international shipbuilding. In fact, CSSC has not been shy in taking credit for China's success in exporting ships. As discussed in the next section, however, deeper participation in the world market was not part of CSSC's master

---

[38] Ibid, pp. 613–614.

[39] Shares of civilian output in total output for the shipbuilding industry were found in Folta (1992), pp. 132, 255.

[40] Subsequent changes in other sectors included the 1988 ministerial regrouping and 1993 corporatization initiative. For a comprehensive discussion of the reorganization experiences of individual defense industries, see Frankenstein (1997), especially p. 11.

plan. Furthermore, there is nothing to indicate that the creation of CSSC was motivated by concerns over the ability to export. Indeed, ship exports had been quite satisfactory prior to the creation of CSSC, with Chinese yards benefiting handsomely from the short-lived but healthy boom in world orders in the 1979–1981 period. As it turns out, China's export orderbook in the early 1980s consisted precisely of the bulk carriers and other basic ship types that industry officials had planned to export. From all indications, in fact, CSSC was established to refocus the industry toward the substantial domestic challenge of meeting China's own commercial maritime needs, especially in light of defense conversion.[41]

According to press reports at the time of CSSC's creation, the industry's main problems involved bureaucratic rivalry, duplication of effort among units, and an overall lack of coordination in research, design, production, and the import of foreign technology. Problems in export were barely mentioned.[42] In fact, CSSC was established as part of a sweeping initiative in which the State Council reduced 52 ministries and commissions to 39 new or restructured entities in 1982. In addition to CSSC, other industrial corporations – e.g., the China National Automobile Industry Corporation – were also established to "help overcome the defects of 'government-run enterprises' by improving economic returns and running enterprises better."[43] As the official *Xinhua* news agency explained it, "China's state shipbuilding industry is [the] latest target of economic reorganization and administrative streamlining."[44] Taken in this context, CSSC's creation had little to do with the specific needs of the shipbuilding industry, especially with respect to exports.

Just as CSSC was not created mainly with exporting in mind, neither did it represent any kind of model for institutional reform. For all the official rhetoric about CSSC and other industrial corporations operating as economic entities, evidence from interviews and press reports overwhelmingly suggests that CSSC actually operated like a reconstituted ministry, albeit one with more rationalized control over the country's shipbuilding facilities. Although CSSC was technically a "corporation" rather than a "ministry," it still directed the industry largely by the traditional means of central control over production planning and the

---

[41] See, for example, *Asian Shipping* (July 1981), p. 39.
[42] See, for example, the front-page editorial in *Renmin Ribao* (*The People's Daily*) in *FBIS Daily Report-China*, 12 May 1982, pp. K4–5.
[43] Ibid, p. K5.   [44] *FBIS Daily Report-China*, 6 May 1982, p. K5.

distribution of inputs and outputs. In fact, this seems to have been by design, as Beijing's objective was not to transform the basic economic system but simply to place all the main shipbuilding facilities under a single jurisdiction for the purpose of improving the industry's performance.

As a commercial entity, CSSC was supposed to engage in independent financial accounting at various levels: the central corporation (CSSC Beijing), the regional corporations, and the individual yards themselves. From all indications, this plan was never fully implemented.[45] More broadly, all of my informants outside the CSSC apparatus – including foreign shipowners who had ships built in China, international bankers who had arranged financing for ships built in China, members of the foreign maritime press, and surveyors for the international classification societies who certify that Chinese-built ships meet international standards – confirmed the image of CSSC as a "corporation" acting like a ministry for most or all of the 1980s. Indeed, even interviews with industry officials cast doubt on certain supposed differences between CSSC and its predecessors.

Truth be told, CSSC's creation actually reflected the larger trend toward recentralization and re-regulation that prevailed in many industries early in the post-Mao period. In its multiseries profile of the newly established CSSC, *Business China* reported that "CSSC has a head office [CSSC Beijing], local branches [regional corporations], and grassroots enterprises [the yards and factories]. Management's authority over local branches and grassroots enterprises is to expand gradually."[46] In other words, the design was to *empower* CSSC Beijing vis-à-vis lower-level units. In fact, the regional corporations (e.g., the Shanghai Shipbuilding Corporation) were entirely new entities formed with the singular purpose of facilitating CSSC's "macromanagement" of the shipbuilding industry.[47]

In this way, the creation of CSSC reflects what Janos Kornai has called the "perfection tendency" in socialist states. While Chinese leaders such

---

[45] For examples of how CSSC initially failed to live up to claims that it represented a new kind of economic enterprise, see Moore (1997), pp. 223–224.

[46] *Business China*, 30 March 1983, p. 48. In fact, the trend prior to CSSC's creation had actually been toward greater decentralization. According to press reports, shipyards were actually increasing their control over production and finances in the final years of the Sixth Ministry and CCSI, its trading arm. For example, yards apparently had at least some freedom to accept export contracts on their own, as well as through the national foreign trade corporation; *Asian Shipping* (July 1981), p. 27.

[47] *ZGHY* 9:4 (Winter 1991), p. 69.

as former State Councilor and Vice-Premier Bo Yibo hailed CSSC's creation as part of an "effort to restructure the management system of China's industry" these so-called reforms entailed only superficial changes, leaving the essence of the command economy unchanged.[48] As described by Kornai, "Although an impression of genuine change is conveyed by official declarations, regulations, and campaigns, the classical system in fact remains unaffected in any of its basic features."[49]

Indeed, the entire reorganization of the Chinese shipbuilding industry in 1982 resonates well with Kornai's description of how socialist states attempt to "perfect" the means of control.[50] First, Kornai identifies the recurrent tendency of these regimes to assign the task of improving economic performance to a new or revamped state institution, such as CSSC. Second, despite the impression of change, direct bureaucratic control remains the basic coordinator of economic production. Kornai describes how this control is often actually *strengthened* through the reorganization process itself, as was clearly the case with CSSC. Third, he notes a pattern in which repeated reorganization campaigns shift the policy emphasis back and forth between territorial and functional principles of control – another tendency present with the creation of CSSC – as territorial authority gave way to functional authority. Fourth, Kornai describes how bureaucratic reorganization is often achieved by alternately (or even simultaneously) splitting up and merging authority. In the case of CSSC, both tendencies were present. On the one hand, authority over the civilian shipbuilding industry, which previously had been fragmented among a variety of institutions, was successfully merged under the CSSC umbrella. Finally, while one might not reasonably expect a complete turnover of leadership personnel, even in an industry reorganization like that which created CSSC, the continuity of industry officials in high positions across this major institutional reconfiguration suggests that the creation of CSSC did, in fact, represent what Kornai has called "spurious reform."[51]

---

[48] For Bo Yibo's comments on CSSC, see *FBIS Daily Report-China*, 6 May 1982, p. K6.

[49] Kornai (1992), p. 396.   [50] Ibid, pp. 396–399.

[51] For example, the first Chairman of CSSC was Chai Shufan, who had been the Minister of the Sixth Ministry of Machine Building at the time it was abolished. Chai was also a former Vice-Minister of Foreign Trade and a former Vice-Minister on the State Planning Commission. The first President and General Manager of CSSC was Feng Zhi, who had been the Vice-Minister of the Sixth Ministry under Chai.

CSSC AND CHINA'S EXPORT SUCCESS: FARSIGHTED ARCHITECT OR UNWITTING BENEFICIARY?

Reviewing its impressive record in the world market, CSSC proudly made the following declaration on the occasion of its tenth anniversary in 1992: "In the past ten years, China has made ship export its priority."[52] While this statement is not entirely disingenuous – the industry did turn to export orders when COSCO's ship orders began flowing overseas in large numbers – it does add a twist of revisionism when CSSC's original policy aims are considered. From the late 1970s through the mid-1980s (i.e., both before and after the creation of CSSC), shipbuilding officials consistently characterized the industry's policy as: "Rely on the domestic market while promoting exports, focus on shipbuilding while diversifying production" (*guonei weizhu, jiji chukou, chuanbo weizhu, duozhong jingying*).[53] While building for export was permitted, and even encouraged with certain restrictions, CSSC clearly intended to concentrate on the construction of domestic ships, both by preference and out of necessity. Similarly, while diversification was also to be pursued as a general industrial goal, CSSC's focus was unmistakably on ship production.

While CSSC understandably wanted the industry's record to appear consistent with its original strategy, a review of its early aims reveals serious distortions in its later rhetoric. In fact, virtually none of the most far-reaching developments in the industry – including the growing emphasis on exports – came about by design. If anything, change in the shipbuilding industry came about *in spite* of CSSC's original plans. For example, the shift in the mid-1980s toward the export of sophisticated vessels such as car carriers, refrigerated containerships, and product-chemical tankers completely contradicted CSSC's initial policy, which unambiguously called for the export of the basic bulk carriers and oil tankers already built by Chinese yards for domestic use. When CCSI had published its *Ships Export Catalogue* in 1980, it indicated no interest in building new ship types, especially not according to the individual specifications of prospective buyers.[54] In fact, it simply listed the types of

---

[52] *ZGHY* 10:2 (Summer 1992), p. 45.

[53] See, for example, *ZGJXDZGYNJ* (1986), p. 239, and an interview with Hu Chuanzhi, Managing Director of CSSC, in *ZGHY* 4:2 (Summer 1986), p. 15.

[54] The official list of "ships offered for export" was reprinted in Dori Jones, "China's Shipbuilding Industry," *CBR* (January/February 1981), pp. 44–45.

vessels manufactured by its main shipyards. Indeed, virtually all of China's ship exports in the early 1980s used Chinese design and technology, including a series of 27,000-deadweight-ton bulk carriers for which contracts were signed prior to the creation of CSSC in 1982. While Japanese or European engines were occasionally imported for use on export ships, the objective was clearly to maximize the Chinese-made content of the vessels.

This basic strategy, in which China sought to export the types of ships it already produced, was continued with no evident change after CSSC was created in May 1982. In its multiseries profile of China's shipbuilding industry, *Business China* reported that "CSSC says it handles the following types of business: building and exporting dry cargo ships and oil tankers up to 100,000 deadweight tons and various engineering vessels."[55] Another article, which appeared in the *China Business Review* later in 1983, told how "recent CSSC catalogues continue to describe ships built for Chinese owners that have never been ordered abroad. . . . CSSC offerings include the familiar 27,000-ton and 36,000-ton bulk carriers. . . ."[56] While some of this behavior may have been due to a lack of marketing experience, CSSC also clearly intended to participate in the world market strictly on its own terms.

Put in the context of this evidence, CSSC's attempt to recast its early foray into the world market as part of a concerted "export drive" rings hollow. In reality, China's success in exporting basic ships in the early 1980s marked not a radical policy change, but rather the fruition of a modest policy initiative dating back to 1975, when China first expressed an interest in entering the world shipbuilding market at the Canton (Guangzhou) Trade Fair.[57] Although China did not win any significant export orders until the 1980–1981 boom in the world market, it exported its first two ships in 1977 and 1978.[58]

The point here is quite simple: Until the recession in the world shipbuilding industry in the mid-1980s, China pursued a consistent policy of supplementing domestic newbuildings with the occasional export order. Moreover, these exports were ships that Chinese yards could already produce with a reasonably high level of local content. From all indications, there was little enthusiasm for taking on unfamiliar projects,

[55] *Business China*, 9 February 1983, p. 24.
[56] Charles Dragonette, "Ship Exports," *CBR* (July/August 1983), p. 36.
[57] United States Central Intelligence Agency (1976), p. 1.
[58] Computer printout supplied by CSSC.

especially if they would require a large percentage of foreign components or substantial foreign oversight of the production process.

From the time of Zhou Enlai's speech in 1970, in which he called for reduced reliance on chartered vessels in carrying China's foreign trade, it has always been an officially stated goal for Chinese yards to meet an increasing share of the country's maritime needs. In fact, even the disruptions orchestrated by the Gang of Four at China's leading shipyards were designed – ostensibly, at least – to defend the industry and highlight its importance. While exports had their place, they were not envisioned as the driving force behind the industry's restructuring. Given the rapid expansion of China's foreign trade, to say nothing of the long lead-time and tremendous expense necessary to construct new shipbuilding facilities, it was a foregone conclusion that China would have to continue buying ships overseas if it was to carry the same percentage of its foreign trade as in the past. There is no evidence, however, of any master plan that called for such extensive purchases abroad that domestic yards would ultimately be left so dependent on exports.

Obligatory rhetoric about reform and opening to the outside world notwithstanding, there was absolutely no indication that either the central leadership or CSSC itself ever intended for the shipbuilding industry to become so fully integrated into the world market.[59] Instead, the idea was for the industry to benefit from selective, controlled exposure to the international industry. Even if some Chinese officials did harbor a long-term ambition for CSSC to become a global shipbuilding power like Japan and South Korea, there was certainly no strategy for China to enter the world market in such a whirlwind fashion, rising from a virtual nonexporter to a country in which more than half of all ship production was consistently exported less than a decade later.[60]

Just as CSSC had never planned to become so dependent on export orders, neither did it intend originally for the importation of ship designs, engines, marine accessories, and even raw materials (e.g., high-tensile steel) to play such an important role in the construction of ships for

[59] On the possibility that CSSC policy statements from the early 1980s did not reflect the true intentions of industry officials, see Moore (1997), pp. 238–240.

[60] Even in 1986, when CSSC's orderbook was severely depleted in the midst of the industry's crisis, its managing director had reiterated the policy of building mainly for the domestic market, indicating a target of only 25 to 33 percent of ship production for export during the Seventh Five-Year Plan (1986–90). See the interview with Hu Chuanzhi in *ZGHY* 4:2 (Summer 1986), p. 97. The same figures were also reported in *Asian Shipping* (July 1986), p. 13.

foreign owners. CSSC officials had always stressed their desire to build ships, even those for export, using a high content of Chinese-made components. While China's shipbuilding industry had been importing foreign technology since the mid-1970s, these efforts were consistent with a policy of limited engagement in the world market. Thus, while the selective import of foreign technology and judicious export of ships allowed the industry to earn foreign exchange and benefit from valuable exposure to international shipbuilding production, its strategy for development never centered on rapid integration into the world market.

Given China's widely acknowledged promise as a major shipbuilding power, it is somewhat puzzling that CSSC officials would embrace a development strategy that seemingly inhibited the industry from realizing its full potential. Why, for example, pursue a policy of exporting only basic ships when orders could probably also be secured (albeit on a discount basis) for more sophisticated, higher value-added vessels? Why settle for limited contact with the global industry when deeper integration could possibly propel China toward the leading ranks of shipbuilding nations? The main reason, according to interviews, was that CSSC resisted any erosion of its control. Specifically, CSSC had no intention of becoming a ship assembler within the international division of labor, one answerable to foreign partners and vulnerable to world forces beyond its control. Since shipbuilding was a large, state-owned industry concentrated in key urban areas such as Shanghai, the central leadership undoubtedly shared these concerns as well. As a Hong Kong shipowner with close ties to CSSC put it succinctly: "State industries like shipbuilding have always been viewed as a mainstay of the socialist economy."

Furthermore, CSSC officials apparently believed that a policy of modified import-substitution would in fact produce a stronger, more independent Chinese industry than an externally oriented development strategy. Specifically, non-PRC informants debunked the notion that CSSC officials were actually closet reformers who preferred greater integration into the world industry but were forced – likely for reasons of political prudence – to adopt a more muted "domestic first, export second" philosophy. From all indications, CSSC was a fairly typical state-run dinosaur in the early 1980s. Finally, it is also possible that the industry's legacy of radicalism from the Cultural Revolution contributed to CSSC's lack of enthusiasm for greater participation in the world market.

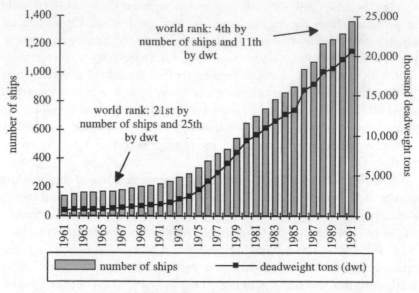

Figure 7.3. China's merchant fleet. *Source: Merchant Fleets of the World,* various years.

CSSC'S STRATEGY FOR THE SHIPBUILDING INDUSTRY: A CREDIBLE PLAN?

Ultimately, the best measure of CSSC's intentions may be the feasibility of its policies. Given the overall situation confronting the industry, were the policies put forth by CSSC basically credible? One issue here concerns the viability of a domestic-first policy. Was it realistic that CSSC concentrate on production for the home market? As Figure 7.3 shows, the early 1980s were a period of vigorous fleet expansion in China, as COSCO tried to keep pace with the continued expansion of China's foreign trade. While COSCO's newbuilding program had been substantial since the 1970s, a particularly ambitious expansion was scheduled to start with the Sixth Five-Year Plan (1981–85), a development that made CSSC's domestic-first policy seem eminently reasonable.[61]

Even if there was sufficient demand, there was also the issue of whether China could rely on its existing technological base and other resources to meet a substantial portion of its need for merchant vessels. In other words, was the shipbuilding industry really capable of pursuing

---

[61] *ZGHY* 3:4 (Winter 1985), p. 49. See also *FEER*, 16 February 1984, p. 35.

a domestic-first policy? While certain vessels required by COSCO may have called for specialized skills unavailable in China, the vast majority of new ships needed for the Chinese fleet were well within the capability of CSSC's yards, especially since China's greatest shipping need in the early 1980s was bulk carriers to carry grain imports. In fact, a detailed breakdown of COSCO's fleet published in 1991 by the international maritime journal *Shipping World & Shipbuilder* revealed that 425 of its 620 ships (71 percent) were bulk carriers, general cargo ships, or tankers; that is, basic vessels well within CSSC's capability.[62] While it is true that a sizable portion of China's fleet expansion in the 1980s involved more sophisticated vessels such as containerships, many of these orders were actually placed *after* CSSC began constructing these ships itself. Moreover, even if none of these higher-end orders had been placed at home, there still should have been plenty of lower-end domestic work for China's yards. In fact, Chinese and foreign maritime observers had always expressed the *opposite* concern: namely, that large domestic requirements would overtax China's newbuilding capacity.

Although the development of China's shipbuilding industry was slowed by the Sino-Soviet split and the political turbulence of the Cultural Revolution, these interruptions did not hamper the industry as much as might have been expected.[63] However inefficient, poorly managed, and technologically backward China's yards were, they could produce basic ships such as bulk carriers and tankers capable of meeting a significant portion of China's transportation needs.[64] In fact, the U.S. Central Intelligence Agency concluded in a 1976 study that "the past decade has shown a dramatic increase in China's [commercial] shipbuilding capabilities."[65] Specifically, the report found that progress in the construction of merchant vessels had far outpaced advances in other sectors of the machine-building industry; most notably, a variety of "major ships" were found to be in mass production in the 1970s after experimental production in the 1960s.

Another question about CSSC's intentions concerns the credibility of its insistence that exports – while welcome – were distinctly secondary to newbuildings for the domestic market. Were there not incentives –

---

[62] *SW&SB* (April 1991), p. 128.
[63] For more on the impact of politics on developments in China's maritime sector, see Moore (1997), pp. 253–258.
[64] For more detail on the specific capabilities of the Chinese industry at the end of the Mao era, see ibid, pp. 248–253.
[65] United States Central Intelligence Agency (1976), p. 1.

such as foreign exchange earnings and access to foreign technology – to privilege exports? First, CSSC already received payment in U.S. dollars for ships ordered by COSCO, thereby eliminating foreign exchange as a primary motivation for export. Indeed, by late 1985, even the provincially owned bureaus of maritime transport (BMTs) were required to pay CSSC half the cost of newbuildings in foreign exchange since they, too, had begun carrying some foreign trade.[66] In fact, even the opportunity to import various kinds of machinery and sign production licenses for foreign-designed engines was not a significant motivation for CSSC to take on export projects, since these same benefits were already allowed on some of its projects for COSCO.[67] In sum, two of the main institutional motivations for export – foreign exchange earnings and access to foreign technology – were largely if not completely absent. As a result, the apparent indifference to foreign versus domestic orders is understandable without even considering the legacy of self-reliance handed down from shipbuilding's experience during the Mao era or suspicions about intensive foreign contact in state-run industry more generally.

Finally, how credible was the industry's commitment to export mainly basic vessels, such as the bulk carriers and oil tankers China was already relatively experienced in building? First, as mentioned previously, this policy apparently did reflect the preference of industry officials: Foreign shipowners, marine engineers, bankers, surveyors, and other non-PRC informants all repeatedly commented on the general conservatism of industry officials and yard managers, particularly in the early 1980s.[68] Second, this policy was also quite feasible given the mini-boom in world demand for basic ships in the early 1980s (Figures 7.4 and 7.5), a time when ship prices reached their highest level in years (Figure 7.6). Even when the world market went sour by 1982, Chinese officials reportedly predicted a recovery by 1985, thereby obviating the need for any change in policy away from the focus on building basic ships for export.[69]

[66] For press reports on foreign exchange payments to CSSC by COSCO and BMTs, see *FEER*, 26 December 1985, p. 56, and *SBR* (February 1986), p. 83.

[67] *FEER*, 26 December 1985, p. 56.

[68] Even in the early 1990s, CSSC officials still expressed some caution and concern about Chinese yards accepting too many orders for sophisticated vessels. While there may be legitimate business reasons for this caution, it also likely reflects the persistence of a basic conservatism within shipbuilding circles (and state-run industry in general). For a press account consistent with this position, see *SBR* (July/August 1991), p. 71.

[69] *FEER*, 5 February 1982, p. 64.

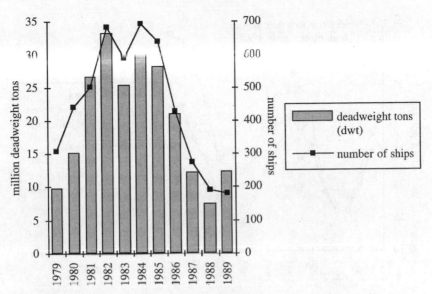

Figure 7.4. World orders for bulk carriers. *Source: New Ship Construction*, various years; *Review of Maritime Transport*, various years.

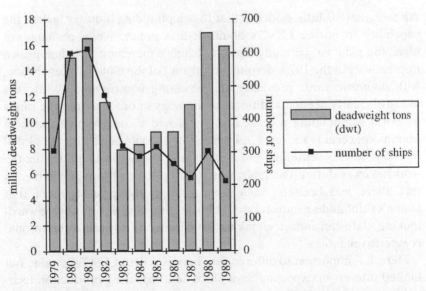

Figure 7.5. World orders for tankers. *Source: New Ship Construction*, various years; *Review of Maritime Transport*, various years.

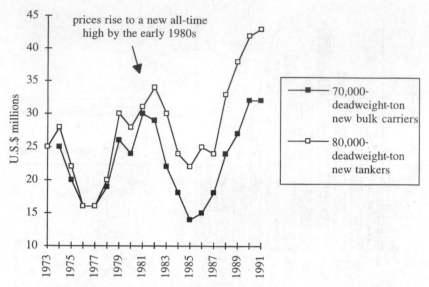

Figure 7.6. World ship prices. *Source: Review of Maritime Transport*, various years.

CONCLUSION

All told, there is little evidence that the shipbuilding industry lacked the capability to pursue CSSC's domestic-first policy. While perhaps not ideal, the plan was certainly feasible. China's merchant fleet had grown impressively in the 1970s despite the turmoil of the Cultural Revolution, with domestic yards providing an increasing contribution. While the industry clearly needed additional technology in order to join the ranks of world shipbuilding powers, CSSC still had a considerable range of options concerning the level of interaction it would seek with the global industry. In this sense, the industry's fast-growing participation in the world market during the 1980s was neither planned nor inevitable. In fact, there had been no indication early in the post-Mao era that China's shipbuilding industry would be anything but yet another inward-looking state-run industry making little progress toward international competitiveness.

Here, it is important to differentiate between, first, CSSC's genuine but limited interest in exporting basic ships and importing production technology to remedy the industry's relative backwardness, and, second, the swift entrance of the Chinese industry into the international division of labor, building ships in response to global market demands rather than in accordance with CSSC's own plans. As a result of the international shipbuilding crisis, which had profound effects on COSCO's pattern of ship procurement, China's yards became significantly integrated into the world market over a relatively short period, even though they remained under state ownership and received negligible amounts of foreign investment. Indeed, as subsequent chapters argue, it was only when chronic GSC deepened into severe GSC as the world ship market fell into recession during the mid-1980s that the process of reform, restructuring, and rationalization began to take form in the Chinese industry.

8

Dangerous Currents: Navigating Boom and Bust Cycles in International Shipbuilding

ONE of the most striking maritime developments in China during the 1980s was the substantially increased dependence on imported ships in expanding the country's merchant fleet (Figure 8.1). Given China's ability to build basic ships in series by the end of the 1970s, shipbuilding officials and foreign maritime observers had expected that Chinese yards would find themselves concentrating on the growing needs of the domestic merchant fleet. Given the tremendous expense of new ships (while falling, prices ranged from U.S. $20–100 million at the time, depending on the size and type of ship), it was doubly surprising that China began to rely increasingly on the purchase of new, rather than second-hand, ships in the world market (Figure 8.2).

Why did COSCO place orders overseas for ships that CSSC's yards were able to produce at home? Indeed, only certain orders for high-tech ships can be explained simply by a lack of capability in China. This puzzle, central to the development of China's shipping and shipbuilding industries, has gone largely unanswered. Commenting on China's imports and exports of cargo ships in 1986, Irwin Heine, an internationally renowned maritime observer, declared that "it is a curious dichotomy in China's shipbuilding policy that CSSC exports the types of ships COSCO needs and [COSCO] will turn around and import the same types from foreign shipbuilders."[1]

---

[1] Heine (1989), p. 48.

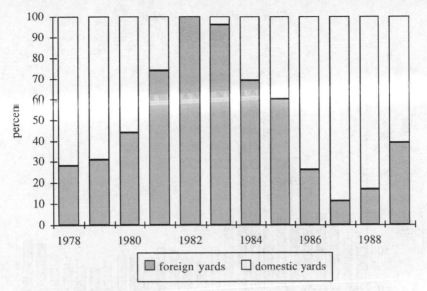

Figure 8.1. New ship orders for the Chinese fleet. Based on the overall size of
the Chinese fleet, the data contained in this series appear to understate the
volume of China's annual new ship orders. That said, the data should still
be useful for tracking trends in the relative shares of foreign and
domestic orders for China's fleet. *Source*: Calculated from data in
New Ship Construction, various years.

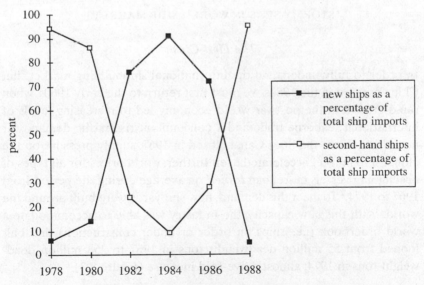

Figure 8.2. Ship imports for the Chinese fleet. *Source*: *Almanac of China's
Foreign Economic Relations and Trade*, various years; *World Trade
Review and Outlook*, various issues.

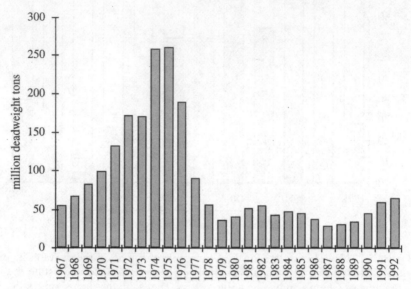

Figure 8.3. World orders for merchant ships. *Source*: *New Ship Construction*, various years; *Review of Maritime Transport*, various years.

STORMY SEAS IN WORLD SHIP MARKETS

The First Crash

In order to fully understand the international shipbuilding market that China entered in the 1980s, we must first return to the early 1960s, when rapid growth in the postwar world economy led to increasing levels of international seaborne trade and a concomitant rise in the demand for new ships. When the Suez Canal closed in 1967, supply pressure on the global ship market accelerated even further; world prices for all types of oceangoing vessels more than *tripled* on average during the period from 1967 to 1974.[2] To meet this demand, new shipyards were built around the world. With this new capacity, the industry was able to accommodate a world orderbook (i.e., ships on order or under construction) that ballooned from 55 million deadweight tons in 1967 to 258 million deadweight tons in 1974, almost a five-fold increase (Figure 8.3).

[2] Table 15, United Nations Conference on Trade and Development, *Review of Maritime Transport 1974* (Geneva: United Nations, 1975), p. 20.

After the world oil crisis in 1973, there was a global economic recession and the demand for new ships collapsed. To make matters worse, ships ordered prior to the oil crisis were actually launched and delivered *during* the recession, causing a massive tonnage oversupply in the international shipping market. Consequently, although international seaborne trade continued to grow modestly through the late 1970s, the era of huge year-on-year additions to the world merchant fleet were over. In short, the halcyon days in international shipbuilding were past.

With the ship market in a virtual free-fall, the world orderbook had by 1978 tumbled all the way back to its 1967 level, losing all the gains of the intervening decade. When the shipbuilding boom collapsed, Japan and Western Europe were left with new state-of-the-art facilities and an expanded workforce that quickly proved redundant. International capacity was estimated to be twice that necessary to meet world demand. Believing that the market would recover by the early 1980s, however, South Korea decided to proceed with its plan to enter the world shipbuilding market on a large scale, one that had been formulated prior to the crisis.

While it is not possible to offer a complete primer on the international shipping and shipbuilding industries here, several observations about the dynamics of these markets are in order. First, the market for ships can be quite volatile, especially due to unpredictable changes in the demand for global shipping services. The shipping industry is particularly sensitive to unanticipated political developments, such as oil embargoes or the closing of the Suez Canal, which can radically alter demand for certain types or sizes of ships or even paralyze the market altogether. Even when the world is relatively free of war and recession, however, basic supply and demand fundamentals can be rather elusive for the ship industry. Since ships are very expensive and take a long time to build – the period from contract to delivery is generally twelve to twenty-four months – there is a almost always a considerable lag between the first signs of undersupply in the market and the appearance of newly built ships. Consequently, an increased demand for shipping services has often evaporated by the time new ships actually hit the water.

When a glut of ships results, fierce competition among shippers drives down freight rates. When the oversupply of ships is truly massive, freight rates may not even be high enough to support new vessel prices that cover the cost of production to shipbuilders. This is exactly the recipe for disaster that the world shipbuilding industry faced in both the mid-1970s and the mid-1980s: the market value of new merchant ships to shipowners was often less than what it would cost shipbuilders to make them.

In this situation, shipbuilders are forced to choose between closing their yards or accepting whatever orders they can secure – and then only at prices below cost.[3] Even if shipbuilders do cut prices in order to keep their yards at least partially occupied, this strategy can only be a short-run response designed to ride out hard times. No shipbuilder, even the subsidiary of a large conglomerate with deep corporate pockets, can tolerate selling below cost indefinitely – at least not without substantial government support. Except for some fairly generic infant industry programs, the world shipbuilding industry had been relatively free of government intervention prior to the mid-1970s. With the steep decline in the world ship market, however, government assistance to shipbuilders increased markedly. Not surprisingly, most countries were unwilling to allow their politically important shipbuilding industries to lose market share.[4] Although there was some attrition, government subsidies at the national level only reinforced the basic problem of overcapacity in the global industry. In fact, by selling below cost, shipbuilders made the cycle of low ship prices and low freight rates all the more vicious.

After the first downturn in the mid-1970s, shipbuilders in Japan and Western Europe, the two main centers of production at the time, undertook restructuring programs to reduce capacity. The Japanese response actually consisted of two distinct initiatives. First, in 1976 the Ministry of Transportation set strict man-hour ceilings, a mechanism designed to encourage efficiency while reducing capacity.[5] By 1978, when it was clear that the decline in orders was not simply temporary, the Ministry adopted a more sweeping initiative in which the government became directly involved in managing the industry's rationalization.[6]

---

[3] Despite a glut of ships and beleaguered freight rates, some shipowners will still always be looking for new ships, either to acquire new tonnage at a bargain or if necessary to replace certain types or sizes of aging ships as they face retirement.

[4] In addition to the obvious national security implications of losing one's shipbuilding industry, many countries also view the industry as central to economic development, functioning not as a profit center as much as part of the national infrastructure. At a more mundane level, shipyards are also major employers in the politically important sector of heavy industry.

[5] Vogel (1985), p. 52.

[6] For an excellent description of the various measures taken, including the establishment of an antirecession cartel and the special purchase of vessels and idle yards by the government, see ibid, pp. 54–55.

In Western Europe, national governments had agreed to eliminate all shipbuilding subsidies by 1975 under the European Community's (EC) Third Directive on Shipbuilding Aid. When the boom years of the 1960s and early 1970s later gave way to recession, however, government assistance was extended, rather predictably, although some effort was also made to encourage capacity reductions. In the end, however, large-scale change was not deemed feasible, given the social and political consequences of possible collapse in the industry.

Overall, then, while employment in the international industry was reduced by as much as one-third with the closing or merger of yards in Japan and Western Europe, the persistence of subsidies ultimately slowed industry adjustment, leaving excess productive capacity after all. To make matters worse, the limited gains from rationalization were largely offset by South Korea's emergence as a major shipbuilder *after* the market's collapse. Despite efforts at structural adjustment during the mid-to-late 1970s, therefore, the global shipbuilding industry entered the 1980s arguably more vulnerable than ever to another downturn.

The Second Crash

While the international industry was mired in recession for nearly fifteen years (1975–1990), this crisis actually consisted of two distinct downturns interrupted by a short-lived recovery in the early 1980s. For a brief period starting in 1979, orders for new ships rebounded modestly and prices recovered even more strongly. After this brief recovery, world shipbuilding again plunged into industrial darkness. As a result of the second oil shock and the ensuing global economic recession, international seaborne trade in 1979 began its first sustained decline in decades (Figure 8.4).[7] Predictably, demand for shipping services followed suit, leaving the market for new ships paralyzed once more.

While the impact on the shipbuilding industry was, as usual, somewhat delayed, prices began an average 41 percent decline across all ship types in 1981–1982, and by the mid-1980s orders had plummeted to levels not seen in more than twenty years (as shown in Figure 7.6).[8] Indeed, the

---

[7] During the first shipbuilding crisis in the 1970s, growth in international seaborne trade had actually slowed rather than stopped altogether. Indeed, it declined for only a single year, 1975; United Nations Conference on Trade and Development, *Review of Maritime Transport* (Geneva: United Nations, annual), various years.

[8] This figure was calculated from data on nine leading ship types including bulk carriers, tankers, and freighters; ibid.

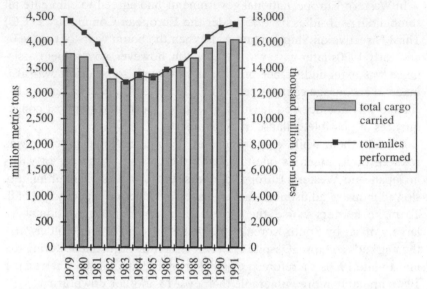

Figure 8.4. International seaborne trade. *Source*: *Review of Maritime Transport*, various years.

absolute volume of ship orders during this slump was ultimately even lower than the level reached during the crash in the 1970s, although it did not fall from as high an initial position. In 1986, a German shipping economist declared this second downturn to be "the lowest the [global] shipbuilding industry has experienced since the depression in the 1920s."[9] He further concluded that "more than 50 percent of world shipbuilding capacity is superfluous."[10] When this idle manufacturing capacity is taken together with the massive tonnage oversupply in the world fleet (Figure 8.5), the total picture suggests that the crisis in the mid-1980s was actually worse than the industry's recession in the 1970s.

With supply again far outstripping demand, it was not surprising that another price war erupted. Backed by government funds, yards simply cut prices in an attempt to "buy" new orders. And unlike before, this time the established industry leaders in Japan and Western Europe also felt

[9] *Asian Shipping* (December 1986), p. 14.

[10] Ibid. By another estimate, 40 percent of productive capacity in the world was unnecessary by 1985; *Asian Shipping* (November 1985), p. 35. Given their dubious record in the 1970s, it should be no surprise that governments the world over again engaged in a subsidy war.

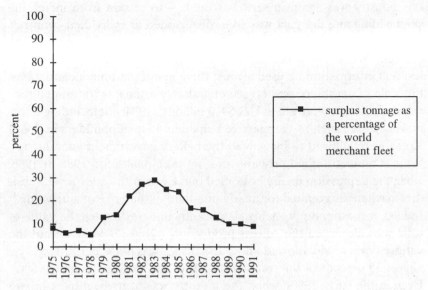

Figure 8.5. Tonnage oversupply in the world merchant fleet. *Source: Review of Maritime Transport*, various years.

increasing pressure from rising competitors in Taiwan, Brazil, and China – to say nothing of South Korea. In Western Europe, the EC adopted a two-pronged approach. First, it participated in negotiations sponsored by the Organisation for Economic Co-operation and Development (OECD) on capacity reductions, principally with Japan and South Korea. Second, it decided to continue providing subsidies as a means to protect the industry from Asian dominance. Overall, shipbuilding employment in Western Europe declined by 62 percent from 1975 to 1990 and available newbuilding capacity in West European yards decreased by 64 percent over the same period.[11] Despite these cutbacks, however, subsidies to help the remaining facilities actually increased, particularly during the height of the shipbuilding depression in the mid-1980s.

Once again, therefore, the major shipbuilding countries failed to stop themselves from synchronized self-destruction. Although they signed an agreement under OECD auspices in early 1983 – when it became clear

---

[11] United States International Trade Commission (1992), p. D9.

the industry was again in serious trouble – to refrain from increasing shipbuilding aid, the pact was soon disregarded as individual countries acted out of fear that they would soon lose their remaining share of the market.[12] While governments never disclosed the total value of their aid, lest that information be used against them in international negotiations, the scale of assistance was no secret: industry estimates for annual subsidies worldwide were put at U.S. $4–5 billion in 1984, not including informal assistance such as the massive bank debt that shipbuilders in South Korea were allowed to incur with the help of government guarantees.[13] What is more, total aid probably did not even peak until 1985 or 1986, when the depression finally bottomed out. Even at the 1984 level, subsidies may have accounted for nearly one-third of the price of a new ship.[14] Indeed, this estimate probably significantly underestimates the value of total subsidies since the "direct production subsidy" – only one of the various types of aid allowed under EC rules – was *alone* permitted to be almost 30 percent of the total construction cost during the mid-1980s.[15] Even in the early 1990s, when the industry was at its healthiest in two decades, official estimates for shipbuilding subsidies in Japan, Germany, and South Korea still ranged as high as 23.5 percent.[16]

As described above, the major shipbuilding nations were not able to manage the necessary (and, in fact, long overdue) contraction of the world industry. When the 1983 OECD agreement failed to maintain discipline within the world shipbuilding community, Japanese shipbuilders took the highly unusual step in 1985 of asking their archrivals in South Korea to cooperate in reducing production.[17] They were, however, rebuffed and Japan was forced to proceed alone. In April 1987, the Ministry of Transportation initiated a program to reduce capacity by nearly

---

[12] Shipbuilders Council of America (1991), p. 3.

[13] The range of alleged subsidies was absolutely staggering. Nonetheless, most forms of aid fall into one of four major subsidy types: ship financing subsidies, ship production subsidies, restructuring-investment aid, and research and development aid. For greater detail on the creative practices used by governments to support their shipbuilding industries, see ibid. In addition, see United States International Trade Commission (1992), p. 44.

[14] These figures are based on estimates reported in *Asian Shipping* (November 1985), pp. 35–36.

[15] Shipbuilders Council of America (1991), p. 9.

[16] United States International Trade Commission (1992), p. xiii. Other estimates are consistent with this general range, including a 1992 figure of 20 percent for EC countries generally. See *The Motor Ship* (January 1992), p. 56.

[17] *SBR* (November 1985), p. 62.

25 percent.[18] It was not until 1988, therefore, after the shipbuilding recession was already over, that Japanese policy had any substantial effect on actual productive capacity in the world industry.

For their part, South Korea's shipbuilders refused to allow hard times in the world industry to deter them from their mission: to challenge Japan for the top spot in global shipbuilding. Entering the world market on the back of low wages, the Korean yards simply were not to be dissuaded in their drive for market share. The strategy was clear: buy your way into the world market with low prices, ride out the recession, and wait for the inevitable recovery during which market share could be translated into handsome profits. To achieve their goals, Korean shipbuilders rebuffed requests by the EC, as well as Japan, to reduce their productive capacity.[19] While there were no capacity increases after an expansion program at the Daewoo yard was completed in 1982, other Korean shipbuilders such as Hyundai successfully raised productivity in the mid-1980s. This accomplishment, which effectively increased their capacity, only exacerbated the problem at the global level. In fact, no plans for actual capacity reduction materialized until the Korean government finally secured promises for significant cutbacks as part of the government bailout of Daewoo in 1989.[20] As far as GSC is concerned, therefore, South Korea provided absolutely no relief during the critical period of the 1980s. In fact, South Korean shipbuilders have admitted rather unabashedly that their aim was to take advantage of the crisis as a means by which to cripple their global competition. Quite by design, then, Korean yards made the international situation even more dire than would otherwise have been necessary.[21]

---

[18] *LSM* (March 1990), p. 10. This program resulted in substantial declines in the number of shipbuilding companies (44 to 26), the number of shipyards (59 to 39), and the number of actual docks (73 to 47); idem.

[19] *LSM* (September 1989), p. 42.

[20] Led by Hyundai and Daewoo, South Korea's shipbuilders did build up impressive market share in the world industry, but at the cost of a crippling debt burden. By the end of 1987, the debts of the four major companies (Hyundai, Daewoo, Samsung, and the Korea Shipbuilding and Engineering Company) was U.S. $5.43 billion. Daewoo, responsible for almost 40 percent of this total debt, was forced to agree to a 50-percent cut in capacity by 1993 in its deal with the government; *SBR* (March/April 1989), p. 49.

[21] Here, it is important to note that most challenges to the competitiveness of South Korean industry, such as the appreciation of the Korean won and wage increases resulting from recurrent strikes, really took force only after the worst of the shipbuilding crisis in the mid-1980s. While Korean yards have faced considerable challenges from the late 1980s onward, they still were in a relatively strong position domestically when it mattered most in the mid-1980s.

COSCO IN A BUYERS' MARKET: EXPANDING CHINA'S
MERCHANT FLEET DURING THE INTERNATIONAL CRISIS
IN SHIPBUILDING

How can we explain China's increased reliance on foreign-built ships in maintaining and expanding its merchant fleet? From the foregoing discussion, it is clear that the most direct explanation can be found in the condition of the international shipping and shipbuilding industries. Courtesy of world economic recession and an accompanying decline in international seaborne trade, the glut of ships in the world merchant fleet during the early 1980s reached levels that were unprecedented in modern shipping history. As shown in Figure 8.5, surplus tonnage stood at an astonishing 29 percent of the total world fleet by 1983. For obvious reasons, this development severely limited the demand for new ships. To make matters worse, the international shipbuilding industry had already been grappling rather ineffectively with a preexisting problem of chronic GSC. The downturn in international shipping only exacerbated this situation.

In an industry characterized by GSC, prices are almost by definition below the cost of production. As Susan Strange has described it, "demand is insufficient to absorb production at prices high enough both to maintain employment and to maintain profitability for all the enterprises engaged."[22] Indeed, the competition among shipbuilders was notoriously cutthroat throughout the 1980s. Too many yards were simply chasing too few orders. Thanks to government financial support, yards all over the world were able to offer steep discounts on ship prices in an effort to retain their market share. Under these circumstances, COSCO's purchase of foreign-built ships is understandable, especially since it was one of the few, if not the only, large shipping companies in the world seeking to expand its merchant fleet during the 1980s.[23] Although it lost its monopoly over China's overseas shipping in the 1980s, COSCO still controlled the vast majority of Chinese orders for oceangoing ships.[24]

---

[22] Strange (1979), p. 304.

[23] Despite the depressed state of international freight rates and the worldwide glut of ships in the 1980s, COSCO's own rapidly growing shipping business was largely insulated from international competition by a number of wide-ranging discriminatory measures. These barriers were not addressed, even preliminarily, until a Memorandum of Consultation on shipping was signed between China and the United States in 1991.

[24] Over the years, COSCO has consistently controlled about 75 percent of China's ocean-going vessels. (The remaining large merchant ships – operated primarily by provincial

This concentrated buying power put it in an especially strong position vis-à-vis foreign yards.

There is no need to catalog on a case-by-case basis the favorable terms COSCO received on ship orders placed overseas during the 1980s; these were widely reported in both the Chinese and foreign press, particularly in the various international maritime publications that closely monitor developments in the shipbuilding market. By successfully pitting competing yards – and, thus, rival governments – against one another, COSCO was able to secure not only rock-bottom prices, but also highly concessionary financing. Typically, COSCO did not even need to secure financing for newbuilding projects; low-interest loans were generally provided, either through public or private channels, in the countries competing for COSCO's business. While this became a fairly standard practice given the ultracompetitive conditions found in the world ship-building industry, China was often able to secure especially preferential arrangements. For example, it ordered a series of five containerships from British and German yards in the mid-1980s at an average cost of U.S. $70 million each. The first two vessels, built by the Govan Shipyard operated by British Shipbuilders, were ordered as part of a £300 million loan package from the British government.[25] China dropped an option for a third ship when the German government offered an even better deal for not one, but two, similar ships. The financing terms for these vessels were so attractive that COSCO ultimately decided to have the fifth ship in the series built in Germany as well, despite having originally committed the project to CSSC's Hudong yard in Shanghai.[26]

This case illustrates quite concretely how intensifying GSC in ship-building had a direct and substantial impact on China's shipping and shipbuilding industries. As COSCO placed more and more of its new-building orders overseas, sometimes even canceling plans for domestic projects, it became increasingly difficult for CSSC to pursue its "domes-tic first, export second" policy. The Sixth Five-Year Plan (1981–1985),

---

maritime bureaus – are engaged in coastal trade.) Until the shipping reforms of the late 1980s, COSCO was responsible for nearly 100 percent of the international shipping conducted by Chinese ships. Despite the swift expansion of its fleet, COSCO's shipping capacity has been unable to keep pace with the huge increase in China's foreign trade. Consequently, COSCO has generally carried only about 40–60 percent of China's foreign trade, depending on surges in imports and exports. For a mid-1980s perspective on COSCO, see the interview with Deputy Managing Director Chen Zhongbiao in *ZGHY* 4:4 (Winter 1986), pp. 80–82. For a later retrospective, see the 1991 interview with Liu Songjin, COSCO's president, in *SBR* (July/August 1991), pp. 68–70.

[25] *LSE* (March 1988), p. 16.   [26] Ibid.

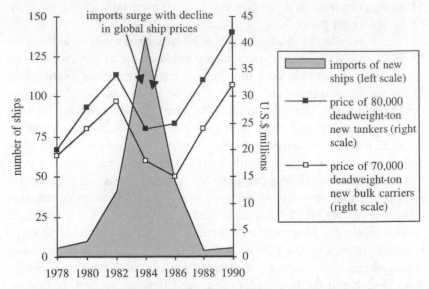

Figure 8.6. China's new ship imports and world ship prices. *Source*: *Almanac of China's Foreign Economic and Trade Relations*, various years; *Review of Maritime Transport*, various years.

which was drawn up prior to the second downturn in the world ship-building industry, called for some 2.5 million deadweight tons of ships – the majority of COSCO's newbuildings – to be built at Chinese yards.[27] With the collapse of the international shipbuilding market, however, this policy never came to fruition. In fact, the shift to overseas buying was synchronized almost perfectly with the emerging collapse of world ship prices (Figures 8.6 and 8.7). By mid-1981, it was being reported in the international maritime press that "China has been ordering at overseas yards on an unprecedented scale."[28] Indeed, the high hopes of domestic yards were dashed by virtual fire sales at many of the world's finest shipyards. For example, CSSC received only six of twenty-two orders for

---

[27] The semi-official magazine *Zhongguo Haiyun* [*Maritime China*] admitted as late as December 1983 that the Plan had called for domestic yards to produce almost 60 percent of newbuildings (by tonnage) for China's fleet; *ZGHY* 1:4 (December 1983), p. 58. The *FEER* also reported a figure of 2.5 million deadweight tons, stating only that "the plan allows for a large percentage of newbuildings to be undertaken by China's own yards." See *FEER*, 16 February 1984, p. 35.

[28] *Asian Shipping* (July 1981), p. 57.

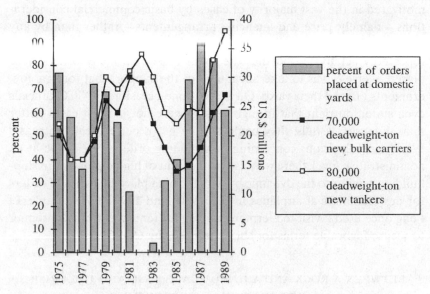

Figure 8.7. World ship prices and the share of ship orders for China's merchant fleet placed at domestic yards. *Source: New Ship Construction*, various years; *Review of Maritime Transport*, various years.

new containerships placed by COSCO in 1983 and 1984, whereas nine went to West German yards and seven to Japanese shipbuilders.[29] Since all of the vessels were relatively similar and the Japanese-built ships were actually the smallest of the group, it is unlikely that CSSC was given so few orders due to any inability to build the vessels. After all, it did receive part of the order. According to one report, the 3.5 percent financing offered on the German ships was critical.[30]

By December 1985, when ship prices had bottomed out, Zhuo Dongming, COSCO's deputy managing director, told *Seatrade Business Review* that the days of massive additions to the fleet were over: "We will now slow down and concentrate on fleet renewals rather than expansion."[31] In a strategic gesture designed to preserve the benefits to which COSCO had become accustomed, he went on to declare that foreign orders would only be considered in the future if overseas yards "offer very favorable terms."[32] In sum, COSCO's overseas orders were

[29] *FEER*, 14 February 1985, p. 50.   [30] *SBR* (February 1986), p. 73.   [31] Ibid.   [32] Ibid. See also *ZGHY* 3:4 (Winter 1985), p. 67.

motivated in the vast majority of cases by basic commercial considerations – namely, price and financing arrangements – rather than by any inability of Chinese yards to build the desired vessels.[33] Indeed, COSCO repeatedly acknowledged that the main reason so many orders were placed overseas was to take advantage of the support that foreign governments offered their yards. On at least one occasion, COSCO officials even stated outright that foreign vessels were not in most cases better than domestic vessels; they could simply get a better deal overseas.[34] While most decisions concerning newbuilding orders were made at an administrative level, there was also an element of high diplomacy in shipbuilding, similar to the dynamic by which China placed batches of orders for new commercial airplanes in the 1980s and 1990s. For example, Li Peng once used a visit to Germany during his tenure as China's premier to secure favorable terms for ship purchases by COSCO.[35]

BETWEEN A ROCK AND A HARD PLACE: CSSC AND THE CRISIS IN INTERNATIONAL SHIPBUILDING

In reviewing the shipbuilding industry's performance in 1986, CSSC publicly admitted that "about 70 percent of local shipbuilding enterprises had idle capacity because of fewer orders from both domestic and international markets."[36] While the effects of the recession may have been felt as early as 1984, by 1986 at least one-third of China's total newbuilding capacity was unused.[37] Courtesy of COSCO's generous distribution of orders to foreign yards, the effects of GSC in the international industry had managed to penetrate China's borders, leaving empty berths at CSSC's yards as well. Indeed, as CSSC's previously full orderbook weakened steadily during the mid-1980s, it became painfully clear that the

---

[33] Another issue was an import tax on foreign ship equipment and machinery used in domestic ship construction. These duties, which did *not* apply to foreign shipowners who had their vessels built in Chinese yards, were an additional disincentive for COSCO to place orders at home. Interviews and press accounts suggest that these import duties contributed, at least in some cases, to the placement of orders overseas, especially when preferential arrangements in foreign yards served as a magnet for COSCO newbuilding projects. This policy was not lifted until the late 1990s, when a special provision was made that allowed a partial rebate on these duties. For more detail, see *The Motor Ships* January 1998, p. 31.

[34] *Zhongguo Xinwen She*, 11 December 1995, in FBIS-CHI-95-238.

[35] "Shipyards Want New Subsidies for China Business," *Frankfurter Allgemeine*, 5 April 1993, in FBIS-WEU-93-069.

[36] *ZGJJXW*, 9 February 1987, p. 3.   [37] Derived from data in *LMA* (May 1987), p. 7.

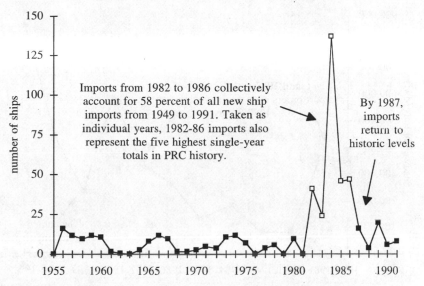

Figure 8.8. Imports of new ships for China's merchant fleet. *Source: Almanac of China's Foreign Economic Relations and Trade*, various years.

Chinese industry was growing increasingly vulnerable to the vagaries of the world market.

No longer able to sit back and entertain orders mainly for basic bulk carriers and oil tankers, China was more or less thrown into competition with industry leaders such as Japan and South Korea. Previously, of course, CSSC had restricted itself to the lowest end of the market, preferring to export the ordinary, unsophisticated ships not actively sought by the world's premier yards. If not for the collapse in the world market for these vessels – bulk carriers, especially – that luxury might well have continued, particularly given the exceptionally low prices China could offer. COSCO's turn to foreign suppliers, depicted in Figure 8.8, obviously ruled out an increased emphasis on newbuilding for domestic use. When CSSC's own export orderbook, built up largely during the world market's mini-boom at the beginning of the 1980s, dried up simultaneously with the flow of domestic orders, the urgency of finding new export orders only intensified. Alas, so, too, did the difficulty of securing new orders. (As Figure 8.9 shows, CSSC was not able to match the deadweight tonnage of its export orders in 1980–1981 until 1987.)

Not surprisingly, CSSC's preferred remedy for hard times was increased import protection. For reasons explored in Chapter 11,

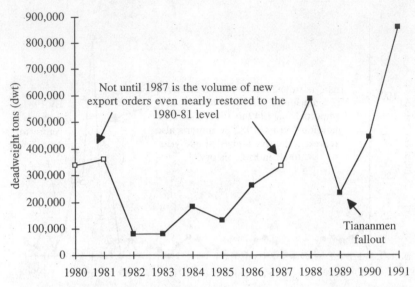

Figure 8.9. CSSC's new orders for export ships. *Source*: *Zhongguo Jingji Nianjian*, various years.

however, this was not forthcoming. According to interviews, it simply was not an option for CSSC to allow its yards to grow increasingly idle. While there was clearly not enough shipbuilding work in the world market to go around, CSSC apparently felt considerable pressure to win whatever orders it could. Even as a state-owned industry, which at that time did not have to fear yard closings or massive layoffs, CSSC could not simply sit around with empty berths.

How could Chinese yards win orders for export in competition with industry giants in Japan, South Korea, and Western Europe – not to mention second-tier shipbuilders in Taiwan, Brazil, and Eastern Europe? At another time or in a different industry, China's cut-rate prices would almost single-handedly have assured China a market niche, if only at the very bottom. Yet with governments around the world committed to the preservation of their national shipbuilding industries, the "natural" price differences that would have favored China were virtually eliminated by the many elaborate subsidy programs.

Unlike the situation in most other industries, then, low prices would only carry China so far in shipbuilding. (As discussed in previous chapters, of course, a similar situation prevailed in textiles.) Even with the introduction of competitive financing terms, a feature that was added only when conditions in the world market made it necessary for China to bid successfully for shipbuilding projects, CSSC still faced real challenges if it wanted to continue exporting ships. In short, severe GSC in shipbuilding exerted tremendous pressure on CSSC to upgrade its goods, adjust its product mix, adapt its management system, and modernize its commercial practices simply in order to survive the cutthroat international competition.

Global Surplus Capacity: The Impact on Development Strategy and Industrial Adjustment in Chinese Shipbuilding

With the world market in extreme distress, CSSC found itself in the unaccustomed position of having to scramble to find adequate work. While there was no formal institutional mechanism that restricted the quantity of export orders that a country could accept, such as the MFA in textiles or VERs in automobiles or steel products, the glut in international shipbuilding capacity had a similar effect. (See Chapter 1 for a more thorough explanation of how the intensifying GSC of the mid-1980s represented a form of *moderate* economic closure equivalent to that found in these other industries.) While the South Korean case demonstrates that a country can increase its market share in shipbuilding over time, these gains were achieved primarily during periods of *chronic* GSC rather than *severe* GSC.[38]

During the hard times of the mid-1980s, a strategy of trying to expand the quantity of ship exports became almost impossible. As Figure 7.1 showed, the average number of ships China exported annually changed little from the early 1980s to the mid-1990s. While China's orderbook did rebound from the lowest point of the crisis by the late 1980s, the effects of chronic GSC persisted in full form. For example, CSSC exported 42 ships from 1992 to 1995, only one more than it had from 1982 to 1985. Not until a swell in world orders in the mid-1990s resulted in a substantial easing of overcapacity in the international industry did the number of ships exported by China increase substantially over the basic level

---

[38] It is also worth noting that South Korea's successful bid for greater market share came at an overwhelming financial cost, one that arguably came into full relief only with the fallout from the AFC. Few countries would be either able or willing to incur such costs. That said, however, the South Korean case does show that GSC represents a slightly more flexible barrier than formal barriers such as textile quotas.

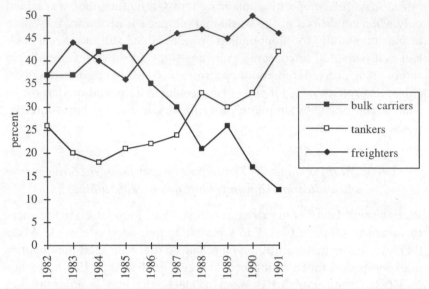

Figure 8.10. World ship orders by vessel type. *Source*: *New Ship Construction*, various years; *Review of Maritime Transport*, various years.

established more than a decade before. (Unfortunately, this relief from GSC proved short-lived due to the economic downturn associated with the AFC.)

In sum, GSC effectively puts a limit on the number of orders that any single shipbuilding nation can reasonably hope to secure. A more realistic, although still difficult, strategy is to maximize the value of each export order by moving production toward more sophisticated, higher value-added ships. When the collapse of the world market for new ships falls disproportionately on basic ship types like bulk carriers and tankers, as it did in the mid-1980s (Figure 8.10), shipbuilders are nudged even further toward making a play for more advanced ship orders. While run-of-the-mill orders for bulk carriers and tankers may still be available, their number is increasingly insufficient to sustain a viable orderbook. In this situation, shipbuilders have little choice but to try to build more advanced ships, even if that strategy entails fundamental changes both at the yard level and within the national industry more generally. As Figure 8.11 shows, tonnage oversupply in the world fleet was, in fact, least pronounced for freighters, the category in which the majority of advanced ships are classified.

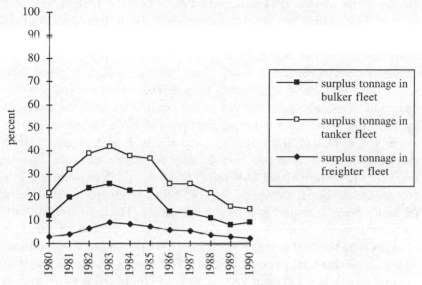

Figure 8.11. Tonnage oversupply in the world merchant fleet by sector. *Source*: *Review of Maritime Transport*, various years.

This, in essence, was the situation in which China found itself as the effects of international recession in the shipbuilding industry grew from the early 1980s to the mid-1980s. By 1984 and 1985, CSSC's orderbook was already becoming dangerously depleted and work scheduled for 1986 and beyond was wholly inadequate. With domestic orders still slumping and the export market for bulk carriers and basic tankers near collapse, CSSC turned largely by default to the healthiest remaining sector of global shipbuilding: high-tech, sophisticated freighters such as refrigerated containerships and roll-on–roll-off ships such as car carriers. Despite the cutthroat competition among shipbuilders, CSSC was able to secure a modest number of orders for advanced ships it had no experience building. The tradeoff for this success included steep price discounts and a willingness to accept significantly higher levels of foreign involvement in the production process.

By all accounts, CSSC proceeded in a decidedly ad hoc manner, exploring the world market for sophisticated vessels rather tentatively until its ever-weakening orderbook required more concerted action. Although CSSC did export a number of small container ships and multipurpose ships starting in 1983, its real entrance into the advanced ship market came in late 1984 and early 1985 when the Dalian Shipyard won its first orders for several highly sophisticated product tankers and shuttle tankers. One important order, from the OSCO Shipping Company of Norway, was for a pair of 69,000-deadweight-ton product-chemical carriers valued at more than U.S. $25 million a piece.[39] To secure this order, CSSC significantly loosened several of its central policy guidelines. First, about 50 percent of the equipment and raw materials for the ships were imported from Europe. The main engines, although assembled at Dalian Shipyard, were actually built with Japanese parts (Kawasaki) under a production license from the engine's Danish manufacturer (Burmeister & Wain).[40] Second, the ships were entirely Norwegian-designed, although CSSC did gain the right to use the design on future projects as part of a royalty agreement. Third, Norwegian sub-contractors were awarded substantial work on the vessels as part of a complex deal reached between CSSC and OSCO. Finally, CSSC offered an attractive financial package in which OSCO was granted a one-year deferral in starting payment on the ships. Perhaps even more impor-tantly, OSCO received a 10-year loan at 9 percent interest from the Bank of China in order to finance construction of the ships.[41]

While CSSC had exhibited some flexibility over the years in securing certain export orders, the contracts for these product tankers marked a significant departure in its policy. The deal was unquestionably good for the development of China's industry, but it did constitute a reversal of CSSC's original development strategy. Most important, the terms of these orders did not prove to be a fluke: similar concessions were made on other ships ordered at around the same time. Although contract details are not always made public for each export order, reports in inter-national maritime publications and the Chinese press suggest a pattern in which CSSC became significantly more flexible simply to win the export orders necessary to fill its yards. According to one report, an offi-cial for a Hong Kong shipping company said that about 90 percent of the equipment for two small containerships built at Shanghai's Zhonghua Shipyard was imported, again primarily from Japan. In addition, the main engines were built in China, but under a license from Sulzer, a Swiss man-ufacturer. The official also reported that the steel plates for the ships were imported. In the same article, a "major Hong Kong owner" claimed that his "China-built" ships were really just assembled in China from

---

[39] *Asian Shipping* (June 1985), p. 10.   [40] Ibid, p. 11.
[41] *Asian Shipping* (June 1984), p. 3.

Japanese parts.[42] These observations are all consistent with comments made by non-PRC informants, many of whom specifically mentioned how China's attractiveness as a shipbuilder increased substantially in the mid-1980s when CSSC became more flexible in order to win export contracts.

The single most prestigious order secured during this period was a deal signed in early 1985 with the National Petroleum Company of Norway for a 115,000-deadweight-ton shuttle tanker. Despite competition from a total of sixty-eight yards worldwide, Dalian Shipyard won the contract through open international bidding, its first such success.[43] This impressive start in product-chemical tankers was soon followed by orders for other high value-added, sophisticated vessels, including a pair of 9,600-deadweight-ton roll-on–roll-off ships specially designed to carry 4,000 automobiles each. The construction of these car carriers, ordered in December 1985 at Shanghai's Jiangnan Shipyard for the Ahrenkiel Shipping Company of Germany, symbolized CSSC's commitment to new, more advanced ship types for export. This kind of newbuilding project, which involved not only a high degree of ship automation, but also state-of-the-art hydraulics and pneumatics, would have been unthinkable in China only a few years before. With its foray into these new ship types, CSSC found itself competing directly – and somewhat successfully – with major shipbuilders in countries such as South Korea and Japan. While CSSC had to be much more flexible in accommodating the production demands of foreign owners than it would have preferred, to say nothing of offering cut-rate prices and competitive ship financing, China was fast becoming an important production base within the international shipbuilding industry.

Despite China's impressive success in gaining a limited foothold in the advanced ship market during 1984 and 1985, CSSC's orderbook continued to deteriorate as domestic and foreign orders alike declined throughout the mid-1980s. In fact, the international maritime journal *Asian Shipping* reported in March 1985 that "when current export orders – a 115,000 product carrier for Norway and some supply boats – are completed, there will be nothing on the export orderbook."[44] While CSSC, like many shipbuilders, tries not to disclose full details of its orderbook, industry officials did acknowledge in late 1985 that newbuilding activity would reach rock-bottom by mid-1986 after a long decline in the world

---

[42] *ZGHY* 3:3 (Autumn 1985), p. 97. [43] *ZGHY* 3:4 (Winter 1985), p. 53.
[44] *Asian Shipping* (March 1985), p. 16.

market that began about 1982.[45] It was no coincidence, therefore, that CSSC's vice president at the time, Wang Longfa, was widely and repeatedly quoted in the international maritime press in late 1985 as saying that "we are prepared to consider any kind of shipowner."[46] Noting that "the organization [CSSC] is well attuned to the requirements of international shipowners – and for that matter the increasingly demanding domestic operators," the semi-official journal *Zhongguo Haiyun* (*Maritime China*) reported that "Wang was frank in saying that CSTC [CSSC's trading arm] will fit a newbuilding with whatever an owner requires whether it be Chinese built and designed, Chinese built under foreign license, or wholly foreign built."[47] As the journal noted, "With the market for bulkers [bulk carriers] and tankers in virtual paralysis, CSTC is very keen to promote China's abilities to build specialized vessels."[48] This apparently explains why "[Wang] was not, at the moment, overly concerned about whether the design built is a Chinese one or one that the owner brings with him."[49]

Wang's comments marked a clear and unprecedented reversal of CSSC's previously stated official policy. While the new course may have been pursued on a de facto basis since earlier in the crisis, these public statements confirmed CSSC's commitment to a new development strategy. Importantly, it also signaled that CSSC understood the ramifications of this strategy for foreign involvement in the industry. As Wang observed at the time, "We have to develop more license import agreements in the future because of the varying requirements of shipowners."[50] In more official form, *Zhongguo Jingji Xinwen* (*China Economic News*) reported in February 1986 that CSSC had indeed adopted a package of "flexible measures to meet customer needs in an attempt to win more foreign orders."[51] For example, there were two new measures involving ship financing: first, whereas the longstanding policy had been cash on delivery, payment could now be deferred; and, second, ship mortgaging was now formally offered by the Chinese themselves, with preferential loans available to eligible overseas buyers. As important as the adoption of these standard commercial practices was for China's

---

[45] For competitive reasons, full details on outstanding orders are often not systematically reported, lest a competing bidder or potential customer gain any bargaining leverage in negotiations over another deal. The mid-1986 low point in CSSC's orderbook was reported in *SBR* (October 1985), p. 45.

[46] For example, see *ZGHY* 3:3 (Autumn 1985), pp. 57, 93, and *SBR* (October 1985), p. 45.

[47] Ibid.   [48] Ibid, p. 95.   [49] Ibid.   [50] Ibid, p. 93.

[51] *ZGJJXW*, 17 February 1986, pp. 11, 19.

export prospects, two additional new measures represented even more fundamental change: first, prospective owners could now freely choose the ship type, design, and equipment of ships to be built by CSSC; and, second, equipment "unavailable" in China could be imported with far fewer restrictions for installation on ships built by CSSC. While these latter measures were not entirely new policies – since CSSC had always imported some equipment and had obviously never been able to dictate all the details of shipbuilding projects to its customers – interviews suggested that these measures did significantly relax the environment in which ship orders were put together.

CONCLUSION

By 1986, therefore, the outline of CSSC's strategy for responding to the steep decline of the world market was increasingly well-formed. COSCO's overseas orders had all but forced CSSC to seek greater participation in the world market itself. The days of building mainly bulk carriers and a few basic oil tankers for a small circle of powerful shipowners (based largely in Hong Kong) was clearly over. As a direct response to the ultracompetitive nature of the world shipbuilding market, therefore, CSSC actively began to pursue orders for more sophisticated, higher value-added vessels from potential customers around the world.

From the beginning, CSSC understood well the crucial link between trying to produce new types of ships and the virtual necessity of introducing advanced technology and management practices from abroad. By early 1986, the semi-official journal *Zhongguo Haiyun* (*Maritime China*) had already made the following observation:

> In view of the sharp decrease in orders in the international shipbuilding market, the shipbuilding industry must improve its ability to compete and meet emergencies. To be well prepared for getting export orders in the future, the industry will try to improve the price, quality, delivery, and service of export ships. . . . The focus will be on producing new types of ships, such as chemical-product vessels, liquid petroleum gas ships, self-discharging coal ships, shallow-draft ships, and energy-saving ships. For this, the shipbuilding industry will go on importing some advanced technology . . . and eagerly seek cooperation in building special types of ships with the outside world.[52]

[52] *ZGHY* 4:1 (Spring 1986), p. 74.

While CSSC's pursuit of foreign technology is certainly not surprising given the general political context of Zhao Ziyang's emphasis on technology transfer during the mid-1980s, the timing of CSSC's response to this broad policy environment was highly industry-specific. Other industries pursued foreign technology both earlier and later than shipbuilding. In CSSC's case, the main impetus for accepting greater foreign involvement in the shipbuilding industry, which was a prerequisite for gaining access to advanced technology, was the harsh reality of the world market. The next chapter examines China's response in greater detail; specifically, it documents CSSC's record in moving upmarket to more sophisticated ships, increasing shiprepair work, shortening construction periods, expanding nonmarine production, and carrying out technical modernization.

9

Chinese Shipbuilding and Global Surplus Capacity: Making a Virtue out of Necessity

DIVERSIFYING THE PRODUCT MIX: THE MOVE UPMARKET IN SHIPS

While Chinese yards had long built a variety of ships, the impact of the global shipbuilding recession on CSSC's product mix for export was unmistakable. As the market for basic ships deteriorated during the mid-1980s, especially the demand for bulk carriers, China quickly came to export mostly advanced ships. (Following convention, this study classifies advanced ships as all vessels except bulk carriers and basic tankers.) Indeed, the share of advanced ships among China's exports increased from 56 percent to 85 percent from the first half to the second half of the 1980s.[1] While impressive in its own right, this jump actually understates the shift upmarket from basic ship types since the "advanced ships" exported by CSSC from 1980 to 1984 were, in fact, lower-end multi-purpose and multipurpose-container ships. Although categorized here as advanced ships for the sake of analytical consistency, these relatively unsophisticated vessels artificially inflated the share of advanced ships in China's product mix during the first half of the decade.

By contrast, the advanced ship category for the second half of the decade included a growing range of truly high-end vessels. Indeed, it was from 1985 to 1989 that China first began to build ultramodern container-ships and partial containerships, including a number of refrigerated carriers. Among this last group, the real milestone for Chinese shipbuilding came in April 1987 when Hapag-Lloyd, the German shipping giant, awarded CSSC a much coveted contract for the *Berlin Express*, a 32,800-deadweight-ton refrigerated containership. This high-tech vessel,

---

[1] Data calculated from a computer printout supplied by CSSC.

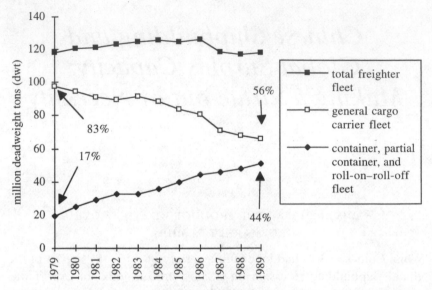

Figure 9.1. Composition of the world freighter fleet. *Source*: *Merchant Fleets of the World*, various years.

more than seven storeys high and longer than two football fields, was designed to carry 2,700 temperature-controlled containers of fruits and vegetables. Shipyards from around the world vied to build the magnificent vessel, with CSSC's Hudong Shipyard in Shanghai finally winning the DM 80 million contract over yards in Germany, South Korea, and Taiwan.

Contrary to CSSC's frequently expressed intentions in the early 1980s, therefore, Chinese yards ended up building mostly freighters and other advanced vessels for export, not bulk carriers and basic tankers. Indeed, the advanced ship category for the period from 1985 to 1989 also includes other high-end vessels such as shuttle tankers, product-chemical tankers, and roll-on–roll-off vessels, none of which had been built by Chinese yards earlier in the decade. In this sense, even the tankers that CSSC did build were increasingly of the high-tech variety, not the unsophisticated oil tankers that had dominated earlier production.

As it turns out, the impact of the world market even extended to China's production *within* particular vessel categories, such as freighters. As Figure 9.1 shows, the composition of the world freighter fleet changed markedly during the 1980s, from one dominated by general cargo carriers to one in which various containerized vessels and roll-on–roll-off vessels were equally well-represented. Since the total size of the world freighter fleet remained virtually unchanged over the course of the decade, this second category of vessels clearly dominated new additions to the fleet. Indeed, CSSC's exports of freighters reflected this trend, as higher value-added containerships and roll-on–roll-off vessels soon greatly outnumbered the general cargo carriers built for foreign shipowners. The role of international forces in bringing about this shift in the product mix was candidly recognized within China, as indicated in the following report from the Chinese press:

> Today, when the world's shipbuilding capacity is greatly excessive and the world's ship market is dwindling, China has gradually gained a place in the international ship market and has displayed a competitive power not to be belittled thanks to the high quality and low production costs of its ships and its good reputation. . . . Since competition in the international ship market tends to become increasingly more acute, China has concentrated its efforts on developing first-rate modern [advanced, sophisticated] ships according to international standards, thus narrowing the gap between China and other countries with a flourishing shipbuilding industry within just a few years.[2]

While the report is somewhat indirect in identifying the causation, it clearly makes the connection between GSC in shipbuilding and China's new emphasis on upscale ships. In fact, the article later described several of CSSC's impressive high-tech orders, implying that the limited number of available orders worldwide had pushed China upmarket. At a CSSC meeting called in April 1986 to discuss the industry's strategy during the Seventh Five-Year Plan (1986–1990), Managing Director Hu Chuanzhi bluntly observed that China needed to diversify both its product mix and its export markets in order to respond effectively to the challenge of a dwindling world market for ships:

> We'll continue to enlarge the number of countries and regions that we will export our products to, so as to build up more and more new markets. In regard to products, we'll strive to take orders for more sophisticated and specialized ships. . . .[3]

[2] *FBIS Daily Report-China*, 18 March 1987, p. K13.
[3] *ZGHY* 4:2 (Summer 1986), p. 98.

This statement underscored just how much the actual policy positions of the industry were affected by the realities of the world market. By all accounts, the Seventh Five-Year Plan for shipbuilding reflected less the original priorities of industry officials than the changing requirements of competing effectively in the international market.[4] For example, the first of CSSC's five "focal points" under the Plan was "to enhance the development of new ship types."[5] In fact, it was later revealed that CSSC had actually begun a project on building new ship types back in 1985, prior to the formal commencement of the Seventh Five-Year Plan in 1986.[6] Chinese sources were surprisingly forthright about the impetus behind this shift in policy. In its coverage of an 1987 interview with Chen Chunshu, president of China United Shipbuilding (CSSC's Hong Kong office), the semi-official journal *Zhongguo Haiyun* (*Maritime China*) acknowledged that "in the last two years, Chinese shipyards tried to build more specialized ships in order to survive the [international] depression."[7] According to other Chinese sources, CSSC developed about ten times as many new ship types from 1985 to 1987 as it had in the entire period covering the Sixth Five-Year Plan (1981–1985).[8]

Although the composition of exports (i.e., ship type) is the best measure of upgrading in the shipbuilding industry, the unit value of ship exports can also be analyzed as a further gauge of China's performance. It should be noted, however, that the unit value of exports is a much more problematic measure in shipbuilding than in textiles. First, it is extremely difficult to collect the data necessary to make accurate calculations of unit values for China's ship exports.[9] Estimates are possible,

---

[4] See, for example, the description of efforts to produce new types of specialized ships according to instructions given in the Seventh Five-Year Plan in *ZGHY* 5:1 (Spring 1987), p. 69.

[5] *ZGJXDZGYNJ* (1986), Section III, p. 131.

[6] *ZGHY* 6:4 (Winter 1988), p. 71.

[7] *ZGHY* 5:3 (Autumn 1987), p. 83.

[8] For the Sixth Five-Year Plan figure, see *ZGJJXW*, 2 June 1986, p. 1. For the 1985–1987 figure, see *ZGJXDZGYNJ* (1988), Section III, p. 112. Since these two periods both include 1985, this obviously means that most of the advances were actually made in 1986 and 1987.

[9] Since CSSC rarely confirmed the value of contracts for individual ship exports, it is impossible to calculate unit values for different types of ships (e.g., bulk carriers and containerships). Without this category-specific information, unit value calculations become imprecise. (Price data on certain ships can be gleaned from sources in the international shipbuilding community – namely interviews and press reports – but there is no systematic record upon which to rely.) By default, the main source of data on the value of China's ship exports are the aggregate figures published by MOFERT in its annual year

and even useful, but the appropriate aim should be to identify trends over time rather than to treat these calculations as precise figures. Second, unit values for more advanced ships are not always higher than unit values for basic ships. In some cases, the monetary value of an especially large bulk carrier or basic tanker might exceed the monetary value of a small sophisticated vessel. Finally, even if precise figures for the unit value of China's export ships were available, we must remember that unit values in shipbuilding fluctuate enormously due to price shifts. Unlike the relative price stability found in most textile markets from year to year, boom and bust periods in the international shipbuilding industry are such that rising and falling prices can easily mask real changes in unit value from product upgrading. As a result, any analysis of unit value must be placed firmly in the context of changing world market prices.

With these caveats in mind, unit values can be used to examine the development of the Chinese shipbuilding industry. In the early 1980s, the average value of CSSC's export vessels actually declined even though world ship prices were rising at the time. For example, while prices for benchmark 70,000- and 80,000-deadweight-ton bulk carriers and tankers rose 21 percent internationally from 1980 to 1982, the unit value of Chinese ship exports fell 18 percent. Moreover, the total value of Chinese ship exports increased by 9 percent over the same period.[10] In other words, CSSC managed to generate higher levels of foreign exchange in the early 1980s only by exporting greater numbers of low-end ships. With ship prices rising, the unit value of Chinese ship exports could have been expected, ceteris paribus, to increase as well. This was clearly not the case, however. Although the downward trend continued when world prices plummeted in 1983 with the recession in the international industry, by the mid-1980s the unit value of CSSC's ship exports had already risen impressively despite further declines in world ship prices. In fact, by 1985 the value per ship exported had recovered fully to the level reached in 1980 when world prices had been 20–50 percent

book, *Almanac of China's Foreign Economic Relations and Trade*. These figures include the value of total ship exports, however, rather than just large oceangoing vessels built by CSSC. In short, in shipbuilding there is no good way to calculate unit value by product category, as was done for textiles. For a rough estimate of the overall unit value of China's ship exports, I have used the quantity of ship exports culled from CSSC data and the figures for aggregate value found in the MOFERT trade data.

[10] Calculated by the author from data in CSSC computer printout; *Almanac* (various years); and *Review of Maritime Transport* (various years).

higher across all ship types.[11] Simply by maintaining the unit value of its exports in the face of plunging world prices, the Chinese industry had responded successfully to the international crisis.

As documented above, CSSC accomplished this feat primarily by diversifying its production toward more advanced ships. Since GSC was truly a worldwide phenomenon – unlike the MFA, which affected several of China's most important markets (e.g., the United States and the European Union), but left others (e.g., Japan) unrestricted – market diversification was a more limited strategy in shipbuilding than in textiles. That said, the crisis in the mid-1980s did spur China to pursue export markets beyond the small circle of customers – dominated by Hong Kong shipowners – upon which it had relied in the early 1980s. Interviews and press accounts confirmed that the difficulty of securing orders during the crisis accelerated CSSC's efforts to expand its export horizons. Due to the Byzantine practices of international ship registry, it is very difficult to track China's ship exports by national destination. That said, CSSC claimed that it had exported ships to 30 countries and territories by the end of 1991.[12] Many of these orders were for smaller, specialized ships Chinese yards would not otherwise have considered. In sum, market diversification played a supporting (but nontrivial) role in China's response to GSC in international shipbuilding, even if CSSC could not simply divert ship production to new markets as readily as in the textile industry.

SPECIALIZATION AMONG CHINA'S LEADING SHIPYARDS

One interesting ramification of product diversification at the national level was product specialization at the yard level. While the industry as a whole produced more types of ships than ever before, individual yards actually made fewer types of ships as the difficulty of newbuilding projects increased markedly. Ultimately, specialization was the only effective way to make use of the machinery imports, technical licenses, and foreign training that were required to build sophisticated vessels successfully. Without concentrating expertise, industrial learning would have been too slow to shorten construction periods, improve quality, and keep costs under control.

---

[11] Ibid. Benchmark international prices for new 70,000- and 80,000-deadweight-ton bulk carriers and tankers fell 41 percent and 21 percent, respectively, between 1980 and 1985.

[12] *Chuanbo Gongcheng*, 7 February 1992, in JPRS-CAR-92-039.

During the 1960s and 1970s, specialization had been very limited within China's shipbuilding community; in fact, the Maoist legacy of self-reliance persisted well into the early 1980s. One of the reasons CSSC was created, after all, was to concentrate authority over all civilian ship-building into one entity, with the hope that it could reorganize an in-dustry in which enterprises were renowned for their all-encompassing production. Even compared to other heavy industries, China's shipyards had been especially notorious for their self-reliance. Beginning in the mid-1980s, however, individual yards became strongly identified with particular types of export ships. For instance, Dalian was known for its tankers (basic oil, product-chemical, and shuttle tankers), Jiangnan for its roll-on–roll-off vessels and bulk carriers, Hudong for its container-ships and basic tankers, and Shanghai for its multipurpose ships and refrigerated containerships.

KEEPING A LID ON CAPACITY: RATIONALIZATION
IN CHINESE SHIPBUILDING

While some new capacity was added to the shipbuilding industry during the 1980s, the focus was clearly on modernizing existing capacity through technical renovation and, where necessary, dock expansion to allow for larger newbuilding projects. (By some measures, the capacity of China's largest yards was inadequate to compete effectively in the world market. By contrast, capacity at small- and medium-sized yards was excessive.) The goal, by all accounts, was to improve China's existing yards – espe-cially the largest yards – in order to meet the challenge of a highly com-petitive world industry. Since the market for new ships was so tight, blind expansion with the aim of increasing the volume of exports (or, for that matter, sales to COSCO) was not a viable option. In this sense, GSC created a strong incentive for CSSC to focus on modernization rather than expansion. Unlike many other industries, which continued to ex-pand capacity in the 1980s, often with the hope of increasing exports, shipbuilding was all but forced to focus on replacing or upgrading exist-ing capacity. The virtual absence of foreign investment opportunities, itself a product of GSC in the world industry, only reinforced the empha-sis on rationalization. (Since the development of the shipbuilding indus-try has never been a top priority in Beijing, a topic discussed further in Chapter 11, government funding for expansion was also quite limited.) While there was little evidence of retired capacity per se during the 1980s, except perhaps in a handful of smaller yards (especially those found in "Third Front" locations far from China's coast), there was an unmistakable emphasis on improving the ability of existing yards to compete more effectively in the world market.[13] All told, China certainly did not add massive capacity like South Korea and Japan had at similar stages in the development of their shipbuilding industries.

GETTING IN TUNE: SHORTENING THE CONSTRUCTION PERIOD FOR NEWBUILDINGS

One the greatest challenges CSSC faced in the depressed world ship-building market of the mid-1980s was to reduce substantially the construction period required for its newbuilding projects. The delivery schedule for Chinese-built ships in the late 1970s and early 1980s had been completely unreliable, adversely affecting the reputation of Chinese yards among foreign shipowners. While CSSC's failure to deliver ships on time had been an ongoing problem, it only became a serious liability when the recession in the mid-1980s turned shipbuilding into a full-blown buyers' market. Previously, some foreign shipowners had been willing to tolerate CSSC's pattern of late delivery, either to secure the lowest price possible or because their need for the ship was not immediate. With the depressed world market, however, customers did not have to tolerate CSSC's unacceptable delays in order to get a good price. While China's prices generally remained the lowest, excellent prices could be found from shipbuilders all around the world, shipbuilders whose yards were extremely reliable in meeting delivery deadlines.

While CSSC did not have instant success in shortening the construction periods for its ships, and even suffered some temporary setbacks due to difficulties encountered in building its first generation of sophisticated vessels, substantial progress was nonetheless made over time. Among CSSC's major yards, Jiangnan Shipyard in Shanghai set the industry standard for reducing delivery times, in many cases halving its construction periods by the end of the 1980s.[14] In fact, improvement throughout the

---

[13] The term "Third Front" refers to the defense industrialization program undertaken in the late 1960s and early 1970s, in which new factories were built in, and some existing facilities relocated to, inland provinces such as Sichuan, Yunnan, Guizhou, and Shaanxi. With American involvement in Vietnam deepening, Mao decided in 1964 that China should reduce its vulnerability along the coast by developing its capabilities deep in the interior. For more detail, see Naughton (1988).

[14] *SBR* (July/August 1991), p. 70, and *SW&SB* (June 1990), p. 219.

industry was so marked that CSSC was reported by the late 1980s to have achieved the unthinkable: numerous *early* deliveries.[15] While this change was likely the result of factors other than simply shortened construction periods – such as a lighter orderbook and greater realism in setting contracted deadlines – the accomplishment is noteworthy all the same.

CSSC BECOMES A DIVERSIFIED MANUFACTURER: THE EXPANSION OF NONMARINE PRODUCTION

Another important aspect of CSSC's response to the international shipbuilding recession was diversification into nonmarine production. As detailed earlier, by the mid-1980s CSSC's orderbook was weakening and newbuilding projects occupied only about two-thirds of CSSC's total shipbuilding capacity. The first substantial indication that yards were turning actively to nonmarine business came in 1985 with reports such as the following:

> Jiangnan has diversified its operations in addition to its main tasks of shipbuilding and shiprepairing. In order to keep up its vitality, the shipyard has taken full advantage of its extensive modern facilities and accepts orders for producing items such as large metal component parts and heavy machinery. . . . Among them were large tunnel borers, large gas tanks, and high-pressure pipes.[16]

Indeed, 1985 was apparently a breakthrough year for nonmarine work in nearly every major yard.[17] By the late 1980s, in fact, the share of nonmarine production in CSSC's industrial output had tripled from the early 1980s.[18] While CSSC had served up the usual hollow rhetoric about diversifying the economy regularly during the early 1980s, its targets in the Sixth and Seventh Five-Year Plans never suggested any substantial commitment to expand nonmarine work, at least not on the scale ultimately seen beginning in the mid-1980s. While it may have been unavoidable

---

[15] Ibid. In 1991, CSSC claimed to have delivered more than half of its large oceangoing ships ahead of schedule; *ZGHY* 10:1 (Spring 1992), p. 59.

[16] *ZGHY* 3:4 (Winter 1985), p. 52.

[17] For more detail, including yard-specific examples, see Moore (1997), pp. 316–326.

[18] *ZGJJNJ*, various years. While data collection was not uniform throughout the 1980s, comparisons for certain years are possible. For example, the share of shipbuilding and marine equipment decreased from 77 percent in 1981 to 47 percent in 1988. The share of shiprepair remained constant at 9 percent, while the share of nonmarine production grew from 14 percent in 1981 to 44 percent in 1988.

given the slump in global newbuilding, CSSC certainly never planned for nonmarine production to prosper at the expense of shipbuilding. By 1987, however, CSSC was already reporting approvingly on the non-marine work undertaken by the yards:

> The shipbuilding industry has now applied the guiding policy of practicing diversified economy. For the last couple of years, it has accomplished a great deal in producing steelwork for tall buildings, machines for underground projects, auxiliary equipment for nuclear power plants, high pressure containers, metallurgy equipment, port machinery, and some light industrial products. In the future it will widen its business scope and increase its activities in other non-ship related areas.[19]

CSSC's praise for these achievements was well-taken since nonmarine production had by 1987 already fulfilled the target set for the end of the Seventh Five-Year Plan (1986–1990).[20] In fact, by the late 1980s the brochures for all of CSSC's major yards read like catalogs for large, diversified manufacturers. In addition to the expected marine-related products, yards were building complete sets of machinery and assembly line equipment, including loading and unloading machinery for coal terminals, generators and blast furnaces, high-pressure vessels for various gases and chemicals, and heavy-duty hydraulic lifts, presses, and cranes. These products ultimately went to industries as diverse as paper manufacturing, textiles, petrochemicals, waste treatment, and tobacco processing. In light industry, CSSC factories produced everything from bicycles and yarn cleaners to gas meters and batteries.

The diversification of CSSC's business into nonmarine production also carried over into exports. For instance, exports of mechanical and electrical products by CSSC's yards more than doubled just from 1986 to 1987. In fact, these exports were actually larger in 1987 alone than for the entire period from 1982 to 1986. Furthermore, the level of exports achieved in 1987 surpassed the target set for 1990 in the Seventh Five-Year Plan.[21] Although figures for CSSC's nonmarine exports are not published regularly in China's statistical yearbooks, they were reported to

---

[19] *ZGHY* 5:1 (Spring 1987), p. 71.

[20] *ZGJXDZGYNJ* (1988), Section III, p. 112.

[21] For more on these figures, see *ZGHY* 6:1 (Spring 1988), p. 77; *ZGJJXW*, 15 February 1988, p. 16; and *China Machinery Industries Yearbook* (1991), p. 70.

have grown six times just from 1988 to 1989.[22] These huge year-on-year increases in nonmarine exports suggest that hard times in the world shipbuilding market may have led not only to an absolute increase in China's nonmarine exports but also to the upgrading of these exports to higher value-added products.[23]

The shift toward nonmarine production also meant greater decision-making autonomy for China's yards. While work on a few large projects was arranged with CSSC's help through the planning system, the vast majority of nonmarine work was apparently produced for the market.[24] In fact, the yards had always been relatively independent in nonmarine production, since it was difficult to make central plans for the myriad activities involving local infrastructure and other regional industrial projects. (Administratively, newbuilding projects were simply far easier to control from the center since the number of large, oceangoing vessels under construction at any given time was relatively small compared to the wide variety of nonmarine production.) Indeed, it was the increasing market orientation of economic activity that accompanied the increased nonmarine work that explains why this diversification can be considered as an important reform in the shipbuilding industry. In one sense, greater emphasis on marine-based production might seem more consistent with both reform and rationalization in an industry such as shipbuilding. For China's yards, however, it could be argued that increased diversification into nonmarine production – a form of "trial by fire" – actually complemented the increasing specialization of vessel production found in ship construction. From this perspective, specialization in shipbuilding combined with diversification into a wider range of nonmarine production served to introduce significant market orientation into the economic lives of the yards, more than either factor could have accomplished in isolation.

---

[22] *China Machinery Industries Yearbook* (1991), p. 180.

[23] Since detailed quantity figures for these many products are not available by producer (CSSC), there is no way to evaluate definitively whether there have been significant increases in the unit value of these exports. Still, one industry yearbook reported in 1991 that "the constitution of mechanical and electronic products exported from the shipbuilding industry has changed from low technological ones ... to high technological ones. ..."; Ibid, p. 70.

[24] One example of a nonmarine project granted to CSSC factories under the state plan was an effort by five enterprises in the Kunming region of Yunnan province to develop an assembly line for tobacco-cutting production. See *ZGJXDZGYNJ* (1988), Section II, p. 10.

SHIPREPAIR: THE SHIFT TOWARD FOREIGN WORK

Another aspect of the industry's response to hard times in world ship-building was an increased emphasis on shiprepair. Since most Chinese yards were equipped for repair work as well as newbuilding projects, this shift was among the most obvious solutions for CSSC's growing problem with idle dock capacity. As in shipbuilding, however, CSSC soon found it necessary to pursue more foreign business, since domestic work proved inadequate as COSCO again sought favorable deals abroad. Facing more and more empty berths, CSSC announced in 1985 that "all shipyards will take on foreign repair work as well as meeting domestic requirements."[25] In short, the dynamics of the world shiprepair market were remarkably similar to those in the world shipbuilding market, in no small measure because the two markets are always so closely linked. Not surprisingly, yards around the world tried to replace their reduced newbuilding business with more repair orders. Even though repair work is less lucrative, stiff competition emerged nonetheless.

In the late 1970s and early 1980s, newbuilding projects were clearly the focus. Not only did shiprepair rank a distant second to shipbuilding, but repairs to foreign ships had virtually no place in the industry (Figure 9.2). If the yards had to do any repair work, so the thinking went, it should only be for the Chinese fleet. In fact, until Chinese yards tried to attract foreign repair business in the mid-1980s, CSSC actually *discriminated* against its overseas clients, systematically charging them higher repair rates.[26]

As part of its increased emphasis on shiprepair, CSSC began to import shiprepair technology – almost from scratch – in the mid-1980s. Without this advanced equipment, Chinese yards could not have competed effectively with modern yards elsewhere in Asia. Shipowners place a substantial premium on a yard's "turnaround time" for repairs since each day that a ship is out of service translates to lost revenue. Given the impending crisis facing CSSC as its orderbook weakened, it is no coincidence that 1985 was consistently identified as the starting point for its effort to acquire advanced technology in shiprepair.[27] Among CSSC's more significant steps, it imported 48 new aerial platforms to replace its traditional scaffolds. It also established some 50 service stations, oper-

[25] *ZGHY* 3:2 (Summer 1985), p. 73.   [26] *Asian Shipping* (May 1988), p. 27.
[27] See, for instance, *ZGJXDZGYNJ* (1988), Section II, p. 10, and *Drydock* (March 1991), p. 19.

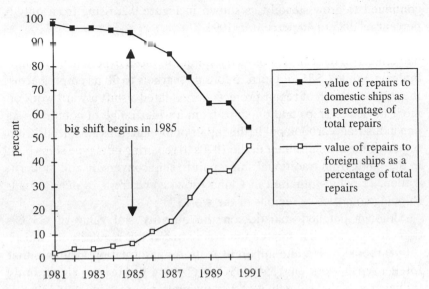

Figure 9.2. Foreign and domestic shares in CSSC's shiprepair. *Source*:
Zhongguo Jingji Nianjian, various years.

ated jointly with foreign marine supply companies, near its yards to facilitate the timely and professional repairs of foreign ships.[28] To further
promote the exchange of shiprepair technology and publicize China's
entry into the world market, CSSC also hosted China's first international
shiprepair exhibition in 1986.[29]

After remaining essentially unchanged in the early 1980s, repairs to
foreign ships rose dramatically after 1985 as China's yards tried rather
desperately to minimize their idle capacity. From a meager U.S. $1.8
million in 1982, the value of foreign repair services increased only marginally to U.S. $4.7 million in 1985. By contrast, the 1985 figure increased
more than tenfold to U.S. $70.7 million by 1990.[30] Although COSCO
signed a long-term agreement with CSSC concerning the repair of domestic ships in 1987, the share of foreign ships in CSSC's repair business

[28] *Drydock* (March 1991), p. 19.
[29] *ZGHY* 4:4 (Winter 1986), p. 92.
[30] *Almanac* (various years). If denominated in Chinese yuan, the increase in the value of
foreign ship repairs is even more pronounced: from 4 million yuan in 1981 to 344 million
yuan in 1991; *ZGJJNJ* (various years).

continued to grow steadily, as shown in Figure 9.2, rising from only 6 percent in 1985 to 46 percent in 1991.[31]

Perhaps more importantly, the slump in global demand for shiprepair had effects on the Chinese industry similar to those experienced in ship-building. While CSSC did turn to foreign markets to fill its empty berths, the relative dearth of repair projects necessitated a shift toward work on more advanced ships and on ships from a wider range of countries. As one industrial yearbook put it, the repair of foreign ships advanced "from repairing the old ships built in the 1970s to repairing new-type ships built in the 1980s, from traditional shiprepair to ship conversion and modern-ization. The ships repaired in China [now] come from 20 main ocean-shipping countries or regions in the world."[32]

Although detailed statistics on the quantity and value of CSSC's domestic and foreign shiprepairs are not reported regularly in statisti-cal yearbooks, it is quite apparent from the information available that foreign repair work enabled CSSC to upgrade its business significantly to higher value-added activity.[33] For example, whereas the unit value of repairs (U.S. $ per repair) for domestic oceangoing vessels declined by almost 25 percent from 1984 to 1986, the figure for foreign repairs actu-ally rose 4 percent over the same period despite international repair prices that were falling steadily due to the worldwide recession in ship-building and shiprepair.[34]

From 1985 to 1989, only once (in 1987) did growth in the *number* of foreign ship repairs outpace the corresponding increase in the total *value* of these repairs. In fact, in 1988 and 1989 the total value of foreign repair work actually grew despite a decline in the number of ships repaired.[35] Thus, the growth in the total value of repairs to foreign ships in the late 1980s came primarily from achieving a higher unit value of repair work (Figure 9.3). While some of this increase might have resulted from work on dilapidated vessels that simply required more extensive repairs, much (or even nearly all) of the increase likely involved complicated work on

---

[31] On the agreement with COSCO, see *PRC Yearbook* (1987), p. 326.

[32] *China Machinery Industries Yearbook* (1991), p. 70.

[33] Even in the various yearbooks which cover the machinery and electronics industry, the presentation of statistics varies from year to year. For instance, figures for shiprepair are not always broken down according to oceangoing vessels, coastal ships, river boats, et cetera.

[34] Data on the number of foreign ship repairs come from *ZGJJNJ*, various years. Data on the value of foreign ship repairs come from *Almanac* (various years).

[35] Ibid.

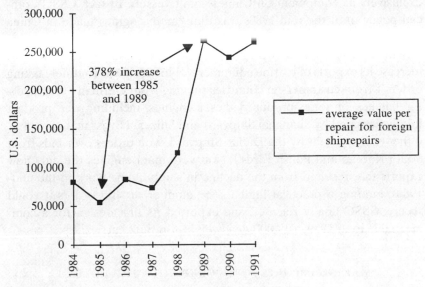

Figure 9.3. Unit value of CSSC's repairs to foreign ships. *Source: Almanac of China's Foreign Economic Relations and Trade*, various years; *Zhongguo Jingji Nianjian*, various years.

more sophisticated vessels. All told, it would be difficult to overestimate the contribution made by foreign ship repairs to CSSC's overall repair business. Although much of the technology imported in the 1980s to facilitate repair projects for foreign shipowners was also subsequently applied to domestic repairs, the daily output value of repairs to foreign ships remained almost twice as high as that for domestic ships in the late 1980s.[36]

CSSC'S GROWING EXPORTS OF MARINE EQUIPMENT

By reducing the number of newbuilding projects realistically available to CSSC, the global recession in shipbuilding also accelerated, and arguably even initiated, the expansion of China's marine equipment exports. Foreign sales of diesel engines and other ship components grew from only U.S. $300,000 in 1984 to over U.S. $40 million in 1991. Until the decline in world shipbuilding, CSSC had sold these products

[36] *ZGJXDZGYNJ* (1988), Section II, pp. 10–11.

exclusively as equipment on Chinese-built vessels. In fact, CSSC's official policy until the mid-1980s was that "main engines made in China could only be exported as parts of ships."[37]

With hard times in the world market, however, CSSC began efforts to increase its exports of marine equipment. By 1990, it was routinely taking orders – from customers in countries ranging from Germany to Brazil – for batches of series-produced diesel engines, including one product jointly designed by Shanghai Shipyard and Sulzer, a Swiss manufacturer. Other engines, built by the Dalian Shipyard, won orders over bids from South Korean and Polish yards.[38] Nor were main engines the only new exports that resulted from the decline in shipbuilding work in the mid-1980s. Finding a practical limit to the number of ship orders it could secure, CSSC finally relented and exported its first design for a commercial ship in 1989, a 17,000-deadweight-ton bulk carrier.[39]

"MAKING IMPORTS FOSTER EXPORTS": THE ROLE OF TECHNOLOGY ACQUISITION

Compared to other aspects of China's response to severe GSC in shipbuilding, such as the increased emphasis on foreign shiprepair and exports of marine equipment, technology imports represented a more continuous phenomenon since these flows actually dated back to the late 1970s.[40] Although foreign technology had been introduced prior to the onset of hard times in the world shipbuilding market, it was only after CSSC entered the market for advanced ship types in the mid-1980s that the scope and depth of foreign involvement in the Chinese industry fundamentally changed its relationship with the international industry. To build the sophisticated vessels for which it had secured orders, CSSC needed advanced equipment. While some components had to be imported as finished products, especially at first, CSSC decided to import as much technology as possible through production licenses and coproduction agreements with foreign manufacturers, a move designed to raise the domestic content of Chinese-built ships in the long run.

---

[37] *ZGHY* 10:1 (Spring 1992), p. 60. [38] *ZGHY* 9:4 (Winter 1991), p. 79.
[39] *SW&SB* (November 1990), p. 380.
[40] Technical exchange with the outside world returned in earnest in 1978 when China signed the original production licenses for several engines with Sulzer of Switzerland and Burmeister & Wain of Denmark. In that same year, Dalian commenced a relationship with Hitachi Zosen of Japan, an agreement that was later complemented by a similar agreement in 1980 between Jiangnan and Mitsubishi Heavy Industries.

The impact of the international shipbuilding recession on China's technology imports can be seen in the number of licenses signed during different periods in the post-Mao period. From all indications, CSSC imported a total of approximately 104 items of technology between 1978 and 1990.[41] From sporadic reports in various industrial yearbooks, it can be determined that about 19 items were imported from 1978 through 1983. The remaining 85 items were, therefore, imported from 1984 onward, with some 63 items (61 percent of the total) concentrated in the period from 1986 to 1990.[42] According to interviews, technology imports apparently tailed off during the last couple of years in this period. If so, the vast majority of technology imports therefore came in a relatively brief period starting about 1985 when CSSC began in earnest to build advanced ships for the international market.[43]

Implementing a policy CSSC officials often referred to as "making imports foster exports" (*yijin yangchu*), the shipbuilding industry set out in discrete stages to learn modern production techniques through license (and, later, coproduction) agreements with various foreign manufacturers.[44] At first, CSSC merely assembled equipment such as diesel engines from imported components, trying to master the technical data along the way. In the second stage, CSSC tried to simulate the technology from abroad, reducing the proportion of imported parts by increasing the domestic content. In the third and final stage, CSSC concentrated not only on simulating foreign technology, but also on using this know-how to develop new Chinese-designed products for use in both domestic and export ships.[45]

With this accumulated technological expertise, CSSC was, by the late 1980s, producing more of the principal equipment – main engines, generators, cranes, and deck machinery – used on ships built in China. While the rate of domestically produced components remained disappointingly

---

[41] See, for instance, *ZGHY* 8:2 (Summer 1990), p. 61, and *China's Shipbuilding Industry in Progress* (1991), p. 24.

[42] While fairly accurate, these figures may not be exact since they are inferred from several different sources. The basic pattern, however, should still hold; ibid. See also *ZGJXDZGYNJ* (1986), Section II, p. 23, and *ZGJXDZGYNJ* (1985), Sections II and III, p. 20 and p. 168, respectively.

[43] Although annual figures were not available, interviews revealed that the rate of technology import slowed by the late 1980s and early 1990s, suggesting that the mid-1980s was in fact the busiest period of technology acquisition.

[44] See, for instance, the interview with Hu Chuanzhi, CSSC's managing director, in *ZGHY* 4:2 (Summer 1986), pp. 13, 97.

[45] *ZGHY* 8:2 (Summer 1990), p. 61.

low for most of the 1980s, especially for the highly sophisticated vessels built for export, the localization of production had improved slightly by the late 1980s and early 1990s. While China's reliance on foreign technology and its use of imported components clearly grew, creating some short-run dependencies, this heightened degree of integration with the international industry also yielded broad benefits for CSSC through the transfer of management practices and the adoption of international maritime standards. Nor should the value of the technology transfer be underestimated. Through scores of agreements with foreign manufacturers, CSSC was able to introduce a variety of advanced production techniques – e.g., mathematical lofting, digitally controlled cutting, and various forms of highly efficient welding technology – as part of the technical transformation of China's main yards. Other new procedures included block outfitting and telescopic assembly; these advances enabled China's yards to build ships section-by-section in different workshops and then assemble them into a finished vessel at the dock.

All told, China emerged from the crisis of the mid-1980s with a stronger shipbuilding base but only marginally greater dependence on foreign equipment. In fact, by one measure – the total value of marine equipment imports – China's position was virtually unchanged at the end of the decade. Indeed, China actually imported U.S. $3 million less in marine equipment in 1990 than in 1982, CSSC's first year as a formal entity.[46] Moreover, what these gross figures do not reveal is the qualitative shift in which imports of complete machinery (e.g., engines and cargo lifts) increasingly gave way to imports of components (e.g., critical engine parts) for more specialized equipment.[47] While published trade statistics do not include quantity figures, since the category "marine equipment" encompasses so many different products, imports appear to have included more items at roughly the same total cost. By these measures, China may have actually even *lessened* its long-term dependence on foreign equipment by the end of the 1980s, this despite an increased emphasis on building specialized ships for export. Even if the actual domestic content of "Chinese-built" ships increased slowly, the advanced capabilities of the industry arguably

[46] *Almanac* (various years).

[47] For a description of this change in the composition of shipbuilding imports, see *ZGJXDZGYNJ* (1988), Section VI, p. 5.

more than compensated for its continued reliance on certain categories of imports.[48]

STEADY PROGRESS IN PERENNIALLY CHOPPY WATERS:
CHINESE SHIPBUILDING SINCE THE EARLY 1990s

Since the early 1990s, when the main focal area of this study ended, the composition of China's ship exports has been more evenly matched between basic and advanced ships. In part, this reflects an international trend in which the newbuilding markets for bulk carriers and tankers have seen a significant recovery in the wake of their utter collapse in the mid-1980s. From this perspective, it is not surprising that China's order-book has returned to a more balanced position consistent with international demand. That said, there has also been continued evidence of product upgrading. First, while advanced ships accounted for only about 50 percent of CSSC's exports between the early 1990s and the AFC, these vessels continued to be dominated by LPG carriers, chemical carriers, containerships, and other specialized vessels rather than the relatively unsophisticated multipurpose ships that dominated the category during the early 1980s.[49]

Second, the unit value of China's ship exports has increased substantially, this despite the greater balance between basic and advanced ship types in recent years. Whatever the limitations of unit value as a measure of product upgrading, CSSC's continued record in raising the value of its ship exports cannot be completely dismissed. During the three-year period from 1993 to 1995, for example, China's exports averaged U.S. $52 million per ship, more than *double* the highest value for any year in the 1980s. (When compared to some of the worst years, unit values in the 1990s had grown as much as three or four times in a ten-year period.) While the unit values of CSSC's ship exports have fluctuated considerably from year to year, the trend is unmistakably upward. While some of this gain surely reflects the higher prices commanded for ship construction after the

---

[48] While CSSC has occasionally reported data on the percentage of main equipment produced in China, a figure that has risen steadily over the years, these statistics can be very misleading since even products "manufactured" in China often contain foreign parts. Since there is little reliable information on the percentage of foreign components in "Chinese-built" equipment, official figures on the nationalization of production may not be very useful.

[49] Data calculated from computer printout supplied by CSSC.

international industry recovered from its hard-hitting recession in the 1980s, much must also be attributed to the product upgrading in the Chinese industry. In fact, the more balanced mix between basic ships and advanced ships strongly suggests that even China's basic bulk carriers and tankers have moved upmarket in recent years.

In addition to improving the quality of existing ship types, Chinese yards have continued to pursue new vessels such as liquid nitrogen gas (LNG) carriers and VLCCs (specialized oil tankers in excess of 250,000 deadweight tons). In August 1999, for example, China secured its first order for VLCCs. The U.S. $370 million contract calls for the construction of five 300,000-deadweight-ton ships, each 1,000 feet long and 190 feet wide. With this order, the Chinese industry surmounted an important psychological barrier that had long separated it from its competitors in South Korea and Japan, the only other two countries currently producing these maritime behemoths.

Market diversification has also proceeded apace. In 1996 alone, first-time orders were either received or completed for shipowners from France, Switzerland, Finland, Taiwan, Japan, South Korea, Canada, Greece, and Malaysia.[50] Since South Korea, Japan, and Taiwan represent the world's first-, second-, and fourth-ranked shipbuilding countries, respectively, it was a major coup to penetrate these markets. That said, China's entree into the newbuilding market for Greek shipowners may well prove to be the most important development in the long run. While time-to-completion will remain a relative weakness for CSSC, as Chinese yards have little prospect of catching South Korean or Japanese yards in the foreseeable future, steady improvement in shortening construction periods continued through the late 1990s.

China's success in foreign shiprepair and marine equipment exports also continued through 1994, the last year for which MOFERT published the necessary data on these activities. While the share of foreign ships in CSSC's repair business leveled off at about 50 percent, the value of foreign shiprepair grew tremendously in absolute terms. In 1993 and 1994, the last two years on record, foreign shiprepair earned U.S. $120 and U.S. $117 million, respectively.[51] As far as marine equipment exports are concerned, foreign sales of diesel engines and other ship components totaled U.S. $157 million in 1994, a figure almost four times higher than the 1991 total.[52]

[50] *China Daily*, 2 February 1999, in FBIS-CHI-97-023.   [51] *Almanac* (various years).
[52] Ibid. *ZGJJNJ* (1997) reports $150 million in marine equipment exports for 1996, suggesting that the 1994 figure was no aberration.

All told, China's shipbuilding industry continued its upward trajectory until the onset of the AFC in 1997. As discussed in Chapter 1, a combination of the regional economic downturn and depreciating currencies in Japan and South Korea affected CSSC's orderbook severely. By October 1998, conditions in the industry were so dire that Beijing announced its intention to reorganize CSSC in an effort to increase the international competitiveness of its shipyards.[53] In July 1999, after nearly a year with no specific plan in place, it was officially announced that two new entities had been formed to replace CSSC: China Shipbuilding Industry Corporation and China Shipbuilding Group Company.[54] China United Shipbuilding remains the agent for both entities in Hong Kong. While the long-term significance of this reorganization remains to be seen, the move did signify the seriousness of the industry's dislocation in the wake of the AFC.

[53] *Journal of Commerce,* 14 May 1999, p. 3B (Maritime). Given its timing, this move may also have been influenced by the renewed emphasis on SOE reform that emerged from the Fifteenth National Congress of the Chinese Communist Party in September 1997. Even more directly, perhaps, CSSC's reorganization may have been influenced by the broader ministerial shake up that occurred in the wake of the Ninth National People's Congress in March 1998. Indeed, one aspect of this government restructuring was an effort to reorganize several defense-related industries.

[54] With Dalian as its core, China Shipbuilding Industry Corporation also controls shipyards in Xi'an, Tianjin, Wuhan, Chongqing, and Kunming. For its part, China Shipbuilding Group Company is headquartered in Shanghai with additional yards in Guangdong, Jiangsu, and Anhui.

10

Market-Oriented Solutions for Industrial Adjustment: The Changing Pattern of State Intervention in Chinese Shipbuilding

A S documented in the previous chapter, China's shipbuilding industry achieved an impressive record of industrial restructuring in coping with severe GSC in the world market for ships. This chapter proceeds by asking the following question: How was all this change accomplished? In particular, what was the nature of the policy response and why was this strategy adopted by CSSC? As its title suggests, this chapter documents the changing pattern of state intervention in Chinese shipbuilding. The first section examines how pressures from the international market contributed to the decline of central planning in the industry. The second section investigates the limited financial decentralization that followed when dilemmas generated by the first wave of reform in the industry created incentives for further change. The third section focuses explicitly on how the industry's export experience led to market-oriented solutions for industrial adjustment. The chapter concludes with an evaluation of reform accomplishments in shipbuilding, as well as a discussion of the changing role played by CSSC's national office (hereafter, CSSC Beijing) in the industry.

THE FIRST WAVE OF REFORM: THE EROSION OF CENTRAL PLANNING

For all the talk about fundamental changes that surrounded CSSC's creation in 1982, including the claim that the "regional corporations and subsidiaries [yards] are fully empowered to negotiate with foreign companies, sign contracts and agreements, organize technological exchanges, and offer technical services," reform in the industry was nothing short of glacial until the mid-1980s.[1] While this is not entirely surprising since nationwide industrial reform did not begin in earnest until 1984, it is worth reiterating that CSSC initially acted much more like a traditional ministry than a new-style "corporation." For example, all work on ship-building projects was allocated directly by the relevant domestic or international planning office at CSSC Beijing until at least 1985.[2] This evidence is, of course, consistent with the argument made in Chapter 7 that CSSC was established primarily to recentralize, rather than weaken, bureaucratic control over the shipbuilding industry.

As it turns out, CSSC did not even begin to decentralize authority over product planning and other business development to the yards until its diminishing orderbook reached a crisis in the mid-1980s due to the powerful combination of chronic GSC and a growing international reces-sion in shipping. By early 1985, *Asian Shipping* and other international maritime journals began filing reports such as the following:

> The China State Shipbuilding Corporation in Beijing has granted more autonomy to local shipbuilding corporations, including the right to negotiate directly with potential customers, signalling China's determination vis-à-vis the world market.[3]

Interviews confirmed that it was indeed about 1985 when China's yards were first granted significant autonomy to negotiate independently with foreign shipowners, overseas equipment manufacturers, marine con-sultants, and the international classification societies that certify the con-struction of ships to international standards. Although this sweeping decentralization was partially revoked later when a few yards entered into disastrous deals, the yards were never again subordinate in the same way. (In fact, the decentralization of economic decision making resumed again fairly quickly.) As the following report from *Zhongguo Haiyun* (*Maritime China*) suggests, the yards were soon left largely to their own devices in finding work:

> In 1986, the continuing depression of the international shipbuild-ing market cast a shadow over China's shipbuilding industry and

---

[1] *ZGHY* 1:1 (March 1983), p. 67.

[2] Every interview, even those with officials from the industry itself, confirmed that orders were strictly controlled by central authorities until the mid-1980s. In fact, even in the early 1990s, CSSC Beijing still had to give formal approval for orders negotiated by the yards themselves.

[3] *Asian Shipping* (April 1985), p. 15.

brought about fierce competition among shipbuilders in the country. The state continued to curtail its general plans and none of the shipbuilding enterprises could get enough work for their building berths. Under such circumstances, Guangzhou Shipbuilding Industry Corporation . . . had no other choice but to diversify its services. . . . It has also improved its management and worked hard to secure contracts for newbuildings. . . .[4]

As early as 1985, less than 60 percent of CSSC's revenues came from goods sold at state-set prices.[5] Indeed, reports about the reduced role of central planning in the shipbuilding industry continued regularly into 1987 and 1988.[6] Although CSSC did not publicly announce its retreat from direct control over all phases of production, distribution, and pricing, the reality of market-oriented reform in the industry was amply clear: "With the relaxation of mandatory planning, enterprises must continue to expand in order to survive. It is important for them to continuously turn out new products that the market needs."[7]

Prior to the onset of the international recession, CSSC had determined both mandatory output targets for the yards and their related input allocations. These, in turn, were based on aggregate targets for the industry approved by the State Planning Commission. In this sense, CSSC was indeed created to supervise centrally run enterprises. As the market situation deteriorated from the early to mid-1980s, however, "mandatory" targets gave way to "guidance" targets. (While the introduction of these reforms in the shipbuilding industry must be understood within the larger context of the industrial reforms begun in 1984, their relatively expeditious implementation – at least compared to most other state-run heavy industries – seems to owe much to CSSC's response to international forces.) At first, the yards apparently gained responsibility mainly for marketing their own products. While the yards were by no means cut off from the CSSC apparatus, including the marketing and sales departments, they no longer formally enjoyed guaranteed procurement for their output. There is little detailed information on precisely how this

[4] *ZGHY* 5:3 (Autumn 1987), pp. 83–84.
[5] For more detail on reform results in CSSC circa 1985, see *Dangdai Zhongguo de Chuanbo Gongye* (1992), pp. 672–676.
[6] For example, *Zhongguo Haiyun* [*Maritime China*] stated rather bluntly that "in 1987 . . . the number of assignments put forward by the state became less and less"; *ZGHY* 6:2 (Summer 1988), p. 80.
[7] *ZGHY* 7:2 (Summer 1989), p. 67.

change in policy was carried out, or what the immediate impact was on the percentage of self-sales, but the yards were by all accounts forced to find more customers for their products independently, even in the case of ships worth tens of millions of U.S. dollars.

With COSCO free to place orders abroad and the market for ships poor in general, central authorities in the industry gradually found that they could not guarantee the purchase of ships produced under the plan. Rather than trying to make sales outside of the plan on its own, CSSC Beijing left this responsibility largely to the yards. From all indications, it tried initially to retain control over many important decisions concerning production, even though the yards were increasingly burdened with marketing their own products. Not surprisingly, this arrangement did not prove satisfactory, and as the market situation continued to deteriorate, "mandatory" targets did in fact weaken into mere "guidance" targets. Over time, even these loose benchmarks became relatively insignificant.[8]

As the market for ships weakened steadily during the mid-1980s, it became increasingly difficult for CSSC to both secure enough orders to prevent the emergence of idle facilities at its yards, and keep the planning system in place as before. As long as the procurement of CSSC's ships was in effect "guaranteed" (i.e., there were enough orders to go around), then it could continue the central allocation of ship orders, thereby maintaining a system of mandatory planning. However, once the purchase of its ships was no longer "guaranteed" – either formally by the state or informally by the existence of sufficient market demand – then it could not continue to impose mandatory plans on the yards unless it was willing to sell the ships on their behalf, something it could not easily do with such weak demand in the domestic and international markets. If CSSC Beijing could not provide enough work for all of its yards, it could either allocate the work it did have and allow the remaining facilities to become idle or essentially cut the yards loose, giving them effective control over most decisions concerning production and distribution. From all indications, CSSC Beijing chose the latter option.

As a result, ship production in China became increasingly market-oriented, although this market was certainly not as freely operating as those in Western countries. This change also applied to ancillary players

---

[8] According to a report in *Renmin Ribao* [*The People's Daily*], the official Party newspaper, by 1989 only 70 of 300 products made by shipbuilding enterprises were even *listed* on state plans, let alone governed by it; *FBIS Daily Report-China*, 6 April 1990, p. 35.

in the industry – e.g., design institutes, training centers, and research facilities – that found themselves orienting more and more of their work to the needs of the market. In the case of design institutes, for example, advanced computer technology actually enabled some of China's larger yards to do more of their own design work. As a result, many of CSSC's design institutes were used only on an ad hoc basis, typically for especially difficult tasks or when a yard's design department was overloaded. While this evolving arrangement often led to better coordination between the yards and the shipowners for whom they were building vessels, it left the design institutes underemployed. In many cases, the dynamics of supply and demand led design institutes to projects wholly unrelated to shipbuilding. The Shanghai Ship Designing Institute, for example, broadened its business by the late 1980s to include systems for air conditioning, fire fighting, and pollution abatement.[9]

Ultimately, the decentralization of authority within the industry was not limited only to sales and production. In order to shorten the average construction period for newbuildings, the yards were also granted more administrative control over the purchase of materials and equipment. In the case of steel, for example, the yards had always needed to plan far ahead for new projects since steel plate was only distributed twice per year through the Ministry of Metallurgy. If a yard needed more steel between deliveries, it was forced to buy it outside of the plan at considerably higher prices. Not surprisingly, most yards tried to order extra steel whenever they could, hoarding this precious supply either for emergency use or to sell later at a profit.[10] Still, given the shortages endemic in state socialist economies, this strategy was not always possible and yards were frequently caught without adequate supplies. So, after several debacles in which export orders for prominent foreign shipowners were embarrassingly (and, due to penalty clauses, very expensively) late, the yards were given considerably more latitude in procuring the raw materials and equipment necessary for ship projects.

The most infamous (and financially costly) debacle involved the desperate attempts of the Hudong yard in Shanghai to acquire steel products for the aforementioned *Berlin Express*, a refrigerated containership

---

[9] *ZGHY* 6:2 (Summer 1988), p. 81.

[10] One surveyor for a major international classification society recalled seeing what he estimated to be 30,000 tons of surplus steel plate "lying around" at a yard in Shanghai in the early to mid-1980s. Chronic problems concerning the timely acquisition of raw materials and equipment for shipbuilding projects in China were raised repeatedly in interviews.

built for Germany's Hapag-Lloyd.[11] At first, steel was to be imported from Japan, until the relevant national foreign trade corporation, China National Metals and Minerals Import and Export Corporation, mysteriously refused Hudong's request. Subsequent plans to obtain the steel domestically were nixed when the shipment, coming from the inland port of Wuhan, was physically stranded in river traffic and could not be transported in time. When CSSC tried again, this time successfully, to import from Japan, the effort was still stymied, in this instance by a requirement that imports of products similar to those made in China be transported by Chinese ships. Due to congestion at Tianjin – hardly the most logical port for receiving goods destined for a shipyard in Shanghai – the ship carrying the Japanese steel had to berth outside the port, further delaying delivery. When the steel finally arrived at the yard, 18 months had already elapsed in the 25-month delivery period stipulated in the contract. This story, which was extensively profiled in the Chinese press, is legendary among those acquainted with CSSC's travails.[12]

While greater freedom in (or, perhaps more accurately, responsibility for) procuring inputs by no means eliminated all of the problems surrounding material supply and late delivery, it did improve the industry's performance. Information about the exact percentage of raw materials that continued to be allocated under the plan is incomplete, but it is clear that informal, market-based exchange increased both among yards and between yards and their basic suppliers (e.g., steel mills). While it would certainly be an exaggeration to claim that problems associated with late delivery in a highly competitive world market single-handedly eliminated the role of central planning in the distribution of inputs, they did diminish its relevance as an effective mechanism for allocating resources in the industry, since greater flexibility and responsiveness was needed for the yards to build quality vessels in a timely fashion for foreign shipowners.

While CSSC had tried for many years, decades actually, to shorten construction periods through the use of various administrative directives, these efforts have difficulty explaining the timing of the industry's successful reduction of delivery times, a process that began – not at all coincidentally – in the mid-1980s when China's orderbook reflected the nadir

---

[11] In the end, a U.S. $3 million penalty (at U.S. $20,000 per day) was assessed for late delivery; *FBIS Daily Report-China*, 20 March 1989, p. 15.

[12] For one account in the Chinese press, see *FBIS Daily Report-China*, 20 March 1989, p. 15.

of the world shipbuilding market. Until that time, all efforts to increase productivity by setting timetables for ship construction had failed.[13] With the global recession in shipbuilding, however, CSSC's yards had no choice but to meet international norms regarding prompt delivery if they were to continue attracting foreign orders.

One mechanism for achieving this improvement in performance was the widespread use of intra-enterprise contracts, bonus systems, and other devices aimed at increasing microlevel responsibility for meeting delivery deadlines and other important criteria. Indeed, departments within the shipyards agreed to cost and quality targets, as well as time deadlines, with bonuses for meeting these goals that constituted up to 40 percent of total pay.[14] More generally, control over a widening array of management decisions was incrementally decentralized to yard directors and, beneath them, department directors. The use of contracts designed to improve responsibility for performance was also extended to relations among enterprises. As early as 1985, for example, quality warranty agreements were established between various equipment suppliers and China's shipyards.[15]

THE SECOND WAVE OF REFORM: DILEMMAS OF PARTIAL REFORM AND LIMITED FINANCIAL DECENTRALIZATION

Even after the system of mandatory planning had all but disappeared, CSSC Beijing still maintained a firm hold on the industry's financial levers. Although CSSC underwent some nominal financial reforms in the early and mid-1980s consistent with programs promulgated nationwide, the industry's centralized system of internal financial management persisted virtually unchanged. Consequently, China's shipyards were not directly responsible for financial losses incurred in their operations. In this sense, they continued to enjoy a fairly soft budget constraint even after they became more responsible for sales and production. Introduced by Janos Kornai, the concept of hard and soft budget constraints addresses the relationship between the profitability of a firm and its long-term survival. Specifically, the hardness or softness of a firm's budget

---

[13] For a discussion of CSSC's use of plans to shorten building periods, see *ZGHY* 10:1 (Spring 1992), p. 59.
[14] For more detail on reform measures in yard management, see *Dangdai Zhongguo de Chuanbo Gongye* (1992), Chapter 38.
[15] Ibid, pp. 676–679.

constraint depends on the credibility of the bureaucracy to tolerate persistent loss making.[16] If the likelihood is high that a firm's losses will be covered, then its budget constraint is said to be relatively soft. Indeed, Kornai argues that the hardness and softness of budget constraints should be conceived in terms of a continuum, not as hard or soft budget constraints in an absolute, dichotomous sense.

Although China's shipyards had made progress by expanding into specialized ship types, upgrading their technology, engaging in more advanced shiprepair, and otherwise restructuring the industry's output, they had little incentive to conserve raw materials, keep costs in line with prices, and raise productivity more generally. Indeed, an increasing number of export orders, such as the high-tech *Berlin Express*, proved to be huge loss-makers for CSSC.[17] In many cases, these financial boondoggles resulted directly from the decentralization of production authority that had occurred during the mid-1980s when CSSC's orderbook became so badly depleted. As mentioned earlier, CSSC Beijing had granted the yards an unprecedented degree of autonomy to negotiate orders with prospective customers. The greater power and flexibility enjoyed by the yards undoubtedly resulted in more (and better) orders for China, but the cost was high indeed: CSSC incurred huge losses simply in order to survive the stormy seas of the global recession.

Ultimately, the financial responsibility borne by the yards was not commensurate with their autonomy over matters such as production and pricing. In this sense, the yards faced a hard market constraint, but a soft budget constraint. Not surprisingly, this combination spelled trouble. The yards took on a variety of newbuilding projects that, while representing excellent opportunities to learn about the construction of advanced ships, would be very costly for a yard in any developing country to undertake, let alone a yard in a partially reformed economy such as China's. While CSSC Beijing did retain some important oversight tools, the shipbuilding industry nonetheless found itself committed time and again to vessel orders for which the yards were ill-prepared, especially at the bargain prices they offered to foreign shipowners. By CSSC's own admis-

---

[16] Kornai (1992), p. 143. The concepts were first raised in Kornai (1980). For a good primer, see Kornai (1992), pp. 140–145.

[17] According to Chinese press reports, the total loss suffered on the *Berlin Express* was U.S. $8 million, including a U.S. $3 million penalty for late delivery; *FBIS Daily Report-China*, 20 March 1989, p. 15. Reports in the international maritime press suggest that many, or perhaps even most, export orders taken in the mid-1980s at the nadir of the market ultimately resulted in big losses for CSSC; *SBR* (July/August 1991), p. 70.

sion, its strategy in the 1980s was generally to win orders simply by offering discounts of 5–10 percent below the prices set by Japanese and South Korean yards.[18]

Without the proper financial incentives in place, these experiments in shipbuilding proved long on learning and short on cost-effectiveness. The acquisition of market knowledge and technical expertise was undoubtedly good for the industry, but the high cost of this education was equally noteworthy. Due to cutthroat competition in the world market, Chinese yards had to offer extremely low prices. Even if a project went smoothly, the profit – if such a thing could be meaningfully measured in China – would surely have been minimal. When problems were encountered, such as technical bottlenecks, raw materials shortages, or penalties for late delivery, the losses quickly mounted. For their part, the yards showed little financial discipline since these losses were largely covered by CSSC. Indeed, this was the crux of the matter. World prices had fallen precipitously during the shipbuilding recession, but the yards felt no real pressure to reduce (or even stabilize) their costs. Consequently, the financial squeeze – to the extent that there were consequences at the industrial level – was felt primarily by CSSC Beijing.

While it is not clear exactly what consequences CSSC ever faced, the scale of its losses was clearly intolerable from the government's perspective.[19] Although published statistics indicate that CSSC always made at least a small profit on its total activities from the early 1980s to the early 1990s, interviews did not support that view.[20] (Several close observers of the industry claimed that official statistics on CSSC's financial performance during this period were substantially embellished.) That said, even these figures reveal the slide in profitability that followed

[18] For an analysis of CSSC's early efforts to enter the export market for ships, including its pricing strategy, see *Dangdai Zhongguo de Chuanbo Gongye* (1992), pp. 608–614.

[19] Interviews confirmed that the government was routinely forced to cover CSSC's losses. This point was implicitly acknowledged by Li Zhushi, vice-president of CSTC, in 1991 when he expressed doubt about the ability and willingness of the government to subsidize CSSC's newbuilding losses in the future. While perhaps unrealistic, CSSC identified financial independence as a goal for the Eighth Five-Year Plan (1991–1995). See *SBR* (July/August 1991), p. 72. For another view on CSSC's perennial deficit, see *LMA* (January 1992), p. 25.

[20] For their part, CSSC officials freely acknowledged that losses were incurred in *shipbuilding* in the mid- to late 1980s, but they also claimed that CSSC actually made a total profit during these years as a result of improved performance in repair work, the manufacture of marine equipment, and nonmarine production. See, for example, the comments of Li Zhushi, vice-president of CSTC, in *FEER*, 7 February 1991, p. 53.

the slump in the international shipbuilding market. (Here as elsewhere, the main value of Chinese statistics is the insight they can provide in identifying trends.) Total realized profit for CSSC fell precipitously in just one year from 430 million yuan in 1985 to 150 million yuan in 1986, plunging further to 90 million yuan by 1988. Not surprisingly, the number of loss-making enterprises within the CSSC system more than tripled during this same period.[21] Reports from the Chinese press confirm that the entire industry, and several yards in particular, were suffering growing losses as early as 1986, especially in their newbuilding activities.[22]

By all accounts, CSSC Beijing tried initially to apply administrative pressure on the yards to improve product quality to international standards, shorten construction periods to meet delivery deadlines, and raise overall productivity to contain costs.[23] In the absence of a hard budget constraint, however, CSSC's exhortations concerning efficiency had the same hollow impact that decades of similar campaigns had achieved in other industries. Ultimately, the buffer between an enterprise and the financial consequences of its behavior remained. Especially as the intensity of the stakes grew for CSSC – as the yards took on difficult, unfamiliar projects in a cutthroat world market, while China's central government wrestled with growing fiscal problems – the pressure to extend greater financial autonomy to the yards mounted.

Before long, financial decentralization was the only practical way to shift more of the burden of industrial adjustment onto the enterprises themselves. At a time of rising losses within state-run industry, CSSC could not afford (politically or financially) to resist the kind of changes embodied in reforms such as the "Contract Management Responsibility System" (CMRS). While it may well have been a reluctant reformer, CSSC Beijing did implement a second wave of reform, in which a limited form of financial decentralization accompanied the earlier devolution in operational control over sales and production. Given the difficulties associated with CSSC's lean orderbook, the timing of CMRS's imple-

---

[21] *ZGJJNJ* (various years).

[22] See, for instance, *ZGHY* 5:1 (Spring 1987), p. 69, and *ZGHY* 5:3 (Autumn 1987), p. 84.

[23] Although mandatory planning gave way to guidance targets rather quickly, CSSC had also apparently used administrative pressure to try to influence production decisions by the yards. For instance, all yards were ordered in 1985 to undertake foreign repair work to compensate for the loss in newbuilding work; *ZGHY* 3:2 (Summer 1985), p. 73. To cite another example, CSSC designated Zhonghua Shipyard as a production base for the export of electrical machinery.

mentation in Chinese yards – 1987 – was no coincidence.[24] As a result of this initiative, as well as related moves, responsibility devolved at two levels: first, from CSSC Beijing to the yards and, second, within the yards themselves as efforts were undertaken to make departments, workshops, and other sub-yard units more accountable for their own performance.

At first glance, it might not appear that conditions in the world industry had anything to do with the adoption of the CMRS in CSSC since this program was first introduced nationally in 1984 at the beginning of a major round of industrial reforms that lasted until 1988. In reality, however, the CMRS was very slow to be implemented. According to data collected by China's State Statistical Bureau as part of a World Bank project, the CMRS had been implemented in less than 20 percent of SOEs by 1987.[25] So, while the shipbuilding industry was far from unique in this respect, it was one of the earlier implementers of this management system. Even though CMRS was not itself a response to specific problems facing the shipbuilding industry, international forces do appear to have been instrumental in facilitating its adoption by CSSC. Hard times in world markets, coupled with low domestic demand from COSCO, made conditions in CSSC favorable for the implementation of nationwide reform experiments.

This case is made all the more compelling by the fact that the shipbuilding industry apparently did not participate fully in earlier attempts at enterprise reform, such as the "Economic Responsibility System" and the "Profit Tax System," introduced in 1981–1982 and 1983–1985, respectively. The available evidence suggests that implementation of these programs in the shipbuilding industry was generally poor. As several studies on Chinese industrial reform have pointed out, these types of programs, even if implemented nominally, did not ensure that the relationship between entities like CSSC Beijing and the yards would experience any real change.[26] Indeed, under both the Economic Responsibility System

---

[24] This was also the year in which CSTC and the China Offshore Platform Engineering Corporation became independent accounting units within the CSSC system. For more on the implementation of the CMRS, see *ZGHY* 6:1 (Spring 1988), p. 77.

[25] A survey of more than 900 urban SOEs was conducted in 1991 and 1992 to collect data on the types of management systems used between 1984 and 1990. For more information, see Jefferson et al. (1999), especially p. 52.

[26] This is the basic conclusion that emerged from fieldwork on industrial reform conducted jointly by researchers from the World Bank and the Chinese Academy of Social Sciences. See, for instance, Byrd (1992a) and Tidrick and Chen (1987).

and the Profit Tax System, there was considerable latitude for enterprises and their supervisory agencies to collectively weaken – or even eliminate altogether – the supposedly strong incentive for enterprises to demonstrate financial discipline.[27] Consequently, even if these reform programs were implemented in some nominal sense in the shipbuilding industry, the core relationship between the government and individual enterprises would not necessarily have been fundamentally transformed. Indeed, interviews suggested that the relationships among different administrative levels within the shipbuilding industry were virtually unchanged until the late 1980s. Not until the CMRS was fully adopted, for example, did the vertical nature of CSSC's relationship with the yards even *begin* to evolve toward a more horizontal relationship, in which enterprises were at least somewhat more accountable for their own financial performance. (Even then, of course, change was both slow and modest.) Although the details varied somewhat from interview to interview, most informants identified 1987 as the first year in which profits and losses became any kind of serious consideration for CSSC's yards. Greater financial accountability is not equivalent to a hard budget constraint, to be sure, but it did indicate progress toward reshaping the structure of financial incentives facing enterprises.

REFORM IN THE CHINESE SHIPBUILDING INDUSTRY: AN EVALUATION

For all the far-reaching change that occurred in CSSC beginning in the mid-1980s, it would be wrong to overstate the extent of reform in China's shipbuilding industry. First, CSSC still had to operate within a larger national economy that was, at best, only partially reformed. As a result, economic activity in the shipbuilding industry certainly cannot be declared fully marketized. In this sense, it is worth noting that progress across the industrial landscape – not just in shipbuilding and not just in SOEs – was limited in a fundamental, albeit arguably uneven, way by the absence of further system-wide institutional reform. Indeed, until a fully functioning regulatory environment – with all of the characteristics of a modern, market-oriented economy – is developed, certain aspects of

---

[27] For example, since profit remittance targets under the first system were revisable and thus subject to ongoing bargaining, the basic objective of the reform was undermined. For more on how the early programs fell short of fundamentally reforming economic relations within state industry, see Byrd (1991).

industrial transformation in CSSC (and all other economic actors) will remain unreachable. Second, even within the confines of the industry itself, reform was limited in certain key areas. As discussed above, for example, the yards were far from facing a hard budget constraint – even if financial discipline had improved in the industry.

These and other caveats aside, the changes achieved in the shipbuilding industry fit fairly well with the practical description of successful reform adopted by World Bank researchers at the conclusion of their decade-long study of Chinese industrial firms in the 1980s: "[A] shift from a system in which planning and administrative directives guided the allocation of resources to one in which resource allocation was determined largely by interactions in the market among autonomous, competitive, profit-oriented economic agents."[28] While the government still exercised a certain amount of administrative supervision over the yards, the yards had gained increasing control over the production and distribution of their own output. There was, for example, no central plan for merchant ships by the end of the 1980s.

Not only were the yards more autonomous and market-driven in their decision making, they were also increasingly cost-conscious by the late 1980s and early 1990s. Since China's shipyards often engaged in competitive bidding for both overseas and domestic orders, CSSC Beijing began to monitor cost data collected from the individual yards. On the basis of this information, it would intervene to invalidate any bid judged to be unprofitable. As a result, the yards developed a strong self-interest in lowering costs since this increased their ability to place bids that would win newbuilding orders in what has remained a highly competitive international industry characterized by chronic overcapacity. Unless they reduced their costs, the yards would have been forced to bid higher in order to win CSSC Beijing's approval. This, in turn, would surely have led to lost orders in some cases.

While life in the state-owned sector of China's economy surely had its privileges – namely a reduced fear of extinction – yards could not simply disregard the need to win new ship orders.[29] Consequently, they learned over time how to price more in line with costs. As a result, by the early 1990s CSSC Beijing needed to intervene much less often than it had only

---

[28] Byrd (1992b), p. 2.

[29] For one thing, CSSC Beijing was unlikely to tolerate anything more than a temporary failure to secure orders. As Byrd (1987, p. 243) and others have argued, industrial enterprises were not able to rely primarily on a strategy of passive dependency for long, even early in the reform era when accountability is often perceived as having been very low.

a few years before.[30] In order to ensure greater attention to costs at the yard level, the relevant departments within a yard signed contracts specifying time and cost targets after receiving a new ship order. While department managers were ultimately responsible for meeting these targets, worker bonuses were also reportedly tied to these intra-yard contracts. While this system was far from perfect, in part because the targets were largely self-set and penalties were applied to bonuses rather than to base pay, the new arrangement still provided for greater accountability than had existed in the past.

The result was a watershed in China's participation in the world shipbuilding market: its exports were at least marginally constrained by cost considerations. Reports in the international maritime press confirm that deals between Chinese yards and foreign shipowners sometimes fell through over price differentials of five percent or less. According to industry observers, Chinese yards would no longer accept orders at no profit, let alone at a loss.[31] Even if this claim must be viewed with some skepticism, especially since it fails to take into account the extent to which Beijing – like governments everywhere – continued to subsidize its shipbuilders, the trend toward greater cost-consciousness is undeniable. As the authoritative publication *Lloyd's List Maritime Asia* declared in 1994:

> Indifference to price is a thing of the past in China. In a small way, Chinese shipbuilders have already started out into the same rat race . . . (as)Japan and South Korea: how to generate enough productivity to keep costs down – and meet worker expectations.[32]

Another experiment in management system reform with major implications for China's shipbuilding industry was the transformation of the Guangzhou Shipyard into a joint stock company in 1992. One year later, it was renamed into the Guangzhou Shipyard International Company Limited and listed on the Hong Kong stock exchange. This experience had a profound, and largely positive, impact on the yard's position in the world industry. According to one international observer, a commercial banker based in Hong Kong, the result of this listing is that "Guangzhou Shipyard has had to bring its operations into the capitalistic system. It had to isolate each expenditure to make efficiencies and to reassure shareholders of the value of company assets."[33] Not coincidentally,

---

[30] See, for instance, *LLMA* (June 1993), p. 25.
[31] *LLMA* (June 1994), p. 51.   [32] Ibid, p. 55.   [33] *SBR* (February 1995), p. 21.

Guangzhou has also proceeded further than any other Chinese yard in terms of adopting foreign (and, in this case, mainly Japanese) assembly processes that have allowed it to improve its position in the international division of labor in shipbuilding manufacturing.[34]

All told, several developments in the industry have served as a source of growing financial discipline in lieu of a truly hard budget constraint. A final example would be the increasing use of foreign loans to finance newbuilding projects for overseas shipowners.[35] As reliance on traditional forms of funding, such as domestic bank finance and government investment funds, lessens, greater financial discipline can be expected from the yards. While this situation is certainly no substitute for a hard budget constraint, it does create pressure for more financially responsible behavior.

RATIONALIZATION IN THE CHINESE SHIPBUILDING INDUSTRY: AN EVALUATION

As the foregoing discussion suggests, China's shipyards began to compete in a manner that reflected a vastly more rationalized industry. Indeed, the relationship between CSSC Beijing and the yards was not the only administrative level at which bureaucratic dynamics were transformed: yard-to-yard and intra-yard relations also changed as the industry adjusted to the evolving reform environment at home while simultaneously responding to hard times in the international shipbuilding market. In the process, competition among yards was transformed from a largely deleterious syndrome of internecine rivalry to an increasingly constructive force. At long last, the yards actually began both to compete where competition was healthy and to cooperate where cooperation was appropriate.

In many ways, it was the dearth of new orders in the world market that led most directly to changes in the way China's yards competed amongst themselves. Prior to the international recession, rivalry among the yards was played out almost exclusively through the politics of patronage, as each yard concentrated on maintaining its clientelist connections with

---

[34] *LLMA* (June 1995), p. 38. In light of these achievements, CSSC announced in 1995 that Guangzhou would be taken as a model yard.

[35] To cite one example, a consortium of 16 foreign banks provided a U.S. $103 million loan to finance the construction of six vessels for Malaysian shipowners worth a total of U.S. $184 million. For more detail, see *Xinhua*, 26 September 1996, in FBIS-CHI-96-189.

CSSC Beijing. From all indications, this competition was characterized by rent-seeking behavior rather than a healthy competition over the allocation of ship orders. As one Hong Kong shipowner put it, there was never any sense of urgency about orders from the yards." Rather, they were consumed with their place in the bureaucratic pecking order. Ultimately, a yard did not evaluate its success solely (or even primarily) in terms of the kind of shipbuilding work it was allocated. Only with the changes described in this chapter was competition over the more general benefits available through the political system transformed into a much more productive rivalry.

At the yard level, many shipyards underwent substantial reorganizations in which loosely related facilities were recentralized into stronger, more coherent shipbuilding entities. In the Dalian area, for instance, several assembly facilities and factories were consolidated into the Dalian Shipbuilding Corporation in 1985.[36] As a result of these reorganizations at the local level, China's shipbuilding activities were considerably more rationalized. No longer did individual yards, and even sub-yard units, attempt to produce everything on their own. Previously, the yards had typically tried to produce everything on site – from the design stage right through to the finished product. Since there was often little or no coordination with other yards and factories, much of the yard's equipment – even the cranes, plate-bending presses, and hydraulic machinery – was often manufactured by the yards themselves. (Indeed, this behavior even extended to sub-yard units, where decrepit machine shops exemplified Maoist self-reliance.)

While the organization of the industry remained imperfect, especially given the shadow CSSC Beijing continued to cast over all shipbuilding activities, a more rationalized industry did begin to emerge in the mid-1980s. (Indeed, there is even some evidence of modest declines in workforce size from the mid- to late 1980s. As it turns out, this foreshadowed the massive layoffs of the late 1990s, when hundreds of thousands of workers reportedly lost their jobs.)[37] Although the yards occasionally

---

[36] Despite the sophisticated new name, the entity was placed under the management of the Dalian Shipyard and is still commonly referred to as "Dalian Shipyard." For the reorganization itself, see *ZGHY* 9:1 (Spring 1991), p. 130.

[37] For the 1980s, see *Dangdai Zhongguo de Chuanbo Gongye* (1992), pp. 653–655, and *SBR* (December 1994), p. 69. For layoffs in the late 1990s, see Smyth (1998), p. 130. According to some reports, CSSC was charged with cutting one-third of its labor force as part of Beijing's plans for SOE reform; *Journal of Commerce*, 9 September 1999, p. 12 (Transportation).

needed prodding from CSSC Beijing, they did begin to cooperate on certain projects in the mid-1980s, with even greater specialization taking form by the late 1980s. In sum, hard times in the international market helped to impel a multilevel rationalization of China's shipbuilding assets, in which the industry simultaneously saw both a *decentralization* of authority from CSSC Beijing to individual yards and a *recentralization* of control over facilities at the yard level. (In the latter case, recentralization – i.e., the consolidation of formerly disorganized shipbuilding facilities into more coherent yards – was often accompanied by the increased use of contract work and other instruments associated with administrative deregulation at the yard level. In this sense, behavior *within* the newly recentralized shipyards was often marked by decentralization.)

Its long shadow notwithstanding, CSSC Beijing's role atop the shipbuilding industry was significantly modified during the 1980s. As one non-PRC informant put it, CSSC Beijing became a "coordinating body," while the yards were transformed from being mere "technical arms" of the shipbuilding industry to virtual "part-owners." In its new capacity, CSSC Beijing served as an all-purpose adviser, at first helping the yards simply to place competitive, professional bids for domestic and foreign orders. Over time, one of CSSC Beijing's most important and challenging tasks became to regulate the heightened competition among the yards and, where necessary, to mediate conflicts between them. Here, its role in training the yards to be more cost-conscious provides an excellent example.

By decentralizing so much operational authority to the yard level, while still retaining a supervisory-cum-regulatory role, CSSC Beijing certainly changed its place in the industry. In fact, PRC informants insisted that CSSC had gradually reduced the "government function" it formerly provided. For their part, industry officials claimed that CSSC Beijing had become as much an agent for the industry as an administrator. From this perspective, its position had evolved from a decision-making center for a centrally planned industry into a technical and marketing resource for an industry comprised of increasingly autonomous shipyards. As such, CSSC Beijing was more responsible in its new role for shaping a long-term strategy for the industry than for day-to-day operations.

Without question, the changing pattern of state intervention in the shipbuilding industry did contribute to a reduction of government intrusion into enterprise activity. Accordingly, the hierarchical ties that have traditionally dominated industrial relations in state socialist systems were undoubtedly weakened. By the same token, however, they were by no means severed altogether. In the view of non-PRC informants, a considerable measure of industrial paternalism persisted in CSSC. While most acknowledged progress toward the transformation of intrastate relations, these observers still regarded the yards as being structurally dependent on vertical administrative ties in certain respects. Although not expressed in these terms, they saw little change in the basic institutional culture of China's shipbuilding industry. For this reason, non-PRC informants were not generally sanguine about the prospects for East Asian–style industrial policy in CSSC or other state-owned industries. In their view, the nature of the Chinese system – even in shipbuilding – is such that government intervention is more likely to serve particularistic rather than developmental goals. While these observations may have revealed their own biases, they do provide a useful corrective to assertions that CSSC Beijing's role had become virtually indistinguishable from that played by industry associations in Western economies. As much as administrative dynamics within CSSC have changed, there have been limits to this process. At the very least, it could safely be argued that the nature of government-industry relations has evolved more slowly than other aspects of change within the shipbuilding industry.

SHIPBUILDING: THE SUCCESS STORY OF A REFORM PIONEER

Its remaining problems notwithstanding, the Chinese shipbuilding industry no longer fit the stereotype of an uncompetitive, stagnant, technologically backward heavy industry by the early 1990s. In many respects, the transformation of the industry had progressed about as far as it could in the absence of more fundamental, system-wide economic reform. While still not subject to a hard budget constraint, neither did China's shipyards resemble the typical state-run dinosaur insulated from market-oriented forces. Indeed, CSSC has become deeply integrated into the world shipbuilding industry in less than a decade, consistently producing about half of its ships for export by the late 1980s. While one must always view "success" stories in the Chinese press skeptically, the shipbuilding industry has been repeatedly singled out for praise, even in reports that appear rather evenhanded. For example, the industry has been hailed for taking the lead among machine-building industries in entering the international market, earning itself national recognition as a "pioneer sector" during the so-called reform decade of the 1980s.[38] For its part, CSSC was touted – perhaps with some embellishment – by *Xinhua*, China's official news agency, as the "first ministry to drop its administrative function and turn into a market-oriented economic entity."[39]

Compared to other industries, shipbuilding's record of reform, restructuring, and rationalization is in fact quite impressive. As the Chinese periodical *Liaowang* observed in 1995, "[a]mong China's several dozen machine-building and electrical industries, very, very few can compete in the international market as the shipbuilding industry can."[40] Moreover, the success of the shipbuilding industry is unusual, if not unique, among defense-related industries. If studies of defense conversion during the 1980s and 1990s are any guide, problems have apparently been more intractable in other industries, including electronics, the defense-related sector which is probably the next most successful in terms of international competitiveness. Many of the generic difficulties experienced in other industries simply do not apply to shipbuilding.[41] While a senior Chinese analyst did include shipbuilding in his examination of defense conversion, he listed no specific adjustments as being urgently necessary for the industry. Shipbuilding was, in fact, the only industry for which no such recommendation was provided, suggesting that CSSC, whatever its warts, was less troubled than its counterparts elsewhere in the defense-related sector.[42]

Consequently, while the impact of GSC on China's shipbuilding industry may have been exacerbated by the fact that CSSC was already suffering from a decline in naval orders due to the low priority of defense among the Four Modernizations, defense conversion does not by itself provide a compelling explanation for CSSC's success in entering the world shipbuilding market. True, defense conversion did mean that production of civilian vessels would be reemphasized. That said, there is no evidence that defense conversion provided the impetus for either the increasing export orientation of CSSC or the relatively high degree of

---

[38] See, respectively, *FBIS Daily Report-China*, 6 April 1990, p. 35, and *FBIS Daily Report-China*, 14 March 1990, p. 32.

[39] *Xinhua*, 10 September 1997, in FBIS-CHI-97-253.

[40] *Liaowang*, 13 February 1995, in FBIS-CHI-95-048.

[41] For a survey of defense conversion in the 1990s, see Frankenstein (1997). (A list of problems in defense-related industries, few of which apply to shipbuilding, is provided by Frankenstein on pp. 24–25.) For an examination of defense conversion in the 1980s, see Folta (1992).

[42] Chai (1997), especially p. 79.

reform, restructuring, and rationalization achieved by the industry. As discussed in Chapter 7, CSSC intended – quite credibly, in fact – to focus on the construction of civilian vessels for the domestic market as the basis of its development strategy. Consequently, only the impact of GSC can serve as the basis for a comprehensive explanation of events in the shipbuilding industry. In fact, as far as the domestic sources of CSSC's evolution are concerned, institutional characteristics of the state, such as the bureaucratic split between CSSC and COSCO, are the most relevant variables. In this sense, industry-specific factors – international and domestic alike – are much more important for understanding outcomes in shipbuilding than broad features of the policy environment such as defense conversion.

Similarly, while the transformation of China's shipbuilding industry was well within the parameters of China's larger reform program, CSSC often found itself on the leading edge within its peer group. While it was certainly no paragon of market-based virtue, the shipbuilding industry had by the early 1990s achieved an impressive record of success compared to both heavy industries such as automobiles and the rest of the defense sector.[43] As this chapter has shown, the imperative of building advanced ships for export provided a significant impetus for reform and rationalization within the industry, whereas earlier attempts as part of national programs for industrial reorganization had been largely ineffective.

Without a blueprint for changing the system, the history of industrial reform in post-Mao China has been characterized by ad hoc measures introduced at various levels of administration. On the whole, initiatives from above have been unevenly implemented. While this may have been especially true of the first phase of industrial reforms launched in 1979 and 1980, it also plagued subsequent rounds of top-down reform, including the second major phase of industrial reform carried out from 1984 to 1988. Indeed, recent history suggests that actual change at the industrial level often depends less on the formal promulgation of reform programs at the national level than on a fortuitous confluence of conditions at the industrial level that leads to their implementation. In the case of the shipbuilding industry, GSC in the world market profoundly shaped conditions at the industrial level.

---

[43] For background on the automobile industry, see Harwit (1994), Mann (1997), Yang (1995), and Byrd (1992c).

11

Who Did What to Whom?: Making Sense of the Reform Process in China's Shipbuilding Industry

EXPLAINING CHANGE IN THE SHIPBUILDING INDUSTRY:
A CASE OF FOLLOWERS AND LEADERS?

Even if we accept that the international environment was a powerful influence in impelling certain changes in China's shipbuilding industry, we must still account for the response within China, just as we did with regard to the textile industry, and pose a similar set of questions. Did the reforms and other policy changes in the industry mainly reflect strategy made by the top leadership to cope with the exigencies of the world market in shipping and shipbuilding? Or were they fundamentally the result of bureaucratic intervention by CSSC Beijing? Or, finally, did the main impulse for change come from below as the yards reacted to changing market conditions at home and abroad? In other words, are the changes that occurred in the shipbuilding industry best conceptualized as the outcome of top-level strategy, mid-level intervention, or low-level demand?

Not surprisingly, actors at each level have tried to take credit for the success of the shipbuilding industry. For its part, CSSC Beijing has long maintained that it orchestrated reform in the industry, directing the yards to undertake various kinds of new responsibilities while simultaneously transforming its own role from a central decision-maker to a marketing agent and technical adviser. By contrast, the yards have claimed – rather predictably – that change was initiated largely from below, beginning with reforms taken at the unit-level. From this perspective, the yards led and CSSC Beijing followed. Although China's top leaders have made few public comments about the shipbuilding industry, usually only at ceremonial ship launchings and during inspection tours, they, too, appear to want some credit. Implicitly, at least, their statements have attributed the industry's achievements to their support for the general policies of reform and opening, not to mention the myriad nationwide programs for enterprise reform issued over the years. From the standpoint of parsimonious explanation, it would be most satisfying (and expedient) to give a stylized account of "who led" and "who followed" in the reform and modernization of China's shipbuilding industry. In the end, however, each of the main players – the top leadership, CSSC Beijing, and the yards – exhibited characteristics of being both a leader and a follower.

Reform from Above: The Role of China's Central Leadership

Following the format used in Chapter 6 to discuss changes in the textile industry, this section suggests that the impact of the central leadership could have been felt in three principal ways: first, the creation of a generally proreform atmosphere; second, the promulgation of (and subsequent support for) various nationwide reform programs; and, lastly, specific actions taken with regard to the shipbuilding industry.

Proreform Atmosphere. The central leadership's commitment to a basic policy of reform and opening was an essential precondition that allowed the course of events to unfold as it did in the shipbuilding industry. As argued in Chapter 6, while this receptive milieu did not lead to uniform change across industries in China, its importance as a necessary (although not sufficient) condition should not be underestimated.

Nationwide Reform Programs. How well can change in the shipbuilding industry be explained by reform measures promulgated at the national level? For example, were reductions in mandatory planning and the administrative allocation of inputs and outputs primarily the result of nationwide efforts at economic reform? Put another way, is shipbuilding a case of reform from above, even if these changes were not directed specifically at CSSC? Without question, the presence of various kinds of reform measures at the national level *facilitated* change in the shipbuilding industry, but the mere *existence* of these programs cannot fully explain either their initial adoption within CSSC or, more importantly, their rather successful implementation over time. This observation is not, of course, restricted to the shipbuilding industry. In addition to the case study of the textile industry presented earlier in the book, this finding is also consistent with other research on Chinese reform. Although there was considerable variation across industries, the World Bank concluded in a decade-long study of Chinese industrial reform that policy packages introduced nationwide in the 1980s often had only a limited effect on change at the enterprise level. In short, implementation was extremely uneven. (CSSC itself had been a laggard prior to the mid-1980s.) While efforts at the top were often an important precursor for reform at the industrial (or even enterprise) level, the World Bank found that other factors were ultimately more important for explaining the timing, sequence, and actual content of change within industrial firms.[1]

In some cases, such as CSSC's adoption of the CMRS, change within the shipbuilding industry did actually follow national reform measures rather closely. Even here, however, the mere existence of a policy package initiated from above cannot explain why implementation varied from industry to industry. Why was CMRS more faithfully adopted in shipbuilding than in other industries? More generally, nationwide reform programs are – at best – incomplete explanations for industry-specific changes. After conducting extensive studies of firms in more than twenty industries, for example, the authors of the World Bank study concluded that the role of central planning was most often reduced "mainly as a result of changing market conditions rather than through explicit reform measures."[2] That is, increases in the share of industrial goods produced for, and distributed by, the market have depended primarily on factors unrelated to official policy packages. Specifically, the World Bank researchers found that the extension of certain privileges to enterprises, such as the right to market their "above-plan" output independently, did not have much effect in the absence of other, more important conditions, such as the emergence of a buyers' market and other industry-specific characteristics that have been shown to impel real improvements in management, productivity, and the use of technology.[3]

In a similar way, the present study argues that while the presence of policy options approved by the central leadership was a vital precondition for change in China's shipbuilding industry, it does not alone provide a satisfactory explanation of this process. After all, the emergence of broad initiatives from above were not sufficient to induce most state-run heavy industries to undertake the degree of reform, restructuring, and rationalization achieved by the shipbuilding industry. Rather, the promulgation of specific nationwide reform programs are perhaps best

---

[1] Byrd (1992a).   [2] Byrd (1992b), p. 5.
[3] For more detail on the World Bank's findings, see Byrd (1992d).

thought of as providing shipbuilding (and other industries) with new courses of action already legitimized from above.

Industry-Specific Actions. To the extent that the central leadership even had a policy for the shipbuilding industry, its treatment of CSSC during the 1980s and early 1990s might best be described as benign neglect. Although CSSC was created to consolidate China's far-flung shipbuilding facilities into a single entity under the direct control of the State Council, it received surprisingly little attention at high levels. While there is no evidence of any conscious effort to disadvantage the industry, CSSC received minimal aid in two key areas: investment funding and protection from foreign competition. Investment details for the industry are sketchy, but it is known that government funding for shipbuilding facilities declined during the 1980s.[4] Not surprisingly, the level of state investment proved to be a persistent sore point between CSSC and the central government, with some of the conflict poorly disguised.[5] Even the marquee example of state largesse in shipbuilding, Beijing's support for the construction of a 250,000-deadweight-ton dock (for VLCC-building) at Dalian Shipyard, revealed the limits of government assistance. Begun in March 1989, the project's completion was delayed for several years due to intermittent funding from Beijing. (In the end, government aid from Japan was reportedly used to help finish the project.)[6] Despite two visits to the shipyard from Jiang Zemin between 1990 and 1994, the project was by all accounts a low priority for the central leadership.[7]

Far more critical than the issue of investment funds, however, was the failure of the central leadership to stem the flood of domestic ship orders that went overseas. Given the collapse in world ship prices, it was

---

[4] CSSC refused for years to provide detailed investment information, as even the Chinese press noted. See, for example, *ZGJJXW*, 29 April 1991, p. 3. Other Chinese sources, however, confirmed information from interviews suggesting that state investment in shipbuilding failed to keep pace with earlier levels. In the Seventh Five-Year Plan (1986–1990), for example, CSSC received only 0.16 percent of total capital investment by the central government, a figure described as "smaller" than that provided in the Sixth Five-Year Plan (1981–1985); *FBIS Daily Report-China*, 13 June 1991, p. 31.

[5] In calling for greater investment in shipbuilding facilities, CSSC officials occasionally blamed inadequate state funding for holding back the industry's development. See, for example, *FBIS Daily Report-China*, 13 June 1991, p. 31.

[6] *LLMA* (June 1994), p. 52.

[7] For a published account, see *SBR* (December 1994), p. 71. Here, I should note that low priority was assigned to maritime infrastructure in general – ports and container terminals, as well as shipbuilding facilities.

certainly understandable that COSCO would consider increasing its newbuilding projects in foreign yards. Yet given the severity of GSC, it is telling that greater import restrictions were not imposed to protect China's shipbuilding industry from foreign competition. Why, for instance, did the central government not insist that COSCO use domestic yards for more of its newbuildings? Although CSSC clearly benefited from the built-in financial subsidization that accompanied state ownership, it was not protected by any overt government scheme in which Chinese yards received preference when orders for the Chinese merchant fleet were placed. This was contrary to the practice in many nations, including Japan and South Korea. Unlike its East Asian counterparts, China's de facto policy more nearly resembled that found in Germany and other Western European nations, where government subsidies to domestic yards were used liberally to underwrite newbuildings for export, but vessels for domestic shipping companies continued to be built both at home and abroad in fairly deregulated fashion.

As discussed in Chapter 7, the low level of domestic orders placed by COSCO in the mid-1980s cannot be explained fully by CSSC's limitations, either in terms of physical capacity or technical expertise. Indeed, CSSC's yards found themselves with substantial idle facilities by 1986, if not earlier. Once it became clear that the flood of ship orders leaving China represented a threat to its own yards, why was CSSC still left more or less to its own devices? Why was COSCO allowed to continue to buy new ships abroad while the domestic industry suffered from insufficient work?

One possibility is that it was simply cost-effective for China to follow this strategy. According to this theory, it was cheaper for China to buy new ships at fire-sale prices overseas – and then cover the losses suffered by its own shipbuilding industry – than it would have been to build these same ships at home. There is, however, little evidence to support this explanation. First, it is doubtful China could have benefited financially from such a policy.[8] While many informants applauded COSCO for taking advantage of the favorable financial terms, export credits, and direct contract subsidies available from foreign yards, they also noted how marked the shift toward imports had been with the slump in the world industry, leaving the Chinese state to underwrite a vastly underutilized shipbuilding industry. As one Hong Kong ship broker put it: "If

---

[8] For a discussion of this issue, see Moore (1997), pp. 382–383.

China had acted more rationally, at least *some* of the orders would have been placed with CSSC."

Second, neither interviews nor press reports suggested that the central leadership had pursued any kind of conscious policy whereby China would import more ships based on a cost-benefit calculation. Although the vast sums of money involved would suggest that an effort to weigh costs and benefits should have been made, some informants felt it was precisely *because* of, rather than *in spite* of, the money involved that these calculations were ultimately immaterial. If there had been less of a financial stake involved, they reasoned, it would have been more likely that a cost-benefit calculation would have entered the decision-making process. While no informants could offer any proof, several implied that ships worth tens of millions of dollars often "leaked" a little money into the right pockets. Perhaps, therefore, there was simply too much money involved for "rationality" to prevail in the decision-making process.

Other informants offered a distinct, but not incompatible, answer based on the observation that top leaders might, to the extent they became involved, simply have made the political choice to leave CSSC unprotected – and cover its losses – rather than change COSCO's behavior. This explanation would emphasize how the fragmented nature of decision-making authority in the Chinese state confers considerable latitude to quasi-ministerial corporations like COSCO and CSSC in setting their policies. In short, this view invokes a bureaucratic explanation of policy making, in which the capacity of the state to undertake certain kinds of policy actions is severely circumscribed in the absence of direct intervention by top leaders, which in turn requires an explicit decision to use precious political capital.

Although few details are available, the evidence seems to support this explanation. By all accounts, COSCO's autonomy from the Ministry of Communications grew as the result of decentralization in the early 1980s. Until early 1982, COSCO had functioned solely as a vessel operator. Ship purchases were actually conducted by the Ministry of Foreign Trade through its National Machinery Import and Export Corporation (known more commonly in the West as MACHIMPEX).[9] Until the decentralization of import and export authority in the early 1980s, the State Planning Commission had formally decided the number and types of vessels

---

[9] See Lauriat (1983), p. 94, and *FEER*, 5 February 1982, p. 62.

to be purchased, although COSCO undoubtedly had substantial input in these decisions.[10] When CSSC was created in May 1982, it took control over every major civilian shipyard in the country, including several that had been run previously by the Ministry of Communications.

While the Ministry of Communications (COSCO's parent) was reportedly not pleased at losing these industrial assets – it did retain some smaller yards engaged primarily in shiprepair – it may actually have been willing to forgo shipbuilding to concentrate on shipping, which it perceived to be a more lucrative business. In fact, several informants strongly implied that this was the case. Specifically, they suggested that a deal was worked out in which CSSC gained control of virtually all of China's significant newbuilding facilities, while COSCO was given unprecedented autonomy over ship acquisitions.[11] While COSCO would still receive some broad targets under the planning system, it would have unprecedented latitude in making decisions not only about the number and types of ships it would purchase, but also about where and when to build new ships for its fleet.[12] While it would be an exaggeration to conclude that this period of bureaucratic reshuffling marked the end of central planning in the production and distribution of ships, it certainly reduced the ability of the state to coordinate outcomes in the shipping and shipbuilding industries.

Indeed, COSCO's independence grew steadily throughout the 1980s, even from the Ministry of Communications itself.[13] This autonomy notwithstanding, COSCO could not be confused with a private, Western-style corporation. Especially in the 1980s, the Chinese state still retained substantial power when it chose to marshal its considerable resources for a dedicated purpose. Why, then, did China's leaders fail to intervene on

---

[10] Middleton (1979), p. 10.

[11] There are no published accounts to confirm such an arrangement, although Chinese sources have acknowledged that shipping and shipbuilding authorities are "authorized to make independent decisions in foreign trade"; *Dangdai Zhongguo de Chuanbo Gongye* (1992), pp. 608–614.

[12] While the Chinese press did not formally report any change in the way newbuilding orders were placed, references appeared as early as 1983 to agreements negotiated between CSSC and the Ministry of Communications for new ships. For instance, it was reported in the semi-official *Zhongguo Haiyun* (*Maritime China*) in December 1983 that CSSC and COSCO had settled on the construction of a number of ships for completion during the Sixth Five-Year Plan (1981–1985); *ZGHY* 1:4 (December 1983), p. 58.

[13] By the early 1990s, COSCO's operational authority had become sufficiently independent that an agreement had been struck in which COSCO began repaying the Ministry for funds it had used in the 1970s to finance fleet expansion. See the interview with Huang Zhendong in *SBR* (July/August 1991), p. 69.

CSSC's behalf given the difficulties the industry was experiencing? After all, products such as automobiles received industry-specific protection from imports on numerous occasions during the 1980s.[14] The mere fact that COSCO could not be "persuaded" to ensure a healthier orderbook for Chinese yards raises questions about the political clout that CSSC enjoyed with China's top leaders. Indeed, several informants indicated that the industry's top patrons in Beijing often had commitments to both the shipping *and* the shipbuilding industries. Thus, when a potential conflict of interest arose, shipbuilding often lacked undiluted sponsorship at the highest levels.

Despite its importance to the national economy, the shipbuilding industry simply never received sustained attention from top leaders. As one Hong Kong shipowner close to industry officials in Beijing put it, "my [mainland] colleagues often complain privately that even a single missile sale to the Middle East commands far more interest within the leadership than a whole series of commercial ship sales to Germany." While this anecdote overlooks compelling geopolitical reasons for leadership attention in the case of missile sales, the point remains that top leaders never became deeply engaged in the affairs of the shipbuilding industry. This stands in stark contrast to an industry such as automobile manufacturing, where individual leaders intervened personally from time to time to settle bureaucratic disputes or overrule past policies.[15] Indeed, strategic plans for the automobile industry were on the agenda at major leadership meetings, such as the annual Beidaihe conference, several times during the 1980s.[16] A final example of direct leadership involvement was the establishment of a short-lived State Council Automobile Leading Small Group in the late 1980s in an effort to coordinate

[14] After an influx of automobile imports in the early 1980s, Beijing put in place an elaborate system of import licenses, quotas, and tariffs. By 1986, these tariffs were among the highest in the world. Import restrictions were further tightened in 1989 and 1994 as part of government initiatives for industrial policy in the automobile sector. In short, Beijing repeatedly provided import protection during the 1980s and 1990s when foreign cars were perceived as inhibiting the development of the Chinese industry. Prior to reductions negotiated as part of China's accession to the WTO, tariff rates on imported vehicles had ranged from 80 to 100 percent in the late 1990s.

[15] Eric Harwit cites one example where Zhao Ziyang and Zhu Rongji intervened to address problems with the Beijing Jeep joint venture. For more detail, see Harwit (1995), p. 161.

[16] Harwit reports that leaders considered the so-called Big Three, Little Three (*San Da, San Xiao*) scheme at the 1988 meeting of the annual *Beidaihe* leadership conference. This plan called for the reorganization of China's automobile industry around three major manufacturers and three minor manufacturers; ibid, pp. 36–37.

national policy for the industry at a higher level.[17] While one might expect automobile manufacturing to enjoy a high political profile, not just in China but across a broad range of countries, the importance of the shipbuilding industry should not be underestimated, especially in East Asia. As a Hong Kong–based business consultant explained it, "Shipbuilding is to East Asia what aircraft manufacture is to the United States and Western Europe." While China was a small player at first, by the mid-1990s it had joined Japan, South Korea, and Taiwan as one of the four largest shipbuilders in the world. Consequently, the relative lack of leadership attention is noteworthy.

In sum, little of the success enjoyed by the shipbuilding industry during the 1980s and early 1990s can be attributed directly to actions taken by the central leadership. On the one hand, there is virtually no evidence that China's leaders planned for the shipbuilding industry to follow its eventual course. Indeed, they never tried to push through far-reaching change in the industry. (At the same time, of course, neither did they apparently resist change once it began to occur.) On the other hand, neither did CSSC benefit from the kind of concerted industry policy enjoyed by industries such as automobile manufacturing.[18] Whatever its official rhetoric at the time, China's de facto policy for the shipbuilding industry was certainly no longer import-substituting industrialization by the second half of the 1980s. Other than the soft budget constraint enjoyed throughout the state-run sector of the economy, which served as an important financial cushion for the industry, Beijing provided little direct support for CSSC. One exception was the availability of preferential financing (namely, deferred loans and low interest rates) to help persuade foreign shipowners to use Chinese yards for their newbuilding projects. A second exception was relief from import duties on equipment used to build ships for export. Both of these measures were introduced to help Chinese yards remain competitive in the cutthroat international market of the mid-1980s. Most importantly, they reflected Beijing's effort simply to keep pace with established practice among shipbuilding countries. Given their widespread use elsewhere, these measures hardly qualify as evidence of proactive government intervention.[19]

---

[17] Ibid, p. 47.

[18] For an excellent overview of state intervention in China's automobile industry through the early 1990s, see Harwit (1995). For an update, see Polly (1998).

[19] For more detail on these measures, see *Dangdai Zhongguo de Chuanbo Gongye* (1992), pp. 608–614, 659.

All told, the biggest role played by the central leadership in the development of China's shipbuilding industry was allowing COSCO such a free hand in purchasing ships for the Chinese fleet. At first, there was little impact on CSSC since domestic demand exceeded the industry's capacity. (At that point, COSCO still chose to keep enough of its newbuilding work at home that CSSC's orderbook was adequate.) When the international market became depressed, however, COSCO's declining orders to domestic yards were no longer sufficient for the traditional planning system to be maintained.[20] Indeed, as explained in Chapter 10, a sellers' market rapidly transformed into a buyers' market. In this sense, it was actually the central leadership that created, however unwittingly, the critical precondition for the sweeping change that occurred in the shipbuilding industry. If not for COSCO's relative autonomy from the planning system, a buyers' market could never have emerged in the wake of hard times in international shipbuilding. Moreover, if not for the lack of explicit import protection, or some other effort to rein in COSCO, the powerful incentives for industrial restructuring and technological modernization emanating from the world shipbuilding market could not have had such a substantial effect on the Chinese industry.

CSSC Beijing in the Reform Process

Another explanation would center on the efforts of CSSC Beijing itself. According to one version of this argument, industry officials were resolved from the start to reduce the growing technological gap that existed between China and the world's leading shipbuilders at the end of the Mao era. As demonstrated in Chapter 7, however, the eventual course of events in the shipbuilding industry was generally inconsistent with the strategy laid out by CSSC Beijing in the early 1980s. Industry officials surely wanted to develop a long-term capacity to build more advanced ships, but there is little evidence that they were prepared either to tolerate extensive foreign involvement in the industry or to relinquish the strict control they enjoyed over production and distribution. Indeed, CSSC Beijing initially had a highly proprietary view of its role in the shipbuilding industry and was therefore reluctant to yield power to the

---

[20] In the years immediately preceding the crisis, it had not mattered much that government procurement of the industry's production was no longer formally guaranteed since COSCO had voluntarily kept enough of its newbuilding work at home for a sellers' market to persist.

yards, let alone foreigners. While committed to developing a strong, modern shipbuilding industry, CSSC showed no inclination whatsoever to become a reform pioneer. In fact, most informants – even those generally sympathetic to the industry's leaders – argued that CSSC was, for the most part, just another state-run dinosaur prior to the crisis of the mid-1980s.

This initial resistance notwithstanding, CSSC Beijing did not forever remain an obstacle to reform. By the late 1980s, in fact, it was probably best characterized as a grudging, but increasingly important, agent of change. In large part, of course, this transformation was due to challenges of industrial adjustment associated with the crisis in world shipbuilding markets. Courtesy of COSCO's generous orders to foreign yards, the effects of GSC had managed to penetrate China's borders, leaving empty berths at CSSC's yards. With little delay, CSSC Beijing adopted several policies designed to facilitate the industrial restructuring necessary to respond effectively to the international crisis in shipbuilding. For example, in 1985 CSSC Beijing ordered all yards to undertake foreign repair work to compensate for the loss of newbuilding work.[21] Similarly, in 1986 certain shipyards (e.g., Zhonghua Shipyard in Shanghai) were designated as production bases for the export of marine equipment and electrical machinery in response to the sluggish newbuilding market. While CSSC's revamped policy goals for the Seventh Five-Year Plan (1986–1990) – to build more advanced ships, to accelerate technology imports, and to expand nonmarine production – may have amounted to little more than a reluctant acknowledgement of realities in the world market, their inclusion in the industry's official strategy did indicate that CSSC Beijing was neither entirely passive nor implacably resistant to change.

Even more importantly, CSSC ultimately adopted increasingly market-oriented solutions to the challenge of industrial adjustment. The policy tools initially available to CSSC Beijing, such as control over production decisions and the allocation of investment funds, were inadequate for the specific tasks facing China's shipbuilding industry. As the number of domestic and foreign orders placed at Chinese yards declined, and as the ships built for export shifted increasingly to specialized vessels, the tools of central planning became increasingly irrelevant as pressures for industrial restructuring and technical modernization

---

[21] *ZGHY* 3:2 (Summer 1985), p. 73.

mounted. As outlined more fully in Chapter 12, the agenda for intensive growth associated with GSC was a poor fit with the state socialist approach to industrial readjustment.

On the whole, central planning is most effective in a sellers' market. In state socialist economies – where industrial ministries such as CSSC have a virtual, if not total, monopoly on production – planning is a viable, if not ideal, mechanism for allocating resources since bureaucrats can control the supply of industrial goods. When a buyers' market begins to emerge, however, planning authorities face a crisis insofar as an outlet for their products can no longer be guaranteed. As described in Chapter 10, unless end-users are compelled to accept delivery by administrative edict, mandatory planning is likely to erode. Under this scenario, production and pricing are increasingly determined by market-like mechanisms as enterprises are left increasingly to their own devices in finding customers for their goods.

In the end, therefore, CSSC Beijing relented – if only by default – to a market-oriented approach when a particular set of international and domestic conditions conspired to reduce the effectiveness of the traditional state socialist approach to achieving industrial adjustment. Unwilling to accept the consequences of persisting with bureaucratic coordination – namely, the responsibility of distributing goods in a buyers' market – it relinquished some of the administrative control it had formerly enjoyed in supervising the industry. Ultimately, CSSC Beijing was unable (and, due to the responsibility it would have entailed, probably unwilling) to effect the necessary changes by administrative edict.

While CSSC Beijing's role as an agent of change was hardly exemplary, it did demonstrate an ability to recognize the incentives facing the industry and fashion a reasonable strategy for coping with an externally imposed challenge. Despite being steeped in a (passive) culture of planning left from decades of tight central control over heavy industries, CSSC Beijing's role as a reluctant reformer warrants attention. For all of its ministerial reflexes, CSSC Beijing did prove to be fairly adaptable.

Reform from Below: The Role of China's Shipyards

Although CSSC did belatedly incorporate several key objectives (new ship types, more repair work, and greater technology imports) into its policy guidelines for the Seventh Five-Year Plan (1986–1990), interviews and press reports indicated that most changes were not undertaken at the explicit instruction of CSSC Beijing. Instead, they were ad hoc, experimental policies adopted more or less independently by the yards. In fact, in some areas – such as reforms in enterprise operation and bold changes in the product mix – the yards clearly exceeded the wishes of CSSC Beijing. Indeed, the most successful cases of product development during the 1980s – many of which carried substantial risk, especially financially – can be traced to efforts initiated by individual yards. In the production of LPG carriers, for example, Shanghai's Jiangnan Shipyard led the way, establishing an international reputation as a reliable, accommodating partner in the construction of these high-technology vessels that were worth U.S. $75–80 million a piece by the early 1990s. By working closely with foreign companies on its initial export orders, Jiangnan was able to progress over time to the most advanced type of LPG carrier. Based on this success, the yard set its sites on one day entering the market for LNG carriers – the most expensive merchant vessels in the world, typically exceeding U.S. $200 million per ship.[22]

While the magnitude of Jiangnan's success in developing LPG carriers was unusual, its experience was still representative of the proactive approach taken by most of CSSC's major yards starting in the mid-1980s. By late 1985 and early 1986, reports began to appear routinely that Chinese yards were undertaking their own marketing efforts to both attract orders and tap the foreign technology needed to build advanced ships.[23] In a front page article in *Zhongguo Jingji Xinwen* (*China Economic News*) in 1987, the director of Shanghai's Zhonghua Shipyard made an unusually open appeal to foreign shipowners and equipment manufacturers, offering favorable terms to partners who could assist in the development of new types of ships. With remarkable candor, the director noted that the yard had empty berths, and he even offered discounts for either multiship orders or multiproduct orders.[24] While this kind of self-promotion was uncharacteristically bold for an SOE in China, after 1985 reports about similar marketing efforts at other yards

---

[22] All figures in this paragraph are representative world prices for the early 1990s as published in *Review of Maritime Transport*, various years.

[23] See, for example, the remarks of yard directors in Dalian and Guangzhou, respectively, in *ZGHY* 3:4 (Winter 1985), p. 53, and *SBR* (February 1986), p. 87.

[24] *ZGJJXW*, 19 October 1987, p. 1. Indeed, by 1987 reports about the vigorous marketing efforts of yard directors were commonplace in the Chinese press. See, for example, *ZGJJXW*, 13 July 1987, p. 2.

were fairly common in both the Chinese media and the international maritime press.[25] Dalian Shipyard, for one, clearly expressed its aim to become a more diversified shipbuilder:

> Dalian Shipyard attaches great importance to the development of new products and technology. It realizes that if it does not press forward with building new types of ships and developing new techniques it will, in the long run, find it difficult to compete in the international market. Therefore, the yard tries to tap outside technology with the aim of receiving new orders.[26]

It was absolutely no coincidence that this statement came after Dalian's whirlwind experience in 1984 and 1985 as a bidder for the few international orders that had been available for sophisticated tanker vessels, three of which the yard secured only by offering steep price discounts and agreeing to unprecedented foreign involvement in the production process. As far as the other major Chinese yards were concerned, they, too, reached the same basic conclusion: pursue more exports, strive for advanced ship types, undertake more repair work, achieve higher quality production, and develop more diversified industrial production.[27] While few of the changes that resulted from this strategy could have persisted without the tacit approval of CSSC Beijing, the yards clearly played an important role in shaping China's response to hard times in the international shipbuilding industry.

In direct response to the challenges encountered in building advanced ships for export, many yards undertook reforms of their own, particularly in the areas of project management and business development. To improve quality control, shorten construction periods, and conserve valuable raw materials, most of the major yards decentralized at least some aspects of their internal management, providing incentives for smaller work units to meet targets on technical standards, safety, and overall productivity.

Dalian Shipyard, by many measures the leading shipyard in China, established several new management practices based on its experience

---

[25] Not surprisingly, these "profiles" of various yards appeared most often in magazines and journals that reached an international audience. Important outlets for these marketing efforts included *Asian Shipping*, *Seatrade Business Review*, *Lloyd's Maritime Asia*, *The Motor Ship*, and *Shipping World & Shipbuilder*.

[26] *ZGHY* 3:4 (Winter 1985), p. 53.

[27] For examples of self-initiated strategies at the yard level, see *ZGHY* 7:1 (Spring 1989), p. 92, and *ZGHY* 8:3 (Autumn 1990), p. 56.

building the first in a series of trademark product and shuttle tankers in the mid-1980s. One such effort was the formation of so-called project groups, a concept around which the production process was to be reorganized. The semi-official *Zhongguo Haiyun* (*Maritime China*) described the origin of this experiment as follows: "In an attempt to cope with the difficulties in constructing the complicated ship structure and in meeting the strict technical requirements concerned, special efforts [i.e., the creation of the project groups] were made to solve these problems. . . ."[28]

Dalian was not alone in introducing such measures. Starting in the mid-1980s, Chinese maritime journals were replete with reports about changes initiated at the yard level. Jiangnan Shipyard, for example, introduced a "policy target" system of management in which production tasks were disaggregated and targets set for each phase of the process. Similarly, at Guangzhou Shipyard, competition was formally encouraged among different production units within the enterprise as part of an ongoing effort to improve quality and raise productivity.[29] According to interviews, yards across the country quietly began to use subcontractors for jobs like painting, sandblasting, and cleaning in order to enhance the flexibility of their production schedules. While this strategy was only necessary during periods of plentiful work, its adoption by the yards marked an important step toward remaking their economic organization more in the image of Japanese and Korean yards.

From all indications, this kind of experimentation with new management practices and production processes was most common in China's largest yards, which were also those most affected by the challenges of building new ship types for export and otherwise coping with the effects of GSC. This finding further supports the notion that international forces provided an important impetus for change in the shipbuilding industry. Press reports indicated that by 1987 sweeping changes in management practices were implemented at the yard level in a variety of areas, including budgeting, product design, and project appraisal – all in order to raise the quality of Chinese-built ships.[30]

For all the genuine dynamism shown by the yards in restructuring the industry's output and undertaking economic reform more generally, it would be misleading to characterize them as incipient entrepreneurs just

[28] *ZGHY* 4:4 (Winter 1986), p. 89.
[29] For more on these reforms at Jiangnan and Guangzhou, see, respectively, *ZGHY* 7:1 (Spring 1989), p. 92, and *ZGHY* 8:3 (Autumn 1990), p. 56.
[30] *ZGHY* 5:1 (Spring 1987), p. 69.

waiting to be released from the bureaucratic shackles of the planning system. Prior to their rather unceremonious baptism into the world market, the yards were, by all accounts, inward-looking, passive enterprises. As Yuan Naichang, director of the Guangzhou Shipyard, observed in late 1985, just before reform in the industry really began to take hold: "[Although] there exists a certain amount of competition between branches [yards], it's not fierce. In China we practice the planned economy."[31] As long as there were sufficient orders (domestic and foreign alike) to go around, competition between the yards was mild, indeed. Only when the industry's orderbook virtually collapsed, and CSSC Beijing in effect withdrew from some of its former responsibilities, did the yards begin to compete actively for work in a constructive, positive way. Consequently, it is probably more accurate to say that responsibility was thrust upon the yards than it would be to say that the yards had sought greater autonomy. This does not mean that the yards did not welcome a certain measure of independence from central control, especially given China's potential to become a major shipbuilder, but nothing suggests that they initially favored the kind of change that eventually occurred.

INTERNATIONAL AND DOMESTIC SOURCES OF CHANGE IN THE CHINESE SHIPBUILDING INDUSTRY

Although the central leadership, CSSC Beijing, and the yards each contributed in their own way to the process of change in the shipbuilding industry, any attempt to assign causal primacy to domestic-level variables would seriously underestimate the role of international forces in providing the original impetus for the reform, restructuring, and rationalization that ultimately occurred within CSSC.[32] To a certain extent, in fact, international and domestic forces were actually working at cross-purposes. While the larger "reform milieu" that characterized China during the 1980s certainly made changes like those found in shipbuilding *possible*, industry-specific variables provided little impetus for change. As documented throughout the case-study chapters, the indus-

---

[31] *SBR* (February 1986), p. 87.
[32] As discussed in Chapter 2, this book rejects the proposition that one set of variables – internal or external – must be chosen over another. In fact, it argues that a complete explanation requires both sets, at least to answer the full range of questions addressed in this study.

try's eventual trajectory was not the result of either special intervention from the central leadership, planned strategy by industry bureaucrats, or efforts by the yards to upset the status quo. Simply put, forces within the Chinese shipbuilding industry generally favored stasis until the crisis in world ship markets. Although the behavior of domestic actors proved critical in shaping the *process* of change – or at least in acting upon the incentives presented by a rapidly changing market environment – factors internal to the Chinese industry do not, on their own, make for a compelling explanation for the basic course of events in shipbuilding that began in the mid-1980s.

Indeed, there is little evidence that key developments within the industry – e.g., the shift toward export-oriented ship production, the increased emphasis on nonmarine production, greater diversification into foreign shiprepair, and efforts to increase imports of foreign technology – were anything but a direct response to the exigencies of the international shipbuilding crisis. Although Chinese analysts do not generally emphasize the impact of external forces on economic reform and development strategy, several accounts of the shipbuilding industry have acknowledged the critical role played by the international environment. One such example is *Dangdai Zhongguo de Chuanbo Gongye* (*Contemporary China's Shipbuilding Industry*), which strongly implies that declining international ship prices during the Sixth Five-Year Plan (1981–1985) contributed significantly to sweeping economic reform and industrial adjustment within CSSC.[33] Indeed, even accounts in the midst of the crisis itself acknowledged the importance of external factors to the transformation of the Chinese industry:

> In view of the sharp decrease in orders in the international shipbuilding market, the shipbuilding industry must improve its ability to compete and meet emergencies. To be well prepared for getting export orders in the future, the industry will try to improve the price, quality, delivery, and service of export ships. First of all . . . the focus will be on producing new types of ships. . . . For this, the shipbuilding industry will go on importing some advanced technology for turning out [a] ship's accessory equipment and eagerly seek cooperation in building special types of ships with the outside world. . . . Secondly, steps will be taken to transform old shipyards. In the five years to come, China's principal shipyards will carry out a technical

[33] *Dangdai Zhongguo de Chuanbo Gongye* (1992), pp. 669–672.

transformation, emphasizing the updating of management, and adopting new technology and new techniques so as to improve the quality of products, to increase the variety of products produced, to shorten manufacture time, and to cut down hours, consumption of energy, and raw materials. . . .[34]

All told, international and domestic factors were, of course, *both* critical in producing the course of events witnessed in the shipbuilding industry. In the absence of severe GSC – and the buyers' market it created – CSSC Beijing would have had little incentive to transfer significant economic authority to the yards. Facing a sellers' market and enjoying full control over all of the major civilian shipyards in China, industry bureaucrats had every reason to resist change. As important as the establishment of a buyers' market has been shown to be in bringing about the marketization of Chinese industries, it does not *by itself* lead ineluctably to the kind or degree of change that occurred in China's shipbuilding industry any more than the mere promulgation of nationwide reform packages guarantees actual change at an industry-specific or firm level.[35] As this chapter has shown, the response at various levels of the political and economic system can matter greatly. For example, the larger environment of reform and opening in China during the 1980s was certainly critical in allowing the course of events to play out as they did within China's shipbuilding industry. Indeed, the central leadership, CSSC Beijing, and the yards each ultimately contributed to the industry's ability to cope with the challenge of industrial adjustment triggered in world markets. While none acted as a true architect of change, in the sense of actively initiating change in the absence of an outside impetus, their responses to the rapid change in market conditions faced by CSSC were instrumental in shaping the industry's evolving path. As discussed in the next chapter, the most critical response was arguably the increased use of the market mechanism by CSSC bureaucrats in coordinating economic activity within the industry.

[34] *ZGHY* 4:1 (Spring 1986), pp. 74–75.
[35] On the role of buyers' markets, see Byrd (1987).

12

External Shocks, State Capacity, and National Responses for Economic Adjustment: Explaining Industrial Change in China

DOMESTIC STRUCTURE AS A SOURCE OF CHINESE POLICY MAKING

What explains the path taken in China to cope with the challenges presented by the MFA in textiles and GSC in shipbuilding? In an effort to construct an explanation that incorporates both the structuring impact of external forces and the mediating influence of internal forces, this chapter will rely heavily on the concept of state capacity, drawing upon the rich body of work developed by scholars in fields as diverse as comparative politics, foreign policy studies, and international political economy.[1] Specifically, three critical aspects of domestic structure are identified from the case studies – the organizational structure of the state, the nature of government-industry relations, and the transitional nature of China's economy during the 1980s and early 1990s – to show a policy "fit" between the particular challenges posed by the outside world and the relatively market-oriented solution for industrial adjustment that emerged in the Chinese textile and shipbuilding industries. In keeping with the book's main theme, Chapter 2 focused conceptually on the catalytic role of the outside world, paying only passing attention to the mediating (but vital) role of domestic structure. Drawing on the

---

[1] The classic, if now dated, review of the literature on state capacity is Skocpol (1985). The concept of state capacity has been used frequently in trying to explain national responses to various kinds of international economic change, such as oil shocks, global recession, and currency upheavals. The literature here is truly vast. Prominent examples include Katzenstein (1978a), Krasner (1978a), Katzenstein (1985), Gourevitch (1986), Loriaux (1991), and Ikenberry (1988).

case-study material, this chapter attempts to redress that imbalance by examining in detail how the specific capacities of the Chinese state shaped the range of adjustment strategies available in responding to the MFA in textiles and GSC in shipbuilding.[2]

Recalling the ideal types set forth in Chapter 1, policy responses for industrial adjustment can be classified according to one of three major approaches: first, a "market-oriented" approach that emphasizes deregulation from direct government intervention in economic matters; second, an "administrative guidance" approach, in which political or bureaucratic decisions replace private, market-based decisions in a selective, discriminating manner; and, third, a "state socialist" approach, in which industrial adjustment is attempted through the planning apparatus by means of central commands and other forms of direct administrative control.

Since the administrative guidance approach represents an intermediate or hybrid response in certain respects, it requires some brief clarification. This approach is often associated with industrial targeting and other state-led policies designed to improve on the operation of free markets by "creating" comparative advantage. Through what Robert Wade has called "government steerage," state officials try to accelerate the development process by raising investment levels and promoting certain industrial activities in line with long-term collective interests (as opposed to short-term individual interests).[3] In contrast to the market-oriented approach, which privileges *allocative* efficiency, the administrative guidance approach emphasizes that *productive* efficiency requires certain (limited) forms of state intervention to overcome market failure. (Indeed, unlike the state socialist approach, this approach seeks to intervene only *selectively* in national economic activity.) In many respects, a real-world archetype of the administrative guidance approach is the *developmental state* policies commonly associated with the postwar economic rise of Japan, South Korea, and Taiwan (hereafter, the East Asian Trio).

---

[2] While an examination of state capacity might ordinarily include international as well as domestic capacities, this study focuses almost exclusively on China's domestic capacities. As discussed in the case-study chapters, China had little ability to change either the MFA in textiles or the highly complex political economy of the world shipbuilding industry. In this sense, China was a "regime-taker" rather than a "regime-maker" in both industries. Consequently, its international capacities were marginal factors in shaping its response to international economic change.

[3] Wade (1990).

Given the presence of a vast economic bureaucracy within the state apparatus and continued state ownership across a wide range of industries (including parts of the textile industry and virtually all of the shipbuilding industry), one might have expected a highly *dirigiste* strategy from China in response to an *external* challenge for industrial adjustment. From this perspective, the leading candidate would likely have been some variant of the traditional state socialist approach associated with the planning apparatus. Failing that, one might at least have expected a state-led strategy, albeit of a more modest variety, in which bureaucratic coordination continued to play a prominent role. Here, a modified *developmental state* arrangement might have been employed to navigate the transition from a command system to a guidance system. Especially in the face of international economic change, one might reasonably have expected a policy shift toward increased, rather than decreased, administrative control, even if this shift was only at the margin.

As documented in the case studies, however, industrial adjustment in textiles and shipbuilding was ultimately achieved through market-increasing policies. Central commands and other forms of administrative control were tried first, to be sure, but in the end deregulation prevailed. While China's response to external challenges in the textile and shipbuilding industries certainly did not approximate the ideal type of a market-oriented approach, the *direction* of policy was clearly toward greater reliance on market coordination of economic activity. So, while the overall level of state involvement in the textile and shipbuilding industries may have remained fairly high in an absolute sense, it did decline substantially compared to the recent past. In fact, the evidence suggests that reform, restructuring, and rationalization in these two industries outpaced change in other Chinese industries. Furthermore, China's response also needs to be put in comparative context. Whereas some countries responded to the imposition of textile quotas under the MFA or hard times in international shipbuilding by increasing state intervention in their industries, China adopted a relatively market-oriented solution, in which the state withdrew significantly from its traditional economic responsibilities.

This chapter argues that domestic structure shapes state capacity in profound ways. In turn, the specific capacities and incapacities of a given state enable and constrain the adoption (and successful implementation) of various policies in response to the challenge of industrial adjustment. As far as the textile and shipbuilding industries are concerned, this chapter argues that a market-oriented approach provided the best policy fit with China's domestic structure. While all three aspects of domestic structure identified above arguably worked against the adoption of a state socialist approach, two aspects – the organizational structure of the state and the transitional nature of China's economic system – proved especially salient. The fragmented nature of political and economic authority across the industrial landscape, coupled with a weakening of the formal planning system, reduced the ability of the state to respond coherently and forcefully with a state socialist approach. Similarly, two aspects of domestic structure – the organizational structure of the state and the nature of government-industry relations – stand out as particularly powerful constraints against China's ability to employ an administrative guidance approach. For example, a so-called East Asian–style industrial policy requires a level of administrative coordination and corporate coherence absent in both the textile and shipbuilding industries. Compared to the alternatives, a market-oriented approach of deregulation provided a better fit between various dimensions of state capacity in China and the nature of the external challenges faced by the textile and shipbuilding industries.

CHINESE POLICY MAKING AND THE ORGANIZATIONAL STRUCTURE OF THE STATE

In the literature on state capacity, many writers have focused explicitly on the organization of the state. From this perspective, the state is viewed not as "a single, integrated, institutional actor but [as] a piece of strategically important terrain which shapes the entire course of political battles and sometimes provides the resources and advantages necessary to win them."[4] As it turns out, this conceptualization is consistent with an important body of scholarship on post-Mao Chinese politics – the "fragmented authoritarianism" literature – in which the state is no longer conceived as the (nearly) monolithic actor it was in both totalitarian models and the so-called Mao- or Deng-in-command literature.[5] For their part, the case studies in this book also support an image of the Chinese state in which the fragmented nature of political and economic

---

[4] Ikenberry (1988), p. 174.
[5] For a comprehensive examination of "fragmented authoritarianism" in China, see Lieberthal and Lampton (1992). For an example of the "Mao-in-command" approach, see Teiwes (1984).

authority places substantial, although by no means absolute, limits on the kinds of policy options available in responding to adjustment challenges. In shipbuilding, for example, it appears that the complex configuration of bureaucratic power at the highest reaches of the state prevented CSSC from receiving the kind of import protection it preferred for coping with the disastrous conditions it faced in the international shipbuilding market. Absent personal intervention by China's top leaders, the institutional capacities of the state were not conducive to a highly coordinated response within the maritime sector. While the available evidence does not permit a definitive conclusion about why the central leadership was unwilling to impose formal import restrictions on ships (or otherwise rein in COSCO), the organizational structure of the state was clearly important in shaping the options China ultimately faced as it sought to manage the crisis in global shipbuilding during the mid-1980s.

Unlike its counterparts in Japan and South Korea (and, arguably, even Western Europe), the Chinese state did not have the institutional capacities necessary to pursue a more *dirigiste* strategy, in which policies for the shipping and shipbuilding industries would have been administered more centrally. In this sense, the split between COSCO and CSSC was the organizational equivalent of a continental divide. As a result, certain kinds of state-led policies – including the type of strategic industrial policy often associated with the maritime sectors in Japan and South Korea – were effectively precluded in the Chinese case. In Japan, for example, the Ministry of Transportation enjoyed wide-ranging bureaucratic control over both the shipping and the shipbuilding industries.[6] As a result, the Japanese state was able to fashion a coordinated policy that provided, among other things, for higher levels of domestic procurement for Japanese-built ships. While this one organizational feature of the Japanese state – unified bureaucratic control over shipping and shipbuilding – does not fully explain how or why such a highly coordinated, state-led industrial policy was both adopted and successfully implemented, it does suggest one reason why it was *possible*. By the same token, the nature of state structure in China did not permit such a policy

---

[6] In fact, Ezra Vogel's assessment of the shipbuilding industry during this period led him to argue that the Ministry of Transportation had actually outperformed the more famous Ministry of International Trade and Industry as a pilot agency for industrial policy; see Vogel (1985), pp. 27–57. For more on the role of the Ministry of Transportation in fostering structural adjustment in the industry, see Chida and Davies (1990) and Woronoff (1992), pp. 103–107.

response. In South Korea, the state decided to carry out a fairly modest public procurement program to stabilize demand for Korean-built ships, but the government's influential position vis à vis the main *chaebol* in the industry (Hyundai, Samsung, and Daewoo) still allowed for a fairly *dirigiste* strategy in response to the crisis in the world shipbuilding market.[7]

As it turns out, the lack of state capacity evident in the shipbuilding industry – specifically, an inability to achieve a highly coordinated policy response across the bureaucratic landscape – appears to have been the norm rather than an exception in China at the time. Indeed, a World Bank research team identified a similar pattern of declining state capacity in their decade-long study of industry-specific reform in China during the 1980s.[8] All told, these findings support the general notion that China's ability to respond to challenges such as GSC in shipbuilding and the MFA in textiles was shaped in a substantial way by the administrative terrain of the state apparatus.

In this sense, it is indeed useful to view the state as a specific organizational landscape over which political struggles are waged. Much as geologists look to the physical record of the past to understand the development of modern-day topography, so, too, must we look at the historically contingent process of state-building in China to explain fully the contours of the "strategic terrain" over which political and economic outcomes are determined today. For example, while the fragmented authoritarianism of the Chinese state is partly attributable to patterns of bureaucratic interest articulation found in all political systems, it is also a function of the particular excesses of the Maoist period (e.g., the policy of extreme self-reliance) and the specific reforms carried out during the Deng era (e.g., the decentralization of economic decision making).

Overall, the case of China's shipbuilding industry does reinforce the general impression that central control over certain industry-specific outcomes has weakened over time. By all accounts, the conduct of politics under Mao – especially during the Cultural Revolution – severely undermined the administrative capacity of the state. In turn, Deng's determined pursuit of economic modernization only reinforced the

---

[7] For a good account, see Amsden (1989), p. 271.
[8] Specifically, they reported a pattern of state passivity in response to the suspension of guaranteed procurement for goods produced by state-run industries, even when those industries were faced with difficult market conditions; see Byrd (1987), p. 255.

fragmentation of political and economic authority begun under Mao. Although one of the main objectives of economic reform under Deng was to *increase* the state's capacity to accomplish a revamped set of regime goals focusing on economic development, the net effect has been to *reduce* the state's capacity to control some (but not all) outcomes.[9] Particularly in economic matters, central control was often weakened during the Deng era, even in cases where the devolution of power extended only to the ministerial level or its "corporate" equivalent. As a consequence of these (and other) processes, the political system in China has become increasingly institutionalized. While there is a long history in post-1949 Chinese politics of coalitional alignments based on the programmatic interest of bureaucracies, the salience of these institutional constraints on the central leadership has grown as the revolutionary guard has died off and as bureaucratic interests have become more entrenched over time.[10]

Given the fragmented nature of political and economic authority in China, the policy-making landscape is often characterized as a bargaining system. While this feature is more than simply a function of the organizational landscape of the state itself, the deep structural divisions within the bureaucratic system (e.g., COSCO versus CSSC) certainly shape the range of policy options available when the country is confronted with an external challenge like the shipbuilding crisis of the mid-1980s. Except in cases where the issue is sufficiently critical to the regime's goals that top leaders become willing to expend the necessary political capital to elicit compliance with edicts issued from above, the fault lines of everyday politics within the state apparatus often preclude certain courses of action.

GOVERNMENT-INDUSTRY RELATIONS IN CHINA: IMPLICATIONS FOR THE CONDUCT OF INDUSTRIAL POLICY

In the literature in comparative politics, one of the main conventions used by scholars interested in the concept of state capacity is an examination of relations between the state and the larger socioeconomic and sociopolitical environment in which the state is situated. Depending on the particular study, this dyadic relationship is most often discussed in

---

[9] For two accounts that interpret reform as an attempt to reassert state control over political and economic outcomes in China, see McCormick (1990) and Shue (1988).
[10] On these general themes, see Bachman (1991, 1992).

terms of "government and business," "public and private," or "state and society." As useful as these dyads have been for examining state capacity in other countries, each falls in some way to capture the essence of this important relationship in China. While observers have devoted considerable attention to the prospect that a genuinely autonomous civil society might emerge in China someday, societal participation is rather minimal in the context of the industrial case studies examined in this book. As a result, the "state-society" relationship emphasized by many scholars, especially those who focus on advanced industrialized countries, is not yet fully applicable to the study of China. Similarly, the "public-private" distinction also remains unsatisfactory in most cases, especially when the subject is a state-owned industry such as shipbuilding.

Even the narrower "government-business" relationship, which has been emphasized in studies of policy making and policy implementation in countries such as Japan and South Korea, needs substantial modification for application to China. Indeed, the fundamental dynamic of state capacity examined in this book is an *intra*state relationship, something each of the previously mentioned dyads fails to capture adequately. In the shipbuilding case study, for example, the most important relationships were those among various levels *within* the state apparatus (defined broadly to include the central leadership, supervisory agencies at the industrial level, and individual SOEs). In this sense, the most appropriate dyad for the study of state capacity in China might be "government-industry" relations – especially the nature of policy networks within the state apparatus.[11] While policy networks are intrinsically interesting in their own right, I am primarily concerned with the institutional capacities they confer upon states to implement specific types of economic strategies.

By most accounts, policy networks in China continued to be characterized by an institutional culture of industrial paternalism during the 1980s and early 1990s. While textiles and shipbuilding were by no means the most powerful examples of this phenomenon – in part because they experienced relatively high levels of reform compared to similar industries – these case studies do nonetheless provide evidence that the legacy

[11] There is a long tradition among comparativists in which arguments about state capacity are framed in terms of policy networks. Two classic examples outside the China field are Katzenstein (1978b) and Johnson (1982). Studies on China that examine policy networks include Barnett (1967) and Bachman (1991).

of state socialism remained strong. Other important changes notwith-standing, the basic nature of government-industry relations in textiles and shipbuilding changed relatively slowly.

As always, the sheer size and diversity of the textile industry makes generalization a perilous endeavor, especially in trying to characterize an aspect of state capacity as broad as "government-industry relations." After all, the share of national textile output produced by enterprises under the administration of MTI (and its successors) declined from 91 percent in 1980 to 53 percent by 1992.[12] Consequently, one problem related to state capacity in the textile industry was simply the decreas-ing scope of centralized bureaucratic control. Even where administrative jurisdiction was not an issue, however, the state's ability to enforce policy was often weak. Here, non-PRC informants consistently depicted government-industry relations as significantly paternalistic in nature. As a result, developmental discipline was difficult to maintain. For example, threats to cut energy supplies and credit allocation to SOEs if they failed to implement directives for industrial rationalization (e.g., spindle retire-ment) were largely ineffective since bank loans continued to be extended to loss-makers. Overall, scarce resources were allocated mainly accord-ing to need, rather than on the basis of strategic goals or meritorious performance.

The persistence of industrial paternalism was equally clear in the ship-building industry. Even if shipbuilding had been a favored sector under government policy, perhaps along the lines of the automobile industry, there is evidence that CSSC lacked the institutional capacities to take full advantage of such an opportunity. Indeed, for all its successes, the inability of CSSC Beijing to impose comprehensive financial discipline on the yards – and to link material rewards to performance more gen-erally – suggests how difficult it would have been to adopt successfully an East Asian–style industrial policy of the kind documented for the East Asian Trio by scholars such as Chalmers Johnson, Alice Amsden, and Robert Wade.[13] Especially with the loosening of administrative control over time, CSSC Beijing experienced ever greater difficulty in eliciting compliance from China's yards.

---

[12] *ZGFZGYNJ* (1982), p.191, and *ZGFZGYNJ* (1993), p. 188. In fact, by 1992 enterprises under MTI's administration accounted for only 21 percent of the total enterprises engaged in textile manufacturing.

[13] On Japan, South Korea, and Taiwan, respectively, see Johnson (1982), Amsden (1989), and Wade (1990).

As described by Janos Kornai, government-industry relations in state socialist systems, including a *reforming* state socialist system such as post-Mao China, are distinguished by a "dual dependency" in which the fate of industry officials and enterprise managers are inextricably linked within the system.[14] Even when reform efforts increase the scope of market coordination, thereby increasing horizontal dependence within the system, vertical dependence remains predominant according to Kornai. Until a truly hard budget constraint is created, incentives associated with bureaucratic coordination generate both paternalistic tendencies from above and demands for paternalism from below. As the case studies of the textile and shipbuilding industries suggest, paternalism can be reduced, but is difficult to eliminate altogether.[15] In China's case, this can be seen more generally in the relative inability of the government to enforce discipline (i.e., punish losers) at either the firm level or the industrial level. As one observer described it, "As an owner, the Chinese state has been amazingly forgiving of bad performance."[16] All told, the institutional culture of policy networks in post-Mao China has provided neither the degree nor the kind of bureaucratic autonomy and corporate coherence necessary for pursuing state-led policies like those often ascribed to the East Asian Trio. Instead, a distinctive pattern of government-industry relations based on dual dependence and particularism persisted largely (although by no means completely) intact during the 1980s and 1990s.

How does the nature of policy networks in China affect the capacity of the state to accomplish certain development tasks critical to late industrialization? Consider the economic agenda studied in this book: industrial adjustment, export upgrading, and intensive growth in the face of hard times in world markets. Like any other institutional culture, the industrial paternalism characteristic of post-Mao China has constrained the adoption of certain policies while enabling others. From the case studies examined here, as well as the general literature on Chinese politics, there can be little doubt that the policy networks that defined government-industry relations during the 1980s and 1990s were not characterized mainly by the kind of rational-legal authority typically

---

[14] For more on dual dependency, see Kornai (1992), Chapter 21.

[15] For an excellent discussion of paternalistic tendencies in socialist systems, including a classification based on five different degrees of paternalism, see Kornai (1980), Chapter 22.

[16] *FEER*, 18 February 1999, p. 15.

ascribed to Japan, South Korea, and Taiwan prior to the revisionist fallout from the AFC. Stated somewhat differently, the autonomy of the Chinese state was not embedded in the more universalistic ties attributed to the *developmental states* of the East Asian Trio. Instead, its (still considerable) autonomy was embedded in particularistic ties of industrial paternalism-cum-reforming state socialism, ties rooted at least partially in the constitution of the Leninist party-state and reinforced by China's political history under Mao and Deng. As a result, bureaucrats often pursued their own narrow self-interest at the expense of broader organizational or national goals; clearly, they were not bound successfully to collective, developmentalist ends.

It is this aspect of government-industry relations – in which the violation of universalistic principles undermines corporate coherence within the state apparatus – that constrains the ability of the Chinese state to pursue, at least successfully, policies modeled broadly on those adopted by the East Asian Trio at similar junctures in their development.[17] (There were, of course, *some* incentives based on bureaucratic interests to achieve essential economic tasks within the Chinese system, but these incentives were often seriously distorted. As a general rule, political expediency prevailed over substantive performance.) While an "administrative" guidance approach was never formally pursued in the Chinese textile and shipbuilding industries, there is ample evidence from the general pattern of state involvement in these industries to suggest that such an experiment would almost surely have failed due to the nature of government-industry relations. Moreover, as discussed in Chapter 13, Beijing's track record in employing East Asian–style industrial policy in other sectors hardly augured well for success in textiles or shipbuilding. In short, there is no reason to expect that these industries would have fared any better.

In contrast to what Pearson has aptly characterized as an "old-style industrial policy inherent in central planning," one designed primarily to protect *uncompetitive* industries, an East Asian–style industrial policy is marked by selective government intervention – in generally market-conforming fashion – to promote *competitive* industries.[18] To borrow a concept from Wade's analysis of Taiwan, East Asian–style industry policy

---

[17] For an extended discussion of the conceptual issues raised in this paragraph, see Evans (1995). For a useful review of Evans and related works by other authors, see Schneider (1998).

[18] Pearson (1999), p. 178.

involves "government steerage" of investment capital to create manufacturing capability in bureaucratically identified strategic sectors. Furthermore, this conception of industrial policy (*chanye zhengce*) is distinct
from the broader notion of economic readjustment (*jingji tiaozheng*)
associated with Chinese reforms early in the post-Mao period.[19]

While the nature of government-business relations in the East Asian
Trio is now often dismissed as "crony capitalism" in the wake of the AFC,
this fails to acknowledge both the positive, developmental aspects of
relational-based governance in these countries and important differences between "crony capitalism" elsewhere in East Asia and "industrial
paternalism" in China.[20] Since this is not the place for a comprehensive
discussion of the lessons that should be drawn from the AFC, except
to say that the "pathologies" of relational-based governance for late
industrialization have arguably been overstated by some observers, the
present study will focus instead on how relational-based governance
differs – not only in degree, but also in kind – between China and its historically high-performing neighbors. One salient difference is the *basis*
of state intervention in enterprise-level economic activity. In China, government and business functions remain closely linked in comparison with
the East Asian Trio, where management decisions are more independent
on the whole and performance standards are more effectively (if still
imperfectly) applied as a condition for government support. Despite
efforts to clarify property rights in recent years, the nature of
government-industry relations in China is still one in which the government too often plays a dual role as both the owner and the manager of
state assets. While the relationship between supervisory agencies and
industrial managers is no longer purely administrative, even in large
SOEs, it does retain a significant element of this dynamic. Reform of the
principal-agent relationship proceeds apace, to be sure, but the separation of government and enterprise functions is far from complete.

Whatever the relevant lessons of the AFC, some of which do correctly
point to serious weaknesses associated with crony capitalism, the term
"public-private cooperation" is still a more meaningful concept for
understanding the organization of economic activity in the East Asian

---

[19] For the definitive work on the 1979–1982 readjustment program, see Solinger (1991).
While this kind of government initiative can certainly be understood as industrial policy
given its focus on shifting investment and production from heavy to light industry, it
differs significantly from the type of industrial targeting examined in the next chapter.
[20] The term "relational-based governance" is borrowed from Smyth (2000). The term is
used here in the sense suggested by popular conceptions of Asian-style capitalism.

Trio than in China. Even after two decades of reform in China, the nature of state involvement in economic activity still does not lend itself easily to a notion of public-private cooperation. For example, while subsidies provided through the fiscal system have been reduced significantly, subsidies provided through the banking system remain an enormous problem – arguably on a scale beyond that found anywhere else in the region.[21] Especially for troubled industries, state-directed credit is absolutely critical. Too often, financial need simply trumps performance-based decision criteria. While there are certainly elements of a soft budget constraint in the East Asian Trio as well, most Japanese and South Korean firms face harder budget constraints than their Chinese counterparts. As long as scarce state resources are diverted primarily to propping up loss-making SOEs, the possibilities for East Asian–style industrial policy in China are severely limited.[22]

That said, the situation in which China continues to find itself reflects something more fundamental than a simple matter of policy choice. As argued in Chapter 13, China has at present only a very limited ability to pursue successfully the kind of strategic industrial policy associated with its high-performing neighbors. Even if a new policy focus were to emerge, one that deemphasized the subsidization of weak SOEs in favor of a more strategic vision for China's industrial structure, the persistence of industrial paternalism would make the successful adoption of an East Asian–style industrial policy difficult at best. Simply put, the Chinese state lacks the institutional capacity necessary to enforce the "reciprocity" – performance in return for government support – widely regarded as essential to the success of *developmental states*.[23] The problem for China, therefore, is not one of relational-based governance per se. (Indeed, as Peter Evans and others would argue, all forms of governance are fundamentally relational-based and differ only in the *nature* of those relations.)[24] Rather, the problem is the *kind* of relational-based

---

[21] Lardy (1998).

[22] While the current priority of subsidizing losers does, of course, represent a certain type of "industrial policy," it essentially precludes – for better or for worse – the broader use of an East Asian–style industrial policy. As discussed in Chapter 13, concerted efforts at industrial targeting have been restricted thus far to a handful of "pillar industries" (*zhizhu chanye*).

[23] Schneider (1998).

[24] Evans (1995). Moreover, even explanations of the Trio's success that emphasize the market-conforming nature of development strategy in East Asia sometimes acknowledge the positive – although in these accounts, much more limited – role played by the state. See, for example, the grudging recognition found in World Bank (1993).

governance found in China, one that is not propitious for the successful implementation of *developmental state* policies. In this sense, the AFC only underscores the dangers of the administrative guidance approach for China. To the extent that the difficulties experienced by Japan and South Korea were in fact associated with weaknesses in *their* relational-based governance, China's brand – which is even less Weberian – is highly vulnerable to weak performance since government-industry relations in China share all of the much-analyzed weaknesses of the Trio's brand, but few of its developmental strengths.

THE TRANSITIONAL NATURE OF CHINA'S ECONOMY

The transitional nature of China's economy in the 1980s and early 1990s made both a state socialist approach and an administrative guidance approach difficult to carry out effectively. Specifically, several features of China's changing economy – ongoing decentralization, new distortions created by partial reform, and chronic resource constraints – undermined China's ability to use either type of state-led approach successfully. While the vestiges of the planning system could be used to undertake broad reallocations of resources across geographic regions or sectors of the economy, the ability of a state socialist approach to achieve a more subtle economic agenda – such as export upgrading, product diversification, and intensive growth within an individual industry – was extremely limited under any circumstances. As modest as they were, the economic reforms of the early to mid-1980s only further weakened the relevance of traditional policy instruments such as planning targets and material balances. As time went on, bureaucratic coordination became increasingly difficult to employ effectively as a means by which to organize economic activity. Indeed, as the case-study chapters document, the standard tools of administrative pressure and central command were unsuccessful in bringing about the kind of industrial transformation required in textiles and shipbuilding. All told, China's economic transition was characterized by declining state capacity to achieve industrial adjustment through a traditional state socialist approach.

Nor did the reform environment of the 1980s and early 1990s prove to be conducive to an administrative guidance approach. On the one hand, the concept of a *developmental state* seemed to be a good candidate for the role of midwife in the transition from central planning to market socialism. Indeed, China's thinly veiled intention to follow in the footsteps of the East Asian Trio as practitioners of industrial policy and conglomerate-building raised the prospect of a more permanent connection between "capitalism with Chinese characteristics" and an administrative guidance approach to industrial adjustment. As it turned out, however, economic transition proved to be a poor milieu for the development of new state capacities necessary for the successful use of an administrative guidance approach. For example, government-industry relations were difficult to remake in the midst of a transition between economic systems. With market institutions in their relative infancy and property rights ill-defined, the institutional culture of the state continued to be one characterized by a significant degree of industrial paternalism. While decentralizing reforms did move forward in certain respects, this often only magnified existing problems. As mentioned before, government funds were devoted primarily to propping up uncompetitive, loss-making SOEs rather than to the development of competitive firms through state-led industrial targeting. Even where policy instruments relevant to East Asian–style industrial policy existed, therefore, declining administrative coherence and resource constraints made the effective implementation of any state-led strategy difficult. To the extent that the reform environment contributed to both problems, economic transition constrained the use of an administrative guidance approach.

STATE CAPACITY, INDUSTRIAL ADJUSTMENT, AND POLICY "FIT": CHINA'S RESPONSE TO EXTERNAL CHALLENGES IN THE TEXTILE AND SHIPBUILDING INDUSTRIES

By the mid-1980s, a variety of domestic factors had begun to reduce the state's ability to pursue the standard state socialist approach to industrial adjustment when faced with external challenges such as the MFA in textiles and GSC in shipbuilding. In addition, this type of policy response was ill-suited for the particular adjustment task at hand, one that emphasized intensive growth and industrial restructuring. In this sense, the international environment constrained China's ability to rely on the planning apparatus to effect industrial change. Even though the planning system was by no means moribund, it simply could not induce the subtle kinds of change in quality, service, and productivity necessary for industries such as shipbuilding and textiles to survive – let alone thrive – in intensely competitive world markets characterized by moderate economic closure. In the absence of this impetus from the outside world, however, the state socialist approach would have been more viable, albeit still suboptimal.

Similarly, all indications were that the Chinese state lacked the specific institutional capacities necessary to undertake successfully an administrative guidance approach in response to GSC and the MFA. At first, of course, China's economic system was insufficiently market-based for an administrative guidance approach even to be plausible. Still later, after reform had proceeded to a point where certain state-led endeavors could conceivably have been characterized as administrative guidance policies – as opposed to traditional planning à la the state socialist approach – these efforts were both few and largely unsuccessful. Due to the nature of government-industry relations, among other political factors, industrial policy in China generally involved the subsidization of loss-making SOEs, rather than the promotion of competitive enterprises.

In terms of existing state capacities, therefore, a market-oriented approach proved to be the most viable option for responding to the external challenges presented by GSC in shipbuilding and the MFA in textiles. While it is theoretically possible to create new capacities through institution-building, such as those necessary for an administrative guidance approach to succeed, the thrust of much recent scholarship in comparative political economy is that the specific capacities of states are largely, if not completely, historical artifacts. Indeed, this theme is strongly represented in the literature on the East Asian Trio.[25] At the very least, state capacities cannot be created overnight, and certainly not in time to cope with any immediate challenge.

Although the lack of mature market-based institutions diminished the full effect of administrative deregulation in China, the state was able to withdraw unilaterally from some of its traditional economic responsibilities. Importantly, this type of response did not require extensive policy coordination within the larger state apparatus. In shipbuilding, for example, industrial adjustment was not predicated on centralized authority over all aspects of the shipping and shipbuilding industries, unlike the more *dirigiste* strategies pursued in Japan and South Korea. Given the fragmented structure of bureaucratic authority over the maritime sector in China (COSCO versus CSSC), the political and institutional capacities of the state actually favored a path of administrative deregulation coupled with increasing market coordination of economic activity.

---

[25] For explicit examples, see Johnson (1982), Cumings (1984), Wade (1990), and Kohli (1999).

Unable to use traditional means in achieving the necessary changes in textiles and shipbuilding, industry officials somewhat grudgingly followed a market-oriented solution to the challenge of industrial adjustment.

THE ROLE OF INTERNATIONAL FORCES IN CHANGING THE PATTERN OF STATE INTERVENTION IN THE CHINESE TEXTILE AND SHIPBUILDING INDUSTRIES

Even if a fit between alternative policy responses and certain dimensions of state capacity in China can be demonstrated, the mere *ability* of the state to withdraw from some of its former economic responsibilities does not by itself explain *why* this happened. Put another way, simply having the capacity to employ a market-oriented solution to the challenge of industrial adjustment does not explain why such a policy was ultimately carried out. What is needed, therefore, is an explanation for why a more market-oriented strategy gained support within the state apparatus, particularly among industry bureaucrats. In the study of state socialist systems, especially those experimenting with reform, there is a critical recurring question: When, if at all, are bureaucrats likely to use the market mechanism to coordinate economic activity? What are the origins of their willingness to make this change? With specific reference to the case of post-Mao China, why did the state withdraw from its traditional economic role more readily in some industries (e.g., shipbuilding) than in others (e.g., automobile manufacturing)?

This book argues that the course of events in China's textile and shipbuilding industries cannot be understood without reference to the external forces that set the underlying dynamic of change into motion. In both cases, the most powerful causal chain runs from moderate economic closure in world markets to industry-specific reform, restructuring, and rationalization. To be sure, the impact of the MFA and GSC was mediated in important ways by domestic structure, as this chapter itself has emphasized. Still, external forces were critical in altering the incentives facing industry bureaucrats. As argued throughout the book, the emergence of an externally driven buyers' market was crucial in both industries. In this way, moderate economic closure in world markets was instrumental in breaking (or at least weakening) the long-noted affinity in state socialist systems between bureaucrats and bureaucratic forms of economic coordination.[26] In shipbuilding, for example, hard times led CSSC officials to abdicate certain responsibilities for the industry's performance, shifting a significant portion of the burden for industrial restructuring and other adjustment tasks onto the shipyards themselves. In this sense, the impact of the international environment was to *enable* a policy of state withdrawal from its former role in the industry by changing the policy preferences of industry bureaucrats. At the same time, their ability to pursue a traditional state socialist policy for industrial adjustment was *inhibited* by the nature of the economic challenge associated with severe GSC – namely, one of intensive rather than extensive growth. In this sense, the effects of international forces included both constraints and enablements.

CHINA IN COMPARATIVE PERSPECTIVE: THE VALUE OF A "STATE CAPACITY" APPROACH

By invoking the concept of "state capacity," this book implicitly argues that the form of political and economic system, while important, does not adequately explain the types of policy responses made in the face of external challenges for industrial adjustment. In this sense, it is the ability of the state to accomplish certain tasks that matters most, not whether a country is broadly defined as democratic or authoritarian, capitalist or socialist, or even market-oriented or centrally planned. To be sure, the type of political and economic system may play an important role in shaping the capacities of the state, but since similar capacities exist across different systems and large differences in capacities are often found within similar systems, it makes little analytic sense to frame the explanation simply in terms of different *types* of systems. Thus, even when the ability to pursue a certain course of action, such as the administrative guidance approach associated with the East Asian Trio, seems to be linked to a particular form of political and economic system, the attributes of this system are still best conceptualized in terms of broader

---

[26] According to Janos Kornai and other scholars of comparative communism, state socialism represents a coherent system in which an "organic link" exists between bureaucrats and bureaucratic coordination, even in reforming systems such as post-Mao China; Kornai (1992), especially pp. 365–368. In no state socialist system, of course, is the economy coordinated solely by bureaucratic mechanisms. Any real-world economy is characterized by a mix of market-based and bureaucratic forms of coordination. Kornai's point is simply that there is a tendency for state socialist systems to reject the increased use of market mechanisms.

analytic categories – e.g., embedded autonomy, internal bureaucratic coherence, technocratic developmentalism – that facilitate comparison across systems.[27] That is, even if variations in state capacity between two or more countries are to some extent derivative of general system characteristics, it is still best to use concepts that transcend the idiosyncrasies of particular systems or country-specific cultures. By taking this approach, our understanding of China's capacities and incapacities extends beyond some jejune statement about "different" systems.

This book therefore endorses not only the concept of state capacity itself, but also a formulation that consciously includes aspects of state capacity other than those that can be attributed narrowly to a particular system. From the case studies, we can see how the dynamics of state-building in recent decades have given rise to specific institutional arrangements (e.g., bureaucratic divisions) in China that reflect the diversity of state structures that can exist even within a particular system (e.g., state socialism).[28] Inasmuch as the origins and dynamics of state capacity can be found in the legacy of past policies, as well as in the type of system, this analysis suggests explanations that are historically contingent and, therefore, path-dependent in some measure.

---

[27] For more on these particular examples, see Evans (1995).

[28] For example, the fragmentation of political and economic authority found among the competing functional bureaucracies in the shipping and shipbuilding industries arguably resulted as much from specific policies carried out under Mao and Deng as from any characteristic inherent to Leninist political and economic systems in general.

13

China in the Contemporary International Political Economy

The major conclusion of this book is that the international environment most propitious for the reform, restructuring, and rationalization of Chinese industries during the 1980s and early 1990s was one marked by moderate economic closure rather than the ideal-typic economic openness assumed by most observers. While this finding must be asserted tentatively given the limited number of cases examined here, evidence from the textile and shipbuilding industries indicates a need for further investigation into the impact of "free trade" and "managed trade" environments on change at the industrial level. Specifically, this book argues that the MFA in textiles and GSC in shipbuilding *accelerated*, rather than *retarded*, industrial transformation and export success. By contrast, the same type and degree of change was less pronounced when the world market was characterized by greater economic openness. For example, the silk sector of China's textile industry – one not subject to quotas until 1994 – lagged noticeably behind other sectors by every measure of industrial restructuring, including export upgrading, product diversification, and technological modernization. For their part, economic reform and industrial rationalization were also comparatively slow in the silk sector.

The remainder of this section provides a brief exploration of broader issues related to this central research finding. First, the discussion expands the empirical focus beyond textiles and shipbuilding to light industries such as toys, footwear, sporting goods, and household appliances. Second, it examines the durability and generalizability of its research findings. Finally, it identifies areas for future study, including additional research projects that will be necessary if the investigation of light industries is to move beyond the highly preliminary analysis offered here.

A Tale of Two Models?

What about the phenomenal success of China's export-oriented light industries? Do they not confirm the conventional wisdom that economic openness in overseas markets is most conducive to economic reform and industrial adjustment in China? After all, many observers would cite the South China "economic miracle" as proof that free trade in these industrial markets has made China's success in consumer goods possible. If only all Chinese industries enjoyed unrestricted access to world markets – so the argument would go – reform, restructuring, and rationalization would be even further advanced in China.

Here, an important distinction must be made between the "new" manufacturing centers of South China and the "traditional" manufacturing centers of East China. (This division is, of course, a simplification made for illustrative purposes. Especially during the 1980s and early 1990s, China's new manufacturing centers – especially those created by FDI – were concentrated largely in South China. By contrast, China's pre-existing manufacturing capacity for light industrial goods – especially products well-suited for export – was located predominantly in East China.) In discussing the impact of the MFA, several informants commented on the superior performance of the textile industry compared to other light industries. In Shanghai, perhaps *the* quintessential traditional manufacturing center in East China, the record of export upgrading and product diversification in the textile industry during the 1980s was reportedly superior to that found in other light industries, mainly due to pressures associated with life under the MFA. At the same time, informants also indicated that this record of restructuring was more uniform across different industries in South China, where the influence of Hong Kong and Taiwan industrialists was so profound. Although no one phrased their comments in terms of treating South China's new manufacturing centers as a special case, their observations were consistent with the notion that light industry in South China and East China represented different models of economic development in the 1980s and early 1990s.

As has been widely acknowledged, the new manufacturing centers of South China achieved strong diversification in both product lines and export markets at an early stage. Furthermore, their exports of light industrial goods such as athletic footwear, electronic games, and household appliances also moved upmarket impressively. In addition, economic activity in these new manufacturing centers was substantially market-oriented almost from their inception. For their part, the traditional manufacturing centers of East China produced similar kinds of products and faced the same free trade environment internationally. That said, economic reform, industrial adjustment, and export success were judged by informants to be considerably slower than in the new manufacturing centers.

From the interviews conducted for this book, therefore, it appears that the South China economic miracle of the 1980s and early 1990s may have been an unrepresentative case as far as the significance of economic openness in world markets is concerned. To what extent was the free trade environment that existed in most light industrial markets responsible for inducing reform, restructuring, and rationalization in South China? Here, the case of East China suggests caution. Put bluntly, it may have been the virtual economic colonization of South China by Hong Kong and Taiwan industrialists that best accounts for the impressive performance of South China's light industries. Indeed, informants repeatedly emphasized the importance of the "front shop, back factory" relationship (*qiandian houchang*) to South China's success. From this perspective, economic change was pushed through by investors from Hong Kong and Taiwan, not induced by a free trade environment, per se.[1] In East China, where this kind of direct, hands-on foreign presence was more limited at first, change comparable to that found in South China came more slowly.

From this perspective, the tremendous attention received by South China's new manufacturing centers – and deservedly so given their export success – may have contributed to the popular misconception that a free trade environment was most conducive to reform, restructuring, and rationalization in Chinese industries during the 1980s and early 1990s. In the absence of explicit regimes (e.g., the MFA) or other forces (e.g., GSC) that have a similar effect in restricting or regulating their access to world markets, Chinese industries faced less pressure to undertake the kinds of change witnessed in the textile and shipbuilding industries. Particularly given the powerful forces of immobilism that often prevailed in China, incentives from the outside world could be (and

---

[1] The classic account of Guangdong's early experience is Vogel (1989). On Fujian, see Hsing (1998).

frequently were) critical. As exemplified by the silk sector, economic openness in world markets reinforced mediocrity in industries that were able to enjoy export growth without undertaking reform, restructuring, and rationalization.

As argued more fully in Chapter 1, if an industry in a partially reformed state socialist economy can increase its foreign exchange earnings through a volume-centered strategy consistent with the system's general orientation toward extensive growth, there may be little incentive for change. In this regard, China would seem particularly susceptible to the classic trap that has long plagued developing countries: newcomers to the world market – driven by the need for foreign exchange – typically focus on short-term gains, a posture that can undermine their ability to trade up the international product cycle for specific industrial goods and inhibit their long-term adjustment to world market trends more generally.

The point here is simply that forces of moderate economic closure restrict the ease of exporting and thereby condition foreign exchange earnings more closely to an ability to move upmarket to higher value-added production. Unlike conditions found in a more market-based economy, signals from the world economy become badly distorted in partially reformed state socialist economies, in part by the operation of the air lock system discussed in this book. Consequently, a free trade environment does not have the same effect in inducing industrial change in China as it might in another country. As described in the case-study chapters, however, forces of moderate economic closure can act as a surrogate for world market signals in industries such as textiles and shipbuilding, providing an incentive for them to adopt a more value-centered strategy. This is why apparent hardships encountered abroad, such as textile quotas and a glut of shipbuilding capacity, can actually enhance the prospects for economic reform, industrial transformation, and long-term export success.

Standing the Test of Time

How durable are the findings in this book? Is managed trade still more conducive than free trade to the reform, restructuring, and rationalization of Chinese industries today, or were the virtues of moderate economic closure restricted to a particular stage of China's reform and opening? While this question cannot be answered definitively on the basis of the time-bound, case-specific research conducted for this study, a few observations are possible. First, the impact of the Asian Financial Crisis on China suggests a logic similar to the argument set forth in this book. To the extent that the AFC has indeed served as an impetus for further reform and opening, its impact – hard times leading to significant economic change – parallels the impact of the MFA in textiles and GSC in shipbuilding. To be sure, evidence concerning China's long-term response to the AFC remains mixed at present. On the one hand, reform rhetoric and formal policy pronouncements have exceeded actual change in the wake of the crisis. Indeed, progress has periodically slowed in areas such as SOE reform. By the same token, the long-term prospects for reform and opening are arguably better as a result of the general lessons China has drawn from the crisis. In this respect, Beijing's willingness to make substantial concessions as part of its bid for WTO accession reflected a recognition that China needs to continue (and even intensify) its economic transition in order to protect its national security. If China lives up to its promises, the AFC may come to be seen as an external shock that contributed significantly to a new stage in China's reform and opening. If so, the role of the international environment will resemble the pattern found in textiles and shipbuilding, one in which discrete external challenges trigger substantial economic change.

While the notion that the outside world continues to serve as an impetus for reform and opening does suggest a point of continuity between the recent past and contemporary events, there are other respects in which this book's findings may indeed be time-bound. Specifically, it is possible – and perhaps even likely – that moderate economic closure may no longer be, or at least soon will not be, the international environment most propitious for the reform, restructuring, and rationalization of Chinese industries. As China's economy becomes more market-based, some would argue, signals from the world economy should increasingly be able to play the dynamic role envisioned by neoclassical theory. In this case, a managed trade environment – its previous benefits notwithstanding – would produce a less efficient allocation of resources in China, thereby actually inhibiting industrial adjustment in some respects.[2] Especially as a member of the WTO, China's economic system may soon converge sufficiently – albeit still very much imperfectly – with market-based norms that the domestic conditions that once

---

[2] As first introduced in Chapter 1, this book has argued that moderate economic closure actually facilitated a *more* efficient allocation of resources in China during the 1980s and early 1990s due to the partially reformed nature of the economic system at that time.

made moderate economic closure beneficial may be diminished or even absent. Moreover, there are reasons to believe that once industrial transformation – as distinct from economic reform – reaches a certain point, individual Chinese industries may be sufficiently competitive in world markets that a free trade environment would be most advantageous both to their further development and to their continued international success. Consider, for example, China's textile industry. As discussed in Chapter 3, many observers believe that the timing of the MFA phaseout will be nearly ideal for China since its industry is now, after the progress documented in this book, increasingly well-positioned to benefit from a free trade environment.

On the other hand, the experience of the East Asian Trio suggests that neoclassical precepts concerning the superiority of modernization through allocative efficiency may require modification, at least when world markets are characterized by moderate economic closure. Specifically, studies by David Yoffie and others have argued that instruments of managed trade (e.g., VERs, OMAs, quotas) have led industries in restricted countries to trade up the international product cycle more quickly.[3] In this sense, modernization through productive efficiency may trump modernization through allocative efficiency. If so, then it is less clear whether moderate economic closure has outlived its usefulness for the reform, restructuring, and rationalization of Chinese industry. This, of course, represents a separate research question altogether, one that will have to await further study. It does serve as a reminder, however, that neoclassical claims about free trade may at least require qualification.

Issues for Future Research

On the basis of the case-study material, the present text has argued that the MFA and GSC led to greater change in the Chinese textile and shipbuilding industries than would have occurred in their absence. To what extent, however, does the *specific* explanation for textiles and shipbuilding provided in this book represent a more *general* proposition about the effects of moderate economic closure on other Chinese industries? As powerful as the causal connection appears to be in these case studies,

---

[3] Yoffie (1983). For more detailed discussion, as well as additional citations to the literature, see Chapter 1.

additional research is needed in order to assert more confidently that this relationship held across the industrial landscape in China during the 1980s and early 1990s. While the research conducted for this study does allow for within-case comparison, thereby giving us greater confidence in its findings, it is still possible that special conditions were present in these cases that restrict their generalizability. Given the small number of cases involved, further research will be especially useful for exploring this possibility.

As far as additional industries are concerned, a good place to start would be the light industries identified earlier in the chapter. While most of these industries faced a free trade environment during the 1980s and early 1990s, specific goods within basic product categories such as footwear, toys, and consumer electronics were subject to quotas in key export markets such as the European Union. While none of these restraints matched the MFA in either the duration or the scope of their coverage (in terms of both the number of individual products covered and the number of countries imposing restrictions), they would nonetheless allow for further testing of the hypotheses concerning free trade versus managed trade environments. This focus would also obviously allow for systematic examination of the South China versus East China inquiry posed rather impressionistically earlier in the chapter. In heavy industry, suitable candidates would include steel and machine tools, two industries that have periodically faced protectionist instruments in world markets. Through these industries, in fact, the research agenda could be broadened to include other forms of managed trade, such as antidumping duties.

To expand the field of study even further, industry-specific cases could also be examined in the transitional economies of Eastern Europe and the former Soviet Union. While the present explanation for events in the textile and shipbuilding industries does assign considerable weight to domestic structure as an important intervening variable for understanding specific outcomes in China, the basic proposition about moderate economic closure leading to industrial reform, restructuring, and rationalization in partially reformed state socialist economies seems ripe for application to other national settings. (Indeed, the analysis of domestic structure provided for the Chinese case could serve as the conceptual baseline for other countries.) In this sense, the book provides an explanation specific to China, but one with broader theoretical implications open to comparative study.

ANOTHER CASE OF "EAST ASIAN MERCANTILISM"?:
CHINESE ECONOMIC SUCCESS IN THE ABSENCE
OF A *DEVELOPMENTAL STATE*

Despite fears that China is following in the mercantilist footsteps of its high-performing neighbors, concerns that persist even in the wake of Beijing's anticipated WTO accession, this book raises questions about China's ability to pursue successfully the kind of strategic industrial policy associated with the East Asian Trio. The Chinese economic juggernaut may indeed continue, as many observers predict, but it is unlikely that China's rise as an industrial power in the coming decades will be the product of a *developmental state* like those often credited with directing the East Asian miracle elsewhere in the region. To be sure, statist accounts represent only one perspective on the sources of East Asia's postwar dynamism, but they are especially important since Beijing has tried rather self-consciously in recent years to pattern the country's modernization after what its leaders regard as an "East Asian" model of development.[4] In neither textiles nor shipbuilding, however, did the state play this kind of role. In fact, as the two case studies in this book suggest, most Chinese "success stories" during the post-Mao era have involved industries where state intervention has declined. By contrast, state-led policies such as the "pillar industries" (*zhizhu chanye*) initiative have enjoyed considerably less success on the whole.

The lineage of China's current industrial policy began with State Council's March 1989 promulgation of a new framework for industrial policy.[5] While this document represented only a first-cut effort to find a new mode of industrial planning consistent with China's market-oriented reforms, the broad outlines of future policy can be detected in the document's identification of specific sectors for government support. Following the formal introduction of the term "socialist market economy" at the Fourteenth National Congress of the Chinese Communist Party

---

[4] Explanations of East Asia's economic dynamism are legion. On the role of the private sector, see Calder (1993). For the essentials of the neoclassical explanation, see World Bank (1993). For an account that emphasizes socioeconomic coalitions and international conditions, as well as the role of government bureaucracy, see Pempel (1999). Arguments about the role of culture can be found in Calder and Hofheinz (1982), Morishima (1982), and Pye (1985). For an explanation that downplays all of the factors considered above, emphasizing instead that economic success has the been the result primarily of an input-driven growth strategy, see Krugman (1994).

[5] "Decision of the State Council on the Main Points of the Industrial Policy for the Present," in FBIS-CHI-89-061.

(CCP) in October 1992, further efforts were made to refine China's industrial policy consistent with the idea of state guidance of market-based economic activity. Specifically, China's leaders were by all accounts increasingly drawn to the notion that their country could follow the East Asian model, patterning its economic system on the institutions and practices of Japan, South Korea, and even Singapore. (Taiwan, for obvious reasons, was not explicitly invoked as a model.) In this way, Beijing believed, Chinese market socialism could also be effectively integrated into the world economy. This move toward an East Asian model culminated in the State Council's June 1994 promulgation of "The Framework of National Industrial Policy for the 1990s," a program under which 56 enterprise groups were subsequently established in the following pillar industries: automobiles and auto parts, petrochemicals, machinery and electronics, aircraft, telecommunications, and construction materials.[6] Indeed, the 1994 statement resulted in a much more targeted approach, focusing on far fewer industries than the relatively broadbrushed 1989 incarnation.

As it turns out, however, China's record in "creating" comparative advantage through industrial targeting has been relatively poor. Consider the machinery and electronics sector. Although exports have increased substantially over time, the World Bank concluded in 1994 that Chinese firms were far from developing a competitive advantage in the production of these goods. Perhaps most revealing, the only area of improvement reported by the Bank was for products associated with processing operations for foreign partners, hardly the centerpiece of the state's effort at industrial targeting. As the Bank's research team concluded, "similar products manufactured domestically [i.e., not as part of a processing arrangement] do not still appear to be competitive in the international marketplace."[7] (Indeed, China remains a high-cost producer for many exports identified as a state priority.) Moreover, the Bank noted that the machinery and electronics sector had a disproportionately high concentration of loss-making SOEs.[8] While this is an imperfect measure of financial viability, given the persistence of serious distortions in China's economy, it does raise questions about the efficiency of

---

[6] For the State Council's March 1994 decision, which was released publicly in June 1994, see FBIS-CHI-94-123. For an official statement on the pillar industries initiative itself, see FBIS-CHI-94-175. This list is consistent with several authoritative sources. See, for instance, World Bank (1996), p. 18, and Pearson (1999), p. 178.

[7] World Bank (1994), p. 132.   [8] Ibid, p. 131.

resource allocation that has resulted from industrial targeting policies and other forms of state intervention in China's economy. Examining the same period as the World Bank, Dic Lo declared that the outcome of industrial targeting for the electronics industry was "mixed, but unsatisfactory on the whole."[9]

Nor have industries such as automobile manufacturing fared any better. By all accounts, support for the automobile industry has been a top government priority throughout the post-Mao era. In Eric Harwit's words, "by the mid-1980s the drive to foster a domestic passenger car industry in China had become nearly unstoppable."[10] In fact, automobiles were the subject of formal initiatives in industrial policy in both 1987 and 1994. Using heavily interventionist policies, Beijing sought to rationalize production capability, meet a series of import substitution goals, and lay the groundwork for future competitiveness in world export markets. Especially in the 1990s, it became clear that Beijing was trying to model these efforts at state-led development after the industrial targeting policies popularized by Japan and South Korea. In 1994, automobile manufacturing was officially named a pillar industry of the national economy. (Indeed, it was generally understood that the automobile industry was first among equals.)

Issued by the State Planning Commission in August 1994 as part of the Ninth Five-Year Plan (1996–2000), the "China Automotive Industry Development Policy" identified as its goal the development of three or four internationally competitive "national champions" by 2010. Using tools such as import restrictions, preferential access to bank credit, subsidized research and development, and priority arrangements for utilizing foreign investment, Beijing sought to take a controlling hand in the industry's development.[11] By all accounts, however, the results have been disappointing. The industry remains fraught with problems, not least of which is the excessive number of remaining manufacturers.[12] Unlike South Korea, where the government successfully intervened to restrict the number of automakers, the ranks of China's vehicle manufacturers actually increased during the late 1980s and early 1990s.[13] Despite the renewed push for rationalization included in the 1994 industrial policy, China's automobile sector continues to be plagued by "a proliferation of

---

[9] Lo (1997), p. 166.   [10] Harwit (1995), p. 35.   [11] Lo (1997), p. 184.
[12] For a good overview of the industry's status, see Polly (1998).
[13] Lo (1997), p. 182.

small and unviable producers."[14] All told, China simply has too many automakers producing too many vehicle models to warrant much optimism about the industry's long-term success. (Furthermore, tariffs on automobile imports are scheduled to fall from a current level of 80–100 percent to 25 percent by 2006 as part of China's accession to the WTO. This, of course, suggests that the Chinese industry will face significant challenges over the next decade.)

As these examples suggest, East Asian–style industrial policy has not yet enjoyed the same success in China as elsewhere in the region. Among many contributing factors, perhaps the most intractable problem Beijing has faced has been its inability to impose strict performance requirements and other disciplinary measures as a condition for government support. As argued in Chapter 12, the Chinese state lacks the institutional capacities necessary to enforce the "reciprocity" widely regarded as essential to the success of *developmental states*.[15] Indeed, this may represent a more profound obstacle for China in its bid to pursue the East Asian model of development than does, say, having a less highly trained corps of economic bureaucrats or an inferior commitment to principles of private property and market-based economic coordination. While considerable progress has been made in the latter areas in recent years, the nature of government-industry relations has proved more difficult to transform. Similarly, while Beijing certainly needs to improve the quality of the policy instruments it wields, the more important difference between China and the East Asian Trio is the institutional capacities state officials possess to implement policies effectively.

What distinguishes China the most, therefore, is the institutional culture of its state, one in which the autonomy of the state remains embedded largely in particularistic ties of industrial paternalism rather than the universalistic ties of rational-legal authority. In Weberian terms, therefore, bureaucracy of the type seen by many as critical to the success of *developmental states* is in undersupply in China.[16] From this perspective, it is the nature of policy networks within the state itself that most constrains China's ability to pursue the corporate, developmentalist goals it seeks through policies such as the pillar industries initiative.

[14] Polly (1998), p. 10. See also *FEER*, 17 December 1999, p. 4.
[15] For a useful review of the *developmental state* literature, see Schneider (1998).
[16] This argument about China is heavily influenced by the general framework provided in Evans (1995).

Neoclassical critics of state-led development may well be correct in pointing out the inherent difficulties of industrial targeting, but in the Chinese case these obstacles arguably pale in comparison to more fundamental issues concerning the nature of government-industry relations.[17]

It is in this light that we should consider China's efforts to develop large enterprise groups (*qiye jituan*) in the image of South Korea's *chaebol*. This strategy, long in planning, was officially enshrined at the Fifteenth National Congress of the CCP in September 1997 as part of the larger *zhuada fangxiao* program ("grasp the big, let go the small").[18] As its name suggests, the central plank of *zhuada fangxiao* is to combine large SOEs into huge conglomerates and allow smaller- and medium-sized SOEs to fade into the private sector. One concrete goal, for example, is to elevate three to five Chinese firms to the ranks of the world's biggest 500 enterprises. To this end, six firms (including Shanghai's Jiangnan Shipyard) were targeted for special support in November 1997.[19] In this sense, *zhuada fangxiao* is the centerpiece of Beijing's strategy for making Chinese industry competitive in an age of global corporations; the objective is to create Chinese multinational corporations (MNCs) comparable not only to South Korea's *chaebol*, but also to American, Japanese, and European MNCs. More broadly, in fact, the aim has been to forge corporate networks comparable to Japan's *keiretsu*, complete with similar kinds of banking relationships. Notably, Beijing has not refuted this strategy in the wake of the AFC. Although debate over *zhuada fangxiao* has been vigorous, and a reverse in course could always materialize, at this writing there have only been modifications to the original program.

Without more effective separation of government and business functions – namely, through further SOE reform – China's strategy of devel-

---

[17] The World Bank refers rather generically to "the danger of targeting" in discussing China's failure to date to achieve satisfactory results in industrial targeting. According to this view, the entire enterprise of "creating" comparative advantage – from regulating import competition and managing foreign exchange controls to providing subsidies for both individual firms and entire industries – is fraught with difficulty; World Bank (1994), p. 132. Although the World Bank has softened its stance somewhat in the 1990s, it still subscribes mainly to neoclassical prescriptions for economic development; see, for instance, World Bank (1993).

[18] Technically, the initiative was only *reaffirmed* at the CCP's Fifteenth Party Congress. It was apparently first proclaimed in September 1995 at the Fifth Plenum of the CCP's Fourteenth Central Committee. For more on *zhuada fangxiao*, see Smyth (2000).

[19] *Xinhua*, 28 September 1999, in FBIS-CHI-1999-0928.

oping large, internationally competitive enterprise groups is unlikely to produce the desired result. Given the persistence of industrial paternalism in China, the nature of policy networks can be seen as constraining the state's capacity to pursue *zhuada fangxiao* successfully. In the absence of sufficient reciprocity, efforts at selective intervention too often degenerate into the subsidization of losers rather than the promotion of winners. In this sense, *zhuada fangxiao* could actually become a drag on economic development, albeit one originally intended to spur industrial transformation in the manner of the East Asian Trio.

Could it be, then, that the single best indicator of industries likely to lag in industrial adjustment and international competitiveness is those identified by the state as a priority? From this perspective, which is wildly overstated, it may actually be an advantage to be left on the industrial sidelines when the state picks "winners" and "losers." In this sense, Beijing's failure to produce, as promised, the next Sony or Hyundai is not entirely surprising. Shipbuilding did of course receive government support, like all state-run heavy industries, but it was no favored sector like automobiles. Even compared to its counterparts in Japan and South Korea, the Chinese shipbuilding industry was not the beneficiary of a farsighted, well-coordinated strategy. Contrary to the premise of *zhuada fangxiao*, Chinese shipyards thrived due to the relative withdrawal of the state from centralized administrative control of the industry.

Another possibility, perhaps even more deleterious for China's longterm development, is that *zhuada fangxiao* could lead to the cooptation of successful industries (or at least certain firms within successful industries). Indeed, there is evidence that the success of the shipbuilding industry has over time increased its attractiveness to Beijing. As mentioned above, Jiangnan Shipyard was one of the six firms targeted for special support under *zhuada fangxiao*. While it could be argued that the reorganization of CSSC in 1999 represents yet another step in the ongoing rationalization of the industry, it most certainly constitutes a recentralization of assets away from the yards. The coordination of management, design, and other yard-level functions into larger units might improve economies of scale and otherwise raise efficiency, but this move still suggests that the state will continue to play a major (and perhaps even growing) role in the industry's development.

By all accounts, industry observers believe that the "new" role of the state bears watching. Even before the announcement of the reorganization, in fact, international maritime journals reported a shift in Beijing's attitude toward further FDI in the industry: "potential foreign investors such as Kvaerner [a Norwegian shipbuilder] have found that the Chinese government is not keen to relinquish its controlling interest in these businesses."[20] From this perspective, the reorganization of CSSC can be seen as an alternative strategy to the concept of increasing yard autonomy and greater participation in the world market. For example, the remarriage of Dalian Shipyard and Dalian New Shipyard – the two entities had been created in 1990 by dividing the assets of a single shipyard – was universally regarded as reducing the chances that these facilities would be able to form a major joint venture project with a foreign shipbuilder.

All told, it appears that the state may now be reestablishing greater control over the shipbuilding industry, at least in certain respects. While it is far too early to reach any conclusions, especially with regard to the likely positive or negative impact of increased state involvement, this example illustrates how a solid foundation for international competitiveness *could* be undermined as an industry's achievements pique the interest of state officials. (What better way to "pick winners" than to, well, pick winners?) This dynamic, which I would call the "irony of success," represents an insidious process in which high-achieving industries (or, in some cases, individual enterprises) find themselves ensnared (or at least coopted) by bureaucratic forces within the state apparatus. To be sure, CSSC and its yards have never been "free" of state control. In relative terms, however, it seems that shipbuilding may be returning more directly into the statist gambit. One question, therefore, concerns how much resistance there will be at the industry level. How easily, for example, will CSSC's successors be seduced by a recent spate of modest government spending on modernized shipbuilding capacity? Will they accede agreeably (or only reluctantly) if Beijing does indeed intend to ride this winner?

Depending on the outcome, both in terms of the state's (still uncertain) intentions and in terms of the ultimate impact on the industry, it is possible that non-CSSC yards may one day become the most dynamic segment of the Chinese industry. As early as 1995, there were reports in the Chinese press that provincial or county-run shipyards were making inroads into CSSC's markets, albeit not for major oceangoing vessels. Still, yards in provinces such as Jiangsu, Fujian, Shandong, and Zhejiang were even exporting small ships to Japan, Singapore, Australia, and

---

[20] *The Motor Ship* (January 1998), p. 31. The article went on to note that Kvaerner had turned its attention to smaller, non-CSSC yards in China.

Indonesia.[21] According to international maritime journals, CSSC did indeed face growing competition from smaller yards by the late 1990s.[22] In fact, foreign companies have in recent years increasingly sought foreign investment in non-CSSC yards. For example, Kawasaki Heavy Industries, a major Japanese shipbuilder, established a joint venture with COSCO to expand a former repair yard (Nantong) in Jiangsu province into a newbuilding facility.[23] In addition to ships built for COSCO, the yard has also secured its first export orders. Along the same lines, South Korea's Samsung Heavy Industries is considering a major joint venture with a yard (Ningbo) in Zhejiang province.[24]

These observations, it should be noted, are not intended primarily as a repudiation of the East Asian model per se – that is, the notion of a *developmental state* promoting large enterprise groups in strategic industrial sectors. Here, the lessons of the AFC have been overdrawn by some observers. (While the ideal-type of universalistic, Weberian ties in the East Asian Trio was undoubtedly stylized in the past, so, too, have the dysfunctional aspects of relational-based governance been exaggerated since the AFC.)[25] Rather, the point is simply that without further change in the nature of government-industry relations, *zhuada fangxiao* is likely to backfire. Not only might *zhuada fangxiao* suffer from the same inherent problems that contributed to the difficulties encountered by South Korea's *chaebol* during the AFC, but government support for conglomerates in China carries with it additional risks – namely, the risk that Beijing will simply end up fostering the growth of enterprise groups that are just bigger, less efficient, and more entrenched versions of the old SOEs. In this sense, *zhuada fangxiao* could magnify the weaknesses of the *chaebol* without accentuating their accompanying strengths.

This analysis has profound implications for the role of the state in China's current and future economic modernization. While it may be premature to write off China's efforts at industrial targeting altogether, there is at present no agent of development within the state apparatus comparable to the Ministry of International Trade and Industry in Japan or the

[21] *Liaowang*, 13 February 1995, in FBIS-CHI-95-048.
[22] *The Motor Ship* (September 1998), p. 29.
[23] Begun as a cooperation agreement in 1996, the relationship became a 50-50 joint venture in 1999. For more detail, see *Business Times* (Singapore), 9 September 1999, p. 1 (Shipping Times).
[24] *Journal of Commerce*, 9 September 1999, p. 12 (Transportation).
[25] Smyth (2000) makes a similar point.

Economic Planning Board in South Korea.[26] (Whatever their virtues, candidates such as the SETC or the State Planning Commission's Department of Long-Term Planning and Industrial Policy currently fall short of this standard.) As the World Bank has pointed out, this owes in part to the decentralized nature of policy making in China, where authority over trade and industry has become dispersed across numerous functional agencies during the post-Mao era.[27] More fundamentally, though, the absence of a pilot agency with a proven track record of carrying out effective industrial targeting – the kind that leads not just to increased exports but also to greater economic efficiency, competitive advantage, and financial profitability – reflects features of China's political economy that transcend the narrow issue of centralized versus decentralized control.

This argument does not, of course, preclude the possibility that China's economy will continue to grow impressively, making it a formidable industrial and trading power in the twenty-first century. If China's economic rise does continue, however, the pathway it takes will likely differ substantially from that taken by the East Asian Trio, particularly with respect to the role of the state in the development process.[28] Whereas many of the industrial "success stories" in its high-performing neighbors involved the strategic intervention of the state *into* market-based processes, this book has emphasized the increasing *withdrawal* of the Chinese state from direct administrative intervention in successful industries such as textiles and shipbuilding. This theme is, of course, consistent with the broader record of China's economic growth and industrial reform in the post-Mao era, one in which the state has largely presided over, rather than actively controlled, the most salient aspects of Chinese development. Ceteris paribus, one might reasonably expect future success to reflect past performance.

As it turns out, additional factors also reinforce the likelihood that China's rise as a world economic power, if it happens, will depend on a pathway quite different from that taken by the East Asian Trio. To the extent that the East Asian miracle in Japan, South Korea, and Taiwan was in fact a function of industrial targeting, several factors in China's external environment raise questions about its ability to pursue an East Asian–style industrial policy. First, China's membership in the WTO will

[26] For two classic works on the role of the state in Japan and South Korea, respectively, see Johnson (1982) and Amsden (1989).
[27] World Bank (1994), p. 134.
[28] For an early statement of this position, see Moore (1996).

severely restrict its opportunities for industrial targeting. As a member of the WTO, China will be subject to a vast body of rules that provide sweeping safeguards against trade practices contrary to liberal norms. Specifically, Beijing will have to undertake broad tariff reductions, eliminate a wide range of import quotas on industrial goods, and discontinue export subsidies as part of its accession agreement. These steps will make it more difficult for China to engage in the mercantilist practices that were associated with the East Asian Trio at comparable stages in their development. Most importantly, perhaps, China's market access concessions were focused on areas of priority concern to its major trading partners. For example, Beijing has agreed to eliminate many specific foreign equity and geographic restrictions in its service industries. More generally, China will accede to the WTO's Basic Telecommunications, Financial Services, and Information Technology agreements. The last agreement is particularly important to Chinese industrial policy given its call for the elimination of tariffs on information technology products, an area of keen interest to Beijing.

Among its other WTO commitments, Beijing has also agreed to eliminate distribution and retailing regulations that serve as de facto protection for domestic producers. In other words, foreign exporters should be able to import directly into China, distribute and sell their products throughout the country, and provide follow-up services. Over time, this will provide a more level playing field for foreign companies conducting business in China. While not all of these provisions relate directly to the specific issue of industrial policy, they do collectively serve to illustrate how membership in the WTO will complicate China's ability to pursue the East Asian model more generally. Not only must China overcome the legacy of industrial paternalism, to say nothing of other domestic impediments, but now WTO membership will only further restrict China's ability to act like a *developmental state*. To be sure, WTO membership may not prevent Beijing from trying to pursue certain elements of an East Asian–style industrial policy, but these practices will at the very least be put to the test of multilateral scrutiny.

Another factor in China's external environment that limits its ability to pursue an East Asian–style industrial policy is the broader phenomenon of economic globalization. Indeed, Beijing's concerted bid to gain WTO accession in the late 1990s reflected, at least in part, the rapid growth of pressures associated with globalization. From both their public statements and their policy actions, it is clear that China's leaders view the wide-ranging set of economic tasks facing the country increasingly within the context of globalization (*quanqiuhua*).[29] While the role of the state remains critical, some high-ranking Chinese officials have openly argued that East Asian–style industrial policy and import-substituting industrialization are not well-suited for the age of globalization.[30] This belief would, of course, help to explain Beijing's willingness to accept the market access concessions necessary for WTO membership. From this perspective, what is needed for China to become more competitive internationally is greater reform and opening. Specifically, one of the main roles of the state as an economic manager is to make China an attractive location for MNCs as they organize the transnational manufacturing networks (also known as commodity chains or production networks) that increasingly dominate world economic activity.

To be sure, the challenges associated with globalization are not all necessarily inconsistent with the pursuit of an East Asian–style industrial policy. As many Chinese analysts have observed, large conglomerates arguably remain critical to national competitiveness in a globalizing world economy. While greater reform and opening may be needed for China to become more fully integrated in the existing transnational manufacturing networks organized by foreign firms, China also aspires to build its own world-class MNCs. Furthermore, industrial targeting can, of course, be focused on export-oriented industrialization. So, while the East Asian model may have lost some of its élan internationally, especially as a result of the AFC, it would be an exaggeration to say that industrial policy has no potential role in meeting the challenge of globalization. That said, it must at least be acknowledged that globalization processes have increased the costs associated with certain policy choices. For example, classic forms of industrial policy – namely, those that serve mainly to protect national industries from international competition – are less likely to be effective in facilitating development in the future. At a minimum, therefore, it can be said that globalization circumscribes the use of industrial policy in certain ways.

BRINGING EXTERNAL FORCES (BACK) IN

The evidence presented in the book suggests that the structuring impact of the international political economy represents one of the most

---

[29] For a detailed discussion of this point, see Moore (2000).

[30] See, for example, the analysis of Long Yongtu, China's deputy foreign trade minister and chief negotiator for international economic affairs (including WTO accession), in his

conceptually important yet inadequately studied issues concerning change in post-Mao China. Just as reform has not been a function solely of imperatives dictated by the international system, neither has it been, as Bruce Cumings once observed, "the product exclusively of causes or processes internal to China."[31] Whether the issue is liberalization of foreign investment laws, the loosening of foreign exchange controls, changes to the foreign trade system, or industry-specific economic adjustment, it is critical to examine the ways in which the international political economy has shaped the set of development strategies and general reform options available to China as its participation in the world economy has grown.

While it is certainly true that domestic politics cannot be reduced conceptually to a mere "transmission belt" or "black box" through which external forces are translated into state policy, the most powerful causal chain in the two case studies examined in this book did originate in the international environment. From all indications, the MFA in textiles and GSC in shipbuilding each served as a critical impetus for reform, restructuring, and rationalization in its respective Chinese industry. Although external forces only *shape* or *condition*, rather than fully *determine*, change within a given country, only by examining the international context can we hope, in Robert Keohane's words, to distinguish the "effects of common international forces from those of distinctive national ones."[32]

Far from eschewing internal factors, however, I argue that domestic structural analysis is essential for understanding China's response to GSC and the MFA. Surely, if one wants to explain the specific course of reform, restructuring, and rationalization undertaken in China's textile and shipbuilding industries, the characteristics of world industrial markets will not alone suffice. Only by examining the nature of contingent factors at the domestic level – the organizational structure of the state, the nature of government-industry relations, and the transitional nature of China's economy during the 1980s and early 1990s – can we understand why China's response to varying degrees of economic openness in world industrial markets followed the particular pattern that it did in textiles and shipbuilding. In short, domestic structure filters the impact of the international environment on China.

article "On Economic Globalization," *Guangming Ribao*, 30 October 1998, in FBIS-CHI-98-313.
[31] Cumings (1989), p. 203.   [32] Keohane (1984), p. 16.

In contrast to existing conceptualizations of the reform process in post-Mao China, the vast majority of which focus exclusively on domestic forces, this book cites the case-study material as evidence of the need for an alternative "political economy of China's reform and opening," one that focuses explicitly on linkages between international and domestic forces. While China's participation in the world economy may have been state-directed at first, the economic, social, and even political forces unleashed as a result of Deng's initiatives have, in certain critical respects, hijacked the process. If Chinese leaders sometimes describe their trial-and-error approach to reform as "crossing the river by feeling for stones" (*mozhe shitou guohe*), then perhaps China's course in the regional and global economy could be described as having been charted in part by currents the state could not completely navigate.[33] While this kind of position can easily be overstated, it also represents a neglected perspective in thinking about contemporary China. Even if one is not prepared to accept "outside-in" approaches in their strongest form, it is difficult to ignore how the path taken in certain provinces (e.g., Guangdong and Fujian) or industries (e.g., textiles and shipbuilding) has been profoundly shaped by factors external to China.

Unlike strictly structural explanations, which bracket the behavior of human agents altogether, the explanation provided in this book allows for the operation of both agency and structure. Truth be told, the book does focus mainly on the structural forces – international and domestic alike – that condition social action. As a macrolevel study focusing on entire industries rather than individual firms, this project does not provide the kind of detailed analysis of human agency found in microlevel studies. That said, my explanation for change in China's textile and shipbuilding industries not only leaves room for the role of human agency but explicitly recognizes its importance. To the extent that this study focuses on the causal power of structural forces, this should be interpreted primarily as a matter of analytical order. As Robert Keohane once put it, "We must understand the context of action before we can understand the action itself."[34] Especially given the dominance of Sino-centric approaches in the existing literature, one aim of this book has been to represent a underutilized approach: an international-centered perspective consistent with Gourevitch's notion of "second-image

[33] For more on this argument, see Moore (1996).
[34] Keohane (1986b), p. 193.

reversed" analysis. Indeed, the outside world has been seriously under-estimated as a source of change in post-Mao China. To paraphrase Marx's frequently quoted aphorism, "Chinese reformers are indeed making history, but not in conditions of their own choosing."

Appendix: Contours of the Research Effort

Within the framework of industry-specific analysis, there are two basic methodological approaches that can be employed: large-n analysis (statistical examination of a large number of cases) or small-n analysis (in-depth studies of a small number of cases). While possible in the abstract, large-n analysis is not an especially good candidate for addressing the research agenda pursued in this book. First, the number of well-recorded case studies involving individual Chinese industries is quite small at present. Consequently, large-n analysis would require primary data collection for many industries. While basic information about many industries is supplied in national, provincial, and ministerial yearbooks, the available data varies widely on several counts: degree of detail, consistency of reporting practices, and the number of possible sources. While data on China's economy has been improving steadily, information remains incomplete in one respect or another for many industries. This was especially true for the 1980s, when reports on Chinese industries were still often superficial, haphazardly documented from year to year, and nearly impossible to verify even by the most rudimentary methods (e.g., comparing different sources). Simply put, there is not enough well-recorded data about a sufficient number of industries in order to conduct large-n analysis consistent with my research agenda.

Second, it can be argued that case-study analysis is simply better-suited for the task at hand. Even if the limitations of large-n analysis did not exist for the study of Chinese industries, small-n analysis would still provide greater opportunity to trace the process by which independent variables affect dependent variables. Put another way, the decisive evidence necessary to establish the causal relationship between degrees of economic openness in world markets and the reform, restructuring, and rationalization of specific Chinese industries is most likely to emerge from detailed case studies where the unfolding of events can be observed more closely. (The role of intervening variables in complex causal chains is especially important here.) This is especially (but not only) true given the data problems described above for large-n analysis of Chinese industries. Even under the best circumstances, large-n analysis cannot provide access to the same kind of data that is available from the in-depth examination of a small number of cases.

Within the larger tradition of a comparatively informed case-study approach, this book uses a mix of congruence testing and process tracing as the centerpiece of its methodology.[1] As far as congruence procedures are concerned, the industries examined in this book allow for significant within-case comparison.[2] As explained in Chapter 1, the gradually expanding, product-specific coverage of quotas under the MFA allows multiple observations on the effects of economic openness and moderate economic closure on change in the Chinese textile industry. While within-case comparison is more limited for the shipbuilding industry, the boom-and-bust nature of the international market does result in periods of greater and lesser restrictiveness in exporting ships. In the lexicon of congruence testing, the shifting intensity of GSC in world shipbuilding – namely, from chronic to severe – allows for variation on the independent variable.

As valuable as the specific characteristics of these industries are for examining the impact of economic openness and moderate economic closure on reform, restructuring, and rationalization in China, this study is not limited entirely to within-case comparisons. Indeed, the study occasionally uses outside comparison to supplement the main focus on within-case comparison. While this kind of comparison is presented mainly for illustrative purposes, references in Chapters 11 and 13 to the widely studied Chinese automobile industry serve as an important benchmark for placing the experience of the shipbuilding industry into broader perspective. Similarly, it is easy to compare the case of China's textile industry to other export-oriented light industries (e.g., toys,

---

[1] The *locus classicus* on the "method of structured, focused comparison" is George (1979). Other useful resources on case-study methodology, with an emphasis on more recent treatments, include Van Evera (1997) and King et al. (1994), especially pp. 128–149.

[2] For more on congruence procedures, see Van Evera (1997), especially pp. 58–64, and George and McKeown (1985), especially pp. 29–34.

footwear, consumer electronics), as many of the interviewees did in thinking about the impact of the MFA on China. In this sense, the "normal situation" among Chinese industries is sufficiently well-known to allow for implicit comparison with the detailed case studies provided in this book.[3]

Neither, of course, are the textile and shipbuilding industries unique to China. Scholars have chronicled the experiences of these industries in many other countries, including both continent-sized latecomers in the contemporary era, such as India and Indonesia (especially relevant for textiles), and smaller countries, such as Japan and South Korea (especially relevant for shipbuilding), which represent earlier generations of industrializing countries in East Asia. These international comparisons provide additional historical and contemporary context for understanding China's recent experience as a developing country whose participation in the world economy has expanded rapidly over the last two decades.

In addition to within-case comparisons (and, to a lesser extent, outside comparisons), the book also relies heavily upon process tracing.[4] A staple of small-n analysis, process tracing involves a detailed reconstruction of the events that led from initial case conditions to case outcomes. In this way, case studies can provide decisive evidence not just about *whether* causal relationships hold, but also *why* they hold. As a result, process tracing can augment significantly either simple congruence testing or large-n analysis. In this book, the case-study chapters examine the chain of events leading from the introduction of an external shock – namely, the imposition of textile quotas under the MFA and the intensification of GSC in shipbuilding – to various changes in the respective Chinese industries. Along the way, evidence is uncovered about how and why the chain of events unfolded as it did.

While process-tracing research on China remains limited in certain respects, especially regarding access to key documents and decision-makers, the ability to elucidate the causal chain through detailed case studies provides an important, and in many ways increasingly effective, tool for studying contemporary China. Specifically, process tracing represents an especially critical (and perhaps the best available) research strategy for evaluating alternative explanations. No study can eliminate

[3] For a similar point, see Van Evera (1997), pp. 46–47.
[4] For a useful discussion on process tracing, see Van Evera (1997), especially pp. 64–66. Other sources include King et al. (1994), pp. 226–228, and George and McKeown (1985), pp. 34–41.

all ambiguity, of course, but the case studies of the Chinese textile and shipbuilding industries provided in Chapters 3–11 do reveal a pattern more consistent with the theoretical argument set forth in this book than any competing explanation.

DATA COLLECTION

The documentary research and interviewing for the book were conducted mainly in Hong Kong, although additional information was also obtained in mainland China and from various sources in the United States. The terms of my dissertation funding (a post-Tiananmen U.S. Fulbright grant) allowed periodic travel to the mainland, but required that I be based in Hong Kong. (The bulk of the original interviews in Hong Kong and China were conducted between October 1991 and September 1992; the final field research for the book was conducted during a trip in August 1998.) In the end, this geographic restriction turned out to be a blessing given the substantive focus of my research and the political atmosphere in China at the time. Indeed, my most productive interviews were conducted in Hong Kong, not only with Hong Kong informants but also with Chinese, American, and European informants. Especially in the early 1990s, interviews in Hong Kong provided access to an unmatched concentration of commercial expertise and an unrivaled willingness to talk openly about issues concerning China's deepening integration into the world economy.

There is little need to elaborate here on the nature of published sources used in the book since this information is fully documented in the footnotes and bibliography. That said, I should note that Chinese statistics, while much improved in recent years, continue to have their shortcomings. This is especially true for the period studied in this book, when data was even less reliable than today. For this reason, I have made every effort to use data, such as export data for textiles and ships, that can be verified by external sources. Indeed, whenever possible I use internationally collected data, such as U.S. statistics for imports under the MFA and international maritime data collected by United Nations agencies, rather than comparable Chinese data. Where the use of Chinese statistics is necessary, this data is better conceived as a tool for tracking trends rather than as a highly accurate source of information.

The formal interviews, which numbered forty-one, were conducted on a confidential basis since the vast majority of individuals requested anonymity. In the case of the textile industry, this desire for anonymity is best understood in the context of tensions between China and its trade partners over quota circumvention in violation of the MFA. As detailed in Chapters 3 and 4, illegal transshipments of Chinese textile products to the United States and the European Union through third countries have contributed significantly to the impression in the West that China is an "unfair" trader. Given the political sensitivity of this issue, not to mention the legal ramifications, it should be no surprise that many potential informants were reluctant to share their knowledge about the industry. While interviewees from China and Hong Kong (officials and businesspeople alike) were perhaps the most reluctant group in this regard, so, too, were many American and European informants. In many cases, interviews could only be arranged by personal introduction. In fact, it proved quite difficult to schedule interviews at first. Over time, however, personal contacts expanded and opportunities for interviews with knowledgeable sources grew appreciably.

In the case of the shipbuilding industry, the desire for anonymity reflects the intimate nature of the international shipbuilding community. Much like a small town, it is difficult for those with close knowledge of the Chinese industry to provide even a general assessment for attribution without everyone knowing about whom their comments were made. In any given year, there are only a handful of major orders to China's leading shipyards. For example, an executive who works for a Hong Kong shipping tycoon would find it difficult to speak candidly on the record about conditions in the Chinese shipbuilding industry since his or her company is likely to have built its new ships primarily at a single shipyard. Even if he or she spoke in general terms, making little or no mention of individual ship orders, particular shipyards, or specific officials in the Chinese industry, the basis for his or her evaluation would nonetheless be clear.

The same holds true for investment bankers, foreign engineers, and other maritime specialists involved in the financing, production, and international certification of ships made in China. These individuals have intimate knowledge about the economic and political administration of the Chinese industry. In many cases, however, their experience is drawn from years of association with a particular Chinese shipyard or a specific overseas shipowner who has built vessels in China. Simply put, these individuals might jeopardize their professional relationships if they allowed themselves to be identified.

As suggested above, the interviewees spanned a wide range of government, business, and academic positions. At the governmental level, they included Chinese, Hong Kong, and U.S. officials. Although businesspeople from Hong Kong outnumbered all others, American, British, Chinese, German, Japanese, Korean, and Taiwanese nationals were also represented. Several academics, business consultants, and journalists were also interviewed, although usually on a more informal basis. Most interviews lasted between 30 and 90 minutes. Each interview followed a prepared set of questions, although the informant was allowed to share extemporaneously whatever information he or she wished. Questions not addressed by the end of the conversation were then typically raised by the interviewer. In the majority of cases, written notes were taken during the interview. Some informants expressed concern about the purpose of written notes, however, and these interviews had to be reconstructed after the fact. In many cases, there was further contact after the initial interview. This rarely lead to a second formal interview, but phone conversations and written correspondence were used to clarify points from the interview, raise additional questions that had come to light after the interview, and explore possible introductions to other informants.

In addition to insisting upon personal anonymity, some interviewees also rejected the idea of being identified generically by affiliation (e.g., Official, Shiptrading Department, China State Shipbuilding Corporation) in a comprehensive list of informants. In order to use the insights and information provided in these interviews, I have respected their wishes. Rather than provide an incomplete list of generically identified informants or generate perfunctory footnotes that provide little information, I have opted simply to convey as much information as possible in the text without violating the anonymity of the source. Most importantly, I have made every effort to substantiate evidence attributed to anonymous interview material by citing corroborating documentary material. By design, in fact, almost none of the argument in this book rests solely on interview material. While China's opening has provided important new opportunities for interviewing, corroboration is critical for all interview material – anonymous and otherwise. In this sense, the interviews should be seen as buttressing the wide-ranging published evidence (industry and trade data, official statements, media reports, and policy-oriented analysis) cited in the footnotes.

Bibliography

BOOKS, JOURNAL ARTICLES, AND UNPUBLISHED MANUSCRIPTS

Aggarwal, Vinod K. (1985). *Liberal Protectionism: The International Politics of Organized Textile Trade*. Berkeley: University of California Press.

Almond, Gabriel (1989). "The International-National Connection," *British Journal of Political Science* 19(1): 237–259.

Amsden, Alice (1989). *Asia's Next Giant: South Korea and Late Industrialization*. New York: Oxford University Press.

Anderson, Kym (1992). "The Changing Role of Fibres, Textiles, and Clothing as Economies Grow," in Anderson, ed. *New Silk Roads: East Asia and World Textile Markets*. Cambridge: Cambridge University Press.

Bachman, David (1991). *Bureaucracy, Economy, and Leadership in China: The Institutional Origins of the Great Leap Forward*. New York: Cambridge University Press.

——— (1992). "The Limits on Leadership in China," *Asian Survey* 32(1): 1046–1062.

Barnett, A. Doak (1967). *Cadres, Bureaucracy, and Political Power in Communist China*. New York: Columbia University Press.

Breslauer, George W. (1997). "The Impact of the International Environment," in Karen Dawisha, ed. *The International Dimension of Post-Communist Transitions in Russia and the New States of Eurasia*. Armonk, N.Y.: M. E. Sharpe.

Brömmelhörster, Jorn and John Frankenstein, eds. (1997). *Mixed Motives, Uncertain Outcomes: Defense Conversion in China*. Boulder: Lynne Rienner.

Byrd, William (1987). "The Role and Impact of Markets," in Tidrick and Chen (1987).

——— (1991). "Contractual Responsibility Systems in Chinese State-Owned Industry," in Nigel Campbell, Sylvain R. F. Plasschaert, and David H. Brown, eds., *Advances in Chinese Industrial Studies*. Greenwich, Conn.: JAI Press. 2: 7–35.

——— ed. (1992a). *Chinese Industrial Firms under Reform*. New York: Oxford University for the World Bank.

——— (1992b). "Chinese Industrial Reform, 1978–89," in Byrd (1992a).

——— (1992c). "The Second Motor Vehicle Manufacturing Plant," in Byrd (1992a).

——— (1992d). "Summary of Research and General Observations," in Byrd (1992a).

322

Cable, Vincent (1990). "Adjusting to Textile and Clothing Quotas," in Hamilton (1990).

Calder, Kent (1993). *Strategic Capitalism: Private Business and Public Purpose in Japanese Industrial Finance.* Princeton: Princeton University Press.

Calder, Kent and Roy Hofheinz, Jr. (1982). *The East Asia Edge.* New York: Basic Books.

Chai, Benliang (1997). "Conversion and Restructuring of China's Defense Industry," in Brömmelhörster and Frankenstein (1997).

Chen, Kun-Tang and K. C. Jackson (1996). "The Statistical Coverage of China's Textile Industry," *The Journal of the Textile Institute* 87, 2 (Part 2): 82–88.

Cheng, Chu-Yuan (1971). *The Machine-Building Industry in Communist China.* Chicago: Aldine–Atherton.

Chida, Tomohei and Peter N. Davies (1990). *The Japanese Shipping and Shipbuilding Industries: A History of their Modern Growth.* London: The Athlone Press.

China Machinery Industries Yearbook (1991). Beijing: China Machine Press.

China's Shipbuilding Industry in Progress (1991). Beijing: New Star Publishers.

Cline, William R. (1990). *The Future of World Trade in Textiles and Apparel.* Washington, D.C.: Institute for International Economics.

Collier, Ruth Berins (1993). "Combining Alternative Perspectives: Internal Trajectories versus External Influences as Explanations of Latin American Politics in the 1940s," *Comparative Politics* 26(1): 1–29.

Crane, George T. (1990). *The Political Economy of China's Special Economic Zones.* Armonk, N.Y.: M. E. Sharpe.

Cumings, Bruce (1984). "The Origins and Development of the Northeast Asian Political Economy," *International Organization* 38(1): 1–40.

(1989). "The Political Economy of China's Turn Outward," in Kim (1989).

Dangdai Zhongguo de Chuanbo Gongye [*Contemporary China's Shipbuilding Industry*] (1992). Beijing: Dangdai Zhongguo Chubanshe.

Dangdai Zhongguo de Fangzhi Gongye [*Contemporary China's Textile Industry*] (1984). Beijing: Zhongguo Shehui Kexue Chubanshe.

Dangdai Zhongguo de Guofang Keji Shiye [*Contemporary China's Defense Science and Technological Cause*] (1992). Beijing: Dangdai Zhongguo Chubanshe.

Dangdai Zhongguo de Haijun [*Contemporary China's Navy*] (1987). Beijing: Dangdai Zhongguo Chubanshe.

Dangdai Zhongguo de Haiyang Shiye [*Contemporary China's Marine Undertakings*] (1985). Beijing: Zhongguo Shehui Kexue Chubanshe.

Dangdai Zhongguo de Shuiyun Shiye [*Contemporary China's Waterborne Transportation*] (1989). Beijing: Zhongguo Shehui Kexue Chubanshe.

Deng, Gang (1999). *Maritime Sector, Institutions, and Sea Power of Premodern China.* Westport, Conn.: Greenwood Press.

Deudney, Daniel and G. John Ikenberry (1991). "International Sources of Soviet Change," *International Security* 16(3): 74–118.

Dickerson, Kitty (1999). *Textiles and Apparel in the Global Economy.* Upper Saddle River, N.J.: Merrill.

Economy, Elizabeth and Michel Oksenberg, eds. (1999). *China Joins the World: Progress and Prospects.* New York: Council on Foreign Relations.

Evangelista, Matthew (1988). *Arms and Innovation.* Ithaca: Cornell University Press.

(1995). "The Paradox of State Strength," *International Organization* 49(1): 1–38.

Evans, Peter (1995). *Embedded Autonomy: States and Industrial Transformation.* Princeton: Princeton University Press.

Fallows, James (1994). *Looking at the Sun: The Rise of the New East Asian Economic and Political System.* New York: Pantheon Books.

Feeney, William R. (1998). "China and the Multilateral Economic Institutions," in Kim (1998a).

Feenstra, Robert (1988). "Quality Change Under Trade Restraints in Japanese Autos," *Quarterly Journal of Economics* 103(1): 131–146.

Feenstra, Robert and Randi Boorstin (1991). "Quality Upgrading and its Welfare Cost in U.S. Steel Imports, 1969–74," in Elhanan Helpman and Assaf Razin, eds. *International Trade and Trade Policy.* Cambridge: MIT Press.

Feenstra, Robert, Wen Hai, Wing T. Woo, and Shunli Yao (1998). "The U.S.-China Bilateral Trade Balance: Its Size and Determinants." *NBER Working Paper Series* No. 6598. Cambridge: National Bureau of Economic Research.

Feinstein, Charles and Christopher Howe, eds. (1997). *Chinese Technology Transfer in the 1990s: Current Experience, Historical Problems, and International Perspectives.* Cheltenham, U.K.: Edward Elgar.

Feuerwerker, Albert (1995a). *The Chinese Economy, 1870–1949.* Ann Arbor: Center for Chinese Studies, University of Michigan.

(1995b). *Studies in the Economic History of Late Imperial China.* Ann Arbor: Center for Chinese Studies, University of Michigan.

Findlay, Christopher, ed. (1992). *Challenges of Economic Reform and Industrial Growth: China's Wool War.* Sydney: Allen & Unwin.

Folta, Paul Humes (1992). *From Swords to Plowshares? Defense Industry Reform in the PRC.* Boulder: Westview Press.

Frankenstein, John (1997). "China's Defense Industry Conversion: A Strategic Overview," in Brömmelhörster and Frankenstein (1997).

Friman, H. Richard (1990). *Patchwork Protectionism: Textile Trade Policy in the United States, Japan, and West Germany.* Ithaca: Cornell University Press.

Fung, K. C. and Lawrence J. Lau (2001). "New Estimates of the United States – China Bilateral Trade Balances," *Journal of the Japanese and International Economies* 15(1): 102–130.

George, Alexander L. (1979). "Case Studies and Theory Development," in Paul Gorden Lauren, ed. *Diplomacy: New Approaches in History, Theory, and Policy.* New York: Free Press.

George, Alexander and Timothy McKeown (1985). "Case Studies and Theories of Organizational Decision Making," *Advances in Information Processing in Organizations* 2: 21–58.

Gilbert, Felix, ed. (1975). *The Historical Essays of Otto Hintze.* New York: Oxford University Press.

Bibliography

Goldstein, Avery (1998). "Structural Realism and China's Foreign Policy: Much (but never all) of the Story," unpublished paper.

Gourevitch, Peter (1978) "The Second Image Reversed. The International Sources of Domestic Politics," *International Organization* 32(4): 881–912.

——— (1986). *Politics in Hard Times: Comparative Responses to International Economic Crises.* Ithaca: Cornell University Press.

Groombridge, Mark A. and Claude E. Barfield (1999). *Tiger By the Tail: China and the World Trade Organization.* Washington, D.C.: AEI Press.

Haggard, Stephan (1990). *Pathways from the Periphery: The Politics of Growth in the Newly Industrializing Countries.* Ithaca: Cornell University Press.

Hamilton, Carl, ed. (1990). *Textiles Trade and the Developing Countries.* Washington, D.C.: World Bank.

Harris, Jennifer, ed. (1993). *Textiles, 5,000 Years: An International History.* New York: H. N. Abrams.

Harwit, Eric (1995). *China's Automobile Industry: Policies, Problems, and Prospects.* Armonk, N.Y.: M. E. Sharpe.

Heine, Irwin Millard (1989). *China's Rise to Commercial Maritime Power.* New York: Greenwood Press.

Hobsbawn, E. J. (1968). *Industry and Empire: The Making of Modern English Society, 1750 to the Present Day.* New York: Pantheon.

Hong, Lun (1982). "China's Shipbuilding Industry," *Almanac of China's Economy 1981.* Hong Kong: Modern Cultural Company Limited, pp. 519–522.

Howell, Jude (1993). *China Opens Its Doors: The Politics of Economic Transition.* Boulder: Lynne Rienner.

Hou, Chi-ming (1965). *Foreign Investment and Economic Development in China, 1840–1937.* Cambridge: Harvard University Press.

Hsing, You-tien (1998). *Making Capitalism in China: The Taiwan Connection.* New York: Oxford University Press.

Hsu, John C. (1989). *China's Foreign Trade Reforms.* Cambridge: Cambridge University Press.

Ikenberry, G. John (1988). *Reasons of State: Oil Politics and the Capacities of American Government.* Ithaca: Cornell University Press.

Ikenberry, G. John, David A. Lake, and Michael Mastanduno, eds. (1988). *The State and American Foreign Economic Policy.* Ithaca: Cornell University Press.

Jacobson, Harold and Michel Oksenberg (1990). *China's Participation in the IMF, World Bank, and GATT.* Ann Arbor: University of Michigan Press.

Jefferson, Gary H., Ping Zhang, and John Z. Q. Zhao (1999). "Structure, Authority, and Incentives in Chinese Industry," in Jefferson and Inderjit Singh, eds. *Enterprise Reform in China: Ownership, Transition, and Performance.* New York: Oxford University Press for the World Bank.

Johnson, Chalmers (1982). *MITI and the Japanese Miracle.* Stanford: Stanford University Press.

Johnston, Alastair Iain (1998). "International Structures and Chinese Foreign Policy," in Kim (1998a).

Kahler, Miles (1992). "External Influence, Conditionality, and the Politics of Adjustment," in Stephan Haggard and Robert Kaufman, eds. *The Politics of Economic Adjustment.* Princeton: Princeton University Press.

Katzenstein, Peter J., ed. (1978a). *Between Power and Plenty: Foreign Economic Policies of Advanced Industrial States.* Madison: University of Wisconsin Press.

(1978b). "Conclusion: Domestic Structures and Strategies of Foreign Economic Policy," in Katzenstein (1978a).

(1984). *Corporatism and Change: Austria, Switzerland, and the Politics of Industry.* Ithaca: Cornell University Press.

(1985). *Small States in World Markets: Industrial Policy in Europe.* Ithaca: Cornell University Press.

Keohane, Robert (1984). "The World Political Economy and the Crisis of Embedded Liberalism," in John H. Goldthorpe, ed. *Order and Conflict in Contemporary Capitalism.* New York: Oxford University Press.

ed. (1986a). *Neorealism and Its Critics.* New York: Columbia University Press.

(1986b). "Theory of World Politics: Structural Realism and Beyond," in Keohane (1986a).

Kim, Samuel S., ed. (1984). *China and the World* (1st edition). Boulder: Westview Press.

ed. (1989). *China and the World* (2nd edition). Boulder: Westview Press.

ed. (1998a). *China and the World* (4th edition). Boulder: Westview Press.

(1998b). "Chinese Foreign Policy in Theory and Practice," in Kim (1998a).

ed. (2000). *East Asia and Globalization.* Lanham: Rowman and Littlefield.

King, Gary, Robert O. Keohane, and Sidney Verba (1994). *Designing Social Inquiry: Scientific Inference and Qualitative Research.* Princeton: Princeton University Press.

Kleinberg, Robert (1990). *China's "Opening" to the Outside World: The Experiment with Foreign Capitalism.* Boulder: Westview Press.

Kohli, Atul (1999). "Where Do High-Growth Political Economies Come From? The Japanese Lineage of Korea's 'Development State,'" in Woo-Cumings (1999).

Kornai, Janos (1980). *The Economics of Shortage.* Amsterdam: North-Holland Publishing Company.

(1992). *The Socialist System: The Political Economy of Communism.* Princeton: Princeton University Press.

Krasner, Stephen D. (1978). *Defending the National Interest.* Princeton: Princeton University Press.

Krugman, Paul (1994). "The Myth of Asia's Miracle," *Foreign Affairs* 73(6): 62–78.

Kurth, James (1979). "The Political Consequences of the Product Cycle," *International Organization* 33(1): 1–34.

Lampton, David M., ed. (2001). *The Making of Chinese Foreign and Security Policy in the Era of Reform, 1978–2000.* Stanford: Stanford University Press.

Lardy, Nicholas R. (1992). *Foreign Trade and Economic Reform in China, 1978–1990.* Cambridge: Cambridge University Press.

(1994). *China in the World Economy.* Washington, D.C.: Institute for International Economics.

(1998). *China's Unfinished Economic Revolution.* Washington, D.C.. The Brookings Institution.

(1999). "China's Economic Growth in an International Context," *The Pacific Review* 12(2): 163–171.

Lauriat, George (1983). *China Shipping: The Great Leap Forward.* Colchester: Lloyd's of London Press.

Levinsohn, James (1995). "Carwars: Trying to Make Sense of U.S.-Japan Trade Frictions in the Automobile and Automobile Parts Markets." *NBER Working Paper Series* No. 5349. Cambridge: National Bureau of Economic Research.

Lewis, John Wilson and Litai Xue (1994). *China's Strategic Seapower.* Stanford: Stanford University Press.

Lieberthal, Kenneth and David M. Lampton, eds. (1992). *Bureaucracy, Politics, and Decision Making in Post-Mao China.* Berkeley: University of California Press.

Lin, Cyril Zhiren (1989). "Open-Ended Economic Reform in China," in Victor Nee and David Stark, eds. *Remaking the Economic Institutions of Socialism.* Stanford: Stanford University Press.

Lo, Dic (1997). *Market and Institutional Regulation in Chinese Industrialization, 1978–1994.* New York: St. Martin's.

Loriaux, Michael (1991). *France after Hegemony: International Change and Financial Reform.* Ithaca: Cornell University Press.

Mann, Jim (1997). *Beijing Jeep.* New York: Simon and Schuster.

McCormick, Barrett L. (1990). *Political Reform in Post-Mao China: Democracy and Bureaucracy in a Leninist State.* Berkeley: University of California Press.

McNally, Christopher and Peter Nan-shong Lee (1998). "Is Big Beautiful? Restructuring China's State Sector under the *Zhuada* Policy," *Issues & Studies* 34(9): 22–48.

Middleton, Ian, ed. (1979). *China: A Seatrade Study.* London: Seatrade Publications.

Moore, Thomas G. (1996). "China as a Latecomer: Toward a Global Logic of the Open Policy," *Journal of Contemporary China* 5(12): 187–208.

(1997). *China in the World Market.* Ph.D. dissertation, Department of Politics, Princeton University.

(2000). "China and Globalization," in Kim (2000).

Moore, Thomas G. and Dixia Yang (1999). "China, APEC, and Economic Regionalism in the Asia-Pacific," *Journal of East Asian Affairs* 13(2): 361–411.

(2001). "Empowered and Restrained: Chinese Foreign Policy in the Age of Economic Interdependence," in Lampton (2001).

Morishima, Michio (1982). *Why Japan Has "Succeeded": Western Technology and the Japanese Ethos.* Cambridge: Cambridge University Press.

Muller, David G., Jr. (1983). *China as a Maritime Power.* Boulder: Westview Press.

Nagatsuka, Seiji (1995). *Recent Trends of China's Shipping and Shipbuilding.* Tokyo: Japan Maritime Research Institute.

Naughton, Barry (1988). "The Third Front: Defence Industrialization in the Chinese Interior," *China Quarterly* 115: 351–386.

(1995). *Growing Out of the Plan: Chinese Economic Reform, 1978–1993.* Cambridge: Cambridge University Press.

ed. (1997). *The China Circle: Economics and Technology in the PRC, Taiwan, and Hong Kong.* Washington, D.C.: The Brookings Institution.

Ng-Quinn, Michael (1984). "International Systemic Constraints on Chinese Foreign Policy," in Kim (1984).

Pearson, Margaret (1991). *Joint Ventures in the People's Republic of China.* Princeton: Princeton University Press.

(1999). "China's Integration into the International Trade and Investment Regime," in Economy and Oksenberg (1999).

(2001). "The Case of China's Accession to GATT/WTO," in Lampton (2001).

Pempel, T. J. (1999). "The Developmental Regime in a Changing World Economy," in Woo-Cumings (1999).

Polly, Laura (1998). "China's Evolving Automotive Industry and Market." *Industry, Trade, and Technology Review.* U.S. International Trade Commission Publication No. 3114.

Putnam, Robert (1988). "Diplomacy and Domestic Politics: The Logic of Two-Level Games," *International Organization* 42: 427–460.

Pye, Lucian (1985). *Asian Power and Politics: The Cultural Dimensions of Authority.* Cambridge: Cambridge University Press.

Reynolds, Bruce Lloyd (1975). *The Impact of Trade and Foreign Investment on Industrialization: Chinese Textiles, 1875–1931.* Ph.D. dissertation, University of Michigan.

Risse-Kappen, Thomas (1995). "Introduction," in Risse-Kappen, ed. *Bringing Transnational Relations Back In.* New York: Cambridge University Press.

Rogowski, Ronald (1989). *Commerce and Coalitions: How Trade Affects Domestic Political Alignments.* Princeton: Princeton University Press.

Rosen, Daniel H. (1999). *Behind the Open Door.* Washington, D.C.: Institute for International Economics.

Rosenau, James (1969). *Linkage Politics: Essays on the Convergence of National and International Systems.* New York: The Free Press.

Sabin, Lora (1992). "The Qinghe Woolen Textile Mill," in Byrd (1992a).

Saunders, Phillip C. (2000). "Supping with a Long Spoon: Dependence and Interdependence in Sino-American Relations," *The China Journal* 43: 55–81.

Schmitter, Philippe C. (1996). "The Influence of the International Context upon the Choice of National Institutions and Policies in Neo-Democracies," in Whitehead (1996a).

Schneider, Ben Ross (1998). "Elusive Synergy: Business-Government Relations and Development," *Comparative Politics* 31(3): 101–122.

Schoppa, Leonard (1997). *Bargaining with Japan: What American Pressure Can and Cannot Do.* New York: Columbia University Press.

Segal, Gerald, ed. (1990). *Chinese Politics and Foreign Policy Reform.* London: Kegan Paul International Ltd.

Shafer, D. Michael (1994). *Winners and Losers*. Ithaca: Cornell University Press.

Shambaugh, David, ed. (1995). *Greater China: The Next Superpower?* Oxford: Oxford University Press.

Shipbuilders Council of America (1991). *Update on World Shipbuilding Subsidies*. Washington, D.C.: Shipbuilders Council of America.

Shirk, Susan L. (1993). *The Political Logic of Economic Reform in China*. Berkeley: University of California Press.

(1994). *How China Opened Its Door: The Political Success of the PRC's Foreign Trade and Investment Reforms*. Washington, D.C.: The Brookings Institution.

(1996). "Internationalization and China's Economic Reforms," in Robert Keohane and Helen Milner, eds. *Internationalization and Domestic Politics*. Cambridge: Cambridge University Press.

Shue, Vivienne (1988). *The Reach of the State: Sketches of the Chinese Body Politic*. Stanford: Stanford University Press.

Skocpol, Theda (1985). "Bringing the State Back In: Current Research," in Peter Evans et al., eds. *Bringing the State Back In*. New York: Cambridge University Press.

Smitka, Michael, ed. (1998). *The Textile Industry and the Rise of the Japanese Economy*. New York: Garland Publishers.

Smyth, Russell (1998). "Toward 'the Modern Corporation': Recent Developments in the Institutional Reform of State-Owned Enterprises in Mainland China," *Issues & Studies* 34(8): 102–131.

(2000). "Should China be Promoting Large-Scale Enterprises and Enterprise Groups?" *World Development* 28(4): 721–737.

Snyder, Jack (1989). "International Leverage on Soviet Domestic Change," *World Politics* 42(1): 1–30.

Solinger, Dorothy (1991). *From Lathes to Looms: China's Industrial Policy in Comparative Perspective, 1979–1982*. Stanford: Stanford University Press.

Spence, Jonathan D. (1990). *The Search for Modern China*. New York: Norton.

Stallings, Barbara (1995). "The New International Context of Development," in Stallings, ed. *Global Change, Regional Response*. Cambridge: Cambridge University Press.

Strange, Susan (1979). "The Management of Surplus Capacity: Or How Does Theory Stand Up to Protectionism 1970s Style?" *International Organization* 33: 303–334.

Sung, Yun-Wing (1991). *The China-Hong Kong Connection: The Key to China's Open-Door Policy*. Cambridge: Cambridge University Press.

Swanson, Bruce (1982). *Eighth Voyage of the Dragon*. Annapolis: Naval Institute Press.

Teiwes, Frederick (1984). *Leadership, Legitimacy and Conflict in China*. Armonk, N.Y.: M. E. Sharpe.

Tidrick, Gene and Jiyuan Chen, eds. (1987). *China's Industrial Reform*. New York: Oxford University for the World Bank.

United States Central Intelligence Agency (1976). *Chinese Merchant Ship Production*. Washington, D.C.: Government Printing Office.

United States Customs Service (1994). *Unraveling the Mystery: Following the Thread of PRC Apparel Exports*. Washington, D.C.: U.S. Customs Service.

United States International Trade Commission (1992). *Shipbuilding Trade Reform Act of 1992.* Washington, D.C.: United States International Trade Commission.

Van Evera, Stephen (1997). *Guide to Methods for Students of Political Science.* Ithaca: Cornell University Press.

Vogel, Ezra F. (1985). *Comeback, Case by Case: Building the Resurgence of American Business.* New York: Simon and Schuster.

(1989). *One Step Ahead in China: Guangdong Under Reform.* Cambridge: Harvard University Press.

Wade, Robert (1990). *Governing the Market: Economic Theory and the Role of Government in East Asian Industrialization.* Princeton: Princeton University Press.

Waltz, Kenneth (1954). *Man, the State, and War.* New York: Columbia University Press.

(1979). *Theory of International Politics.* Reading, Mass.: Addison-Wesley.

(1986). "A Response to My Critics," in Keohane (1986a).

Whitehead, Lawrence, ed. (1996a). *The International Dimensions of Democratization.* New York: Oxford University Press.

(1996b). "Three International Dimensions of Democratization," in Whitehead (1996a).

Woo-Cumings, Meredith, ed. (1999). *The Developmental State.* Ithaca: Cornell University Press, 1999.

World Bank (1988). *China: External Trade and Capital.* Washington, D.C.: World Bank.

(1991). *World Development Report 1991.* New York: Oxford University Press.

(1992). *China: Strategies for Reducing Poverty in the 1990s.* Washington, D.C.: World Bank.

(1993). *The East Asian Miracle.* New York: Oxford University Press.

(1994). *China: Foreign Trade Reform.* Washington, D.C.: World Bank.

(1996a). *The Chinese Economy: Fighting Inflation, Deepening Reforms.* Washington, D.C.: World Bank.

(1996b). *Poverty in China: What Do the Numbers Say?* Washington, D.C.: World Bank.

(1997a). *China 2020: Development Challenges in the New Century.* Washington, D.C.: World Bank.

(1997b). *China Engaged: Integration with the Global Economy.* Washington, D.C.: World Bank.

Woronoff, Jon (1992). *Japanese Targeting: Successes, Failures, Lessons.* Houndsmills: Macmillan Press, Ltd.

Yang, Xiaohua (1995). *Globalization of the Automobile Industry: The United States, Japan, and the People's Republic of China.* Westport, Conn.: Praeger.

Yoffie, David (1983). *Power and Protectionism.* New York: Columbia University Press.

Zhang, Jialin (1989). "Protectionism: A Curse for Both China and the United States," in Richard H. Holton and Wang Xi, eds. *U.S.-China Economic Relations: Present and Future.* Berkeley: Institute of East Asian Studies, University of California.

Zweig, David (1995). "'Developmental' Communities on China's Coast," *Comparative Politics* 27(3): 253–274.

(2000). "Hungry for Linkages: Domestic and External Demand for China's Internationalization, unpublished manuscript.

NEWSPAPERS, PERIODICALS, AND ANNUAL PUBLICATIONS

Almanac of China's Foreign Economic Relations and Trade (*Almanac*)

Asian Shipping

Beijing Review

Business China

China Business Review (*CBR*)

China Trade Report (*CTR*)

Drydock

Far Eastern Economic Review (*FEER*)

Foreign Broadcast Information Service, Daily Report-China (FBIS-CHI)

Foreign Broadcast Information Service, Daily Report-Latin America (FBIS-LAT)

Foreign Broadcast Information Service, Daily Report-Western Europe (FBIS-WEU)

Guoji Maoyi Wenti [Issues in International Trade] (*GJMYWT*)

Joint Publications Research Service (JPRS)

Lloyd's List Maritime Asia (*LLMA*)

Lloyd's Maritime Asia (*LMA*)

Lloyd's Ship Manager (*LSM*)

Lloyd's Shipping Economist (*LSE*)

Merchant Fleets of the World (U.S. Maritime Administration, annual)

The Motor Ship

New Ship Construction (U.S. Maritime Administration, annual)

New York Times

PRC Yearbook

Review of Maritime Transport (United Nations Conference on Trade and Development, annual)

Seatrade Business Review (*SBR*)

Shipping World & Shipbuilder (*SW&SB*)

South China Morning Post (*SCMP*)

Textile Asia [*Yazhou Fangzhi Yuekan*] (*TA*)

Textile Outlook International (*TOI*)

U.S. Imports of Textiles and Apparel Under the Multifiber Arrangement (U.S. International Trade Commission, annual)

World Trade Review and Outlook (*WTR&O*)

Zhongguo Fangzhi Gongye Nianjian [*China Textile Industry Yearbook*] (*ZGFZGYNJ*)

Zhongguo Haiyun [*Maritime China*] (*ZGHY*)

Zhongguo Jingji Nianjian [*China Economic Yearbook*] (*ZGJJNJ*)

Zhongguo Jingji Xinwen [*China Economic News*] (*ZGJJXW*)

Zhongguo Jixie Dianzi Gongye Nianjian [*China Machinery and Electronics Industry Yearbook*] (*ZGJXDZGYNJ*)

Index

administrative deregulation, 50, 291; as policy option, 19, 30; in textile industry, 117; *see also* market coordination

administrative guidance approach, as industrial adjustment strategy, 29–33, 277–79, 286, 289, 291, 293

advanced ship types, 166–67, 185, 210, 211, 213, 217–22, 230, 232–33, 235–36, 267, 271

AFC: *see* Asian Financial Crisis

Africa, role in transshipment of Chinese textile exports, 97–98

Agents of change: *see* reform from above, reform from the middle, reform from below

Agreement on Textiles and Clothing (ATC), 65, 69–70, 71

agriculture, as loser in China's WTO entry, 78

Ahrenkiel Shipping Company, Germany, 213

air lock system, 28, 73, 120–21, 134, 137, 158, 298; *see also* industry-trade coordination, lack of

aircraft industry: *see* aviation industry

allocative efficiency, 277, 300

all-or-nothing conceptualization, 39–43, 49, 56

Almond, Gabriel, 54

Amsden, Alice, 284

antidumping duties, China as target of, 27, 112; as form of managed trade, 19, 301; *see also* dumping

APEC: *see* Asia Pacific Economic Cooperation forum

Asia Pacific Economic Cooperation (APEC) forum, 17

Asian Development Bank, 17

Asian Financial Crisis (AFC), 4, 131, 286, 289; China's currency policy and, 54;

diminution of East Asian model and, 312; impact on shipbuilding industry, 15–16, 163, 165, 210, 235, 237; impact on textile industry, 15–16; as impetus for reform and opening, 299, 306; lessons of, 309

Asian Shipping, 213, 239

ATC: *see* Agreement on Textiles and Clothing

athletic shoes: as a buyer-driven industry, 159; Chinese export industry, 4, 18, 297; *see also* footwear

Australia, ship purchase from China, 308

automobile industry: as heavy industrial counterpart to shipbuilding in China, 57, 168, 257, 265, 284, 292, 307, 317; industrial policy in China and, 266, 303, 304–5; Japan's response to VERs with the United States, 7–8, 72; as loser in China's WTO entry, 78, 305; in South Korea, 304; as subject of managed trade, 7–8, 72

Automobile Leading Small Group, 265

autonomous export rights: *see* direct export rights

aviation industry, 173, 176; industrial policy for, 303

Bank of China, 212

basic ship types, 166–67, 179, 182, 183, 185, 187, 210, 217–22, 235–36

Beidaihe conference, 265

Beijing, 147, 148, 151, 223, 251, 303, 307, 308

Belgium, textile industry in, 83

Berlin Express, 217, 242, 245

black market, in textile quotas: *see* quota trading

BMTs: *see* bureaus of maritime transport

Bo Yibo, 181

333